Grass Grows

"Bridger's book is a gift to all who love   ican West. What they may find is that the West they love is   that tells them more about their human selves—who the,   n the place they love. Any book that can do that is worth reaung.'

—Daniel Wildcat

"*Where the Tall Grass Grows* offers a refreshing perspective that will certainly be discussed by Indians and non-Indians alike...a must-read for anyone who wants to know how we as Indian people were turned by Hollywood and politicians from 'Noble Redmen' into the 'Savage Indians.' This book is the truth and everyone should read it."

—J. R. Mathews, executive director,
Native American Productions,
and former chairman of the
Quapaw Tribe of Oklahoma

Other books by Bobby Bridger

A Ballad of the West
Buffalo Bill and Sitting Bull: Inventing the Wild West
Bridger (autobiography)

Where the Tall Grass Grows

Becoming Indigenous

and the Mythological Legacy of the
American West

Bobby Bridger

FULCRUM

GOLDEN, COLORADO

Library of Congress Cataloging-in-Publication Data
Bridger, Bobby.
  Where the tall grass grows : becoming indigenous and the mythological legacy of the American West / Bobby Bridger.
       p. cm.
  Includes bibliographical references and index.
  ISBN 978-1-55591-454-7 (pbk.)
1. Indian mythology--West (U.S.) 2. Indians of North America--West (U.S.)--History.
3. Frontier and pioneer life--West (U.S.)--History. 4. Indians in popular culture. 5. Indians in literature. 6. Indians in motion pictures. I. Title.
  E78.W5B75 2011
  398.2089'9--dc23

                           2011020027

Printed in the United States of America
0 9 8 7 6 5 4 3 2 1

Design by Jack Lenzo
Cover images: skull © Kurtwilliams | Dreamstime, parchment © sharonj430 | flickr creative commons, grass © Martin Pettitt | flickr creative commons

Fulcrum Publishing
4690 Table Mountain Dr., Ste. 100
Golden, CO 80403
800-992-2908 • 303-277-1623
www.fulcrumbooks.com

Contents

Acknowledgments

I wish to thank my friend of thirty-six years, Barbara Deloria, who took the first draft of this manuscript to her late husband's friend, editor, and publisher at Fulcrum Publishing, Sam Scinta. I was initially somewhat intimidated to be working with Vine Deloria Jr.'s editor and publisher, but Sam's genuineness and friendly personality quickly allowed me to relax and discover it was truly a pleasure to work with him. Sam never insisted on anything editorially; instead he skillfully led me to make decisions about the manuscript myself. Sam's vast knowledge of American Indian history and culture inspired perceptive suggestions and notes that invariably helped to further develop and more clearly articulate themes throughout my text.

I also want to thank Barbara and Vine's son Philip for taking time from his very busy schedule to read my manuscript. Phil's suggestions helped me with the fine-tuning of many historical facts and his insight and notes were invaluable to the ultimate trajectory of the book by encouraging me to dig deeper into the development of my themes and clarify their logical implications and consequences.

I also wish to thank the book's first editor, Faith Marcovecchio, who read early drafts of the manuscript and offered the splendid notes that helped me recognize, clarify, and define the eventual three-part structure of the book. And I want to thank Haley Berry, who did the final editing and polished things up very nicely stylistically, and Jack Lenzo, whose beautiful design provided an elegant visual expression of the essence of the book. Finally I wish to thank my wife, Melissa, and son, Gabriel, for their loving patience and understanding while I was "in the woodshed" so often with "the book."

Introduction
Becoming Indigenous

In Nebraska the first Sunday each August is an official holiday proclaimed to honor the state's Poet Laureate in Perpetuity and the United States' official Prairie Poet Laureate, John G. Neihardt. Neihardt Day centers on festivities seventy-five miles north of Omaha in the poet's adopted hometown, Bancroft. Completed in 1976, the circular John Neihardt Center is easily the most modern building in the tiny farming village. Every Neihardt Day, however, Bancroft's population swells as local farmers and merchants leave shops and soy bean and corn fields to greet visitors arriving from all over the world to celebrate the poet and his many contributions to western history and literature.

In 1978 I performed my epic ballad about Jim Bridger and the mountain men, *Seekers of the Fleece*, for Neihardt Day festivities. Immediately after my performance the executive director of the Neihardt Center, Marie Vogt, informed me that noted playwright Christopher Sergel wanted to meet me, and she whispered incidentally that Mr. Sergel owned the theatrical and film rights to Neihardt's classic, *Black Elk Speaks*. A charming gentleman from Connecticut, Chris Sergel was familiar with Neihardt's epic verse as well as *Black Elk Speaks*, and he quickly recognized the poet's influence on *Seekers of the Fleece*. We chatted a bit, discussing our backgrounds in show business and how we each came to discover Neihardt's work, before Chris suddenly asked me to join the production team he was assembling to produce an American Indian stage play and feature film based on Neihardt's classic. I told Chris I would be honored to assist his efforts with *Black Elk Speaks* and accepted the invitation.

But there was even more life-altering serendipity in the air that very special day: No sooner had I accepted Mr. Sergel's offer than Marie Vogt asked me to become the official Balladeer in Residence of the John G. Neihardt Center, an honor I also immediately accepted, and a title I still proudly hold. There were nevertheless ulterior motives attached to Ms. Vogt's offer: Aware of my friend-ship with Dakota author Vine Deloria Jr., she immediately implored me to ask Vine to come to Bancroft to speak about Neihardt and the Sioux. I was as surprised as Marie when Vine accepted her invitation to speak at the 1980 Neihardt Day celebration.

Vine's speech in Bancroft focused on his introduction to the 1979 University of Nebraska Press edition of *Black Elk Speaks* and an explanation of his already-famous remark that the book had become an "American Indian Bible." Vine pointed out that Neihardt's *Black Elk Speaks* and *When the Tree Flowered*, along with Black Elk's recollections in *The Sacred Pipe* by Joseph Epps Brown, form the core of a North American Indian theological canon that will someday challenge the Eastern and Western traditions as a spiritual and moral perspective of reality. He emphasized this theme with the comment that if any great religious classic has emerged in this century or in North America it had to be judged in the company of *Black Elk Speaks*. While acknowledging that *Black Elk Speaks* had in the 1970s become familiar to millions of non-Indian readers globally, Vine nevertheless stressed that the most important aspect of the book is its impact on the contemporary generation of young Indian people searching for their roots in "universal reality." He emphasized that Christianity and Buddhism both took centuries to create the theological and philosophical frameworks to properly express the universality their founders envisioned, and he suggested that the current generation of Indian college students could very well produce a generation of theologians destined to attend the birth of a new religious tradition based on Black Elk's teachings.

The central theme of *Black Elk Speaks* is the holy man's vision in which he prophesied a reunification of the Sacred Hoop of Nations. But Black Elk had an even more profound epiphany when he realized his reunification vision of the Sacred Hoop of Indian Nations was only one of *many* nations coming together in harmony. Vine's remarks about contemporary Indian people seeking a "universal reality" through *Black Elk Speaks* reminded me that from 1964 to 1967 he was the executive director of the National Congress of American Indians (NCAI). Founded in 1944, NCAI was the first successful "Pan-Indian" political congress in the history of North America, and it certainly was one of the first indications that Black Elk's unification prophecy was revealing itself in Indian Country even while the holy man was still alive.[1]

As a non-Indian, however, Vine's remarks about the significance of *Black Elk Speaks* to young Indian religious seekers and leaders made me wonder what role *non-Indians* played in this new, evolving Pan-American Indian culture. Since meeting Vine in 1975 and becoming close friends with him I had assumed that my responsibility as a non-Indian in late-twentieth-century America was simply to continue developing my western epic ballads as a faithful student of the American West privileged to have as my mentor the man contemporary American Indian people affectionately referred to as "the Head Red," or "Uncle Vine."

Vine's three years as the elected executive director of NCAI convinced him that most of the problems Indian people faced in the twentieth century had *legal* origins. So when his term at NCAI ended in 1967, Vine entered the University of Colorado Law School, and while studying for that degree he published his landmark best seller *Custer Died for Your Sins: An Indian Manifesto* in 1969. The next year Dee Brown's *Bury My Heart at Wounded Knee* was published, and, though originally published in 1932, Neihardt's *Black Elk Speaks* was soon "discovered" by mainstream audiences. Suddenly scores of other books and blockbuster films about American Indians began skyrocketing to the top of box-office and best-seller lists, indicating both Indians and non-Indians had begun a serious reexamination of the five-hundred-year-old relationship. When American Indian Movement (AIM) activists seized a church at Wounded Knee in 1973, however, American Indians instantly became front page news all over the world. Vine's 1974 book *Behind the Trail of Broken Treaties* chronicled events leading up to the 1973 incident at Wounded Knee as well as the earlier American Indian seizure of Alcatraz Island in 1969.

On that hot August Nebraska afternoon in Bancroft, after concluding his speech and mingling a few moments with the audience, Vine signaled for me to walk up the gentle slope of the natural amphitheater of the Neihardt Center's landscaped grounds to meet him at the poet's old writing cabin. The tiny, one-room building had been immaculately restored in 1967 to become part of the center's attractions. Vine and I sat in silence on the cabin's wooden porch and watched the large crowd break into smaller groups as people chatted and meandered around the lovely Lakota prayer garden before departing. Remaining silent, Vine rose from the porch and I followed him into Neihardt's cabin. An ancient wood stove stood proudly in the center of the stark, neatly-painted room. Neihardt's old typewriter and its lone companion, a kerosene lantern, sat atop a plain wooden table. A straight-back chair was shoved close to the table's edge.

"It takes strict discipline to retreat to a room like this day after day to write," Vine said, taking a drag off his ever-present Pall Mall. He paused a while and took another long drag from his cigarette before speaking again. "You know?" he exhaled, "We should do something to acknowledge Neihardt."

We returned to the porch, and after pausing there for a few more moments of silent reflection, we headed farther up the hill-side to attend a party scheduled for the presenters at Marie Vogt's nearby home. Vine stopped, flicked the ember off the end of his cigarette, stomped it, and field-stripped the unfiltered butt.

"Maybe an anthology," he said.

"An anthology?"

"Yeah. I could invite ten or fifteen writers to contribute an essay about Neihardt. We could convince a publisher to donate portions of the book's profits to the Neihardt Center? Whaddaya think?"

Of course I thought Vine's idea was great. To my thinking, John G. Neihardt's five meticulously researched epic poems, *The Song of Three Friends*, *The Song of Hugh Glass*, *The Song of Jedediah Smith*, *The Song of The Indian Wars*, and *The Song of the Messiah*—collectively titled *A Cycle of the West*—remain without peer in American literature. When American Indians walked across the continent from San Francisco to Washington in 1978 to peacefully present grievances to legislators, they entered the Capitol under a banner that read, "We Come from the Land of Black Elk." The old long-hairs among the Lakota often remarked that Neihardt was the single *washichu*, or white man, who spoke *their* heart.

But Vine's notion of an anthology had only begun to take shape in Neihardt's writing cabin. Before we reached Marie's party Vine paused again, tossed his head back, and laughed with pleasure at his rapidly blossoming idea.

"Actually, we should do *three* anthologies! Neihardt, Frank Waters, and Dee Brown!"

Thus began the concept of a trilogy of tribute anthologies devoted to three literary lions of the twentieth-century American West. Within weeks Vine had convinced twelve writers and Howe Brothers Publishing Company in Salt Lake City to publish an anthology celebrating Neihardt's life and work. *A Sender of Words: Essays in Memory of John G. Neihardt* was edited by Vine and published in 1984 with proceeds donated to the Neihardt Center. In 1994 the University of Ohio's Swallow Press and twenty-one writers published the second anthology in the concept, *Frank Waters: Man and Mystic*, also edited by Vine. Having based my epic ballads on Neihardt's work, I understood why Vine asked me to contribute an essay to the Neihardt anthology, but I was pleasantly surprised in 1992 when he insisted that I contribute an essay to the Waters anthology. Soon I found myself frantically digging through Frank's impressive body of work searching for a theme to explore in the essay.

A few weeks after I accepted the invitation to write an essay for the Waters anthology, Vine had granted me permission to publish his essay "Sacred Lands and Human Understanding" in *Hoka Hey!*, a quarterly sixteen-page tabloid magazine I had founded and had edited and published from 1985 to 1994. Upon reading Vine's essay I realized I kept returning to his quote of Lakota philosopher Luther Standing Bear's criteria concerning the process for non-Indians to *become* indigenous to North America: "The man from Europe is still a foreigner and an alien," Standing Bear observed, "...but in the Indian the spirit of the land is vested; it will be until other men are able to divine and meet its rhythm. Men must be born and re-born to belong. *Their bodies must be formed of the dust of their forefathers' bones.*'"[2] In "Sacred Lands and Human Under-standing," Vine elaborated on Standing Bear's observations of the non-Indian's five-hundred-year presence in North America: "Although non-Indians are born in North America, they are not indigenous to North America and they remain strangers in a land they do not understand. They have not had sufficient time to set down roots that will enable them to understand America or themselves. American Indians are indigenous because we have paid attention to what the land is saying to us and where there are sacred places we have become a member of the community of those places, where there are holy places we have paid utmost respect, and where we have consecrated the land with our lives and blood we have truly become native to this land."[3]

Having been born in the United States during the waning days of World War II, I had never once considered myself a for-eigner—much less an *alien*—to North America until reading those remarks. Nevertheless, Standing Bear's criteria and Vine's analysis for becoming indigenous to North America forced me to recon-sider my fundamental identity as a non-Indian American. Yet even as I continued to ponder this troubling question, the pressing issue of the Frank Waters essay deadline kept whispering in my ear until I eventually decided to make becoming indigenous the theme of my essay and compare several of Frank's well-known works, such as *The Man Who Killed the Deer*, *The Book of the Hopi*, and *Masked Gods*, to Standing Bear's criteria. While researching and writing "Frank Waters: Becoming Indigenous" for the *Frank Waters: Man and Mystic* anthology I became progressively aware that this essay about becoming indigenous was indeed only the seed of a much larger premise that I intended to continue researching.

In 1996 I was still exploring the implications of Standing Bear's and Vine's thoughts on becoming indigenous while also maintain-ing my livelihood as a recording artist, touring singer-songwriter, actor, and theatrical producer. My focus throughout 1996, how-ever, was a very serious looming deadline to complete my third attempt to compose an epic ballad about William F. "Buffalo Bill" Cody. The debut of my one-man theatrical show of the ballad was

scheduled for July 2, 1996, in the Coe Auditorium of the Buffalo Bill Historical Center (BBHC) in Cody, Wyoming, as part of
festivities celebrating the sesquicentennial of the American icon's
birth. Once composition of the epic ballad was completed I would
immediately begin round-the-clock rehearsals in preparation for a
month-long run of the ninety-minute-long work in the historical
center's Coe Auditorium.

In mid-June 1996, after twenty-five years of research and two
destroyed earlier drafts of musical works based on the life of William F. "Buffalo Bill" Cody, I completed *Pahaska*, the third and
most troublesome epic ballad of my trilogy, *A Ballad of the West*.
There were many reasons the *Pahaska* ballad had proved more problematic than its companions, *Seekers of the Fleece* and *Lakota*. To
begin with, having become an actor as well as a producer in Chris
Sergel's stage adaptation of *Black Elk Speaks*, I had spent much of
the 1980s deeply involved with his effort to mount an American
Indian production of that drama. Toward that end, I had joined
the board of the American Indian Theater Company (AITCO) in
Tulsa, Oklahoma, to help recruit and train Indian actors for the
production. I was also cast in two prominent roles in the 1984
AITCO production of *Black Elk Speaks* starring the late David
Carradine as Black Elk and the late Will Sampson as Red Cloud.
Moreover, as we developed the production in the early 1980s Chris
had introduced me to the late renowned playwright Dale Wasserman, author of *Man of La Mancha* and the stage adaptation of *One
Flew Over the Cuckoo's Nest*. For nearly two years I worked directly
with Dale at the Eugene O'Neill Theater Center in Connecticut
and at his home in Los Angeles to create the leading role of "the
Drifter" in his musical comedy *Shakespeare and the Indians*. Even
though I loved performing in the musical, and particularly working with Dale Wasserman, after a six-month run of *Shakespeare and
the Indians* in Omaha I had to decide whether to continue with
Shakespeare or focus my attention on *Black Elk Speaks*. I chose
Black Elk. Yet even after I pulled out of *Shakespeare and the Indians* my schedule was still overwhelming; when I wasn't working on
Black Elk Speaks with Chris, or in Tulsa with the American Indian

Theater Company, I was touring America or abroad with my own one-man shows of *Seekers of the Fleece* and *Lakota*. All this activity left little time or circumstance to write.

In spite of my hectic pace during the 1980s, completion of *Pahaska* was complicated by the fact that more skillfully than any other personality of the nineteenth century, William F. Cody blurred the line between fiction and reality. Even more significantly, the deeper I probed into the life of Cody seeking a unique angle from which to present his life in ballad form, the higher rose my opinion of the man. Consequently, at the beginning of my third attempt at *Pahaska* in 1995, my perception of William Cody had changed from one shaped by youthful misconceptions to one of genuine respect. Because of Cody's commitment to raising the world's awareness to the humanity of Plains Indians when the pervasive attitude of his day was that they were savages, I had learned to regard Buffalo Bill as an authentic hero. Since the Lakota called Cody *Pahaska*, or "long-hair," before he became known as Buffalo Bill, I gave my epic ballad that title also and designed its structure to draw upon the mystical possibilities of Cody's unique relationship with Plains Indians and their subsequent invaluable contribution to the design and success of his *Wild West* show.

Immediately upon the completion of *Pahaska* and its theatrical run in Cody, I began work on a manuscript that would eventually be published as *Buffalo Bill and Sitting Bull: Inventing the Wild West*. In the book I continued my exploration of Cody's relationship with the indigenous people of the Trans-Missouri region and structured a parallel account of Cody's life alongside the history of the Lakota—particularly Sitting Bull. *Pahaska* reflected Buffalo Bill Cody's heroic mythology and his creation of the *Wild West*, while celebrating Cody in an epic, Homeric—or better, Neihardtic—context. I continued that theme in my book. In the book I also emphasized that Cody and the organization he created had a major impact on the shaping of the American personality in the nineteenth and early twentieth century. In the fall of 1998 I submitted the first draft of my manuscript of *Buffalo Bill and Sitting Bull: Inventing the Wild West* to the University of Texas Press.

Having been attracted to the mythology of the Trans-Missouri region and its impact on American culture for over forty years, I should have known the assumption that I had concluded my explorations of the region's impact on the American character was premature. In fact, my best friend's son was about to address the subject of American identity in a manner that would turn my entire thinking about the subject upside down.

In 1998 Vine and Barbara Deloria's eldest son, Philip, published his first book, *Playing Indian*, in which he offered landmark insight into the very meaning of American identity. Philip accomplished this by cleverly examining the pre-Revolutionary period forward through American history, noting instances such as the Boston Tea Party, when rebellious colonialists dressed as Indians to express acts of civil disobedience. Intertwining such revelations throughout US history with articulate, crystal-clear evidence and sharp critical analysis, Philip proved the American personality was indeed largely created and molded by non-Indians *role-playing as Indians*.

When *Playing Indian* was published I had already spent thirty-five years in beaded buckskins and coyote headdress performing on stage in various incarnations of a mountain man, or "frontiers-man"; I once joked to a fellow actor in New York that I had never played a role in the theater that didn't require wearing moccasins. My rationalization for donning these costumes, of course, was that I was depicting characters in my trilogy of one-man shows, or in other playwrights' productions with western themes, and the attire only served to enhance the experience for the audience. Nevertheless, according to the younger Deloria's criterion, I had made a career of "playing Indian," albeit unwittingly. The thought had never occurred to me that in portraying all of those historic personalities I had been employing the same tactics in precisely the same way non-Indians had to define American identity since arriving in the "New World."

So Philip's book introduced a very personal motivation to understand more about Standing Bear's standards for "becoming" indigenous. Even with the notion imprinted now in my awareness, however, I still had to make my living "playing Indian," and

audiences expected to see me in costume, so I continued wearing beaded buckskins and performing my shows. But as I toured
the country and discussed Standing Bear's criterion for becoming
indigenous to North America with a truly diverse range of people
and cultures, I was also increasingly convinced that the complex
issue was deeply embedded within the American public's spiritual and mythological misconceptions of itself and was perhaps
the underlying cause of many worsening environmental concerns.
Consequently, Standing Bear's assertion that "In the Indian the
spirit of the land is vested; and it will be so until other men are able
to divine and meet its rhythm" rang with the shameful reality that
immigrants clearly have failed to divine the rhythm of this hemisphere and have tragically "soiled the nest."

The soiled nest metaphor was of course deeply embedded in
American consciousness by 1971's "weeping Indian" public service
announcement. It is important to remember, however, that Iron
Eyes Cody's moving performance in the Keep America Beautiful
organization's public service message was created to announce the
debut of an annual Earth Day and as such ultimately was a Madison Avenue advertisement designed as a preemptive effort to assimilate an increasingly militant environmental movement that was
making its first appearances during that era. The crying "Indian"
character, Iron Eyes Cody, was played by actor Epera de Cortii, a
first-generation Sicilian-American from Kaplan, Louisiana. Having made his career portraying American Indians and acting as
technical advisor on countless Westerns since the 1920s, de Cortii was instantly recognized by television audiences because of his
many movies; indeed, it could be argued that Iron Eyes Cody is
the representation of Phil Deloria's definition of "playing" Indian
in the twentieth century. Yet this does not diminish the fact that
the metaphor of Iron Eye Cody's presence was spiritually potent;
the weeping Indian's powerful depiction of non-Indian America's
contamination and toxic waste left little doubt that the respect and
honor of indigenous people was the first step to the solution of
America's environmental malfeasance. Perhaps this not-so-sublim-
inal message is why most baby boomer Americans can still vividly

recall minute details from that television advertisement. Yet in spite of repeated and increasingly dire warnings from nearly every field of science over the past fifty years, what was soiling the nest in the 1960s has brought us to the brink of environmental catastrophe in the twenty-first century. Equally troubling, the oil and chemical companies and other international conglomerates responsible for most of this ecological turmoil now use the term "green" with the same heartfelt sincerity as the Sierra Club.

So, being part of the Woodstock/baby boomer generation myself, after the publication of *Buffalo Bill and Sitting Bull: Inventing the Wild West* in 2002 I started asking friends and associates if they considered themselves "indigenous" to North America. Of course the immediate response was, "Only *Indians* are indigenous!" Yet when asked if that response meant that they considered themselves foreign, or alien, non-Indian Americans invariably refused to think of themselves as such. When my questioning reached this point some people immediately became defensive and avoided responding by accusing me of setting them up with trick questions. Most simply went into a knee-jerk response and recalled parents' and grandparents' origins and history as an explanation of pedigree and heritage. A large percentage could recall only superficial information about their grandparents, and a surprising number could recall nothing of their family history before their grandparents.

After September 11, 2001, and the blizzards of American flags, the eruption of red-versus-blue super-patriotism, and the rise of evangelical "rapturists" and their political church, it occurred to me that this complex notion of becoming indigenous was rapidly becoming timely. When the US border issue rose to intense national prominence and WASP "minute men" began swarming on our southern border scouting for illegal immigrants, I started imagining Tecumseh and Sitting Bull saying to some of those right-wing vigilantes, "You think *you* have an immigration problem?"

Even while the notion of becoming indigenous in modern America continued to intrigue me, the anthology trilogy Vine had conceived in 1980 remained only two-thirds complete. Since the Neihardt anthology had been published in 1984 and the Waters anthology exactly a decade later in 1994, I assumed Vine would continue the symmetry of the tradition and conclude the trilogy in 2004. So in 2003 I suggested to Vine that we should begin plans for Dee Brown's anthology. For good measure, I said, "Maybe we should consider a fourth anthology after that; maybe one on Alvin Josephy?" Vine replied ominously, "You'll have to do those."

Vine died on November 13, 2005. In the weeks before his death he was too ill to know that his old friend Alvin M. Josephy Jr. had preceded him in death by less than a month. Indian Country would never be the same after the loss of both men. A few weeks after Vine's death I was reading Josephy's autobiography, *A Walk Toward Oregon: A Memoir*, and it occurred to me that two of the three men that Vine had selected to honor with anthologies were non-Indians; even though we never actually spoke about it—whether intentionally or not—on some level Vine had evidently intended the trilogy of anthologies as a way to recognize non-Indian efforts to bring the Indian perspective of the history of the United States into the light. This realization started me thinking about creating a collection of mini-biographies of non-Indians such as Neihardt, Dee Brown, and Alvin Josephy, each of whom certainly exemplified Luther Standing Bear's criteria for becoming indigenous to North America.

Then in June 2006, exactly a decade after my debut of *Pahaska* and four years after the publication of *Buffalo Bill and Sitting Bull: Inventing the Wild West*, another moment of serendipity arrived when I was invited by planners of the annual convention of the Western Writers of America (WWA) to join a symposium panel to speak on the subject "Writing about Buffalo Bill." I was delighted to learn the panel would comprise several authors who had recently published books about Buffalo Bill, including George Moses (*Wild West Shows and the Images of American Indians: 1883–1933*), and Louis S. Warren (*Buffalo Bill's America*). Former senior curator of the BBHC—and generally recognized as the foremost living Buffalo Bill scholar—Paul Fees, former WWA president Loren D. Estleman, and the senior curator of the BBHC, Juti Winchester, were also seated at the dais. Many noted authors, journalists, historians, and aficionados were also in the audience. As the annual WWA convention happened to be in Cody, Wyoming, that year, the panel discussion was appropriately held in the BBHC's Coe Auditorium.

The seriatim structure of the panel gave me time to become sufficiently intimidated by each august speaker's remarks—and of more immediate concern, their vast knowledge and insightful analysis left little about Buffalo Bill to discuss superficially when it was my turn to speak. So I decided to begin by calling attention to the fact that in the decade since the 1996 debut of my *Pahaska* ballad on the very stage upon which we now sat, ten major books about Buffalo Bill—including my own—had been published.[4] Moreover, I emphasized that nearly all these books had one thing in common: each in some way referred to "The Indians," an essay that the late Vine Deloria Jr. wrote in the early 1970s. "The Indians" was filled with numerous fresh and positive perspectives on Buffalo Bill's unique relationships with American Indians—or more significantly, American Indian relationships with William F. Cody and his *Wild West*. Commissioned by the BBHC in 1971, Vine's essay was written as American Indians were taking an increasingly militant political stance on the national stage to address their grievances, and I noted that after Vine's generally positive insight into the relationship of Plains Indians with Buffalo Bill, historians became more inclined to reexamine the unique microcosm of American society reflected by the cultural diversity and racial harmony within Cody's *Wild West*.

Next I noted that since Buffalo Bill reached the peak of his popularity at the turn of the twentieth century, the synchronicity of so many authors and historians reevaluating Cody's life at the turn of the twenty-first century seemed to me mythologically important *because* of his relationships with Plains Indians. I explained that early into my research into Plains Indian culture I was introduced to the Falling Star creation myth of the Lakota. Among many other mystical aspects of the culture, upon encountering the Falling Star myth I began to realize that the unique landscape of the Trans-Missouri gave birth to the creation mythology of the tribes of the Great Plains and upper Rockies. This inspired the notion that when Euro Americans first encountered the Trans-Missouri while crossing the continent during the Great Migration of the nineteenth century, the very same landscape also produced the first genuine collective "Old World" mythology in North America. America's western expansion into the Tran-Missouri region figured importantly in the beginning of the Civil War, and the fact that America immediately returned to the region with a renewed meta-phorical intensity after the Civil War to create the Transcontinen-tal Railroad as a symbol of national unity is a clear implication that this region held vital mythological significance to non-Indian *and* Indian culture. Moreover, the mythology, religion, and culture of the nineteenth-century Plains Indian—particularly as expressed in Neihardt's *Black Elk Speaks*—has since the mid-twentieth century been absorbed and spread by instantaneous electronic media and modern travel throughout a Pan-Indian culture of Indian nations within the United States as well as around the world. Equally sig-nificant, the enduring global success of Buffalo Bill's *Wild West* and Hollywood's Western movies have led the world to assume all American Indians are from the Trans-Missouri, that all Indians wear feathered war-bonnets, smoke peace pipes, and live in tipis—all cultural and religious accoutrements of Plains Indians. This led me to conclude the Trans-Missouri region to be the very cradle of America's collective mythology—the sacred place our indigenous *and* immigrant nations will always return to when we need to col-lectively reinvent ourselves.

Focusing on the panel's theme, "writing about Buffalo Bill," I noted that the synchronicity of such diverse and positive new interest in Buffalo Bill indicated that we might be subliminally reexamining Cody in an attempt to reinvent our collective heroic perception of ourselves as a nation as we entered the uncertainties of the new mil-lennium—especially after the events of September 11, 2001.

In closing, I crossed a dangerous heretical threshold in post–World War II concerning the twentieth-century American hero. I mentioned that since the room was full of writers of historical fic-tion—potentially screenplays—about the American West, I wished to share a dichotomy that had intrigued me for several decades:

Buffalo Bill was a legitimate American hero who became the first global celebrity, whereas his metaphorical grandson, John Wayne, was an international movie star who became an *illegitimate* American hero. I paused briefly to see if denigrating the Duke set any trigger fingers itching in the audience. Hearing only sparse laughter in response, I felt it was safe to continue and suggested that, like volunteers for a hypnotist's act, we had collectively and willingly agreed be bamboozled by Hollywood mythmaking machinery into the co-creation of the heroic John Wayne. When this remark elicited a big laugh from the audience I decided to leave them laughing, thanked the WWA for inviting me to speak about Buffalo Bill, and concluded my remarks. At that very moment, however, I knew the time had finally arrived for me to trace the period in the history of the American West from the end of Buffalo Bill's life through John Wayne's career in order to compare their legends and mythologies and explore the circumstances in which their heroic archetypes overlapped.

I began by reading historian Robert G. Athearn's *The Mystic West in Twentieth-Century America*, a book that perfectly underscored my theory of the mythological implications of the Trans-Missouri and reminded me why I felt this comparison of Cody and Wayne was necessary:

> The myth is set firmly in…that ephemeral region between the Missouri and the Sierras. But those who try to assess and explain its strength and longevity often underestimate the obvious— that this myth's appeal and implications are more national than regional. The South has a literature of its own and writers who deal with it as an entity; so has the East. But there is a difference. Americans admire Faulkner and love *Gone with the Wind*, but they do not spend millions to dress like Rhett Butler. Nor have they stood in line, generation after generation, to buy paperbacks and watch B movies about cotton pickers and pellagra. There are westerns, but there are not southerns. The West alone seems to be a national possession. Its experience speaks for all Americans, not just for those who live there.[5]

Philip Deloria's insight into America's history of "playing Indian" immediately combined with Robert Athearn's remarks concerning the national singularity of the artistic medium of the Western—particularly the Western movie—and made me wonder if the transformation of authentic hero Buffalo Bill into his metaphorical grandson and false hero, John Wayne, wasn't somehow bizarrely connected to this notion of becoming indigenous. Upon considering John Wayne and his role as twentieth-century America's archetypical Western movie hero and right-wing icon, I was reminded yet again of the conflicting principles these Trans-Missouri mythologies continue to propagate in the twenty-first century; it is no coincidence that even though *Black Elk Speaks* was originally published in 1932, the book began its ascension from the shadows of history thirty years later in the early 1960s. There is a historical symmetry to the fact that Wayne's long film career began with *The Big Trail* in 1931, and, though originally published a year later, *Black Elk Speaks* vanished during the peak years of John Wayne's career, only to be rediscovered by the counterculture movement during the early days of the Vietnam War at precisely the moment that the Duke's reign as *the* Western movie star began a gradual decline and his stature as hero of conservative America skyrocketed. The chronological synchronicity of this mythological metamorphosis of John Wayne from heroic movie star to international right-wing icon, and the "rediscovery" of *Black Elk Speaks* during the unprecedented counterculture and civil rights movement of the 1960s, indicated there was perhaps an even more direct connection to the notion of non-Indians becoming indigenous to North America. Yet even though the mythological insight of the Lakota holy man's teaching appears to be extending in spiritual form into the twenty-first century, thereby instantly reaching throughout the entire world in the digital age, there remains the reality that since the nineteenth century a powerful and radically different non-Indian mythology has also emanated from the Missouri River country. This ubiquitous mythology celebrates the creation of the "American character" while crossing the Great Plains in pursuit of Manifest Destiny during the nineteenth century. Moreover, this mythology was skillfully embedded in the culture's subconscious from the beginnings of the motion picture industry and perfected and perpetuated throughout John Wayne's long career; indeed, as Robert Athearn noted, from its inception Hollywood discovered that the Western could be successfully employed to romantically project "core" American values such as freedom, equality, opportunity, and overcoming harsh adversity—and in doing so sell a lot of tickets. Thus pioneer conquest of the tall grass plains, Rocky Mountains, and North America's indigenous people quickly became Hollywood's favorite metaphor to represent the emigrant creation of a collective American identity. In addition, the legacy of John Wayne's definitive and defiant "Western" heroic mythological archetype of the American personality has continued to flourish through the conservative policies of his political protégés from the rise of Barry Goldwater throughout the cold war era to Ronald Reagan and forward to George W. Bush, the so-called neocons of the late twentieth century, and the Tea Party movement of the early twenty-first century. Consequently, the non-Indian western mythology emanating from the Trans-Missouri has *everything* to do with the unique development of the American understanding of human nature, and, blessed with the ability to shape-shift with the changing times, this "cowboy" persona continues to define us as a nation.

Therefore, in order to examine both the Indian *and* non-Indian mythology originating from the Trans-Missouri, as well as Black Elk's unification prophecy emanating from the same landscape, I decided to construct a concise narrative history of Plains Indians intertwined with the careers of Buffalo Bill and John Wayne that would chronicle the time spans of both of their careers in show business. Since Buffalo Bill and John Wayne were both products of media, however, I realized that I would also need to create another narrative chronicling the connections of the two icons from the perspective of media analyst Marshall McLuhan's insight that "the medium is the message." In other words, if the advent of any new medium introduces a dramatic shift in the culture, it most certainly affects the creation of the heroes of that era and, conversely, the hero's reflection of the times.

The late media theorist Neil Postman adds a vitally important mythological semantic to consider when applying McLuhan's famous adage to personalities such as John Wayne and Buffalo Bill. Postman believes Marshal McLuhan's aphorism requires clarification because it may lead one to confuse message with metaphor. While metaphor creates a cognitive map between concepts in order to connect the abstract with the concrete, message indicates an unambiguous statement about the world. Postman warns that the forms of our media, "including the symbols through which they permit conversation," do not create such statements. "They are rather like metaphors," Postman concludes, "working by unobtrusive but powerful implication to enforce their special definitions of reality. Whether we are experiencing the world through the lens of speech or the printed word or the television camera, our media metaphors classify the world for us, sequence it, frame it, enlarge it, reduce it, color it, argue a case for what the world is like."[6]

Considering that most of the technological advances that created Buffalo Bill mythology occurred as a result of the benchmark accomplishment of the Industrial Revolution—the construction of the Transcontinental Railroad (and that truly colossal undertaking is yet another example of the creation of non-Indian mythology born from the Great Plains landscape and connected with the Indian mythology of the very same landscape)—a book based on the origins and intertwining of these various histories in the specific region eventually started to take shape in my thoughts.

Once I decided to include a McLuhanist/media element to the examination of Cody, Wayne, and the mythological legacy of the Trans-Missouri, it dawned on me that I had traveled full circle yet again on this search: In 1970, while *Custer Died for Your Sins* was perched atop US best-selling charts, Vine Deloria Jr. published *We Talk, You Listen: New Tribes, New Turfs*, in which he explored the impact of media on Indian and non-Indian culture in America from a McLuhanist perspective. McLuhan's declaration that instant electronic communication was changing civilization from a "print" culture into a new "oral" culture intrigued Vine and suggested possibilities for new tribal civilization in America as well. At this realization I embarked on a journey to revisit Vine Deloria Jr.'s body of work.

Although many aspects of the American heroic archetype born in the Trans-Missouri in the nineteenth century were indeed solidly based on fundamental human principles and were genuinely born of a nation challenging itself by encountering and overcoming hardship with profound courage and sacrifice, it will be necessary for parts of this book to confront the authenticity of some of the most sacred iconic expressions of the old mythological legacy of the American West. The mythologies of the Indian and non-Indian fiercely collided in the Trans-Missouri during the nineteenth century, and this conflict has continued in various forms of legal, social, religious, technological, cultural, physical, and mythological violence ever since. Yet it also remains that even with this five-hundred-year history of conflict duly noted, Black Elk's vision prophesized a reunification of the hoops of many nations and races. Considering this, as well as Luther Standing Bear's criterion for the non-Indian to become indigenous to North America, the continuing mythological discord emanating from the Missouri River Country poses several important questions: Does a creative synthesis of these opposing perceptions of reality through the wisdom of Black Elk's spirituality offer contemporary America mythological transcendence? And if so, how do we process, understand, incorporate, and reconcile Black Elk's mythology with the dominant non-Indian mythmaking that subdued the indigenous nations of North America and plundered her natural resources, but in doing so, created unprecedented opportunities for western civilization? Is reconciling these apparently contradictory mythological perceptions a pathway for non-Indians to eventually become indigenous to North America? And finally, is *Black Elk Speaks* altering the mythological concept of the American hero, and, if so, what role does the Indian play in the evolution of the heroic archetype?

My exploration of these multiple complex questions immediately required a brief examination of the early history of America's western expansion in order to create a composite portrait of the heroic template born in the nineteenth-century Trans-Missouri and the mythological legacy created by legendary individuals and landmark adventures and accomplishments of that time and place. Given mountain man Jim Bridger's propensity for participating in pivotal historical events throughout the nineteenth-century American West, I decided to employ my distant relative as a guide through this portion of my exploration. To balance this examination of the beginnings of non-Indian mythology in the American West I wove into the aforementioned narratives of Buffalo Bill, John Wayne, and Plains Indian history, mini-biographies of noted Plains Indians Sitting Bull, Luther Standing Bear, Charles Eastman, and Vine Deloria Jr., as well as non-Indians John G. Neihardt, Mabel Dodge Luhan, Upton Sinclair, John Collier, Frank Waters, Alvin Josephy, Dee Brown, and other individuals whose clear alternative mythological visions over the span of a century pulled back the veil and exposed much of the sentimental and dramatic propaganda Wall Street, Madison Avenue, Washington, and Hollywood posed and sold us as the American myth.

I have structured this book into three sections. Part 1 recalls the meeting and unique relationship of John G. Neihardt and Lakota Holy Man Black Elk, before embarking on an exploration of the United States' western expansion into the unknown territory of the Louisiana Purchase and the creation of the frontiersman as the American heroic archetype. The first section also surveys the rise of media and its impact on entertainment and the role the arts and sciences played in definitive events of the emigration era, the Industrial Revolution, the Indian wars, and the creation of American mythology. Part 2 continues the exploration of the evolution of American heroic iconography into the twentieth century by means of an amalgamation of technology, media, entertainment, and the creative visionaries who invented America's motion picture industry. The second section reviews the American Indian's transition into the twentieth century while introducing important non-Indian pioneers who championed Indian rights, and, with the inclusion of a deconstruction of the American cowboy, also chronicles the rise of the cinematic team of John Ford and John Wayne as the twentieth century's leading purveyors of the Western genre in motion pictures. Part 3 surveys the often tumultuous relationship between Indians and non-Indians in the late twentieth century following the rise in awareness and activism that occurred throughout America during the counterculture and human rights movements of the 1960s. The third section also explores the impact of publishing and motion pictures on the transformation of the American Indian mythological archetype from villain to hero at the turning of the twenty-first century and a new millennium.

It is my hope that in uniting these multiple complex themes, personalities, and eras into a single statement, this book will reveal that the fates of both cultures are ultimately interdependent and the Indian and non-Indian have been bound in an ironic "captivity narrative" since the very beginnings of their relationship in North America. Finally, I hope this book will reveal that a creative synthesis —and possible reconciliation- of these conflicting mythologies has been occurring in the American entertainment industry since Sitting Bull realized celebrity as a survival tactic and joined Buffalo Bill's *Wild West*.

PART ONE

Maybe it was the sheer space that seemed so fascinating to the whites. Or maybe it was the style of the Plains culture with its nomadism, its horse herds, hunters, warfare, and apparently aimless, leisurely movement over the land. Or maybe it was the immensely colorful costumes of these people who seemed to play at life with a sort of fierce artfulness. At bottom, maybe it was the sense that was to be gained over and again that the tribes loved this life, thought themselves the privileged and elect of all creation to be permitted the gusty, wide-skied joy of their world. This made them seem arrogant to the whites, but it also compelled a kind of admiration that yet lingers in our culture.

—Frederick Turner, *Beyond Geography: The Western Spirit against the Wilderness*

Chapter One
Flaming Rainbow, the Word Sender

He is a word sender. This world is like a garden. Over this gar-
den go his words like rain and where they fall they leave it a little
greener. And when his words have passed, the memory of them shall
stand long in the west like a flaming rainbow.[1]

—Black Elk, describing his adopted son John G. Neihardt,
whom he dubbed Flaming Rainbow because
there is no word in his language for "poet"

On April 27, 1971, erudite host Dick Cavett devoted his entire
ninety-minute network broadcast to an intimate conversation with
John G. Neihardt. It was the first time in the history of the medium
that a television talk show had ever devoted an entire program to a
single guest, and the result was that worldwide sales of the ninety-
year-old epic poet's 1932 biography of a nineteenth-century Plains
Indian mystic, *Black Elk Speaks*, instantly soared. A year later Neihardt told a friend that more copies of the book had been sold after
his appearance on the *Cavett Show* than had sold from 1932 until
1970.[2] Neihardt died November 3, 1973, finally having reached a
vast international audience in his twilight years.

Black Elk's teachings have become increasingly important
throughout the world since Neihardt's 1971 appearance on the
Dick Cavett program. In 1984 preeminent Lakota anthropologist
Raymond J. DeMallie expanded upon Vine Deloria Jr.'s observation that *Black Elk Speaks* has risen to the status of becoming an
"American Indian Bible" when he suggested that "the book might
better be considered an American Indian Rosetta Stone, for it
serves both Indians and non-Indians of today as a way into the traditional native American culture of the nineteenth century, a key
to translation from modern English into older American Indian
modes of thought."[3]

Neihardt's wife, Mona, suggested the title *Black Elk Speaks as Told through John G. Neihardt*, but his working title of the *Black Elk* manuscript was *The Book That Wouldn't Die*. Neihardt's working title reveals much about the personality of the poet himself, the life of Lakota holy man Black Elk, and the unique growth to fruition of the book.

Black Elk first started hearing voices calling him in 1868 when was still a very young child. He told Neihardt that when he was five years old his grandfather made him a bow and some arrows. One day he was riding on horseback and observed a thunderstorm moving in from the west. As he rode into the woods along a creek he noticed a kingbird sitting on a limb. Black Elk stressed to Neihardt:

> This was not a dream, it happened. And I was going to shoot at the kingbird with the bow my Grandfather made, when the bird spoke and said, "the clouds all over are one-sided." Perhaps it meant that all the clouds were looking at me. And then it said, "Listen! A voice is calling you!" Then I looked up at the clouds, and two men were coming there, headfirst like arrows slanting down; and as they came, they sang a sacred song and the thunder was like drumming. I will sing it for you. The song and drumming were like this:
>
> "Behold, a sacred voice is calling you;
>
> All over the sky a sacred voice is calling."
>
> I sat there gazing at them, and they were coming from a place where the giant lives (north).But when they were very close to me, they wheeled about toward where the sun goes down, and suddenly they were geese. Then they were gone, and the rain came with a big wind and a roaring.
>
> I did not tell this vision to any one. I liked to think about it, but I was afraid to tell it.[4]

Then, when Black Elk was nine years old, he suddenly fell unconscious and slipped into a coma for twelve days. During those twelve days Black Elk was summoned to a council of the Six Grandfathers representing the earth and sky and the four cardinal points—collectively in Lakota theology *Wakan Tanka*, the Great Mystery, or the six omnipotent powers of the universe.

The Grandfather of the west gave young Black Elk a cup of water, the Grandfather of the north gave him an herb; the Grand-father of the east gave Black Elk a peace pipe; and the Grandfather of the south gave him a red stick. In the vision the Grandfathers eventually took Black Elk to "the high and lonely center of the earth" so that he could "better see and understand" what was being presented to him. There, the Grandfathers granted him six powers: the power to make live, the power to destroy, the power to heal the sick, the power to sustain his nation, the power to make peace, and the power to understand. He was recognized as a "younger brother" by the Six Grandfathers—in Lakota theology this act of recognition by the Six Grandfathers acknowledges Black Elk as the Grandfather representing mankind—and was informed that "all the wings of the air and the stars shall be like relatives." While at the summit, Black Elk was presented with a precognitive view of four future generations of the Lakota people, including the generation that would soon experience cultural annihilation. Then he was instructed to thrust the red stick into the ground, whereupon it immediately grew into a tall cottonwood tree with leafy branches filled with songbirds. Immediately, happy animals and people began to gather under the tree's protective limbs. Then, Black Elk told Neihardt,

> I was standing on the highest mountain of them all, and round about me was the whole hoop of the world. And while I stood there I saw more than I can tell and I understood more than I saw; for I was seeing in a sacred manner the shapes of all things in the spirit and the shape of all shapes as they must live together as one being. And I saw that the sacred hoop of my people was one of many hoops that made one circle, wide as

daylight and starlight, and in the center grew one mighty tree to shelter all the children of one mother and one father. I saw that it was holy.[5]

In 1887, after surviving the Indian wars and the beginning of the reservation era, twenty-four-year-old Black Elk went to Europe with William F. "Buffalo Bill" Cody's *Wild West* production. The holy man was introduced to Queen Victoria, who pronounced the Sioux some of the "finest looking" people she had ever seen. When Cody's *Wild West* troupe departed Great Britain, however, Black Elk and four other Sioux men somehow missed the boat and were left stranded in England. Speaking no English, the quartet were promptly arrested and after a bit of deliberation by the authorities, placed in a copycat Western show called *Mexican Joe's Wild West* that was following in Buffalo Bill's wake. Mexican Joe (Shelley) took Black Elk to France with his show and, after that, to Germany. Eventually slipping away from the Mexican Joe circus, Black Elk wandered back to Paris, where in 1889 he was living with the family of a French woman who had befriended him.

One morning the holy man suddenly slipped into such a profound comatose state that doctors were summoned. When no breath or pulse was detected in Black Elk, doctors assumed him dead and a coffin was ordered. While comatose, however, Black Elk experienced what paranormal researchers describe as astral projection, in which he flew within a cloud at phenomenal speeds across the ocean until he soared over his homeland and was able to identify specific beloved features of the Great Plains. As soon as he looked down and recognized his parents at Pine Ridge, however, the cloud turned and sped back in the direction from whence it had come. When Black Elk returned to Paris and suddenly regained consciousness, he learned that Buffalo Bill's *Wild West* was in Paris and that Cody was searching for him.

"So they took me to where he had his show, and he was glad to see me," Black Elk told Neihardt. "He had all his people give me three cheers. Then he asked me if I wanted to be in the show or if I wanted to go home. I told him I was sick to go home. So he said he would fix that. He gave me a ticket and ninety dollars. Then he gave me a big dinner. Pahuska [Black Elk's pronunciation of Buffalo Bill's Lakota name] had a strong heart."[6]

Cody hired a policeman to accompany Black Elk and make certain the holy man returned safely to Pine Ridge. When Black Elk arrived in South Dakota in 1890, however, Pine Ridge was anything but safe; the Messiah or Ghost Dance movement was spreading rapidly throughout the fledgling reservation system. Black Elk immediately recognized similarities in the Ghost Dance and the power vision of his youth, and in order to answer his many questions about the movement, joined the large numbers of Sioux embracing the new religion. An American Indian interpretation of the Christian Rapture, the Ghost Dance religion threatened and confused Indian agents and other non-Indian leaders, who feared another rise of militant insurgency. These misunderstandings— and perhaps the vengeance of the US Army's 7th Cavalry—led to the massacre at Wounded Knee in December 1890.

Black Elk's cabin in Manderson on Wounded Knee Creek was only a few miles from the location of the fighting, and hearing all the shooting that sad morning, he raced on horseback to defend his people. Black Elk arrived at Wounded Knee after most of the atrocities had occurred, but fierce skirmish fighting was still taking place around the perimeter of the massacre site as soldiers chased down fleeing Lakota people to kill them. Before the morning ended, Black Elk was severely wounded in the stomach, but somehow he had managed to save the lives of a few of his people. Some Lakota believe that Black Elk, having been granted the mysterious "soldier weed" power to destroy by the Six Grandfathers, could have single-handedly annihilated the forces of the military that day with a wave of his hand. Instead, upon witnessing the carnage Black Elk wanted nothing more to do with killing; he immediately relinquished any destructive urge within himself and returned the power to destroy to the Grandfathers. Forty years later he poignantly described the aftermath of the massacre to Neihardt with these often-quoted remarks:

I did not know then how much was ended. When I look back now from this high hill of my old age, I can still see the butchered women and children lying heaped and scattered all along the crooked gulch as plain as when I saw them with eyes still young. And I can see that something else died there in the bloody mud and was buried in the blizzard. A people's dream died there. It was a beautiful dream.[7]

Except when seeking interpretation from a medicine man, the Lakota believe that when a person reveals details of their power vision to any other person they thereby *give away* the power of their vision to that person. For forty years, slowly going blind yet all the while clinging to his vision, Black Elk waited for the empathetic Neihardt to appear so that he could relinquish responsibility and give his power vision to the poet. Black Elk most certainly realized that many of the meanings of his vision might be skewed when translated into a foreign tongue and printed in books that would be read by non-Indians, yet the holy man also understood his vision was for *all* people, and to give it away was also in keeping with the larger Lakota religious concept that everything in the circle of life is related and part of the never-ending act of giving away.[8]

Black Elk choose to give his power vision to Neihardt because he instantly recognized in the poet a man who had broad and deep sympathetic experience with Plains Indians. Aside from being a Homeric poet, Neihardt was a Socialist who recognized that a pure form of socialism manifested itself throughout Plains Indian culture. Moreover, Neihardt had rejected the materialism of the dominant Euro American culture to pursue artistic and spiritual values. Black Elk also recognized that, like himself, Neihardt was an active explorer of the paranormal. Both men were mystics.

Mirroring Black Elk's boyhood experience, when Neihardt was nine years old he developed a very high fever and suddenly slipped into a coma. During the coma Neihardt experienced a dream in which he heard a voice encouraging him onward as he saw himself flying in space at terrific speeds with his hands and arms extended. Since Neihardt had created a crude turbine engine a year before, when he was only eight years old, his family had assumed that he would become an inventor. Neihardt, however, awoke from the coma and immediately announced he was going to be a poet.

In 1900, still in his teens and inspired by his love of the Hindu *Vedas*, Neihardt published his first book, *The Divine Enchantment*. In 1907 he published his first collection of poetry, *A Bundle of Myrrh*. Written in free verse and considered erotic for the times, the book was shunned in America but was immediately well-received in France, where it came to attention of Mona Martinsen, the woman who would soon become Neihardt's wife. A native of New York, Martinsen was a gifted artist, studying in Paris as a star pupil of the famous master sculptor August Rodin. She fell in love with Neihardt's poetry and sent him a letter that initiated regular correspondence. The pair of artists fell in love through their letters and, having never set eyes on each other, agreed to marry. In 1908 Mona returned to her home in New York and caught the train to Omaha to begin fifty years of marriage with her poet.

In 1911 Neihardt abandoned blank verse and lyric poetry in favor of narrative, heroic verse. The next year he began what would eventually become sixteen thousand lines of heroic, narrative epic poetry chronicling and celebrating the "mood of great courage" of the Indian and non-Indian people of the nineteenth century Trans-Missouri. Between 1915 and 1941 Neihardt published the five epic poems that collectively comprise his masterpiece, *A Cycle of the West: The Song of Hugh Glass* in 1915, *The Song of Three Friends* in 1919, *The Song of the Indian Wars* in 1925, *The Song of the Messiah* in 1935, and *The Song of Jed Smith* in 1941.

Black Elk Speaks was actually a diversion from Neihardt's twenty-six years of work on *A Cycle of the West*. In the summer of 1930 Neihardt began research for *The Song of the Messiah*, the work that would eventually become the final poem in the chronological sequencing of the five "Songs" comprising *A Cycle of the West*. That August Neihardt and his son, Sigurd, traveled to Pine Ridge Reservation with hopes of meeting an old medicine man in order to gain a broader understanding of the spiritual aspects of the Messiah movement that swept through Plains Indian tribes at

the close of the Indian wars in the late 1880s and led to the massacre at Wounded Knee. Unlike today when one can freely drive
onto the "rez," Neihardt and his son had to obtain permission from
Bureau of Indian Affairs (BIA) agents to enter Pine Ridge Reservation. Once on the reservation Neihardt and Sigurd were required
to report immediately to the Indian agent there to specify their
intentions. The Indian agent at Pine Ridge told Neihardt about an
old "long-hair" named Black Elk, a "kind of preacher" who lived
at the edge of the reservation in Manderson, a three-building town
on Wounded Knee Creek. The agent said that the old man had
participated in the Ghost Dance movement, was a second cousin
of Crazy Horse, and was present at the Wounded Knee Massacre.
Neihardt knew a Lakota interpreter named Flying Hawk who lived
in Manderson, so, continuing their quest, he and Sigurd immediately drove there. Flying Hawk agreed to introduce them to Black
Elk, but he warned that the old man probably wouldn't speak with
them. Puzzled, Neihardt asked the interpreter to explain. Flying
Hawk replied that the old man was nearly blind, but also "peculiar";
that only a week earlier a nice woman from Lincoln, Nebraska, had
driven up to Pine Ridge and requested a meeting with Black Elk to
talk about Crazy Horse so that she could write an article about the
great warrior. The old man explained he did not wish to talk about
such things and politely turned her away.

When the Neihardts and Flying Hawk drove up to Black Elk's
cabin the old man was outside sitting on the ground under an
arbor of pine boughs. Both Flying Hawk and Sigurd commented
that it seemed like Black Elk was expecting Neihardt. Soon after
they were introduced Neihardt noticed some of Black Elk's curious
Oglala friends lingering about the cabin. Experienced in Indian
Country, Neihardt had come with an ample supply of cigarettes,
so he politely invited them to join the session by silently offering smokes. Soon the group sat on the ground together, smoking
behind silent language barriers.

"Black Elk, with his near-blind stare fixed on the ground,
seemed to have forgotten us," Neihardt wrote in his preface to
Black Elk Speaks, "I was about to break the silence by way of getting

something started, when the old man looked up to Flying Hawk, the interpreter, and said (speaking in Sioux, for he knew no English): 'As I sit here, I can feel in this man beside me a strong desire to know the things of the Other World. He has been sent to learn what I know and I will teach him.'"[9]

The holy man was sixty-seven years old and concerned that he would soon journey to the spirit world having failed to fulfill the powerful vision he experienced as a child. After visiting for nearly five hours, during which time Neihardt attempted to get the old man to talk about some of the more famous military events and personalities of the Indian wars, Black Elk offered only "fragmentary references" to the "other world." Neihardt sensed the old man could not respectfully speak about such matters before the present company of Indians, and he wisely waited for the old man to tell him what to do next.

Black Elk suggested that Neihardt return the following year when the grass was a certain height: "There is so much to teach you," the old man told Neihardt. "What I know was given to me for men and it is true and it is beautiful. Soon I shall be under the grass and it will be lost. You were sent to save it, and you must come back so that I can teach you."[10]

In May 1931 Neihardt returned with two of his daughters, sixteen-year-old Enid and twelve-year-old Hilda. Black Elk invited four of his old "long-hair" friends, Standing Bear, Fire Thunder, Chase In The Morning, and Holy Black Tail Deer, to assist with interpretation, to underscore the religious significance of the telling of the vision, and to validate his story. The interviews were conducted over a sixteen-day period with Neihardt's trained court stenographer daughter, Enid, taking notes grammatically spoken to her by her father after first being interpreted by Black Elk's son, Benjamin, or by Standing Bear.

Originally published in 1932, *Black Elk Speaks*—as told *through* John G. Neihardt—was well-received critically by history aficionados, anthropologists, and ethnologists but failed to capture the general public's attention and was eventually remaindered. Then in 1950, the year Black Elk died, the noted Swiss psychologist

Carl Jung happened upon a copy of *Black Elk Speaks* in Zurich. Fascinated with the classic archetypes represented in the book, Jung immediately urged a Swiss translation and sent his assistant, Carol Bauman, to the University of Missouri to interview Neihardt. Between the years 1950 and 1954 Jung and Neihardt corresponded frequently.[11] After Swiss and German translations of *Black Elk Speaks* were published, other European translations quickly followed, and through word of mouth the book began to steadily attract increasing numbers of young readers. European interest in *Black Elk Speaks* inspired renewed American curiosity that blossomed with a 1960 edition of the book, published just as the baby boomer generation was coming of age.

In Jungian terms, a synchronicity clearly had occurred between Black Elk and post–World War II America. *Black Elk Speaks* communicated in a very personal way numerous timely messages for the counterculture, and for many readers the book was their very first encounter with an alternative religion. Equally significant, this religion was native to North America and explained to readers by a gentle American Indian holy man. Vitally important during the beginning of the great civil rights movement, the book also gave young Indian activists a "means of distinguishing themselves and their issues from the protests and issues of other racial minorities and was an easy reference to use when attempting to describe the life which Indians had lost because of government manipulation."[12]

Black Elk Speaks continued to attract attention as the youth, civil rights, and environmental movements swelled and coalesced throughout the 1960s. Then, in 1969, Vine Deloria Jr. published *Custer Died for Your Sins: An Indian Manifesto*, and the book shot to the top of international best-seller lists. Whereas the Deloria book rallied the burgeoning American Indian and non-Indian youth movements, Dee Brown's *Bury My Heart at Wounded Knee*, published in 1970, was destined to unite with *Black Elk Speaks* and *Custer Died for Your Sins* to create the blossoming of a new literary era in Indian Country. Soon after the publication of *Bury My Heart at Wounded Knee*, television talk show host Dick Cavett began quoting passages from the book on his program, igniting sales.

Dee Brown was the first to humbly admit, however, that *Bury My Heart at Wounded Knee* was indelibly influenced by the work of John Neihardt. Published in 1948, the book that put Dee Brown on the path to *Bury My Heart at Wounded Knee*'s unprecedented literary success twenty-two years later was his *Fighting Indians of the West*, a collection of military archive photographs of nineteenth-century American Indians. Describing how he assembled the book with his partner, Martin Schmitt, Dee wrote in his 1984 essay, "The Power of John Neihardt,"

> In arranging our text and illustrations in a chronological narrative we gave no conscious thought to the epic poetry of John Neihardt, which had sung of the incidents we were trying to depict, yet I know now that we were influenced subconsciously by Neihardt's vision. Both of us had read and re-read *The Song of the Indian Wars* so it was natural for us to break away from the old stereotypes of American Indians that had dominated our history and literature for more than a century…During the following twenty years I published several other books about the west, some concerned with the same events that Neihardt dealt with in his poems…it was as if I were following a well-marked pathway designed by a pioneer trail blazer, although I was not conscious of the fact that I was doing so at the time I chose to write the books. The culmination of the Neihardt influence was *Bury My Heart at Wounded Knee*, his voice being mixed in with the voices of many Indians who spoke poetic prose while I wrote that book.[13]

When Neihardt appeared on the Cavett show in April 1971, *Black Elk Speaks* was perfectly positioned to fulfill the trust the old Sioux placed in John Neihardt nearly four decades earlier. Dee Brown put the event in precise historical context later when he told Dick Cavett that "the greatest thing he had ever accomplished was to bring John Neihardt east of the Mississippi River."[14]

When Dick Cavett first heard the talk circulating around John Neihardt and *Black Elk Speaks*, it instantly reminded him of his high school science teacher in Lincoln, Nebraska. During class

Julius Young often spoke with great fondness about his dear friend, poet, and historian John G. Neihardt. So Cavett naturally contacted Mr. Young to ask if he knew how to reach Neihardt. Mr. Young replied, "Indeed I do, he's living in my basement."[15]

Julius Young and his wife, Myrtle, were two of Neihardt's oldest and dearest friends. In 1923, before the days of state-sponsored historical markers, the trio traveled to Lemon, South Dakota, to erect their own monument to mountain man Hugh Glass at the nearby forks of the Grand River. The inscription read: "1823–1923 This alter to courage was erected by the Neihardt Club August 1, 1923 in memory of Hugh Glass who, wounded and deserted here, began his crawl to Ft. Kiowa in the fall of 1823."[16]

In the late 1960s Julius and Myrtle Young traveled to Neihardt's Skyrim farm outside of Columbia, Missouri, to convince their old friend to return to Lincoln to work on an autobiography. In 1958 Neihardt had lost his beloved wife Mona, and by the late 1960s his cataract-scarred eyesight was rapidly fading, making writing extremely difficult. At Skyrim his daughters Enid, Hilda, and Alice and several favorite students cared for him while he held court with numerous well-wishers and wisdom seekers.

Determined, the Youngs felt a Neihardt autobiography was imperative and convinced their old friend to begin the work in their home in Lincoln. Since Neihardt's daily writing habit was to write throughout the morning and review his work in the evening, they devised a system in their basement incorporating a blackboard-sized wall complete with cup hooks on which enlarged letters could be hung that would enable Neihardt to construct sentences and review his work. The result of their efforts was the publication of two parts of a proposed six-part biographical series, *All Is But a Beginning: A Youth Remembered, 1881–1901*, published in 1972, and *Patterns and Coincidences*, published in 1978, five years after Neihardt's death.

"John Gneisenau Neihardt was born almost a decade before the close of the Indian Wars, and I can never get my mind around this and the fact that I know him," Dick Cavett wrote in his 1972 introduction to *All Is But a Beginning*. "Or that I once sat in a quiet Nebraska living room with him on a Sunday afternoon, sipping beer with a man who, after talking about his impressions of the televised moon walk, could begin the next sentence with, 'When I was a deckhand to Captain Marsh on the *Expansion*...' Because of something I had just read I realized, with a jolt, that he meant Captain Grant Marsh, whose steamer *The Far West* brought home the wounded survivors of Major Reno's command after the Custer battle. It was a few minutes before I regained my equilibrium."[17]

Cavett's exclamation of wonder in Neihardt's presence was a natural reaction—perhaps reflections of the poet's own joyful sense of wonder at having lived so long a life. Neihardt was certainly aware that a long-awaited important moment had finally arrived when Cavett offered the invitation to appear on his program. From the beginning, Neihardt was an unusual personality, apparently conscious of a calling, a sacred destiny; few children announce at nine years of age that they intend to become a poet. Neihardt commented on this aspect of his life at age ninety-two in the introduction to his final book, *Patterns and Coincidences*:

> I have long thought and previously remarked in a wondering exploratory manner that somehow there are dynamic spiritual patterns in our cosmos, that destiny is a matter of being caught up in such a pattern, apparently by accident, and of being compelled to strive for its realization in the stubborn stuff of this world, be it for good or ill.[18]

Is the destiny of *Black Elk Speaks* manifesting in a "dynamic spiritual pattern" such as Neihardt pondered? Visionary thinkers, religious scholars, psychologists, historians, and authors such as Carl Jung, Vine Deloria Jr., Raymond DeMallie, and Dee Brown have speculated for the past sixty years that the social and spiritual impact of *Black Elk Speaks* will last throughout the ages. Because of the profound implications of such assertions, many brilliant scholars have gone to great lengths to determine which part of *Black Elk Speaks* was purely Black Elk's voice and which parts were created by the poet Neihardt. Complicating this discussion, during his two-year sojourn in Europe Black Elk visited the shrines of

Christendom seeking knowledge of the religion of the non-Indian, and this quest lead to his subsequent conversion to Catholicism in 1904. Some scholars argue this resulted in the holy man's ultimate fusion of Plains Indian religion into a hybrid form of Christianity in *Black Elk Speaks*. Some have argued that as a product of western civilization Neihardt was subliminally influenced by his own culture and thereby blindly emphasized Black Elk's Christian allusions and symbols in the book, whereas others have argued that at the time of their meeting, Neihardt was already without peer in the non-Indian world because of his vast and deep knowledge of Plains Indian history and culture and was thus guilty of poetically imposing his pro-Socialist agenda on native culture.

Such critical argument and analysis is of course important to understand *Black Elk Speaks* as a theological and ethnographical classic. Yet this discussion seems to move further away from the very simple point that a hybrid of the two religions and cultures is precisely the point of *Black Elk Speaks*; the uniting of a mystical Plains Indian holy man and non-Indian Homeric poet *as one voice* expressing the vision of a reunification of *both* cultures' "broken hoops" is of singular importance when considering the mythology legacy of the American West. Viewed from this perspective the very simple message of *Black Elk Speaks* is unification of the cultures. Thus the blended voices of an Indian and non-Indian in *Black Elk Speaks* create a mythological metaphor as well as an oral history to guide those who wish to explore the early—and future—encounters of the two cultures meeting where the tall grass grows.

Assuming that *Black Elk Speaks* is by Neihardt's definition being manifested in a "dynamic spiritual pattern in our cosmos," and that "destiny is a matter of being caught up in such a pattern," then it follows that *Custer Died for Your Sins, Bury My Heart at Wounded Knee*, and the torrent of literature and motion pictures about Indian/non-Indian relationships—old and new—that followed those landmark books are also part of a dynamic spiritual pattern that began the moment Europeans first arrived in North America.

Chapter Two
Across the Wide Missouri

*If the vision is true and mighty, as I know, it is true and mighty yet;
for such things are of the spirit, and it is in the darkness of their eyes
that men get lost.*[1]

—Black Elk

In 1803 President Thomas Jefferson initiated an era of expansion
that would ultimately define America as a nation. By 1820 western
expansion would develop into divisive sectionalism in the United
States, but in 1803 the young nation had only recently survived its
first revolutionary rumblings, an aftershock of 1776. A two-party
system of politics had emerged after the political squabble, and
in his farewell address—more worried about partisan divisiveness
than western expansion—George Washington cautioned that this
development caused him great concern; he feared that a two-party
system might eventually tear apart the nation's unity.

The 1800 presidential election nearly proved Washington pro-
phetic. A dangerous electoral struggle was finally resolved with Jefferson's extremely narrow election in the House of Representatives
in 1800, and America emerged with a two-party system of representation in spite of the first president's admonition; the Federalist
and the Democratic-Republican parties now directed the political
fate of the young nation.

As America developed into a nation to be reckoned with on the
world's political stage, the Jeffersonian era coincided with Napoleon's rise to power in France. Earlier Jefferson had served as America's minister to Paris, and the two men became good international
political friends until Napoleon's devious global ambitions forced
Jefferson into a delicate diplomatic situation in the North American
West. As a result of the French and Indian War in 1763, France had
lost most of its North American empire to Great Britain and Spain,

land east of the Mississippi going to the former and west of the Mississippi to the latter. Napoleon had failed in his effort to seize control of a section of the British Empire in India in 1798, returned from the campaign through Egypt, conquered Italy, and was turning his armies toward Germany when his advisors reminded him of France's past glory in North America. Napoleon recognized Spain's decline as a world power as well as America's growing global influence, so he sought to regain France's former holdings in North America in order to attack the British Empire from another front. In what would prove to be a precognitive remark, President Jefferson commented to US Minister to Paris Robert R. Livingston that if France decided to involve itself in North America again it would "change the face of the world."[2]

Bernard DeVoto elaborates on Napoleon's influence on the course of young America's history: "Singularly little ever got written down about the new French Empire in North America. Of the men who have tried to conquer the world, no other had a mind commensurable with Napoleon's, which was infinitely subtle and much concealed from scrutiny. It played with continents as with dice, with nations as with the markers of the game, and seems to have produced intricate and detailed plans as instantaneously as a reflex. Clearly, his design for the colonial empire in North America which would challenge and eventually overturn the British Empire was as specific as that by which he blueprinted the political and juridical reorganization of France."[3]

In October 1800 Napoleon signed a peace agreement with the United States and the very next day forced Spain to cede Louisiana to him in the secret Treaty of San Ildefonso. The peace agreement and the treaty certainly "changed the face of the world" from French, British, and American perspectives. Combined, the actions provocatively reintroduced the greatest military power on the globe—directed by a man who made no secret of his intention to conquer the world—to the western boundary of the republic that was only twelve years old.[4]

Unaware of the San Ildefonso agreement between France and Spain, in the fall of 1802 Jefferson was shocked when, ignoring the

Pinckney Treaty of 1795, which guaranteed the United States access to the port of New Orleans, Spanish authorities suddenly closed the Mississippi River and the port of New Orleans to US commerce. Napoleon had only recently flirted with military involvement in a major slave rebellion in Haiti, so Americans immediately suspected that the dictator's aggressive chicanery on the Mississippi and in New Orleans was part of a military operation to control the Gulf of Mexico. Western US extremists immediately urged President Jefferson to declare war against France. Smelling blood, Jefferson's political opponents in Washington joined western frontiersmen crying for a fight with France. Hoping to force the president into a potentially embarrassing political dilemma, New England Federalists, usually opposed to western expansion, aligned themselves with western extremists. If Jefferson responded to Napoleon with force he risked an international war; yet if he did nothing he would lose the vital political support of the West. Jefferson chose instead a diplomatic option: he would attempt to *buy* New Orleans from Napoleon.

Jefferson selected two excellent representatives to negotiate with Napoleon: the ardently pro-French Robert R. Livingston, and James Monroe, a fellow Virginian who had the confidence and support of western frontiersmen. If they failed to secure from France minimum rights to shipping in the Gulf of Mexico, Monroe and Livingston were ordered by Jefferson to proceed immediately to England to attempt to structure a military alliance with Great Britain against France.

The plan did not have time to be implemented. Napoleon abruptly changed his mind about his North American empire and, through his minister of finance, offered to sell *all* of the Louisiana Territory to the United States. Taken by surprise, Monroe and Livingston were not certain they even had the authority to structure a treaty to purchase Louisiana. Both realized, however, that they had to move quickly or the impetuous dictator might change his mind yet again and withdraw the offer. Monroe and Livingston concluded that the president and Congress could reject the transaction if they disapproved, and the two agreed to the deal on April 30, 1803. For the present-day equivalent of $15 million—$2 million in cash and the assumption of $13 million of French debt to Spain—the United States had instantly more than doubled its domain.[5]

President Jefferson could now justify an interest in exploration of the American West that had intrigued him since the infancy of the republic. While minister to Paris, Jefferson had become involved with a failed expedition to explore the western portion of North America by departing from Europe and traveling through Russia (in the late eighteenth century the southeastern border of Russia was the current northern border of California) to reach the headwaters of the Missouri River. By 1792, as secretary of state, Jefferson proposed to the American Philosophical Society that money should be raised to engage a competent exploration team to approach the American West from the east by ascending the Missouri River. In 1803—before purchasing the Louisiana Territory from France—President Jefferson "sent a confidential message to Congress concerning the establishment of trading houses on the Indian frontier" and at the same time proposed sending an exploratory party to "trace the Missouri to its source" and on to the Pacific. Congress approved the president's plan and the money to fund the "voyage of discovery," led by his friends Meriwether Lewis and William Clark.[6] The explorations of Lewis and Clark provided fundamental information about the United States' new possession—primarily, that the Pacific coast could be reached by an overland water route. Lewis and Clark were, however, also following specific instructions from Jefferson to seek out and engage in peaceful commerce with the indigenous people they encountered on their expedition.

The voyage of discovery followed an intertwined North American river system across the continent to the Pacific Ocean. Upon their return the explorers nevertheless described the West as a vast, hostile region where civilized society could probably not exist. They estimated it would take perhaps as many as ten generations of Americans to unite the coasts and begin to populate the entire continent as a nation. The explorers informed the president that the most positive news they could glean from the unknown territories of the American West was that the region offered an immense, foreboding boundary to prevent an invasion by a military foe. This information was soon corroborated by another exploratory expedition launched the very year of Lewis and Clark's return from the Pacific. Whereas Lewis and Clark traveled over the Great Plains following a water route, in 1806 Jefferson sent Zebulon Pike on the first truly overland US expedition into the unknown southwestern portion of the continent. Pike returned after two years with descriptions of the region that supported the long-held assumption of "the Great American Desert." The popular concept of the desert had existed in written records for two hundred years before that time; Great Plains historian Walter Prescott Webb informs us that the language of period maps reveals that the Great American Desert existed in the records from 1820 until 1858, and in published accounts and in the public mind it "continued to live until after the Civil War."[7]

In spite of such discouraging reports, Jefferson and his fellow architects of the American experiment were heavily influenced by the European Age of Enlightenment and continued to regard unknown North America as the divine blessing of a "second Eden." Revolutionary era heroes like Washington and Jefferson had established a prevailing sense of historical legitimacy in the United States, and a general attitude of optimism for the new culture in the making existed throughout the country; indeed, Lewis and Clark's voyage of discovery echoed the religious legalese of the "doctrine of discovery" Europeans rationalized in the process of making such land deals as the Louisiana Purchase without bothering to invite the indigenous tribal people of the globe to become involved in the transactions.

In fact, few Americans have reflected on exactly *how* colonization was morally justified by European Christians. Instead, mythological stories such as the first Thanksgiving have skillfully promoted the romantic notion that the indigenous people of North America were appreciative of European arrival and indeed eager to receive the blessings of civilization. Christian Europeans were, in reality, forced to deal with theological questions concerning the morality—indeed, the spiritual legality—of taking lands claimed by aboriginal inhabitants. Thus exploration, colonization, and settlement required concepts by which Europeans could relate to North American natives, and Christians naturally developed legal theories that gave them all the power in negotiations.[8]

In 1550, faced with the moral implications of stealing land outright, the Christian nations of Europe found it necessary to hold a sanctimonious debate concerning the New World and Indians in which Spanish, English, French, and Swiss intellectuals unanimously agreed upon Rome's papal resolution—the doctrine of discovery. This doctrine became a cornerstone of international law—as defined by European nations—for several centuries. The legal and religious rationalization of the doctrine of discovery allowed the discoverer of "unoccupied lands" around the globe a right to claim title of the land against other European nations. Benevolently, the theological legislation granted Indians in the Americas and other indigenous peoples of the world "aboriginal title."

"Aboriginal title," treaty authority Vine Deloria Jr. explains, "is a legal concept ultimately endorsed by the Supreme Court of the United States, which describes the nature of ownership of land held by the Indians within the legal framework of the Anglo-American judicial system. It is a concept which has its origins outside of the courts of Anglo-Saxon heritage. Since it is a pragmatic, politically created concept of the European powers, in discussing it we are forced to use the western perceptions of what the Indian use of land and ownership meant. This required that we reject our knowledge of the Indian civilizations and consider Indian rights in light of what Europeans imagined them to be in the European system."[9]

Deloria's interpretation of Euro American use of written English law and the printed word to define its relationship with Indians is supported by the fact that from its very beginning, the foundation of American culture and jurisprudence was based on the printed word as well as on oration based on the printed word. Here it is important to note also that as an unprecedented event in the history of civilization, the United States was founded by intellectuals and scientists, many of whom Richard Hofstadter reminds us were well-educated in classical philosophy and "who used their wide reading in history, politics, and law to solve the exigent problems of their time."[10]

American Indians were the very first "exigent problem" faced by the collective reasoning of the enlightened visionaries who conceived and constructed the remarkable US Constitution. In their initial interactions, colonialists like Thomas Jefferson generally assumed that Indians would eventually be assimilated into Euro American culture but placed Indians in one of three categories. "Praying Indians" were those who quickly converted to Christianity and were living in towns segregated from non-Indians. "Frontier Indians" dwelled on the western fringe of civilization, often causing trouble but remaining weak and vulnerable against the more powerful whites. The third group was of course the stronger, still "wild," and potentially violent tribes living beyond the reaches of civilization. Jefferson did not believe Indians and whites could live together peacefully. Instead, he believed the smaller Indian populations would eventually be absorbed by racial intermingling and marriage. Still, rather than allowing nature to take its course, the author of the Declaration of Independence and the immortal words "all men are created equal" was indeed the very first man to suggest removal of Indians from their ancestral lands in order to protect them from abuse by non-Indians; it was Thomas Jefferson who first sought, but failed, to remove the Cherokee Indians from their homeland to territories obtained through the Louisiana Purchase. Jefferson's segregation concept would of course become morally and legally controversial when it was actually implemented during the administration of President Andrew Jackson. Old Hickory's Indian Removal Act of 1830 "sanctified" the forced removal of tribes from their ancient lands in the southeastern section of the continent to the "Indian Territories" west of the Mississippi River and created an indelible stain on our nation's honor by launching the removal of the Choctaw and Cherokee Nations known as the Trail of Tears.[11]

Problematic as the legal and moral issues created by legislation and treaties were destined to become, however, the psychological relationship the Euro Americans entered into with the indigenous people of North America was perhaps even more complicated. The very presence of Europeans in North America was an indication of the psychological problems inherent in the situation, for upon breaking away from Europe it became immediately imperative for colonialists to define themselves as citizens of the New World. To counter any European notions that American democracy was simply a mob of hooligans rebelling against the monarchy, early colonial efforts to determine a mythic national character—a collective American identity—focused on military heroes like Washington, scholars like Jefferson and his friend Benjamin Franklin, gentleman-farmers, intellectuals, patriots, prominent statesmen, and other sterling personifications that embodied virtue, principles, and independence. Yet at the turn of the nineteenth century, as the leaders from the Revolutionary period began to pass with time, Americans sought a new generation of hero—an "American Adam"—to explore, to conquer, and to dwell in this new Eden.

Even before Revolutionary War, characters like Daniel Boone had donned Indian buckskins and begun blurring the lines between fiction and reality to create a new "American Genesis" mythology. Born in 1734, Boone was already dead by the 1820s, when American entrepreneurs first began to ascend the Missouri River on fur expeditions designed to penetrate the heart of the American West. But during Boone's long, colorful lifetime the original American frontiersman ventured into the Appalachian Mountains, opened the famous Cumberland Gap, and initiated the migration of more than two hundred thousand colonialists into the regions south of the Northwest Territory and the Ohio River in what would become Kentucky and Tennessee.

By 1806, western pioneers along the Ohio River had gotten glimpses of another variation of the American Adam in the form of a skinny, thirty-year-old man who violated treaty boundaries by venturing into northwest Indian Territory, went barefoot year-round, allegedly wore a burlap coffee sack for a shirt and a tin pot for a hat, and was noted for sleeping in hollowed-out logs. John Chapman was nicknamed Johnny Appleseed by pioneers along the Ohio River as he lazily floated in two dugout log canoes lashed together. One of Chapman's canoes usually contained a small pile of apple seeds that he had meticulously covered with moss and mud to prevent their drying in the sun. With a single bushel of those precious seeds Chapman could plant more than three hundred thousand apple trees along the Ohio and its tributaries.

Even though Euro American frontier legends (and later, romantic animator Walt Disney) portrayed Chapman as a naturalist and a socio-agricultural bridge between Indian and non-Indian culture, botanist Michael Pollan reveals that Chapman was in reality a pioneer American businessman. Pollan notes that by planting apple orchards in the wilderness, John Chapman was more accurately a pragmatic real-estate agent than pantheistic nature boy and suggests that Johnny Appleseed was planting signposts of civilization for settlers heading west from the colony states. Chapman was completely aware that pioneers who followed him down the Ohio River would arrive at a choice location he had hand-picked for an orchard and thus designated as a prime setting for homesteading. Consequently, Chapman's nurseries of apple orchards would become mature advertisements for his real estate ventures by the time settlers set eyes on them. Pollan also notes that the apples Chapman was planting were not the sweet, delicious varieties we are familiar with today. Instead, the apple trees Chapman was planting were destined to produce bitter crab apples, perfect for making cider. Because of the fear of diseases, most pioneers drank cider rather than water, and Johnny Appleseed was essentially creating an alcohol trail for Euro Americans to follow into the wilderness. Perhaps of even more fundamental importance, with his apple trees Chapman, like any good salesman, was selling memories and token assurances to settlers of the past they had left behind, providing a comforting sense of civilization in their adventure in the wilderness.[12]

Johnny Appleseed's fermented apples may have made the wilderness experience more comfortable for early pioneers, but fur is what inspired entrepreneurs to head west. By pioneering very successful commercial ventures in the fur trade, the British and French had already established a healthy colonial presence in the

Great Lakes and Mississippi and lower Missouri River regions of the interior. In 1808, two years after Lewis and Clark returned from their expedition, New York fur shop owner John Jacob Astor requested and received permission from President Jefferson to organize the American Fur Company. In 1811, on the Columbia River in what was known as the Oregon Territory, Astor founded the first US community on the Pacific coast. It exploded into one of the most phenomenally successful financial empires in North America, even rivaling Great Britain's Hudson's Bay Company in Canada. Yet even as the fame of Astor's wealth spread throughout the East, Americans remained blissfully ignorant of the West. Most citizens still lived in the rapidly growing eastern population centers, and the general public's opinion of the West as the Great American Desert remained popular until an unlikely footnote in fashion changed the course of history: men in European and American cities began wearing stovepipe hats. The finest of these hats were made from the fur of beaver, and the price of beaver pelts exploded. By 1821 reports of millions of beaver in the Rocky Mountains began to buzz throughout America and Europe.

Nestled at the confluence of the mighty Missouri and the muddy Mississippi, St. Louis was the last city on the edge of civilization and the first city on the edge of the frontier. Established in 1809, Manuel Lisa's Missouri Fur Company was the most successful St. Louis operation in the early fur trade on the Missouri River. By 1812, at the Three Forks of the Missouri River in what is now Montana, a rogue explorer and entrepreneur, Major Andrew Henry, built the first fort west of the Mississippi River. Indians promptly burned it to the ground.

John Jacob Astor's fur empire on the north Pacific coast and Great Britain's Hudson's Bay Company in Canada were extremely successful, yet in reality the United States interior fur trade was completely dependent upon friendly socioeconomic relations with Indians. Cordial relationships were not always possible, and many of the friendly tribes did not trap beaver. Major Henry, the British, the French, and a few independent traders like St. Louis's Manuel Lisa and Pierre Chouteau persisted, however, and trading with less-friendly Indians in the region who *did* trap and trade fur, they began to establish commerce on the upper Missouri. In 1821 Major Andrew Henry returned to St. Louis seeking a financial backer and partner to fund a trading expedition to the headwaters of the Yellowstone. His timing was finally perfect. By 1822 demand for beaver pelts was at its peak, and it was suddenly economically feasible to risk a major commercial expedition into the unknown territory.

Andrew Henry found his partner when he met General William Ashley, a St. Louis politician who needed money to fuel his political aspirations of becoming governor of Missouri. Throughout the early 1800s Ashley had watched rogue traders like Manuel Lisa and Pierre Chouteau ascend the Missouri River with a relatively small investment and return with a fortune in fur.

Ashley and Henry placed an ad in the Missouri Republican in March 1822 seeking "100 enterprising young men," and they quickly filled their quota. Jedediah Smith, Hugh Glass, Mike Fink, James Clyman, William Carpenter, Thomas Fitzpatrick, William and Milton Sublette, Jim Bridger, and others destined to become legendary characters in early western history were among the men who joined the expedition. Ashley and Henry's partnership set in motion one of the most significant events in American history: it was the first organized group of free, enterprising Euro Americans to venture into the interior of the American West to live there.

Following Lewis and Clark's lead, early explorers—American traders or French singing voyageurs—stayed on the rivers much the way modern Americans travel interstate highways. The men of the Ashley-Henry expedition became known as mountain men simply because they were the first to depart the rivers and venture into the mountains on horseback and foot. Within twenty years of their entry into the West, the path they opened would become the trail of a phenomenal migration across the continent. Aside from exploring the upper Missouri and establishing relationships with Indian tribes of the region, by creating commercial enterprises with indigenous people the mountain men established the United States as an economic power in the Rocky Mountains. This was important, as Great Britain, France, Spain, and even Russia were challenging the United States' ability to actually claim military dominance of the region. Indeed, many of these colonial powers—especially Great Britain—surreptitiously instigated many of the problems between the American mountain men and Indian tribes of the upper Rockies in efforts to undermine their successful commercial entry into the region. Moreover, because their basic needs were all that concerned them, Indians did not make good commercial hunters or trappers.

Yet the price of fur—specifically beaver pelts—was skyrocketing in major European and American markets, and this created fur entrepreneurs like Ashley, who quickly came to depend upon a wild group of young, flamboyant, devil-may-care, non-Indians who could coexist in a precarious economic relationship between Indians and businessmen. The arrangement between the trappers and the St. Louis entrepreneurs was essentially a Rocky Mountain version of the old agricultural form of debt peonage known as sharecropping—a financial arrangement Indians could not imagine. When the smoke cleared in the Rockies, however, the American mountain men prevailed economically—and martially.[13]

Aside from establishing economic and military dominance when no US army existed anywhere near the remote region, these men had no idea that by entering the unknown territories of the upper Rockies they were also becoming active participants in the creation of a new American mythology. In his landmark book *The Hero with a Thousand Faces*, mythologist Joseph Campbell defined the central heroic myths of every culture as proceeding through three distinct phases: "A hero ventures forth from the world of common day into a region of supernatural wonder; fabulous forces are there encountered, and a decisive victory is won; the hero comes back from this mysterious adventure with the power to bestow boons on his fellow man."[14]

As previously mentioned, D. H. Lawrence, Philip J. Deloria, and other scholars who have pondered the creation of the American personality have observed that simply by being in North America, colonists suffered a psychic crisis because their very presence indicated their desire to define themselves as separate from their European roots, yet as civilized Christians they could not wholly embrace the heathen "Indian" implication of adapting to the natural environment of the New World. In *America's Prophet: How the Story of Moses Shaped America*, author Bruce Feiler notes that throughout the Middle Ages Catholics were not allowed to read the Bible directly and that the Reformation and the invention of the printing press finally brought Bibles into the hands of every-day people. Yet because of the domination of the Catholic Church, oppressed Protestants began to closely identify with the story of Moses leading the tribes of Israel through the desert. Feiler notes that in particular the Puritan sect of Protestantism that colonized America strongly identified with Moses and the Israelites fleeing from an Egyptian king and crossing the Red Sea, because they were crossing the ocean to flee from King George. Feiler continues this analogy to suggest that frontier characters like Daniel Boone represented the American version of Moses leading a chosen people through the wilderness into their promised land.[15]

Defying such psychological, cultural, and religious barriers, the men of the Ashley-Henry expedition of 1822 and 1823 most certainly embraced the indigenous culture of North America while they also clearly met Campbell's standards as mythmakers; indeed, inhabiting the indigenous culture of North America to become a mythmaker is what would eventually distinguish the very fine line between "playing Indian" and "going native." Because of their absolute immersion into Indian culture, the mountain men would thus become recognized as the very first collective manifestation of American freedom and individuality in the heart of the "wilder-ness" of the New World. Since they were totally immersed in the Indian culture in order to survive, the greatest compliment one could pay a mountain man was, "I took you fer an Injun."

Historical events ultimately proved that General Ashley's instincts to pursue his political aspirations on the frontier were on target; the rise of the "first frontiersman president," Andrew Jackson, to the highest office in America directly coincided with the Ashley-Henry expedition. Old Hickory's ascension to the presidency began with America's squabbles with Great Britain over the North American fur trade and conflicting claims upon Indian lands as these controversial issues soon exploded into the War of 1812. Even though that war essentially ended in a stalemate, Americans could rightfully claim one certain victory: the Battle of New Orleans. Andrew Jackson had already earned his flinty reputation as an Indian fighter defeating the Creek Indians in Mississippi and Alabama and the Seminoles in Florida, but during the War of 1812, when he learned the British were moving toward New Orleans, he raced to the Crescent City with his backwoods buckskin brigades to greet and soundly defeat them. Even as Old Hickory's forces were engaging British General Pakenham's redcoats in battle, negotiations for a peace treaty between America and Great Britain had already concluded in Belgium; a five-man American commission led by John Quincy Adams and Henry Clay had structured a peace agreement with commissioners from Great Britain *before* the first shot of the Battle of New Orleans was fired. Communications of that era were so rudimentary that word of the peace agreement did not reach Jackson and Pakenham before their forces started shooting each other. Even though Jackson's famous victory in New Orleans had absolutely no effect on the outcome of the War of 1812, the battle nevertheless defined him as an American frontier hero, and this celebrity launched his political career.

Since pre-Revolutionary days, frontiersman hostility towards what they viewed as elitism had been seething and bubbling barely below the surface in American culture, and the presidential election of 1824 caused this antagonism to suddenly boil over. After campaigning as a champion of the frontier and winning the popular vote in the campaign of 1824, Andrew Jackson lost the election in the House of Representatives to John Quincy Adams, son of the second US president, John Adams. The election of Adams over Jackson intensified the strained elitism issue as Old Hickory's populist following was enraged and viewed the decision in the House of Representatives as a rejection of a "man of the people" by the politically powerful and overeducated. The stage was set for a cultural revolution.

Anti-elitism exploded in 1828 during the second presidential campaign between Andrew Jackson and John Quincy Adams. The son of a president and former Harvard professor, Adams symbolized to ordinary Americans the privileged European intellectualism they increasingly renounced. Jackson, on the other hand, was the obdurate military hero from Tennessee who had won the Battle of New Orleans in the War of 1812 and represented the quintessential American—a willful and pragmatic frontiersman. The first major populist movement in American presidential politics swept Jackson into office with a mandate. Once elected, Jackson broke precedent and became the first president to invite the general public to his inaugural ball in the White House. The cultural war in America was officially declared with Jackson's symbolic action. The hoi polloi eagerly accepted Old Hickory's invitation, and thousands swarmed into the "people's house," broke rare and fragile china, and stood in muddy boots on ornate chairs in order to get a better glimpse of the new president. Fights soon broke out, and Jackson himself barely escaped injury at the hands of well-wishers and was forced to flee the riot as the mob ultimately wrecked the White House. The throngs of people were eventually able to be dispersed like livestock only by being lured outside with food and refreshments on the White House lawn.

Neal Gabler links the White House riot with the birth of American entertainment and describes the 1828 election of Jackson as

> a deliberate, self-conscious expression of cultural hostility—a willful attempt to raze the elitists' high culture and destroy their authority by creating a culture the elitists would detest. In this view, trash was a choice, a choice made precisely *because* it seemed so antithetical to Culture and *because* promoting it would infuriate the aristocrats, so that there was actually a cause and effect between how much the elitists decried entertainment and how much entertainment flourished. Or, put another way, whatever else it was, mass entertainment may have begun as the democrats' revenge against the elites they despised.[16]

Reading and storytelling were of course early forms of American entertainment, but dance and musical contests, theatrical performances, museums, freak shows, and literary publishing efforts also reflected the young nation's robust creative personality. The rise of Jackson's "frontiersman" persona punctuated the transition of American entertainment into the genesis of the culture of celebrity that would by the late twentieth century become so pervasive that it would overwhelm virtually every aspect of American society. While the dawning of modern media also began in the 1820s with the rapid rise of populations in the East creating increased newspaper circulation, the romantic representation of the mountain man of the American West was destined to become imprinted in the general public's consciousness by the 1840s when "penny newspapers" evolved into "dime novels" and forever intertwined Jim Bridger protégé Kit Carson's name into the American mythological fabric. Yet it was during the frontiersman phase of Jackson's tenure—1828 to 1836—that several of the Ashley-Henry expedition's ranks, such as Jim Bridger, Jedediah Smith, and Hugh Glass, started to become famous in the East.

The 1822 Ashley-Henry expedition was ultimately a financial failure, and by 1823 the partners faced bankruptcy. Their "enterprising young men" had originally signed on as river traders, a livelihood that consisted of setting up a trade blanket at specific locations on the river and waiting for curious Indians to arrive. The tribes of the upper Missouri River who trapped beaver, fox, wolves, and coyotes, remained loyal to the early French traders, yet few of the Indians of the region trapped animals for fur, and when Ashley and Henry's expedition arrived in the region, only a very few inquisitive, but suspicious, Indians came to trade fur with the Americans.

So Ashley made a historic decision. He would return to St. Louis and gather another one hundred young men, resupply, and return the following year to rendezvous with Major Henry at a specific location and time. In the meantime Ashley ordered his partner to send the young men out into the mountains as trappers. This single act initiated major interaction between the Indian tribes of the upper Missouri and the United States, while it also began the process of providing the first intimate knowledge of the landscapes of President Jefferson's purchase nearly a quarter-century earlier.

Upon entering the Yellowstone country, however, the expeditioners entered a region that had been fraught with bitter, intertribal warfare since antiquity. The Absaroka (Crow) tribe held the crown jewel of the upper Rockies: the Yellowstone. Naturally, all the other regional tribes wanted the Crow's land, and the Crow were in a constant state of defending themselves at all points on the compass: from the southeast, the Arapaho; from the southwest, the Shoshone; from the north, the Blackfeet; and from the east, their greatest enemies, the powerful Lakota. So when the mountain men arrived in the Yellowstone country in need of allies themselves, they found an eager counterpart in the Crow; the Americans brought horses and guns to the Crow, and the Crow offered the Americans sanctuary in the midst of the dangerous tribes.

By becoming allies with the Crow, however, the mountain men made enemies of one of the tribe's most hostile foes —the Blackfeet. To avoid the dangerous Blackfeet in the north, the traders—now trappers—headed south, where they formed new friendships and alliances with the Shoshone. It was from the Shoshone that they heard stories of large colonies of beaver farther south. In 1824 a small party of trappers "discovered" a pass over the Wind River mountain range that was actually pioneered a decade earlier by John Jacob Astor's Astorians and their bold overland expedition returning from his Oregon colony. The Ashley-Henry trappers christened the route the South Pass. In less than twenty years this route would become the major passageway through the northern Rockies as hundreds of thousands of immigrants crossed the South Pass en route to the Pacific coast. More timely and crucial to the Ashley-Henry Fur Company, however, as they exited the pass and continued south, Jim Bridger, Jedediah Smith, the Sublette brothers, William and Milton, and others came upon the Seeds-ske-di (Prairie Chicken) River. There, the exploring trappers discovered one of the largest interconnected systems of beaver colonies in the world. For twelve years this area supplied the world with pelts, until the beaver in the region were trapped to the brink of extinction and demand plummeted as fashion favor shifted from felt to hats made of silk.

Yet the discovery of the Seeds-ske-di was only the beginning. As previously mentioned, the early traders used the rivers like modern Americans use interstate highway systems. Ashley and Henry's dream of a phenomenal beaver harvest had come true, but the colony was many hazardous miles away from the "highway" of the Missouri River and the marketplace.

The French word *rendezvous* adds a romantic, sometimes mysterious, patina to the rather mundane meaning of an appointment to meet at a specific time and place. But Ashley's use of the word during the fur trade era was absolutely pragmatic. When Ashley was forced to return to St. Louis for more men and supplies, he and Henry made a second historic decision: they agreed to meet at a specific place in the foothills of the Uinta Mountains, at an exact time in the spring—a rendezvous. This act created a brilliant organizational structure that soon made them fabulously wealthy, but it also established the first major social and commercial interaction between Americans and the indigenous peoples of the upper Missouri. The mountain men would gather annually at various locations in the Rockies for rendezvous, where traders would arrive from St. Louis with supplies, and two weeks of robust commerce and merrymaking would ensue. Their favorite location was a mountain "hole," or high-altitude, grassy prairie completely ringed by snowcapped mountain peaks. A rendezvous required vast grass prairies to feed the large numbers of horses and mules as, at its peak, huge tipi cities would emerge. The rendezvous of 1830 drew more than four thousand Indians and several hundred trappers.

The mountain men would bring a year's worth of pelts on a fur caravan across the plains, deserts, and mountain ranges to rendezvous. Traders would bring such things as guns, gunpowder, blankets, foodstuffs, traps, trinkets, and whiskey. Firewater and the precious circumstance of social interaction certainly encouraged the tradition, but "yarning" was already a popular pastime throughout the eastern United States during the early nineteenth century, and at rendezvous the mountain men developed the art form to its highest standard. Jim Bridger was a natural-born yarner who at rendezvous developed into a master. For example, he once described a canyon so large that when he camped there he would prepare his bedding at the edge of its cliffs, yell, "Jim Bridger, git out of them covers!" and then go to bed, and eight hours later the echo of his voice would return and wake him. A generation later, on a theatrical stage, inspired by the mountain men he had admired as a child and emulated as an adult, William F. "Buffalo Bill" Cody would develop the art of yarning to the level of mythology, but the embryonic form of the Western was itself created and perfected around the fires of trapper rendezvous.

Early in the Ashley-Henry expedition, Andrew Henry had pioneered an alternate, tributary river route to avoid the fierce upper Missouri. The expedition departed the Missouri and followed the Grand River southwest to the Power River Country, and then on into the upper Rockies and the Yellowstone, thus avoiding thousands of miles over the northern portions of the Great Plains. After the rendezvous system was in place and functioning successfully, however, it became imperative to find an even quicker route to get the fur back to St. Louis. Soon, acting on Shoshone advice, Thomas "Broken Hand" Fitzpatrick descended the North Platte River to the Missouri River and returned in record time to St. Louis with a season's beaver harvest.[17]

Aside from the party, however, rendezvous was first and foremost a time for the mountain men to replenish their supplies. Trappers would often spend a year's worth of earnings in two weeks at rendezvous before heading back out into the mountains for another fifty weeks. Thus the rendezvous system encouraged and continued the deep exploration of the landscape and indigenous culture of the region. Indeed, many of the mountain men married Indian women at rendezvous. These Indian women became the centerpiece of the success of the rendezvous system and, one might argue, of the fur trade itself. Without the invaluable assistance of Indian women, American mountain men and their rendezvous system could not have survived the transition into the indigenous culture of the Rocky Mountains. Indian women's knowledge of the customs and languages of various tribes and locations of beaver colonies was priceless. They taught mountain men Indian languages, informed them where to go, and warned them where *not* to go. At the peak of the fur trade era a mountain man like Jim Bridger commanded a small brigade of trappers working in a large region either individually or in little groups. Each member of the trapping brigade returned with his harvest to a central hearth—headed by Bridger and, ultimately, his Indian wife.

Chapter Three

The Road of the Emigrants

They told us that they only wanted to use a little land, as much as a wagon would take between the wheels; but our people knew better. And when you look about you now, you can see what it was they wanted.[1]

—Black Elk

By the late 1830s silk had replaced beaver pelts as the choice material to make the world's finest hats, and with the western beaver population also severely diminished, the bottom fell out of the American market. Facing the end of the fur trade era in 1841, Jim Bridger headed east to his home state of Missouri. Only thirty-seven years old and already recognized as America's premiere mountain man, Bridger had spent over half his life in the Rocky Mountains. Nineteen years earlier, like the majority of the hundred youngsters who signed on with the historic Ashley-Henry expedition, he had ventured into the West as a callow eighteen-year-old; few of Bridger's teenage companions on the expedition lived past the age of twenty-five. A survivor, in the fall of 1824 Bridger accepted a hazardous mission to ride a bull boat down the rapids of the Bear River and became the first white man to see the Great Salt Lake. Bridger had also participated in the discovery of the phenomenal beaver colonies along the Seeds-ske-di River by the Ashley Henry trappers and profited from the successful financial system that accompanied it. He had been an integral part of the team of explorers that had unwittingly established an American presence and economic toehold in the region for the young United States, forced competing European colonial powers to depart, and allowed the western expansion of the American population to truly begin.

In 1841, more than any living man—red or white—Jim Bridger was said to be in possession of the broadest knowledge of the unknown territory of the American West. Still, as Bridger's occupation suddenly vanished, his geographic sagacity and comprehension of Indian language and culture seemed useless and only contributed to his doubts concerning his abilities to earn a living in the society he had rejected as a youth. Having survived two Indian wives, Bridger was also a widower with several children to support, and his best options to care for his family appeared to be back in Missouri. So he decided to return to St. Louis and become a blacksmith, an occupation he had trained for as a boy.

Following Broken Hand Fitzpatrick's overland fur caravan route east along the North Platte River in 1841, Jim Bridger headed to Missouri and his uncertain future. Bridger certainly realized the fur trade era had affected America, but he could never have imagined the magnitude of historical events already set in motion in the East during the preceding decade. While Bridger was heading east, the population of the United States had already begun what would soon swell into an unprecedented, massive western immigration. Ironically, this western migration also included the forced removal of entire nations of Indian people from the southeastern portion of North America.

At the beginning of the 1830s President Andrew Jackson had signed into law Thomas Jefferson's earlier notion of segregating Indian and non-Indian people. In his first message to Congress on December 8, 1829, President Jackson called upon southern legislators to send him a bill that would allow him to adopt Indian removal as official government policy. After intense debate in which eastern congressmen denounced the legislation as a corruption of American honor, the Indian Removal Act was enacted on May 28, 1830.

The result of Jackson's legislation was that throughout the 1830s massive numbers of Indian tribes were forcibly removed from the southern Ohio and Mississippi valleys to the western plains. Perhaps the most famous of these tribes were the Cherokee, Creek, and Choctaw. In the last half of the 1830s sixteen thousand Cherokee walked from their ancestral homes in Georgia, the Carolinas, and Tennessee to their newly assigned lands in the Indian

Territory. Likewise, the Choctaw were forced to surrender all their land east of the Mississippi—more than ten million acres—and relocate to Indian Territory.

During the spring of 1831, when Jackson's Indian Removal Act was in the first stages of enforcement and the Choctaws and Creeks were being relocated to Indian Territory, a twenty-six-year-old Frenchman named Alexis de Tocqueville and his companion Gustave de Beaumont arrived in the United States. The young men had been sent by the French government to study the US prison system, but both were astute social scientists and eager to analyze why republican representative democracy blossomed in America when it had withered and failed to take root elsewhere. The two French sociologists traveled extensively throughout the United States observing every minute aspect of American culture. When the pair returned to France, de Tocqueville wrote *Democracy in America*, which immediately became popular in both the United States and Europe and even today remains one of the most probing early psychological examinations of the young American nation. Alexis de Tocqueville was greatly impressed with many aspects of American society—but particularly with the rapid expansion of the population on the western frontier. His *Democracy in America* strongly suggests this occurred because of the equality of the citizens of the United States: "Amongst the novel objects that attracted my attention during my stay in the United States," de Tocqueville writes, "nothing struck me more forceably [sic] than the general equality among the people…it creates opinions, gives birth to new sentiments, founds novel customs, and modifies what it does not produce,…I perceived that this equality of conditions is the fundamental fact from which all others seem to be derived and the central point at which all my observations constantly terminated."[2]

De Tocqueville observed that the "gradual and continuous progress of the European race toward the Rocky Mountains has the solemnity of a providential event," which led him also to conclude that because of the equality of the population of the United States, a "great democratic revolution was going on amongst us." Yet in one of history's great ironies, the entire indigenous population of the southeast portion of North America was being removed from their ancestral lands at the threat of violence, and it was all based on an idea first suggested by the man who wrote the immortal line, "All men are created equal."

Still, the great westward migration de Tocqueville defined as being motivated by equality had begun. On the prairie along his way east, Bridger encountered a small group of bewildered travelers en route to the Rocky Mountains and beyond —to Oregon Territory. Lost and in desperate need, the group convinced Bridger to change his plans and instead guide them across the prairie and through the mountains. Jim Bridger had unwittingly discovered a way to remain in the West; he spent the next twenty years directly involved in the business of guiding travelers along what he defined as "the Emigrant's Road." In a December 1843 letter Bridger had someone write to his friend and fellow trapper Pierre Chouteau, he reported: "I have established a small fort with a blacksmith shop and supply of iron in the road of the emigrants on Black's Fork of Green River which promises fairly."[3]

America's original fur trade historian, Hiram M. Chittenden, says of the founding of Bridger's trading post and blacksmith shop, "In the year 1843 James Bridger, whose name will always be prominent in the annals of Western adventure, built a post on a tributary of Green River, a water of the Pacific Ocean, for the convenience of the emigrants. It was the first trading post beyond the Mississippi ever built for this purpose, and its establishment marks the beginning of the era of emigration into the Far West."[4] Jim Bridger had become the first guide of what would eventually become one of the most celebrated migrations of humanity in world history. From 1843 to 1869 approximately three hundred thousand emigrants traveled the Oregon Trail linking the world to the pristine heart of North America.

Much of the inspiration for the migration originated in the mind of Hall Jackson Kelley, a Boston school teacher, textbook publisher, surveyor, and vociferous advocate for the termination of a joint occupation treaty between the United States and Great Britain concerning "the Oregon Country." A romantic inspired by the publication of the journals of the Lewis and Clark Expedition and the phenomenal success of John Jacob Astor and his American Fur Company, Kelley urged the complete "Americanization" of the Oregon Country. Kelley began to lobby Washington, but in 1818 Congress extended the Oregon Country Joint-Occupation Treaty with Great Britain for ten years. Undaunted, Kelley created the Oregon Colonization Society, developed around a vision of Americans—as their pilgrim forefathers crossing oceans into the unknown New World—crossing and linking the North American continent by land. Kelley claimed providence was shaping America's destiny.[5] Decades later, in 1845, New York journalist John L. O'Sullivan, inspired by years of conflicting newspaper editorials arguing the virtues and folly of overland travel to Oregon, coined the term *Manifest Destiny*.

Before Great Britain and the United States entered the joint occupation treaty in 1819, the Oregon Country was claimed simultaneously by four nations: Spain, Russia, Great Britain, and the United States. Oregon Country boundaries extended from the 42nd parallel north at the northern border of California to 54° 40' north, the southern boundary of Alaska. Spain relinquished its claim to Oregon in 1819 in the very same treaty that ceded Florida to the United States and defined the southern boundaries of the Louisiana Territory. Russia's continuing claims to the territory inspired President James Monroe to issue his famous Monroe Doctrine in 1823, in which he announced to the world that the United States would no longer tolerate colonization in the Western Hemisphere. Newspapers and periodicals in Great Britain were consistent in their opposition to US claims to the Oregon territory, though most called for the dispute to be settled by arbitration rather than force. British journalists argued that it was impossible for the United States to colonize Oregon by land and too expensive to accomplish by sea, and therefore called their claims superfluous.[6]

Some prominent American journalists were also opposed to overland travel to Oregon for the purpose of colonization. Dispelling the national myth associated with his iconic "Go West Young Man" remark, Horace Greeley is perhaps the best example of a negative viewpoint concerning the colonization of Oregon. The editor of the *New York Daily Tribune*, Greeley has been consistently depicted in nationalistic American mythology as a powerful advocate of westbound emigration. Greeley's position concerning Oregon, however, fell in line with eastern opponents of western emigration. The noted pioneer journalist acknowledged American claims to Oregon Territory but advised against risking conflict with Britain by attempting to colonize the region. Greeley believed that not only would efforts to settle Oregon be financially prohibitive, but the region itself would not prove as valuable as those in favor of colonization maintained. Furthermore, Greeley believed the distance to Oregon alone prevented it being effectively included in the Union. Greeley's columns repeatedly urged the United States and Great Britain to relinquish their claims to Oregon in order to allow the territory be settled and developed as an independent nation.[7]

While Greeley editorialized against overland travel to Oregon, Americans nevertheless continued flocking into the Trans-Missouri. Whereas most of the first emigrants were political and philosophical followers of Hall Jackson Kelley and the Christian missionary Jason Lee, increasingly more religious sects began to join the western movement. Describing religion in the United States, Alexis de Tocqueville observed that "Americans combine the notions of liberty and religion so intimately in their minds that it is impossible to make them conceive of one without the other." By the mid-nineteenth century evangelical Protestantism—a form of Christianity that Neal Gabler has noted could have been born only in the tolerant environment of American democracy—was the most popular religious movement in America, yet conventional nineteenth-century European Christians would probably not have even considered evangelical Protestantism as worship. Conversely, American worshipers embraced the connections between evangelicalism and entertainment. Walt Whitman observed that working-men attending revival meetings in the 1830s behaved as if they were at the theater and referred to the gatherings as "amusements." European visitors commented that houses of worship were apt to be confused with the theaters and cafés; indeed, once a community began to take shape on the frontier, the first building to go up after the church was often a theater.[8] Underscoring frontier America's deep ties to the printed word and the subsequent blending of literature, theater, and religion, de Tocqueville wrote in *Democracy in America* that "there is hardly a pioneer's hut does not contain a few odd volumes of Shakespeare." The French sociologist fondly recalled reading Shakespeare's *Henry V* for the first time in a log cabin in America.

Because of increasing political pressure from all fronts, however, by the 1840s the Oregon Territory had become a national political issue. Democrats under the leadership of James K. Polk made western expansion the major issue of the 1844 presidential campaign. Born in North Carolina, Polk was a meticulous micromanager who in his mid-twenties followed his political mentor, Andrew Jackson, to Tennessee. He served fourteen years in the House of Representatives—four as Speaker of the House. A Scotch-Irish Presbyterian lawyer, Polk ran for president under the promise that, if elected, he would serve only one term. He also promised to annex Texas and California and coined the phrase "54-40 or Fight" to emphasize his opinions concerning the Oregon Country.

Once elected, Polk kept all of his campaign promises. Using skillful high-stakes diplomacy and military brinksmanship, as well as war itself, Polk bluffed the British out of Oregon, annexed Texas in 1845, and, through the Treaty of Guadalupe Hidalgo ending the war he initiated with Mexico, brought California, New Mexico, and the entire Southwest into the possession of the United States. When he left the White House in 1848 Polk had acquired more than one million square miles of land, extending US boundaries from the Atlantic to the Pacific Ocean. No president other than Jefferson had acquired more land. Exhausted, Polk died three months after leaving his promised single term as president.

To understand the impact of Polk's land acquisitions requires a brief return to the 1830s and the peak of the fur trade era. Nathaniel Wyeth, Boston businessman and follower of Hall Jackson Kelley, had made a fortune cutting ice from Massachusetts ponds and shipping it to the Caribbean. Wyeth grew impatient with Kelley and moved on his own to colonize Oregon. He recruited rugged New England outdoorsmen, scientists, sea captains, and Methodist evangelical Jason Lee—who had received a "call" to minister to the Indians beyond the Rockies—and created his own commercial, scientific, religious, and political expedition to Oregon. In 1832 Wyeth met Jim Bridger's partner in the Rocky Mountain Fur Company, William Sublette, in Independence, Missouri. Wyeth accompanied Sublette to rendezvous and was astonished to discover the broad knowledge of the region the American mountain men had obtained. He immediately made arrangements with the Rocky Mountain Fur Company to be their principle trader the following year at rendezvous. After the 1832 rendezvous, Wyeth's expedition headed on to the Willamette Valley in Oregon. Convinced he was on the verge of creating an American settlement in Oregon, Wyeth returned to Boston in 1833 to gather more men and supplies. He made record time returning overland from Independence to rendezvous only to discover his trade connections with the mountain men had disintegrated because of a previous financial arrangement between the Rocky Mountain Fur Company and its chief rival, the American Fur Company, to regulate their competition for beaver pelts to specific regions. Consequently, the Rocky Mountain Fur Company reneged on the deal with Wyeth and used another trader to supply rendezvous trade goods. Furious with the mountain men, Wyeth took his supplies and headed to Oregon. Wyeth's supplies were indeed very much needed by the expedition he had deposited in Oregon; arriving there he learned that two supply ships he had commissioned to Vancouver had met with disaster at sea. In 1834 Rocky Mountain Fur Company partners William and Milton Sublette, Robert Campbell, and Jim Bridger honored their agreement with the American Fur Company and closed out all posts competing with their rival and moved to a new region to do business. The Sublette brothers and Campbell immediately began construction of a new post on the Laramie River they dubbed "Fort William." By 1840, however, everyone had begun calling it "Fort Laramie."

Wyeth spent the next few years stumbling around the Rockies attempting, but failing, to establish the lucrative business connections he desired and needed to support his dream of a settlement in Oregon. He did, however, establish a colony of New England Protestants, missionaries, and scientists in Oregon, map the lush Willamette Valley, and, following fur trade era routes, bring solid proof to the eastern United States of an overland route linking the East and West Coasts.[9]

Then in the late 1830s the East was rocked by a great economic depression that heavily affected the middle and lower classes and, ironically, assisted Wyeth's colony in Oregon. Coincidentally, Wyeth's colleague in the project, missionary Jason Lee, returned to the East Coast on a tour extolling the advantages of colonizing Oregon. Because of the precarious financial climate in the East, Lee was successful in gathering courageous souls to return with him to the Willamette Valley. In the spring of 1841 Lee and five hundred followers departed Independence, Missouri, and headed across the Great Plains to the missionary's colony in Oregon. What began as a trickle was about to become a flood.

In 1842 the bottom also fell out of the American grain market, dispossessing thousands of young farmers and plunging the country into a deeper economic depression. Perhaps financial hardship made the two-thousand-mile trek seem less intimidating, but in 1842, 112 people under the leadership of Elijah White left Independence to join Jason Lee's colony in Willamette Valley. In 1843 a nine-man commission met in a barn at Lee's mission to draw up a resolution that announced: "We the people of Oregon territory, for the purpose of mutual protection and to secure peace and prosperity among ourselves, agree to adapt...laws and regulation, until such time as the United States of America extend their jurisdiction over us."[10] That same year the first organized wagon train of one thousand people left Independence for Oregon.

In 1844 four hundred emigrants joined wagon trains heading to Oregon. In 1846, however, the Great Potato Famine dispersed thousands of Irish fleeing their homeland with hopes of discovering a new life in America. The massive number of Irish immigrants is reflected in the years 1845 to 1847, when five thousand people departed in wagons from Independence heading west for California now as well as Oregon. In spite of the incredible numbers of impoverished Irish emigrants, however, the migration remained primarily a middle-class movement.

Inspired by a Boston exhibition of George Catlin's paintings of the Trans-Missouri and its native people, and by the migration that was increasingly becoming recognized as a social phenomenon, in 1846 a writer from New England embarked on a solo adventure into the west. Francis Parkman's *The Oregon Trail* remains one of most authentic portraits of the period. Parkman vividly describes a scene around St. Joseph, Missouri, in 1846 in which thousands of emigrants were camped on the prairie about eight or ten miles outside of the community while still more new arrivals were in a steady stream out from Independence to join them. Parkman describes the camps as being in a state of "great confusion," with emigrants holding intense meetings, arguing and unable to decide upon leaders to guide them across the prairie. Parkman also rode from the emigrant camps outside of St. Joseph down to Independence and found that bustling community to be crowded with scores of shops and an "incessant hammering and banging from a dozen blacksmith's sheds, where the heavy wagons were being repaired, and the horses and oxen shod." Parkman discovered the streets of Independence were crowded with men, horses, mules, and wagons filled with healthy-looking women and children peering from canvas covers. Parkman observes some "very sober-looking countrymen" and comments that "the emigrants, however, are not all of this stamp. Among them are some of the vilest outcasts in the country. I have often perplexed myself to divine the various motives that give impulse to this strange migration; but whatever they may be, whether an insane hope of a better condition in life, or a desire of shaking off restraints of law and society, or mere restlessness, certain it is, that multitudes bitterly repent the journey, and after they have reached the land of promise, are happy enough to escape from it."[11]

As the migration continued to swell, the massive number of emigrants was dramatically affecting the tribal culture of the far West. The impact of the migration was perhaps most keenly felt by

Plains Indians who nomadically followed the ancient north/south migratory path of one ancient, gigantic herd of buffalo. The massive human migration suddenly crossing the Great Plains—east to west—cut a line directly through the middle of Indian and buffalo country, and by the 1850s trouble began to surface. Still, Plains Indians did not always fight emigrants as in modern stereotype. In truth, many emigrants—particularly early ones—would not have succeeded crossing the continent without Indian assistance. Usually Indian help came through the diplomacy of experienced guides such as Jim Bridger and other "plainsmen" like him. In the beginning, peaceful relations between native people and emigrants were often accompanied by a shared sense of common purpose. This is not to say Indians were not angry, suspicious, and concerned about the rapidly increasing numbers of Euro Americans entering their homeland and disturbing ancient natural patterns of entire ecosystems. Yet a delicate diplomacy prevailed as trouble with Indians became increasingly hostile with the enormous numbers of people crossing the plains. The situation soon called for military intervention.

Since the days of tension over the Oregon Country, Great Britain and other colonial powers had taunted the United States over its inability to mount and march an infantry to defend its northwestern boundaries. Polk's wars of acquisition had entrenched the American military along southwestern borders between the United States and Mexico. Once the military entered the Great Plains and Rocky Mountains, Bridger worked almost exclusively for the government as a scout.

By 1849, the beginning of peak migration years, gold was discovered in California. Around the same time an unscrupulous land speculator, Lansford W. Hastings, published *The Emigrants' Guide to Oregon and California*. Rapidly, tens of thousands converged on Independence, camped in enormous prairie cities of white tents, bought and sold supplies, organized wagon trains, and waited for spring grass to reach the proper height for oxen to graze en route.

The quicker one arrived in the California goldfields, the better one's chances of wealth. Most could not afford expensive sea passage to California, and if trouble occurred on a sea voyage the trip to California could take even longer than by land. The fifteen-thousand-mile sea journey around Cape Horn usually took six months. Sometimes a ship might take a month to "round the Horn," besieged by terrible hazardous storms. The route that employed the Isthmus of Panama was several thousand miles shorter, yet equally perilous, as the traveler was exposed to deadly tropical diseases. Moreover, often a traveler might survive the crossing through the jungle only to have to wait a month for another ship bound for California.

During this intense and expansive era a young man named Cornelius "Commodore" Vanderbilt rose to great fame and wealth. As a youth Vanderbilt had earned his living running a Staten Island ferry service in New York and had already become very wealthy during the early days of the steamship era. But when Panama created a railroad line across the country to the Pacific, Vanderbilt was among the first to urge the creation of a water route—a canal—crossing through Nicaragua instead of Panama. Of course Panama eventually built the canal, but it was at Vanderbilt's initial urging, while his steamship business grew increasingly wealthy with one-way charters from New York to San Francisco and the goldfields.

Just north of Independence amid bluffs overlooking the Missouri River, St. Joseph sprang up almost overnight as forty-niner's looking for any head-start to the California goldfields flocked there to prepare to cross the plains. In the spring of 1849, fifteen thousand wagons left St. Joseph.

Soon wagon trains were leaving daily from the end of April until the end of May. Several days' journey west from St. Joseph, emigrants on the "St. Jo Trail" merged with those leaving from Independence. Emigrant diaries describe a great junction having huge numbers of wagons coming down both forks, meeting amid swirling dust, and forming a single line streaming on endlessly. It seemed as if all humankind was rolling westward.

Chapter Four
The Iron Cyclops and the Lightning Slingers

I had never seen a Washichu then, and did not know what one looked like; but every one was saying that the Wasichus were coming and that they were going to take our country and rub us all out and that we should all have to die fighting...I remember once that I asked my grandfather about this. I said, "When the scouts come back from seeing the prairie full of bison somewhere, the people say the Wasichus are coming; and when strange men are coming to kill us all, they say the Wasichus are coming. What does it mean?" And he said, "That there are many." [1]

—Black Elk

By the late 1840s a tipi village of Lakota known as "hangs-around-the-fort people" surrounded Fort Laramie, and the outpost had also become the major gathering place on the road of the emigrants. The appearance of US military at Fort Laramie in the early 1850s nevertheless pushed the increasingly tense diplomatic Indian situation in the West out of balance. Plains Indians' hostility toward emigrants escalated from the moment US troops entered the region. While Plains Indians' lifestyles, religion, and culture were being dramatically affected by the increasing presence of emigrants and the US military in the West, the continent itself was also radically changing. East of the Mississippi River, the northern section of America had been transformed by industrialism. Tobacco, originally the staple crop of the colonies, was replaced by king cotton and, as a result of that plant's affinity for southern climates and terrain, prosperity was spreading throughout that region. The hunger for new land was exploding across western frontiers in both the North and South. Complicating matters, each of these sections of the country had also developed socially and culturally in radically different ways: the North, with its factories and cities, was developing a pronounced class system with upper-class industrialists amassing fortunes by exploiting an expanding lower-class work force; the wealthy aristocratic planters of the agricultural South were becoming increasingly dependent upon slave labor to support their massive operations; the western pioneer's restless, nearly nomadic, hunger for land appeared insatiable; and a wild, lawless society was rapidly developing on both the northern and southern fringes of the frontier.

The Trans-Missouri presented a formidable natural barrier that for a time halted the entire westward movement. The geographical impediment of the Great Plains had a more dramatic economic and cultural impact on the South than it did on the North; the northern economy was based upon individual ownership of land and free labor, a system that was only slightly altered when it entered the Great Plains region, leaving its essential character unchanged. The South's economy, however, was founded almost totally on cotton and the plant required a large population of slave labor to plant, grow, and harvest it. Equally significant, the agrarian economy of the South was hemmed on the west by lack of water just as surely as it was bound on the north by cold. Consequently, the landscape of the Trans-Missouri shifted the cultural balance between the North and the South, giving the advantage to the northern section of the United States and making its ideals, rather than those of the South, national.[2]

While the Daniel Boone/Andrew Jackson/Davy Crockett archetype of the American frontiersman was born in the reality of the continent's eastern primordial forests, in 1823 James Fenimore Cooper's *Leatherstocking Tales*, featuring his fictional heroic character Natty Bumpo, first appeared in the book *The Pioneers*. Aside from writer John Filson's exaggerated descriptions of the life of Daniel Boone, James Fenimore Cooper's novels mark the earliest literary documentations of the unique social process taking place on the frontier of American culture. It is significant that as western expansion in both the northern and southern sections of the country was momentarily halted at the Trans-Missouri, the colonial, Anglo-Saxon-dominated, eastern section of the country became directly involved politically in the creation of a national mythological "identity."

In 1819—the same year that the United States entered into the Joint Occupation Treaty with Great Britain concerning the Oregon Territory—all these sections and diverse perspectives had entered into such intense disagreement over western expansion and the issue of slavery that elder statesman Thomas Jefferson remarked, "This momentous question, like a fire bell in the night, awakened and filled me with terror. I considered it at once as the knell of the union."[3] Of course the ever-diplomatic Kentucky Senator Henry Clay's famous Missouri Compromise—which proposed that in order for a territory to be admitted to the Union as a slave state it had to be accompanied by the admittance of a territory also seeking admittance as a free state—temporarily calmed the storm.[4]

By 1833 English activists were successfully abolishing slavery throughout the British Empire, thus intensifying the movement to do the same in the United States. Increasingly the issue of free or slave state rolled across the Great Plains in pioneers' wagons as the numbers of emigrants swelled. Heightening the issue, as more middle-class Americans and emigrants headed west, the United States boundaries expanded with them. Whether new western states would enter the union as free or slave states became increasingly controversial, and this argument led to legislation intended to divide the immense territory of Jefferson's Louisiana Purchase in order to cope with the slavery issue and western expansion. The well-intended Kansas-Nebraska Act of 1854 sought peace in the West but accomplished the opposite as the legislation set the stage for the Civil War.

"Eastern preemption of the West became a powerful nationalizing force," historian Alan Trachtenberg explains. "Longfellow's Song of Hiawatha, a product of mid-century Boston, was an early shot in the campaign (which included the Civil War) to imagine a continental nation with origins in the West among the Indians. High among the binding elements in this developing campaign—the military metaphor is apt—were ideas of race and white supremacy, of the rightness of divisions between rich and poor among whites themselves, of Anglo-Saxon superiority over recent immigrants, and of America's 'Manifest Destiny.'"[5]

Sponsored by Senator Stephen Douglas of Illinois, the Kansas-Nebraska Act repealed Henry Clay's Missouri Compromise. The legislation also carved out two new territories from the lands of the Louisiana Purchase, both of them north of the thirty-four-year-old dividing line of 36° 30' north. Significantly, however, the legislation declared that citizens of the territory had the right of "popular sovereignty" to vote to become a free or slave state upon entering the Union.

New, intense arguments erupted throughout the country concerning the moral and constitutional implications of western statehood, slavery, and the popular sovereignty aspects of the Kansas-Nebraska Act. Perhaps the most volatile region of sectional divisiveness was at the threshold of the Oregon Trail in Kansas Territory. Northern abolitionists and southern pro-slavery forces flooded into the area, mixed with the unusual number of violent desperados, ruffians, and social outcasts also pouring into the territory, and created a violent predecessor to the Civil War. The territory became known as Bleeding Kansas as violence escalated and rapidly spread to the rest of the nation.

Douglas's ultimate intention in championing the Kansas-Nebraska Act had been to create new western states that would unify all the feuding sections of the United States into a colossal technological effort to build a transcontinental railroad. Douglas, like many progressive Americans of the era, was eager to link the Atlantic and Pacific coasts with a railroad. As a bonus, the transcontinental railroad would also solve Washington's old logistical dilemma of rapidly dispersing military forces to the nation's most remote western regions.

The idea of a railroad was a relatively new one in the United States. On July 4, 1828, the Baltimore and Ohio Railroad opened with a crude, undependable locomotive—the *Tom Thumb*—built by Peter Cooper in New York. In 1833, merchants in Charleston, South Carolina, financed a 136-mile railroad that at the time was the largest in the world. By 1840 there were nearly three thousand miles of track in the eastern section of the continent; by 1850 the United States had nine thousand miles of track. By 1860 thirty thousand miles of track had been laid, mostly in northern states, and railroads linked the Atlantic Ocean to the Mississippi River.[6]

The earliest advocate of a transcontinental railroad was a New Yorker eager to conduct business in the Orient. When businessman Asa Whitney traveled to China, it had taken him a year to sail around the Horn and cross the Pacific. Whitney believed there was a fortune to be made trading in the Orient if Americans, with control of the Pacific coast, could build a railway across the continent. In 1845 Whitney offered to build and pay for the railroad himself if the government would grant him a strip of land sixty miles wide across the continent on which he might lay his tracks. He offered to pay ten cents an acre for the land. After a nationwide campaign promoting his idea, Whitney met Senator Thomas Hart Benton.

Whitney could have found no more important ally for his concept than Senator Benton, who was also particularly interested in the Orient and had had some success pioneering commercial passageways. At the beginning of his twenty years in the Senate Benton championed a public works bill through legislation that created a national road of commerce stretching from his home state of Missouri to New Mexico. Benton's route became famous as the Santa Fe Trail. Senator Benton was a powerful proponent of low tariffs and free trade and, like Whitney, envisioned a profusion of Asian goods one day entering the United States through western ports such as San Francisco and Puget Sound. Like Hall Jackson Kelley, Senator Benton was well-read on the subject of empire and theorized that all empires in world history had become powerful by achieving direct access to Asian trade.[7]

Senator Benton initially favored government financing and control of a transcontinental railroad, yet he quickly converted to Whitney's dream of the railway being created by free enterprise. Learning of Whitney's bold proposal, however, New England's shipping industry, doing booming business sailing people and goods around the Horn, quickly joined with the coaching industry of the western frontiers, and both groups fought a well-financed and organized campaign against Whitney's idea. The visionary businessman soon ran out of money.

Nevertheless, because of Senator Benton's influence in Congress and his passion for western expansion, the idea of independent industry teaming with the government to create a transcontinental railroad had taken root. In 1853 Congress passed a bill ordering the Secretary of War to make surveys for a Pacific railroad. By 1856 government engineers had laid out five possible routes to cross the continent. At this point, however, like everything else happening in the country, the issue of a transcontinental railroad was becoming entangled in sectionalism: the North wanted the railroad to initiate in Chicago or St. Paul; the South preferred New Orleans or Memphis.[8]

Intrinsic to the relationship of time and space, speed became a dominant concern of pioneers challenging the immenseness of the nineteenth-century Trans-Missouri. Swiftness of communication became the motivation that inspired the significant temporal technological advances of the American Industrial Revolution. As the population of the United States expanded to the Mississippi River, the ability to communicate with family, friends, and business associates in the East remained a relatively simple process. After the population in California exploded following the 1849 gold rush, however, vast numbers of people were separated by a continent, and the need for both coasts to be in constant communication intensified and magnified exponentially.

Today we tend to think the gold rush happened instantaneously with people flooding into California. Yet a closer examination of the time it took for news to travel to the East Coast reveals the communications problem the people of the era faced when encountering the Trans-Missouri; it took ten months for news of the discovery to reach the East Coast. When President Polk mentioned the California gold strike in his message to Congress in December 1848, however, the rush was on. By summer 1849, sixteen months after the initial discovery, thousands set out from Independence and St. Joseph for California.[9]

Once in California, emigrants found themselves separated from all news of loved ones and business associates. The sense of isolation was exaggerated by mail delivery that was so painfully slow that any news from the East was months old by the time it arrived. Nevertheless, old news was better than no news, and signal flags would announce when mail steamers arrived in San Francisco Bay so that settlers could rush to the post office to wait in line for hours, often simply on the hope of mail arriving for them. As the numbers of emigrants multiplied, little villages and mining camps sprang up so quickly that it soon became impossible for the postal system to keep up with the population. Literally tons of unclaimed mail began to pile up in San Francisco, as mail would often arrive so late that the intended recipient would have left the city long ago to race to the latest goldfield that had emerged.[10]

In the 1850s there were only two overland routes linking Missouri and the Pacific coast: the Butterfield Route and the Central Overland Route. John Butterfield was an upstate New Yorker who had been successful developing a stagecoach and mail delivery line between Ithaca and Syracuse. A friend of President James Buchanan, Butterfield secured mail contracts to develop a line running from St. Louis and Memphis to Fort Smith, Arkansas. From Fort Smith the route proceeded through Indian Territory to El Paso, Texas, then on to Yuma, Arizona. From Yuma the route forked, with one route heading west to Los Angeles and the other north to San Francisco. Sometimes called the Ox-Bow Route, Butterfield's line was 2,800 miles long and took twenty-five days to deliver mail from Missouri to San Francisco, yet it avoided the snowy winters of the Great Plains and Rocky Mountains of the Central Overland Route; indeed, the Central Route could be traveled only six months of the year because wagons and coaches could not risk the treacherous mountain passes and blizzards.

Mail routes, like the proposed transcontinental railroad routes, had become increasingly entangled with the issue of secession throughout the 1850s. Southern representatives in Congress naturally supported the Butterfield Route; if war broke out, the route would enhance the possibility of their controlling the southern

portion of the continent from Atlantic to Pacific. Northern congressmen's hands were tied with the reality that the Central Route had
failed to prove plausible. With no realistic alternative, the Butterfield
Route prospered, creating an obvious potential military strength for
southern concerns as civil war loomed on the horizon. Complicating
matters, even though California had been admitted to the Union as
a free state, there were powerful and vocal forces brewing there in
favor of secession. Some even called for California to secede as a new
nation with ties to neither northern nor southern agendas.

In 1860, backed at tremendous financial risk by the shipping
empire of Leavenworth, Kansas businessmen William Russell,
Alexander Majors, and William Waddell, the following advertisements appeared in San Francisco's newspapers, announcing the
creation of the Pony Express: "Wanted—Young, skinny, wiry fel-
lows, not over 18. Must be expert riders, willing to risk death daily.
Orphans preferred. Wages, $25 a week."[11]

The Pony Express shortened the time required to get a letter
from New York to San Francisco from twenty-five to ten days. The
greatest single accomplishment of the Pony Express, however, was
the delivery of President Abraham Lincoln's Inaugural Address to
the citizens of California on March 17, 1861—only thirteen days
after his inauguration. Still, it is of greater significance that the
Pony Express provided news to California during a most critical
time in American history, keeping the state informed and connected to the Union at the eve of the Civil War.[12] Yet in spite of
its critical role linking communication between the East and West
Coasts of North America during this era, William F. Cody biographer Don Russell suggests that the Pony Express would very
likely have remained a mere footnote in American history if Buffalo Bill had not included it in his *Wild West* a quarter-century
after the service's demise. As Cody presented it in the *Wild West*
arena, the Pony Express provided a romantic and extremely visual
display of the equestrian skills required on the frontier as well as a
splendid metaphorical example of American ingenuity and prob-
lem-solving. The Pony Express thus remains in the twenty-first
century a powerful frontier metaphor representing the genesis of

America's obsession with conquering time and space that has cul-minated today in instant global communications. With its obvious link to the entertainment business, the Pony Express also contrib-uted greatly to the non-Indian American mythology born in the Trans-Missouri by symbolizing much of modern humans' obses-sive preoccupation with speed—particularly swiftness of the com-munication of information.

Even as the brave boys of the Pony Express were risking their lives racing time across the western portion of North America, however, the poles and wire that would unite the nation with a new form of electric communication were being hurriedly constructed along the very same route that the swift riders braved on horseback. From the West heading east and from the East heading west, those poles and wires were being laid simultaneously along the archetypi-cal trail that followed Thomas Fitzpatrick's fur trade route and Jim Bridger's "Emigrant's Road" and that in five years would become the course of the Transcontinental Railroad.

Telegraphy began in 1837 when a renowned New England art-ist named Samuel Morse offered a presentation of his experiments with electronic communication at a Manhattan university. A for-mer student at the school, Alfred Vail, attended Morse's demonstra-tion and approached him afterward with a proposal to develop and refine his idea for 25 percent of the profits. Vail improved Morse's crude prototype and created the famous "dot-dash" system for sending messages that would soon become known as Morse Code. Soon thereafter the pair offered a demonstration at Franklin Insti-tute in Philadelphia that was attended by several members of Con-gress, and in 1843 President Martin Van Buren signed legislation granting Morse and Vail thirty thousand dollars to construct an experimental telegraph line from Washington, DC, to Baltimore.[13]

Underscoring Neal Gabler's thesis that the genesis of America's modern entertainment culture of celebrity began during the era of Andrew Jackson's anti-elitist presidency, Neil Postman notes that the arrival of "penny newspapers" preceded Morse's telegraph by only a few years and that Benjamin Day of the *New York Sun* and James Gordon Bennett of the *New York Herald* had "already begun the process of elevating irrelevance to the level of news" by focusing on sensational events like crime and sex. Postman also skillfully connects the innovation of the telegraph with the pioneer American newspaper industry by observing that the *Baltimore Patriot* used the very same Washington-to-Baltimore telegraph line Morse had constructed to provide its readership "information about action taken by the House of Representatives on the Oregon issue."[14] Even today when the telecommunications industry wishes to suggest the immediacy of news it often uses the iconic "dot-dash" sound of Morse code accompanied by graphic zigzag lightning bolts.

Postman continues his assessment of the impact of the telegraph on American society and culture with the observation that even though the invention contributed greatly to the American obsession of conquering time and space, the success came at enormous cost. Postman notes that when Morse prophesied that telegraphy would make "one neighborhood of the whole country," he did not foresee his invention "[destroying] the prevailing definition of information and, in doing so [giving] new meaning to public discourse." Postman reminds us, "Among the few who understood this consequence was Henry David Thoreau, who remarked in *Walden*, 'We are in great haste to construct a magnetic telegraph from Maine to Texas; but Maine and Texas it may be have nothing important to communicate.'" Postman reminds us again of Marshall McLuhan's famous aphorism, pointing out that "Thoreau, as it turned out, was precisely correct. He grasped that the telegraph would create its own definition of discourse; that it would not only permit but insist upon a conversation between Maine and Texas; and that it would require the content of that conversation to be different from what Typographic Man was accustomed to."[15]

Postman observes that in both oral and typographic cultures information is important only when it stimulates *action*. But the situation created by telegraphy that would soon be intensified in other rapid technological advances in the Industrial Revolution made the relationship between information and action both abstract and remote. Postman concludes, "For the first time in human history, people were faced with the problem of information glut, which means that simultaneously they were faced with the problem of a diminished social and political potency."[16]

Telegraphy rendered Americans socially and politically impotent because it introduced a revolutionary new language—one based on fragmented, impersonal headlines. Whereas prior to the telegraph much cultural emphasis had traditionally been placed upon clear, detailed description—preferably rendered in lovely, floral penmanship—each dot-dash headline now stood alone in stark, singular context, leaving the receiver of the information to provide meaning—right or wrong—to the remark. The meaning of "facts" was thus fundamentally altered as the traditional typographic, chronological format of the sequential printed page surrendered to the telegraphic quest for speed.

Of course Indians dealt differently with the problem of quickly communicating information to one another over the vast distances of the Great Plains; the indigenous people of the tall grass prairies used smoke signals. Smoke signals essentially required the same brevity of expression as Morse and Vail's dot-dash system, yet that very succinctness fit the oral and visual cultures of the Plains Indians perfectly, often communicating more subtle information to its recipient than a telegraph headline could express to a person separated by a continent from loved ones and accustomed to reading descriptive, sequential letters from home.

Telegraphic communication continued to slowly spread throughout the East during the 1850s until in 1860 Congress passed the Pacific Telegraph Act authorizing the US Post Office Department to spend forty thousand dollars a year to complete and maintain an overland telegraph line across the continent. The same year the state legislature of California authorized six thousand dollars a year toward the same end. A contract was won by the president of Western Union, Hiram Sibley, to begin construction of the line heading west from Omaha. Sibley negotiated an agreement with Omaha freight tycoon Edward Creighton to survey the lines and design the framework of the first Transcontinental Telegraph System. Creighton, it should be noted, was an outspoken champion for Indian rights, a trait that alienated him from many friends and his own brother. Even though he was a devout Catholic, Creighton was particularly outraged with Christian proselytizing among the tribes of the Trans-Missouri.

On July 2, 1861, Creighton dug the first post hole and aimed the telegraph line straight along the route of the Oregon Trail—the same as Broken Hand Fitzpatrick's mid-1820s fur caravan route from rendezvous. The Overland Telegraph Company simultaneously headed east with poles and wire from Carson City, Nevada. The two lines would meet in Salt Lake City.[17]

On October 24, 1861, eight months after the Pony Express raced Lincoln's Inaugural Address across the nation at what was then considered incredible speed, the transcontinental telegraph was completed. The Pony Express was officially discontinued two days later. Alexander Majors and William Waddell's initial dire forebodings concerning their partner William Russell's vision of a Pony Express were right on target, however, and the effort bankrupted their financial empire.

Meanwhile, as the telegraph increasingly linked the continent in communication, young men like Thomas Edison learned Morse code and took great pride in referring to themselves as "lightning slingers." Within thirty years many of these young lightning slingers, their imaginations impregnated with the magnetic wonders of electricity, would introduce revolutionary new forms of communication, and by the century's end Edison would forever alter storytelling, mythmaking, and the evolution of the American heroic archetype with his light bulbs, phonographs, and moving pictures.

Yet even as technological innovations were changing the ways Americans communicated, the art of diplomacy was breaking down. The controversial issues of slavery and western expansion continued to heat up and by mid-century centered intensely on a young Republican lawyer from Illinois.

In 1860 Abraham Lincoln campaigned for president promising free land for settlers in the new western territories and a railroad to the Pacific Ocean. Lincoln's campaign slogan said it all: "Vote Yourself a Farm." Southern politicians promised to secede from the Union if Lincoln was elected, and they kept their promise, opening fire on Fort Sumter shortly after Lincoln's inauguration. In 1862, a year into the Civil War, President Lincoln pushed both the Homestead Act and the Railroad Act through Congress. The Railroad Act created unprecedented government subsidies and grants to stimulate industrialists to finance the transcontinental railroad, while the Homestead Act offered 160 acres to any US citizen, or anyone intending to become a US citizen, under the conditions that they paid a small fee to register the claim and then lived on the land for five years.

In 1862, aware of Lincoln's desire to build a transcontinental railroad, western businessmen sent railroad construction engineer Theodore Judah on a second visit to Washington to explore the possibilities of the government assisting them financially with their vision of a Central Pacific Railroad. Judah's second visit to Washington was much different from his first. Lincoln had assembled an impressive lobby to support his railroad bill in Congress. The dream of the Central Pacific Railroad had become part of a much larger, rapidly growing vision to unite the continent. With the passage of the Railroad Act, Theodore Judah telegraphed his associates in Sacramento, "We have drawn the elephant. Now let us see if we can harness him."[18]

Judah knew that passing legislation to build a railroad was the first, and perhaps easiest, step of laying tracks across the plains, mountains, deserts, and rivers. To complicate matters, the Confederacy was winning the first important battles of the Civil War and, although Lincoln's support of the railroad was obvious, the president was consumed with the essential task of ending the conflict and preserving the Union.

Ironically, Lincoln had been among the first politicians to view a transcontinental railroad as the way to end the sectionalism that had divided the Union for a half-century. Lincoln and the founders of the Republican Party believed a transcontinental railroad would unite the industrial North with the agrarian South and West, while also linking the Atlantic and Pacific coasts. In 1859, while visiting Council Bluffs, Iowa, to review some property he had obtained as a fee for a case he litigated for a railroad company, Lincoln ventured across the Missouri River to Omaha and by chance he met a young engineer named Grenville Dodge. The military surveyor and law-yer discovered they shared many ideas concerning the western route of a transcontinental railroad. Dodge was in fact returning from a survey expedition for his employers, Farnham and Durant, on the Platte River and in the Black Hills. On this expedition Dodge met Jim Bridger, who became his close personal friend and from 1865 to 1866 was his guide for the surveys that indeed became the route of the Union Pacific Railroad from Omaha to Utah.

Lincoln's Homestead Act of 1862 was designed to open the heart of North America to massive Euro American colonization. When combined, Lincoln's Homestead Act and Railroad Act had a devastating impact on Plains Indians and the buffalo/horse culture of the nineteenth-century American West. The two acts of legisla-tion were intended to work together like a patchwork quilt, with the railroad companies owning one patch of the quilt and settlers the next. The logic of this design promised to bring industry, agri-culture, and population to the region simultaneously. Accordingly, the Railroad Act ultimately turned over 130 million acres of land, valued in the 1860s at $123 million to the railroad companies. The government also provided bonds loaned to the railroad companies amounting to $65 million. As the race to completion intensified, incentives amounting to $16,000 for every mile of track laid in a valley and $48,000 for every mile of track completed in the moun-tains drove the two railroad companies at a fever pitch. Lincoln's efforts to unite the continent with a railroad and abolish the issue of slavery had, ironically, devastated the ecosystem of the heart of the continent and given birth to an era of greedy robber barons that would only be broken apart by Theodore Roosevelt at the turn of the twentieth century. On May 10, 1869, a golden spike united the Atlantic and Pacific coasts at Promontory, Utah. The road of the emigrants was now made of steel.

Chapter Five
A Fierce Artfulness

You have noticed that everything an Indian does is in a circle, and that is because the power of the world works in circles, and everything tries to be round. In the old days when we were a strong and happy people, all our power came to us from the sacred hoop of the nation, and so long as the hoop was unbroken the people flourished. The flowering tree was the living center of the hoop, and the circle of the four quarters nourished it. The east gave peace and light, the south gave warmth, the west gave rain, and the north with its cold and mighty wind gave strength and endurance.[1]

—Black Elk

Settler journals are brimming with terrified accounts of the first Euro American contact with the Great Plains. These primal fears were motivated in large part by the fact that the austere oceans of endless prairies were starkly different to a people familiar with the forested, mountainous landscapes of Europe and eastern America. In 1931 historian Walter Prescott Webb referred to the *physical* impact of the landscape of the Trans-Missouri region on American culture and noted that in Europe as well as the eastern portion of North America, settlement was based on plentiful wood and water, resources rare on the Great Plains. Yet beyond those vast and mysterious tall grass plains was the "promised land"; on the other side of the immense space, plentiful wood and water returned to the settlement equation.[2] There, in Oregon and California, the hope of resources was as boundless as the founding fathers' democratic principles regarding a free society.

Nourished like an exotic flower by Washington politicians and businessmen on both coasts, Anglo-Saxon mythology flourished in the Trans-Missouri during the years following the Civil War because emigrants crossing the plains were continuing proven eastern settlement patterns from colonial New England—mythologized from the Puritan era forward—and connecting them with visions of a future global empire beyond the Pacific. The image of humble, yet determined pilgrims risking life and limb while laboring to cross the Great Plains as quickly as possible in pursuit of their dream thus became *the* defining metaphor of the American myth. Subduing the wilderness landscape and the powerful warrior societies of the indigenous tribes of the Trans-Missouri promised the fulfillment of America's collective vision of a manifest destiny as well as the restoration of the nation's shattered attempts to unify its post–Civil War mythological identity. The migration of humanity across the Great Plains in the nineteenth century was among the largest in the history of the world, and each settler carried the hope and promise of the United States' constitutional democracy implicit in the founding fathers' words and actions. Yet perhaps even more than the Euro American's addiction to natural resources that fueled his quest for "progress," the mythological obsession to culturally "conquer" the Great Plains physically and spiritually created the primal instinctive opposition of its indigenous people where, aside from the Apache and Comanche wars in the deep Southwest, Indian resistance to the invasion quickly became the most violent.

After a decade of peaceful coexistence between Plains Indians and settlers crossing the Trans-Missouri, conflict first reared its head after the gold strike in California in 1849. In place of the humble, religious, farming families that preceded them throughout the 1840s, fanatical Euro American males suddenly began crossing the plains in increasingly great numbers. These men were desperate to get to the goldfields as quickly as possible and thus were deaf and blind to Indian concerns. Tragically, these growing hordes of men failed to honor the fundamental manners their modest emigrant predecessors had maintained while trespassing and poaching on Indian land, and violence followed in their wake.[3]

Newspaper editors throughout eastern America also fanned the flames of discontent with sensational claims that a few savage Indian tribes were selfishly attempting to hoard all these natural resources for themselves when the exploding and progressive population of the United States would put the land to better use. Misunderstandings and depredations by both American Indians and Euro Americans continued to escalate throughout the 1850s, but the era of the Indian wars was officially initiated with a three-pronged military expedition deep into the Lakota Powder River country in the summer of 1865 by Civil War hero General Patrick Connor. Designed to shock and awe the Lakota with the military might of the United States, Connor's wretched orders from Washington were explicit: "You will not receive overtures of peace or submission from Indians, but will attack and kill every Indian male over twelve years of age."[4]

Yet even while Connor headed north from the route of the Union Pacific lines and moved into the Powder River territory of the Lakota, more trouble was brewing directly south of the railroad in Colorado; indeed, the Indian wars exploded in the spring of 1866 when a crazed Methodist minister named J. M. Chivington was appointed colonel in the Colorado militia. Chivington believed he was on a "mission from God" to kill Indians and took it upon himself to order his troops to murder and then mutilate the corpses of 105 Cheyenne women, children, and old men who sought protection under a white flag of truce at Sand Creek. Enraged, the Cheyenne immediately sent a war pipe to their powerful Oglala Lakota allies. Oglala Lakota warrior-chief Red Cloud smoked that pipe, thereby committing himself to avenging the murders of his Cheyenne cousins and allies.[5]

Jim Bridger had hardly returned to his farm in Missouri after being conscripted by the Connor expedition into the Powder River country in Wyoming Territory when he learned of the massacre and mutilations at Sand Creek. Shocked at the news, he predicted a swift and terrible retaliation from the Cheyenne and their Lakota and Arapaho allies. Even though Bridger had strongly resisted becoming involved personally, his participation in the Connor expedition had already drawn him directly into the conflict. Unaware of Connor's despicable orders and with profound misgivings, Bridger had agreed to act as scout for General Connor's misguided expedition into the Powder River country as a personal favor to his friend General Grenville Dodge. The old mountain man instantly disliked the general, and the pair quarreled frequently from the very beginning of the expedition. Once in the Powder River country, however, Bridger heard a spirit wolf howling and, recognizing it as a bad omen, made one last attempt to persuade Connor to abort the expedition. Incredulous, Connor had no intention of listening to such superstitions, and Jim Bridger left him to his fate and returned to his Missouri farm. Soon thereafter General Connor and the world first learned the name and military genius of Sitting Bull. Deep in the Powder River country, Sitting Bull's forces turned Connor back at every turn, sending him home in defeat with his glorious Civil War record in tatters.

While reprehensible, it takes little imagination to see *why* Washington sent General Connor into the Powder River country in a shameful attempt to murder the entire male population of the Lakota. While the transcontinental railroad raced to unite the continent with the steel rails of fluid communication and corporate commerce, gold had been discovered in Virginia City, Montana. A surveyor named John Bozeman pioneered a trail north from Fort Laramie and the Oregon Trail that went straight through the ancient Lakota Powder River country between the Big Horn Mountains and the Black Hills. Prospectors promptly swarmed into the region along the Bozeman Trail, igniting the Sioux into full-scale armed conflict. Oglala Lakota warrior-chief, Red Cloud declared war on the invaders in what soon known became known as the "Red Cloud Wars". Red Cloud's frequent attacks on emigrants and prospectors brought traffic to the goldfields to a halt in Montana, and the name of the route quickly changed to the Bloody Bozeman. The United States responded by cutting deeper into Lakota territory, building a series of forts along the Bozeman Trail.

Jim Bridger had always encouraged white men to stay out of Lakota territory—especially the Powder River country between the Big Horn Mountains and the sacred Black Hills. Immediately conscripted as the Indian wars exploded, Jim Bridger became chief of scouts for Colonel Henry Carrington, commander of Fort Phil

Kearny in the heart of Powder River country on the Bloody Bozeman. At ten dollars a day, Bridger's pay was more than Colonel Carrington received and more than twice the income of a junior officer. But Bridger was "a walking encyclopedia of Indian lore and readily available to any man who needed him" and was virtually indispensable to Carrington's command.[6]

Still, not everyone wanted to listen to the old mountain man's sage advice. No doubt more than a tad chagrined at Bridger's salary when compared to their own, many young West Point graduates, fresh from Civil War glory, were also eager to continue ascending through the ranks in military campaigns against Indians. As Red Cloud's forces surrounded Fort Phil Kearny in the fall and winter of 1866, Captain William J. Fetterman—having repeatedly ridiculed Bridger's judgment and called attention to the old man's failing eyesight—arrogantly ignored Bridger's advice *and* Colonel Carrington's orders and allowed a young, previously unknown Sioux warrior named Crazy Horse to lure him into a deadly trap that cost the lives of three officers, seventy-six enlisted men, and two civilians as well as his own. The Fetterman Massacre on December 21, 1866, was the worst defeat the United States military had experienced in its ninety-year history.

Soon after Fetterman's command perished, a blizzard descended on the region, and without the firewood the troops had been assigned to retrieve, Fort Phil Kearney was shivering cold. But the people inside its walls were also shivering with fear that Red Cloud's forces were preparing to attack the fort to torture and kill them all. Jim Bridger informed them the only way to prevent the attack they feared was to quickly retrieve the bodies of the slain men in order to prove to the Sioux that they were brave and powerful. Bridger personally led the group to gather the dead and return them to the fort without incident.

The direct political result of the Fetterman Massacre was that a commission headed by Commissioner of Indian Affairs Nathaniel G. Taylor, and veteran Indian fighter, General William S. Harney, sided with the increasingly popular eastern liberal perspective that it had become cheaper to "feed rather than fight the Sioux," and convinced the US government to sue for peace; the Oglala Lakota warrior-chief Red Cloud had become the first American Indian to win a declared war against the United States.

Red Cloud made his demands perfectly clear: he wanted all white men out of his country—especially prospectors. After the sound military drubbing he had delivered US troops on the battlefield, Washington was finally willing to meet his demands. On April 29, 1868, the United States of America signed the Fort Laramie Treaty, promising the Lakota, in perpetuity, all their ancestral homelands—especially *Paha Sapa*, the Black Hills. Red Cloud believed the Lakota's sacred lands were finally safe. Of course non-Indian politicians, businessmen, and military leaders realized the completion of the Transcontinental Railroad would render the Bozeman Trail obsolete.

Why did Red Cloud and the Lakota consider the Black Hills, the Big Horn Mountains, and the Powder River territory sacred? In their groundbreaking *Lakota Star Knowledge: Studies in Lakota Stellar Theology*, Ron Goodman and his Lakota research team led by Stanley Red Bird answer this question by offering insight concerning the religious language underscoring the political speeches of such important historic Lakota leaders as Red Cloud. Goodman and Red Bird remind us that all religions speak in symbols and that the Lakota leaders constantly spoke "God Speech." Revealing much of the God Speech of the Lakota, Goodman's studies of Lakota constellations and related matters helped him and his young Sioux research team appreciate that the Lakota's need to move freely on the plains was primarily religious. Red Cloud's last speech to the Sioux people in 1903 makes this religious expression of mobility implicit:

'We told them [government officials] that the supernatural powers *Taku Wakon* had given to the Lakota, the buffalo for food and clothing. We told them that where the buffalo ranged, that was our country. We told them that the country of the buffalo was the country of the Lakota. We told them that the buffalo must have their country and the Lakota must have the buffalo.'[7]

Goodman believes Red Cloud's repeated use of the word *must* emphasizes that the Lakota leader was referring to his people's "religious duty and not merely economic necessity or political control." Goodman explains that Red Cloud was directing attention to the need for religious freedom and that the Lakota were "following the sun on earth, that following the sun and the buffalo was part of living in harmony and balance with the sacred powers of the universe."[8]

Goodman and Red Bird's research focuses on the fundamentals of Lakota mythology, its origins in the Trans-Missouri landscape, and why the Lakota were indeed "following the sun on earth." Goodman informs us that most Lakota activities were time-factored. For example, there was a specific time to hunt buffalo, a time to sew new tipi covers, to gather the willow bark smoked in a sacred pipe, to tell certain stories, and so on. As difficult as it is for modern non-Indians to comprehend, there is no Lakota word for religion. Although it appears to the non-Indian that Lakota rites and rituals have a recognizably religious nature, to the Sioux themselves these are simply the intensification of daily activities, *all* of which must be lived in a sacred manner. The entire "Lakota way of life," or *Lakol Wicoh'an*, is their religion.[9]

Lakol Wicoh'an is firmly rooted in oral tradition. Goodman and Red Bird define the stories of Lakota oral tradition as sacred literature and believe they, like other scriptures, must be understood on four levels of awareness that correspond to our physical, emotional, intellectual, and spiritual natures. They explain further that the Lakota scriptures are related to the four stages of life: childhood, youth, adulthood, and old age. The Lakota believe that understanding can eventually come to any earnest seeker, as one matures through the stages of childhood, youth, and adulthood, but the spirits alone can provide us awareness in old age. Ultimately, all four levels are one truth.[10]

According to Lakota creation mythology, the most superior of the Gods is Inyan (rock). Inyan is *Wakan Tanka* ("the Great Mystery") and *Wakan Tanka* is Inyan. Inyan had no beginning because he "was there when there was no other." In the beginning Inyan was "soft and shapeless like a cloud" and wanted to use his power, but there was "no other that he might use his powers on." In order to create another, Inyan was forced to use part of his being. Inyan let his "blue blood" flow to establish earth, the stars, and everything else.[11]

"The Creation Myth of the Falling Star" was first published by Neihardt in his classic collection of Sioux stories that form an important section of the Black Elk canon, *When the Tree Flowered*. But Goodman and Red Bird also focused their research on this definitive formation of Lakota mythology. The Falling Star myth concerns a supernatural being conceived of man and a star who arrives on earth from the heavens to establish order. The Lakota always preface telling the story of the Falling Star with the remark that the oldest person who ever told the story heard it from his grandfather. Also, traditionally, it is only appropriate to tell the story after dark. The story begins with two young Lakota women out one night gazing at the stars. One young woman said, "See that big beautiful star. I wish I could marry it." Not be outdone by her sister, the other woman picked another star and announced her wish to marry it. Instantly, two men encased in light appeared to the women and telepathically instructed them to put their arms around them. Following the star-men's instructions, the two women were suddenly transported into the star world, where these two stars became their husbands and the wives soon became pregnant.

One day the women were out on the plains of the star world, digging up wild turnips. One of the pregnant women pulled out a turnip and opened a hole in the star world. She looked down and saw the earth and her old village and became homesick and decided to return to earth. She made a rope from turnip braids and let herself down through the hole. Unfortunately, the braid was not long enough to reach the earth and she panicked and fell. The crash killed her, but her baby was born, survived, and was raised by a meadowlark. The Lakota believe meadowlarks speak their language, so the baby, now named Fallen Star, grew up speaking Lakota too.

Fallen Star aged in days rather than years and a light emanated from him. The meadowlark grew old and took him to a Lakota band where he settled for a while and eventually was recognized as Fallen Star, the protector, the bringer of light and higher consciousness. Fallen Star traveled from one Lakota band to another, establishing order among the people and the animals. For example, there is a story of a band camped near Harney Peak in the Black Hills, where every day a red eagle would swoop down, seize a girl child, and carry her to the mountain top to slay her. The men try to kill the red eagle, but the great bird outwits them at every turn. They pray for Fallen Star to help them, and after seven days (and after seven girls have been killed), he arrives. Fallen Star kills the eagle and places the spirits of the seven girls in the sky as the constellation Pleiades—in Lakota, *Wicincala Sakowin*—"seven little girls."

Another Fallen Star story tells of a band camped near the site of Devils Tower. A brother and sister are chased by giant bears. As they flee, Fallen Star's voice directs them to a knoll. The bears surround the children and begin to close in. Fallen Star commands the earth to rise up and lift the children out of the reach of the bears, which claw at the hill as it lifts. The clawed hill becomes Devils Tower. Later, a bird carries the children back to safety, back on earth.[12]

The Lakota experienced the sacred through a concept Goodman and Red Bird define as "mirroring." Similar to the ancient Chinese philosophy of "as above, so below" developed as Taoism through millennia of study in the *I Ching* and Confucianism, the Lakota envisioned a sacred, interactive relationship between the star world and their earth world on the Great Plains. Like the Chinese, the Lakota also emphasized "as below, so above"; traditional Lakota believed that ceremonies were being performed in the heavens, and when ceremony in the stellar world is mirrored simultaneously on earth, a hierophany occurs in which "sacred power can be drawn down; attunement to the will of *Wakan Tanka* can be achieved."[13]

As the constellations of the heavens were the visible "scriptures" of the traditional Lakota at night, important land forms such as the Black Hills and Devils Tower "mirrored" those stellar scriptures during the day. The general public assumes the Plains Indian was nomadic because of the horse and ancient buffalo migratory

patterns, and to a degree this is true. Much of Goodman's information predates the horse in North America, however, and indicates
Plains Indians were *walking* nomadic trails long before equestrian
travel. In fact, Goodman's work reveals that most Lakota activities
were timed to coincide with stellar movement, and every aspect of
Lakota life was designed to reflect what was happening in the heavens. When the sun was in a specific Lakota constellation the people
would travel to a specific location to perform a specific ceremony.
Lakota certainly followed buffalo, but they were nomadic *because
of the stars.*[14]

When considering stellar scriptures and the fact that the Lakota
culture was rooted in the oral tradition, it is important to remember
communications theorist Neil Postman's observation that "the wise
Solomon, we are told in First Kings, knew three thousand prov-
erbs. In a print culture people with such talent are thought to be
quaint at best, more likely pompous bores. In a purely oral culture,
a high value is placed on the power to memorize, for where there
are no written words, the human mind must function as a mobile
library. To forget how something is to be said or done is a danger
to the community and a gross form of stupidity."[15] Furthermore,
the noted psychologist Carl Jung revealed that the great religions of
the world, by necessity, use symbols, or archetypes, to express what
cannot be expressed in words. With these two observations noted,
Goodman informs us that the Lakota believe the "inner shape of
a star to be an inverted tipi." Goodman examines the classic conal
shape of the Lakota tipi—a word that, incidentally, means "to live"
in Lakota—as the living, breathing example of "as above, so below/
as below, so above" and likens the act of building a tipi as "nothing
less than recreating or replicating a world." Viewing the body of
the tipi below and the poles above, one can see a clear inverted geometric image of Lakota mirroring from the archetypal perspective
of Lakota stellar theology in the twin equilateral triangular shape
of the tipi; the equilateral triangular shape above representing "star
sites" and the triangle below representing "earth sites." Recognizing that triangles representing star sites and earth sites combined
to represent the "inner shape of a star," we begin to understand

what Goodman means when he says that "in everyday life, living inside a tipi symbolizes living inside the sun. The traditional tipis were made of buffalo hides. The buffalo is the embodiment of solar power in the animal world. Physically and metaphysically, when the Lakota lived in a tipi they were "living inside the skin of the sun, of a star."[16]

Aside from the traditional, colorful, geometric quill and bead-work designs of the Lakota, the same principle—the converted conal shape of the tipi becoming the inner shape of a star and the hierophantic archetype of mirroring heaven and earth—also explains more about another central, vital ceremony of the Lakota: the Sun Dance.

Sun Dancers' breasts are pierced and physically attached with leather thongs to the top of a tall forked pole made from a Cotton-wood tree. Thus dancers create a tipi, offering prayers and making sacrifices while dancing around the holy tree of life. The conal vortex of power becomes a "tipi of praise" as the dancers, through prayer and sacrifices, rebuild the primal star and, indeed, recreate life.[17]

Despite the example of Christ's bloody sacrifice, non-Indians, even sympathetic ones, have been slow to comprehend the willing surrender of blood and flesh of the Plains Indian Sun Dance cer-emony. Non-Indians have also never quite been able to fully com-prehend Indian generosity as exemplified by traditional "giveaway ceremonies," in which a participant literally gives away all their possessions. That someone would willingly give away all their pos-sessions has always baffled anyone with the slightest hint of Euro-pean genetic coding.

The Giveaway and Sun Dance ceremonies are values and rituals Plains Indians divined from the stars. Ron Goodman points out a Lakota constellation known as "The Hand" that occurs in Orion. (Orion's belt is the wrist of the hand, while Orion's sword is the thumb. *Rigel* becomes the index finger, while the northernmost star in *Eridanus Eridnus Beta*, becomes the little finger of the hand.) Goodman says, "The Lakota interpret the annual disappearance from the night sky of 'The Hand' constellation in the spring as a divine signal of the impending loss of the earth's fertility."[18]

To fully comprehend the "earth reality" created through the Giveaway and Sun Dance ceremonies as mirroring "stellar reality," we must return again to Lakota oral tradition and the Fallen Star. Lakota oral scriptures tell of a selfish chief who through his greed threatens to alter natural order among the people. In order to teach the chief a lesson, the *Wakinyans*, or "thunder beings" that possess the power to make live or destroy, tears off the selfish chief's arm and hides it among the stars.

Soon thereafter Fallen Star arrives in the chief's village and, attracted to a particular young woman, announces his intention to marry her. When he speaks to the woman, who is the daughter of the one-armed chief, she informs him that the *Wakinyans* have hidden her father's severed arm, and she will marry only the man who is able to recover it.

So Fallen Star goes in search of the chief's arm. Traveling from village to village, Fallen Star meets spirits who give him gifts and words with special powers. The gifts and words will enable Fallen Star to change his shape and escape from the *Wakinyans* once he finds the chief's arm. Throughout his journey Fallen Star seems to be in the Black Hills area, but simultaneously he appears to be traveling in a stellar reality.

Fallen Star reaches the thunder beings, and by changing into a wren and finally into a man he is able to outwit the *Wakinyans* and *Iktomi* (a "trickster spider") and recover the selfish chief's arm. By using all the powers he was given by helpers along the way, he is able to flee. He restores the arm to the chief and marries the daughter, and they have a son. [19]

The Fallen Star story is pregnant with meaning. Symbolizing the loss of masculine regenerative power to fertilize the earth, the selfish chief loses his right arm. In retrieving the chief's arm, Falling Star claims this regenerative power. The young daughter is interpreted as a fertile Mother Earth. The son born to Falling Star and the daughter is the renewal of heaven and earth.

Goodman says, "The fact that the Fallen Star is sometimes in the sky and sometimes on earth symbolically links the two and reinforces the people's living according to precepts set forth in the sky.

"What the old chief loses involuntarily, the Sun Dancers vow to recover. They overcome chaos, death, and the earth's infertility...hope to recreate and renew the world by voluntarily sacrificing their own blood. Symbolically, they are also recovering the chief's lost arm."[20]

Non-Indian America nevertheless considered Plains Indian ceremonies like the Sun Dance—indeed, the continent itself—as wild and pagan and therefore destined to be overwhelmed by Christianity and the march of civilized mankind. Euro Americans had become enchanted by the technological sirens of progress and were now egotistically wedded to the colossal task the young nation created for itself as an opportunity to heal its wounds from the Civil War and simultaneously express to the rest of the world that the United States had conquered time and space.

By the mid-nineteenth century Daniel Boone, Jim Bridger, Andrew Jackson, Kit Carson, Davy Crockett, and other buckskin-clad heroes had pioneered a very clear heroic trail away from the European role model and created the prototypical image of the "American Adam in Eden." When the Transcontinental Railroad was being constructed in the era following the Civil War, however, the criterion for slipping on the beaded buckskins and becoming a national hero had subtly shifted. Telegraphy, photography, journalism, advertising, and the American entertainment industry were rapidly coalescing into what would eventually become "mass media," and the new buckskin hero would have to have the ability to adapt to each of these emerging forms of media to rise to recognition. Even more fundamentally significant, however, the landscape upon which this unique American mythological drama was unfolding was already showing the first signs of the profound and permanent negative effects of the non-Indian's technological invasion. The frontier was vanishing.

Chapter Six

A Star Appears

Pahuska [Buffalo Bill] had a strong heart.[1]

—Black Elk

One personality perfectly embodies the mythological blending of the Indian and Euro American, the nineteenth-century Trans-Missouri landscape, and the rise of modern multimedia in America: William Frederick "Buffalo Bill" Cody. Cody was born February 26, 1846, during the first phases of the emigration era and the western expansionist policies of the Polk administration. Cody's father, Isaac, moved his family from Iowa to Kansas after giving up his dreams of making it to the California goldfields. The Cody family arrived in Kansas Territory immediately after the 1854 passage of the Kansas-Nebraska Act had embroiled the region in bloody warfare over the issues of western expansion and slavery. Isaac managed to keep his political views to himself for a while, but he was destined to become a victim of the pre–Civil War era and the environment of "Bloody Kansas." When Isaac and young Will ventured into Leavenworth for groceries and chanced upon a pro-slavery rally, Isaac was forced by the mob to stand on a soapbox and reveal his opinion on the matter. Isaac bravely stated he believed Kansas should be a free state and was immediately stabbed twice in the back by a pro-slavery ruffian. Nine-year-old Will Cody witnessed the attack and, with the help of a sympathetic grocer, managed somehow to drag his bleeding father into the man's nearby store to prevent the enraged mob from killing him.

With his wounded father unable to provide for the family, Will Cody went to work riding mules as a messenger boy for Russell, Majors, and Waddell, the famous shipping firm that would soon create the Pony Express. The boy made such a positive impression on the "bullwackers," or teamsters, working for the shipping firm that one of them asked William Russell to allow young Cody to work for him accompanying their freight wagon trains across the Great Plains from Leavenworth to supply such faraway posts as Fort Laramie and Fort Bridger. Surviving hostile Indian attacks, floods, droughts, tornados, and other dangers, the boy made his third journey to the upper Rockies and back to Leavenworth before his twelfth birthday. Lakota playmates nicknamed Will Cody *Pahaska*—"long hair"—when he was interacting with them at Fort Laramie during his preadolescent years and began to wear his hair long like them.

Cody, of course, first gained notice in the eastern population centers of the United States in the mid-1860s after he won his famous alliterated sobriquet killing buffalo to feed the workers on the Kansas/Pacific Railroad line. By 1867, however, the Kansas/Pacific completed its route, and Buffalo Bill Cody suddenly found himself out of work. So he went to Fort Larned, Kansas, and signed on for the first time as a civilian scout with the military.[2]

Even as he first became famous, Americans believed Cody was singularly responsible for having decimated the massive buffalo herds of North America. So it is important to emphasize here that Cody ended his days as a buffalo hunter in 1867 when he began his career as a scout for the military. When searching for one person to blame for the wanton killing that pushed the buffalo to the brink of extinction, however, the trail often leads to the man who was Cody's commanding officer when he became a scout for the 5th Cavalry: General Philip Sheridan.

When Columbus entered this hemisphere it is estimated that the great North American buffalo herd numbered in excess of 80 million. More than 40 million buffalo were slain, however, between 1830 and 1890 alone. The fact that this period coincides with America's Indian wars era is no accident; indeed, these remarks by Philip Sheridan were widely circulated in the media during the Indian wars: "These men [buffalo hunters] have done in the past two years and will do more in the next year to settle the vexed Indian question, than the entire regular army has done in the past thirty years. They are destroying the Indian's commissary, and it is a well-known fact that an army losing its base of supplies is placed at great disadvantage. Send them powder and lead, if you will; for the sake of a lasting peace, let them kill, skin, and sell until the buffaloes are exterminated. Then your prairies can be covered with speckled cattle and the festive cowboy, who follows the hunter as a second forerunner of an advanced civilization."[3]

Philip Sheridan first implemented what was known in the nineteenth century as "scorched earth" warfare in Virginia's beautiful Shenandoah Valley as a strategic effort to hasten the end of the Civil War. Aware the Confederate Army was living off the land, Sheridan pledged to "strip the valley so that even the crows would have to carry their own rations" and proceeded to burn the Shenandoah Valley, thus starving his enemy and delivering the vital Virginia victory to Grant and Union forces.[4]

Similarly, General William T. Sherman coined the phrase "War Is Hell" as a rationale when he employed scorched earth tactics with deadly precision and ignited a conflagration in the Union Army's wide wake across the entire southeastern region of America as part of his famous March to the Sea. By the time he turned Atlanta into an inferno Sherman had broken the will of the Confederacy and initiated the end of the Civil War.

The Indian wars on the Great Plains had not been going well for the United States Army when General Sheridan made his remark about the "Indian's commissary." To its great embarrassment, the US War Department had discovered that the Indian tribes of the Great Plains and upper Rocky Mountains were masters of guerrilla warfare, and traditional military tactics learned at West Point and perfected during the Civil War did not work against them. In battle after battle American generals with previously glorious military careers had been disgraced by the skillful, unorthodox strategies of the Plains tribes. Exacerbating the situation, the chain of command of the United States Army during this period was filled with ambitious West Point graduates, many veterans and heroes of the Civil War with eyes on the White House. Indeed, one of their own, Ulysses S. Grant sat in the Oval Office. Spoiling for a fight that would bring national headlines, vainglorious young Army officers were eager to rid the West of its "vexed Indian problem."[5]

Even worse than a politically ambitious military, a wide-ranging economic depression followed the Civil War. As the depression deepened in America's urban centers, the promise of boundless natural resources enticed Washington to renew efforts to shape and vigorously market a new dream of hope for the future of the United States. President Grant and the US Army attached great significance to the realization of beloved slain President Abraham Lincoln's vision of a transcontinental railroad, but corporate America also had a powerful economic motivation to complete the undertaking. Delayed by the Civil War, Lincoln's Railroad Act of 1862 had been written to fit like hand in glove with its companion legislation, the Homestead Act of 1862. Working in coordination with Lincoln's legislation, American business was eager to complete the promised patchwork quilt of land grants sixty miles wide stretching across the Great Plains and fill them with immigrant farmers and consumers.

As Indian resistance proved much more clever and intense than anyone had anticipated during the creation of the Transcontinental Railroad, Generals Sherman and Sheridan brought a jaundiced, deadly, military perspective to the situation, and they quickly realized that the environmental warfare techniques employed in the Civil War would work equally well in the western campaigns. Sheridan observed that the previous unsuccessful military campaigns against Indians had taken place in the spring and summer—precisely the time that Indian people traditionally made war against each other; the warring tribes were quite accustomed to fighting during these periods of the year and then retreating to their lodges during the winter months for healing, storytelling, and preparing for future combat. Sheridan turned this pattern upside down; his cavalry would attack during the winter months.

Next on Sheridan's agenda was the Indian "commissary." Destroying the great buffalo herds became as important as it had been to incinerate the pristine Shenandoah Valley and a huge portion of southeast North America. If Sheridan could not whip Plains Indians on the battlefield, he would starve them into submission. As the railroad inched across the prairie grasslands, buffalo hunters—with the general American public's "powder and lead" support—took Sheridan's advice with a religious vengeance that brought many of the tribes of the Great Plains and upper Rockies, as well as the buffalo, to the verge of extinction. As the 1860s drew to a close the completion of the Transcontinental Railroad finally united the coasts. In doing so, however, it also divided the ancient migratory path of the North American buffalo, splitting what had been one massive herd into two separate herds and thrusting essential environmental and social connections throughout the immense ecosystem into chaos. The heart of the continent was finally laid bare. The coup de grâce, Lincoln's Homestead Act, introduced the plow to the immense grasslands and continued the process of replacing the Indian and buffalo with Sheridan's "cowboys and speckled cattle."

In the 1840s Jim Bridger's protégé, Kit Carson, had become a national hero scouting for Senator Thomas Hart Benton's son-in-law John C. Freemont's expeditions deeper into the unknown West. In the late 1850s Jim Bridger also became a scout for the military in the American West. Emulating mountain men and plainsmen such as Bridger and Carson who preceded them into the West, Will Cody and other scouts wore beaded buckskins and long hair in deference to Plains Indians people who preferred not to cut their hair. Aside from distinguishing them as civilians rather than military men, the flamboyant costume visually represented their relationship in war and peace with the indigenous people, culture, and landscape. General George A. Custer quickly adapted the costume of the civilian scouts and donned beaded buckskins and grew his hair long for a while. (By the time of his death at Little Big Horn, however, Custer had shorn his locks and returned to traditional military apparel.)

Even though hostile war parties still roamed the region and depredations by both Indians and non-Indians were increasing in 1867, most of Cody's initial scouting experiences were without much adventure. After a quarrel with a quartermaster over a horse, Cody quit the scouting business and for a while vanished into the Trans-Missouri landscape.

During the summer of 1867, after the Fetterman Massacre the preceding winter, General William T. Sherman formed the Harney-Taylor-Sanborn commission to structure a peace plan with the Plains Indians. The commission was influenced by liberal easterners whose research had proven it was less expensive to feed the Sioux than to fight them, and many the treaties of this era clearly reflected this perspective. The Medicine Lodge Treaty of 1867 was signed by headmen with less power than Cheyenne warrior-chiefs Roman Nose and Tall Bull, and, as such, were hollow. Red Cloud signed the Laramie Treaty of 1868 himself, however, and though individual hostile war parties occasionally terrorized various regions of the Trans-Missouri, the Red Cloud Treaty, as it became known, temporarily resolved the Indian wars.

Unable to find work, Will Cody rode into Fort Hays, Kansas, seeking employment as a scout on the very day General Sheridan arrived at the post. Soon after his arrival at Fort Hays fate tapped Cody on the shoulder, and he volunteered to make a dangerous night ride through hostile Indian Territory to deliver important dispatches for General Sheridan. Extremely impressed with Cody's courage, and even more with his successful ride, Sheridan appointed Buffalo Bill chief-of-scouts of the prestigious 5th Cavalry.

Soon after Cody won the coveted scout's position, occasional playwright, temperance lecturer, and all-around rascal Ned Buntline stumbled upon him at an army post. Buntline was looking for gunfighter-scout Wild Bill Hickok, but after initially confusing Buffalo Bill with Hickok, Buntline shrewdly realized the ambitious young Cody was more malleable and thus more of "the future" of the West, whereas the rigid and unmanageable Hickok would remain forever locked in the past.

Buntline certainly knew what would appeal to the everyday American at the theatrical box office, in the penny press, and in dime novels. In May 1849, nearly a decade before meeting Cody, Ned Buntline had been involved in an infamous yet pivotal event in the theatrical history of America that connected the increasingly divisive psychological impact of Jacksonian Democracy on culture in its distinct parallels to Old Hickory's 1829 presidential inaugural ball for the common man at the White House. Although twenty years separate the two incidents, the similar motivations of both events strongly support the notion that the genesis of popular entertainment in America began with the anti-elitist mob's destruction of the White House.

Arguably the most magnificent theatrical palace in America, the opulent Astor Place Opera House opened in New York City on November 22, 1847. Named after fur trade tycoon John Jacob Astor, Astor Place attracted the elite, wealthy, intellectual classes of New York society to opera and classic stage productions, yet also filled the cheaper balcony and gallery seats with polite, less-affluent patrons. The harmony that united the economic classes at the Astor Place was interrupted, however, when in early May 1849 the renowned British Shakespearean actor William Charles Macready was engaged to begin a two week run of Shakespeare's "Scottish play."* Macready was a classic Shakespearean, highly trained and *very* British—indeed, posh—and, to Jacksonian egalitarian standards, elite.

With what would soon prove to be fateful timing, the Broadway Theater booked American Shakespearean actor Edwin Forrest to appear as Spartacus in *The Gladiator*. Unfortunately, Forrest's run of *The Gladiator* would coincide with Macready's run of Shakespeare's bloody Scottish family drama. Forrest had become famous for his more expansive, "American" approach to acting that was considered by many to be more expressionistic and natural than Macready's classical British style. Initially the actors apparently held each other in high esteem, but, when pressed by penny newspapers to define their differences, lines were drawn, and by the time the competing shows opened the two actors had become polarized symbols representing the conflict between British and American acting technique. On May 8, 1849, young provocateurs sneaked into Macready's audience at the Astor Place and began to boo, whistle, hiss, and create such a general disturbance that the actor had to halt his show.

---

* Those of us in the theater are superstitious about speaking the name of this play aloud. Theater tradition refers to it instead as Shakespeare's "Scottish play."

Edward Zane Carroll Judson, also known as Ned Buntline, was one of those rowdy hooligans. Buntline was a member of the "Know-nothing" nativist political movement that believed the massive numbers of Irish Catholics immigrating to America in the late 1840s were infiltrating the United States at the order of the Pope to take over the country. Buntline also headed a group called the American Committee that, among other activities, sermonized to crowds gathering for performances at the Astor Place and put up billboards and handed out broadsides all over Manhattan with headlines such as "Shall Americans or British Rule in This City?" Soon organizations such as Buntline's American Committee had made contact with the penny presses and cheap newspapers of the lower classes, and in order to sell more papers and expand circulation, the rags began exaggerating the "feud" between the two actors.

On May 10, 1849, a group of nativist louts infiltrated the balcony and gallery of the Astor Place again and created such a ruckus they forced Macready to stop his performance for a second time. The police were waiting for them this time, however, and they successfully rounded up the rabble-rousers and escorted them out of the theater—only to be greeted outside by a nativist mob estimated at ten thousand that had been informed of what happened in the theater and rushed to the defense of their comrades. Enraged, the mob began throwing bricks at the theater and the police. More police were summoned, but the riot rapidly escalated to the point that local militia had to be called in to assist the police. The militia fired a warning shot over their heads, which only forced the mob to surge them with more rage. Then shots were fired directly into the throng. When the Astor Place riot ended, twenty-two people had been killed and more than one hundred wounded. Buntline spent a year in prison because of his leadership role in the riots.[6]

The Astor Place riots were a violent expression of the dramatic economic and cultural divisions that began to surface in urban America during the mid-nineteenth century. While Jacksonian Democracy sharply delineated the difference between frontiersmen and "elitist" Americans influenced by aristocratic European civilization, the political reasoning expressed itself in urban environments as a class struggle between rich and poor, nativist and immigrant. The ironic result of the rise of the "common man" expressing himself politically in the theater was, however, that after the Astor Place riots the upper classes increasingly sought to remove themselves from the hoi polloi and simply built more extravagant theatrical palaces and raised ticket prices high enough to prevent ruffians like Ned Buntline from breathing the same air they breathed. With the wealthy safely sequestered in their entertainment fortresses, refined behavior naturally became more subdued and attentive in upper-class, "legitimate" theaters. Hissing and booing, throwing vegetables and coins at performers, and other diversions such as open prostitution in the balcony sections nevertheless remained part of the theatrical experience of the lower classes until well into the vaudeville era of the early twentieth century.

The Astor Place riots further segregated the audiences but also segregated the types of entertainment the different social classes of audiences preferred. Prior to the riots, variety programs had historically shared the stage with tragedy and farce and unified the different economic classes of the audience. After the riots, however, variety show and farce were relegated to their own venues in vaudeville and minstrel shows, saloons and beer gardens, the circus, and burlesque. In 1880, thirty years after the Astor Place riots, the dramatic divisions in popular entertainment were evidenced by the fact that there were twenty-five playhouses in New York City seating between one thousand and two thousand patrons, and more than half of those were situated in affluent neighborhoods. Each of the twenty-five playhouses charged one-dollar admission, four times that at other theaters. There was a larger group of theaters that catered to the Protestant middle class and an even larger group that charged a quarter and presented vaudeville, minstrel shows, and cheap melodramas for the lower-middle and working classes.[7]

When he met Buffalo Bill Cody, Ned Buntline was intimately familiar with every strata of the American entertainment world of the mid-nineteenth century. Aside from his well-deserved reputation as a scalawag, Buntline was also a serial bigamist who had shot a man in a duel over a woman in Nashville and had survived the subsequent hanging only when the rope broke. Buntline often earned his living as a temperance lecturer, so he obviously knew his way around the saloons and beer gardens. And his occasional efforts at writing plays also had made him aware of the formidable psychic tools of the theater and the wide-ranging entertainment appeal of the cheap melodramas so popular among lower-class audiences. His experiences with broadsides and newspapers taught him to use language the "common man" could relate to, and, like everyone else in the nation, the dime novel had introduced him to the heroic American archetype emerging from the edge of the frontier in the persona of mountain man Kit Carson. When he met Cody in the late 1860s, Buntline was no doubt seeking a personality that could attract the attention of the exploding "penny paper" and dime novel circulation in eastern urban centers and appeal to the common man.

During the first fifty years of American history, most newspapers were broadsheets devoted to advertising and sensational political editorializing. In 1833, however, at the beginning of Andrew Jackson's second term in office, Benjamin Day founded the *New York Sun*. When most newspapers of the period cost six pennies, Day founded what is today considered the "tabloid" press by blatantly appealing directly to a mass audience and dropping the cost of a paper to a single penny. Day's formula worked, and penny press readership skyrocketed as eastern urban populations were brimming with new opportunities and jobs that lured many away from the farm and into the city.

The difference between the penny papers and the traditional press was content; the six-penny papers were the occasionally published editorial opinions of ongoing current events, but the penny papers were published daily. The very first such publications in the country, the penny papers offered consistent, daily perspectives of the city, the nation, even the world. Rather than being lectured about what some erudite editor believed, readers could now learn about life around them from real people's experiences and immediate events.[8]

Pioneer newspapers such as the *New York Herald* quickly adapted to the tactics of the penny presses and began to incorporate sensational stories such as grisly murders, melodramatic love tri-angles, and trashy criminal investigations from everyday events alongside their editorial opinion pages. Scottish-born owner-pub-lisher of the *New York Herald* James Gordon Bennett was perhaps the most innovative at adapting the devices of the penny presses to legitimate daily newspapers. A friend of General Philip Sheridan, Bennett was also instrumental in dramatically expanding Ameri-ca's awareness of Buffalo Bill Cody.

By 1872 the Indian wars had made Cody a hero as the chief of scouts of General Sheridan's 5th Cavalry, and Ned Buntline's dime novels had made him famous throughout America as "Buffalo Bill." Sheridan insisted that Cody accept James Gordon Bennett's persistent invitations to come to New York for a visit, and Buffalo Bill went east for the first time. Even though Cody confused the date and failed to show at a gathering of important movers and shakers Bennett had arranged especially for him, a mutual friend intervened and saved the moment for the befuddled plainsman. Eastern "swells" began queuing up to travel to the Great Plains to hunt buffalo with Cody from the moment the scout became friends with Bennett. Bennett, like Cody, was a master of erasing the lines between imagination and reality; indeed, Bennett had become so skilled at sensationalist journalism during the Civil War that generals had complained that his newspapers had the power to prolong the war in order for readers to be able to continue reading the accounts of thousands killed, wounded, and maimed in battles that never occurred.

Bennett's critics, peers, and rivals such as Horace Greeley pro-claimed his legacy to the newspaper business was "odious sensa-tionalism." Yet Bennett obliterated any lines dividing imagination and reality while simultaneously blurring any distinctions separat-ing diverse forms of entertainment such as journalism, theatrical drama, and the dime novel. In short, by *inventing* the news, Ben-nett confused the realms of perception so thoroughly that no one would ever be able to resolve the confusion.[9]

While Bennett was inventing news as entertainment and entertainment as news, Cody, like Jim Bridger, Kit Carson, and most survivors on the American frontier, was supremely gifted in the art of reinventing himself. Obviously inspired by Bennett's ability to manipulate media, Cody adopted the newspaperman's concept of "news as entertainment" to recreate himself—and his unique perspective of the vanishing frontier for the American public. Upon seeing an actor playing "Buffalo Bill" on stage, Cody realized American audiences would rather see the real thing than someone pretending, and the everlasting worldwide phenomenon of the "Wild West" truly began with this epiphany. But the seminal moment of the Western arrived when Cody took the stage for the very first time in Buntline's *Scout of the Plains* and completely forgot his lines. In a panic Cody resorted to yarning to hold his audience and the dramatic shift from the Shakespearean "the play's the thing" to the American "the *star*'s the thing" occurred in that instant. But it is important to emphasize that as William F. Cody blurred the line between truth and fiction, the resulting mythology he was creating was based in physical reality. Like Bridger, Carson, and the other mountain men he idolized, with their exaggerated attempts to describe the magnificent scale of the American West, Cody realized that yarning about western adventures could hold almost anyone's attention. Only now, unlike his predecessors who embellished their majestic-scale reality to spin grandiose adventure tales around the light of a campfire, Cody had a theatrical stage with modern lighting, comfortable seating, and, most important, people *paying* him to tell his stories. Moreover, by incorporating the theatrical arts he was simultaneously obtaining an education in the very basic tools of the yarning trade, tried and proven true for centuries. Most important, as his fame as "Buffalo Bill the hunter" spread, Cody realized that the general public strongly associated him with the destruction of the very West he cherished and adored. This bitter insight most certainly led him to want to change this perception of himself in the public's mind, and he realized he could best accomplish that in the theater.

Even as Cody began his theatrical career in the early 1870s, however, rumors of large amounts of gold in the Black Hills began to circulate throughout the West. Exhibiting blatant disregard for the Laramie Treaty of 1868, in 1874 Washington ordered General George Armstrong Custer on a secret reconnaissance into the Black Hills to search for gold. Meanwhile, even as Custer was stirring up trouble in Indian Country, Cody was becoming a national phenomenon in dime novels and on the stage. Yet while the name Buffalo Bill was being bandied about by media moguls such as James Gordon Bennett in elite gentlemen's clubs and newspapers, newsboys on the streets below those ivory towers simultaneously hustled the streets of Manhattan, Philadelphia, and Boston singing the praise of Buffalo Bill in dime novels. Immigrants pouring into the country in increasingly greater numbers arrived asking "What is an American?" and were quickly led to those same dime novels and the adventures of Buffalo Bill to find the answer. Poring over the simple language of Buntline's purple prose adventures of Buffalo Bill, immigrants were also learning to read and write English. Buffalo Bill and two other creations of the Industrial Revolution—modern media and advertising—had simultaneously begun their rapid rise to prominence in American culture.

However, as tensions mounted throughout the early 1870s and Indian troubles escalated again after the US government broke the Laramie Treaty, Cody was eager to return to military service. Cody thus began a period of spending his winters in the theater portraying himself and his adventures in melodramas and his summers scouting for the Sheridan and the 5th Cavalry. It was during this period that Cody effortlessly erased the line between fiction and reality.

Meanwhile, General Custer's entry into the Black Hills flagrantly violated the Laramie Treaty, and the Sioux would never forgive the desecration. The Lakota's sacred Black Hills were holy grounds for ceremony, introspection, and renewal of religious and cultural tradition. Because of this, the region had been very specifically set aside in the treaty, and the Lakota were promised *Paha Sapa* eternally; no white man was to be allowed there without the strict permission of Lakota leaders. Custer's shameful mission infuriated the Lakota. Worse, however, was Custer's leaking a report in the East that the Black Hills were "filled with gold from the grass roots down."

Lakota holy man Black Elk often referred to Harney Peak in the Black Hills as "the center of the universe." Describing the Lakota mythological perspective of the Black Hills in *Lakota Star Knowledge: Studies in Lakota Stellar Theology*, Ron Goodman describes an immense circle of stars defined with Castor and Pollux in Gemini, Procyon in Canis Minor, and Sirius, Rigel, Pleiades, Capella, and Beta in Auriga. Goodman says the circle of stars encompass a space proportionately the size of a polar cap on the earth's globe.

"The Lakota refer to this group of stars as *Can Gleska Wakon*, or 'The Sacred Hoop,'" Goodman says. "*Can Gleska Wakon* is mirrored on earth as the Black Hills." Goodman relates the Lakota myth of the Great Race between the "two-legged and the four-legged." The mythical purpose of this race was to decide which would be hunted and eaten, and it took place in the red clay valley that encircles the entire Black Hills area. (Fortunately for us two-leggeds, the Magpie outwitted the Buffalo and won the race.)

The Lakota also refer to this enormous circle of stars as *Ki Inyanka Ocanku*, or "the race track." The race track on earth is mirrored in the stars as "the Sacred Hoop." While the Black Hills already existed at the time of the great race, containing "everything that is," the hills were lifted higher by the turmoil of the racing animals. The red clay was created by the blood of the trampled animals.[10]

Oblivious to such mythological awareness, a wave of gold-crazy prospectors flooded into the Black Hills in violation of the Laramie Treaty and reignited conflict between the United States and the Sioux. After feeble attempts to remove the thousands of miners from the Black Hills in 1875, the US government sent representatives with offers to buy the Black Hills. This perfidious action backfired, causing most Lakota to further distrust the government; the "Great White Father" had promised the Black Hills to them for eternity only seven years earlier. Once again diplomacy failed, and the region erupted into full-scale war.

In the spring of 1876, military leaders in Washington ordered a pincers maneuver designed to kill all the hostile Sioux and force the survivors onto a compact, manageable reserve. In May, with great excitement, Buffalo Bill announced from the stage in New

York that he was ending his theatrical season early in order to hurry to join the 5th Cavalry as part of the troop movements taking place in the Trans-Missouri. Yet on July 3—the eve of the nation's centennial celebration—shocking news arrived of yet another inconceivable military defeat on the western plains: General George Armstrong Custer and the 7th Cavalry had been annihilated at Little Big Horn. The entire population of the United States entered a collective state of shock following the news of Custer's defeat. In a panic, western journalists predicted Indians would soon begin methodically attacking all white settlements on the plains, and a dark, paranoid cloud descended over what had been intended to be a festive time for the young nation. Then, less than three weeks after Little Big Horn, hope arrived with more riveting news from the Great Plains: Buffalo Bill Cody had defeated a Cheyenne war chief named Yellow Hair in hand-to-hand combat and claimed the "first scalp for Custer." This controversial event remains one of the most singular instances in American history of the absolute obliteration of *any* separation between theater and reality. The fact that it punctuated one of the most dramatic mythological milestones in our national narrative—the Battle of Little Big Horn—served to launch Cody's celebrity to international status and set the stage for him to actualize a vision that would forever connect him with the mystic Lakota prophet, Sitting Bull.

Chapter Seven

The Showman, the Medicine Man, and the Messiah

Maybe if I could see the great world of the Wasichu, I could understand how to bring the sacred hoop together and make the tree bloom again at the center of it.[1]

—Black Elk

Jim Bridger's eyesight was fading even as he served as Colonel Henry Carrington's chief of scouts at Fort Phil Kearney during the Red Cloud War. Soon after the Fetterman Massacre and the Laramie Treaty of 1868, the cataracts that plagued Bridger had virtually robbed him of his vision. Because of his rapidly approaching blindness, Bridger's Shoshone daughter, Virginia, traveled to Fort Bridger, retrieved her father, and returned with him to their farm in Little Santa Fe, Missouri. Since ascending the Missouri River with the Ashley-Henry expedition in 1822, Bridger had been the foremost participant in pivotal events in the history of the nineteenth-century American West beginning during the fur trade era and spanning through the emigration and Indian wars eras. As Bridger biographer Stanley Vestal observed, however, Jim Bridger lived the last thirteen years of his life "sadly ignored" by historians and journalists of the day.[2] He died at age seventy-seven on July 17, 1881, at the eve of an era in the history of the Trans-Missouri that would be indelibly imprinted by the Lakota mystic warrior Sitting Bull.

In 1911 the first American Indian physician *and* published author, Charles Eastman, wrote about medicine men: "It is well-known that the American Indian had somehow developed occult power, and although in later days there have been many imposters, and, allowing for the vanity and weakness of human nature, it is fair to assume that there must have been some even in the old days, yet there are well-attested instances of remarkable prophecies and other mystic practice."[3] Eastman continues for a full chapter in *The Soul of the Indian* listing instances of Lakota prophets and prophecies and urging in-depth study of the matter, but he is not the only Indian or non-Indian authority to recall such practices, particularly among the Sioux.

"In order to understand the spiritual/intellectual journey of the Indian elders, we must start where they begin their quest for understanding," Vine Deloria Jr. explains. "There were two paths that led them to make sense of their world: empirical observation of the physical world and the continuing but sporadic intrusion of higher powers in their lives, manifested in unusual events and dreams." Often a medicine man's dreaming power centered on particular animals or birds, as creatures often brought answers to important questions in dreams. Others received messages from animals while fully awake; Sitting Bull, for example, often received messages from birds and was believed to understand and speak their language. Aside from interpreting meaning from powerful dreams, from a lifetime of careful, detailed observation of the physical world around them Indian elders and medicine men noted the subtle yet fundamental effects that the orderly, simple processes of natural life had on people, religion, and culture. Moreover, Deloria explains that by judiciously observing the clever behavior and development of all forms of life from multiple perspectives, Indian spiritual leaders realized "that a benign personal energy flowed through everything and undergirded the physical world. They understood their task was to fit into the physical world in the most constructive manner and to establish relationships with the higher power, or powers, that created and sustained the universe."[4]

There was no greater prophet among the Lakota than Sitting Bull. He was revered by the Sioux throughout his life for his ability to predict the future. For example, Sitting Bull prophesized the Plains Indian victory at Little Big Horn with eerie detail two weeks prior to the actual event; indeed, the Lakota placed such value on Sitting Bull's prophecies that when word arrived in their camps on Little Big Horn that Crazy Horse had halted the powerful General

George Crook's progress many miles away on the Rosebud River and held his forces under seige, everyone immediately recognized that even though this was a remarkable development, it was *not* the great victory of which Sitting Bull foretold; in Sitting Bull's vision soldiers were falling upside down into their camp. As the soldiers fell, Sitting Bull heard a voice saying, "I give you these because they have no ears." The chief's vision was to every Lakota a clear indication that soldiers would be *coming into their actual camp to die.*[5] In fact, even while Crazy Horse held Crook in a stalemate on the Rosebud, Custer was pushing the 7th Cavalry double-time and riding through the night to get to the Lakota, Cheyenne, and Arapaho encampments on the Little Big Horn River with hopes of finishing the battle before any of his comrades had the opportunity to get there to share in the glory.

Sitting Bull was too weak from the Sun Dance that inspired his prophecy to participate in the actual Battle of Little Big Horn. Yet even today most assume him to be the man who killed Custer, and in the mythological sense this is most certainly true. It should be noted, however, that there was a second aspect of Sitting Bull's Little Big Horn prophecy that pertained specifically to the Lakota themselves and this part of his prophecy returned to haunt them: the medicine man also warned the Lakota not to desecrate the bodies of the fallen soldiers of his vision, or they would suffer. Lakota women unfortunately ignored Sitting Bull's dire warnings and immediately after the slaughter of the 7th Cavalry, swept upon the battlefield and mutilated the corpses of the slain soldiers.[6]

Bloodthirsty for vengeance after the Battle of Little Big Horn, America's military viciously pounced upon the Lakota. Merciless generals, advanced weaponry, legal semantics, the loss of important leaders, and starvation finally bludgeoned the fierce Lakota into submission. Never defeated on the battlefield, the ascetic Oglala Lakota military strategist Crazy Horse was murdered soon after surrendering in 1877. This deceitful act of violence reinforced a wide-ranging suspicion among the Lakota that the true purpose of the reservation was to gather Indians together in one place and un-arm them so that the US military could murder the entire population en masse.

Therefore, in a brilliant military retreat following Crazy Horse's murder, Sitting Bull wisely fled to Canada, where he remained with a large band of followers for five very difficult years. With their bravest military men and wisest tribal leaders either brutally subjugated or surreptitiously murdered, the Lakota people were finally subjected to the full wrath of Washington's domination.

In the autumn of 1876, immediately following the Battle of Little Big Horn, the "duel with Yellow Hair," and the "first scalp for Custer," Buffalo Bill's celebrity exploded beyond the boundaries of the United States. Fundamentally united now with the birth and explosive global growth of mass media, Cody's fame spread quickly around the world. Naturally blessed with such remarkable historical timing, by 1882 Cody was uniquely prepared to synthesize the past, present, and future, obliterate the lines between reality and fantasy, and create unique American mythology. A decade of experience in the theater had prepared Cody to realize his vision of exhibiting his beloved West at the precise, ephemeral moment of its passing into history. Now a master of reinvention, Cody was burning with inspiration to recreate legendary historical events from the initial clashing and eventual blending of the cultures of the Plains Indian and the Euro American. To accomplish this, and because of the necessity of presenting equestrian aspects so intrinsically related to the majestic scale of the history of the Trans-Missouri, Cody was forced to escape the rigid confines of the theater's proscenium structure so that real horses, Indians, and buffalo could thrill uninitiated audiences in outdoor arenas.

During his winter 1882 theatrical season in Manhattan, Cody met with Nate Salsbury, a former song-and-dance man who shared his vision of a spectacular outdoor exhibition featuring equestrian arts depicting western American history. Financially strapped, the pair agreed that it would be best to wait until they had enough money to risk such an extensive and expensive undertaking, but Salsbury nevertheless agreed to explore possibilities of taking the show to Europe. Fate intervened in June of 1882, when Cody was suddenly presented with an opportunity to experiment with the concept. Cody and his old scouting friend from the Indian wars, Major Frank North, had bought a ranch in North Platte, Nebraska, and christened it Scout's Rest. Neighbors in the small prairie community asked Cody to help with a July Fourth "Old Glory Blowout." So Cody hired Indians and local cattlemen and even rounded up a small buffalo herd. Although he was already recognized as a skilled marksman himself, Cody hired a local dentist-sharpshooter named W. F. Carver to do trick shooting. Earlier, Cody had spotted the old Deadwood stage rotting on the side of the road and, instinctively realizing the old Concord coach's historic value, bought and restored it and used it in the show. In five years the monarchs of Europe would stand in line like children at an amusement park to ride the Deadwood stage while being pursued by painted Plains Indians on horseback.

The Old Glory Blowout was a success. Tiny North Platte, Nebraska, proved Cody and Salsbury's concept was indeed possible and could make money. Meanwhile, early in the summer of 1882, after facing starvation and the steady dwindling of his loyal but aging band of exiles, Sitting Bull decided to return to the Dakota plains and surrendered to authorities at Fort Randle, South Dakota, on July 19, 1882—only fifteen days after Cody's Old Glory Blowout in nearby North Platte.

Change had shifted the political balance in Sitting Bull's favor while he was in Canada. Unlike Crazy Horse, who was murdered when he surrendered, during five years of exile Sitting Bull had become too famous to assassinate; Canada was a member of the British Commonwealth, and after the major international media incident Sitting Bull created by seeking and receiving asylum there, it would be difficult for Washington to murder Sitting Bull and justify it in the world's court of opinion—particularly in Great Britain. So the power brokers and politicians were forced to accept Sitting Bull's surrender instead as a symbolic indication that violent resistance by indigenous people was finally over. Even though settlers had continued to homestead while the chief was in exile in Canada, the absence of Sitting Bull's military leadership meant the heart of the continent was now truly open to be safely settled by the agrarian culture so vigorously promulgated by Washington and the railroad barons.

Though the American West had once been viewed as infinite as the imagination, it was now ready to be parceled into 160 acre tracts. Idealistic farmers, manipulated into believing that "rain follows the plow," were now encouraged to take full advantage of Lincoln's Homestead Act twenty years after the initial passage of the legislation designed to alter the entire ecosystem of the Trans-Missouri. The natural tall grasses of the region would now be replaced with corn, beans, cows, and pigs. Eastern bankers and politicians were delighted that their efforts to impose a European agrarian structure upon the Great Plains were finally taking root with emigrant farmers, and they accelerated financial investments along the lines of the Transcontinental Railroad. Cody supplied the mythological pieces of the puzzle when he assumed the role as the first buckskin hero of the mass media era, and the capitalistic economic organization and distribution system of corporate America was now in place in the Trans-Missouri for unprecedented fortunes to be made.

Sitting Bull, now a prisoner of war, was assigned to an Indian agent named James McLaughlin. By the turn of the twentieth century McLaughlin would rise to great importance in the Bureau of Indian Affairs, but in 1882 he was only beginning his career with the important assignment as Sitting Bull's warden. A Scottish Canadian, McLaughlin was married to a Lakota woman and used her intimate knowledge of Sioux religion and culture to wither and break the tribal will and bonds of Indians in order to convert them to Christianity and the way of life that awaited them on the reservation. Needless to say, McLaughlin and Sitting Bull were destined to lock horns. Sitting Bull, however, was much smarter than the Indian agent, and his extraordinary intelligence had been profoundly tested, tempered, and sharpened throughout his experiences during the Indian wars and his Canadian exile. So it was a relatively simple matter for the clever Sitting Bull to outwit McLaughlin—something he did frequently and with great mischief.

The dynamics of the relationship between McLaughlin and Sitting Bull shifted when Wall Street financier Jay Cooke and Northern Pacific Railroad representatives requested permission to bring Sitting Bull to St. Paul, Minnesota, as part of festivities surrounding the appearance of President Chester Arthur to encourage the construction of a northern route across the continent. McLaughlin welcomed the opportunity to get the meddlesome old chief out of his hair for a few days. Sitting Bull promptly agreed to let himself be exhibited on the long shot that he might be able to meet with the president and personally express his grievances to the "Great White Father."

Of course Sitting Bull was prevented from meeting with President Arthur, but Buffalo Bill perceived Sitting Bull's visit to St. Paul as potential box office gold. He asked for—and was immediately denied—permission to exhibit Sitting Bull in his show. Persistent, in 1885 Buffalo Bill made a second request to exhibit Chief Sitting Bull, and this time fate and Cody's timing were in synchronicity. By 1885 James McLaughlin had lost so many important political squabbles with Sitting Bull that the frustrated Indian agent was eager to remove the medicine man from the reservation so that he could no longer interfere with McLaughlin's plans to convert Indians and assimilate them into the dominant culture; the Indian agent immediately granted Cody permission for Sitting Bull to join the cast of the *Wild West*.

During the Indian wars Cody's scouting partner, Major Frank North, had played an important role defeating the mighty Lakota by employing their ancient enemies, the Pawnee, as scouts. Because of his close relationship with Frank North, Cody had expediently cast Pawnee Indians in his company prior to Sitting Bull's joining the *Wild West*. To ensure harmony in the troupe, however, once Sitting Bull joined the *Wild West* it was immediately understood that the days of Pawnee performers in the ensemble were over; the moment Sitting Bull became involved with the *Wild West* it was determined that members of the Sioux, Cheyenne, or Arapaho tribes—paradoxically, the very confederacy that fought the US military until the bitter end—would be the exclusive Indian performers employed in the production from that point forward. Sitting Bull's participation in the show would thus have a profound mythological impact reaching well into modern times; at the very moment conservative military and evangelical forces in America were trying to stamp out the religion and culture of the Plains Indian, the *Wild West* show began showcasing and celebrating them as a "worthy foe," thereby ironically providing them a window of opportunity for preserving their religion and culture. To be sure, Cody's *Wild West* would have survived and prospered if Sitting Bull had never become part of the troupe. But the combination of the most famous Indian and non-Indian Americans on the planet launched the concept into immediate, lasting, mainstream success. The unprecedented American triumph of the *Wild West* also quickly spread to Europe, and even though the old chief had departed the show by that point, his powerful legacy remained in place. Because of Sitting Bull and the Lakota presence, the additional casting of Cheyenne and Arapaho performers—Sioux allies—also allowed these tribes to become globally famous; soon the nations of the world recognized the religion and culture of Plains Indians as the definitive example of American Indians. Equally significant, as veterans of the *Wild West*, members of the Lakota, Cheyenne, and Arapaho tribes—such as Lakota Luther Standing Bear—adapted to show business and were later among the first Indian performers to make the transition from the *Wild West* shows to the fledgling Hollywood film industry.

All this occurred because of the relationship between Cody and Sitting Bull. One could argue that during his lifetime Sitting Bull formed friendships with only three white men. The first was also the first white man to interview the medicine man and make his name known to the outside world, Father Pierre De Smet. The second was Major James M. Walsh, a compassionate Canadian Mountie who befriended Sitting Bull during his exile in Canada. The third was Buffalo Bill. As a bonus for joining the Wild West, Cody gave the old chief a gray Stetson and a trick horse—a splendid and thoughtful gift for any Lakota of that era. Whereas P. T. Barnum or any other impresario of the period would have exhibited Sitting Bull in a crass, vulgar manner, Cody demanded respect for Sitting Bull's dignity as a chief and, showing great wisdom and sensitivity, made it clear to audiences that any differences between him and Sitting Bull were completely resolved. Cody accomplished this by writing brief essays in the *Wild West* playbills calling for equal rights for American Indians. Cody also showcased Sitting Bull in a singular role in the exhibition, during which the chief rode around the arena alone under the banner that read, "Foes in '76, Friends in '85." The chief had to endure hisses and boos from the audience, but it is a testament to audiences' love of Buffalo Bill, the *Wild West*, and the brilliant directness of Cody's foe/friend phrase that there were no attempts to assassinate Sitting Bull during the time he was involved with the production. After a short period in *Wild West*, Sitting Bull's fame rivaled—perhaps surpassed—Buffalo Bill's; the old chief even started earning a very healthy income signing his autograph after the shows.

Despite his success in the show, Sitting Bull's primary responsibility as a chief was his people, and reports of McLaughlin's increasing progress during his absence from Standing Rock Reservation greatly concerned him. During the time Sitting Bull had been away from the reservation McLaughlin had assembled a barely competent Indian police force. Composed of men jealous of Sitting Bull's enduring influence among the Lakota, McLaughlin's notion of "Indian police" was, as was all of his thinking, based on ancient divide-and-conquer strategies that enabled him to more easily manipulate the Sioux to his will. Of course McLaughlin's ultimate purpose was to clear the way for government treaty negotiators, land speculators, and mineral prospectors to enter Standing Rock and take advantage of the leaderless, confused tribal people in order to whittle away at the edges of Lakota lands. Sitting Bull realized he was needed by his people and after only one season with the *Wild West* returned to the reservation in 1886 to deal with McLaughlin and the talk of new congressional legislation in Washington.

The Dawes General Allotment Act of 1887 most certainly set in motion events that precipitated Sitting Bull's return to the reservation. US Senator Henry L. Dawes of Massachusetts designed the legislation to fundamentally reflect the decades-old Euro American rationalization that small populations of Indians were selfishly clinging to vast amounts of land and resources that could be put to more appropriate use by the larger population of the United States. Senator Dawes's legislation was written and enacted to abolish legislation that had stood for sixty years in order to redistribute American Indian land previously reserved in treaties with the US government.

Even though the Dawes legislation was intended to affect tribal people throughout the United States, its initial thrust was aimed at the Cherokee, Chickasaw, Choctaw, Muscogee-Creek, and Seminole tribes. Known as the Five Civilized Tribes because they had so readily adapted to the ways of the Euro American, these tribes had been the target of legislation that established Oklahoma as Indian Territory sixty years earlier.[7] In 1828 Georgia was the largest state in the union and engaged in conflict with the Cherokee Nation over rapid non-Indian encroachment into their ancestral lands. The establishment of Indian Territory in 1828 anticipated the Indian Removal Act of 1830 and was clearly intended to work in tandem with the earlier legislation to grant President Andrew Jackson authorization to order the infamous forced Trail of Tears march of the southeastern tribes to Indian Territory. After the surrender of Sitting Bull, however, the United States deemed the Indian wars officially over and possession of the continent *theirs*, so Washington was now ready to restructure the calculus of land allotment for the entire reservation concept. The driving force behind the Dawes legislation was the fact that the United States was also facing the second major economic collapse it had experienced since the completion of the Transcontinental Railroad, so the notion of opening up more land to settlement quickly gained favor with Americans.

The first post–Civil War economic failure occurred in 1873 after the sudden collapse of the house of cards built by the greedy robber barons of the Transcontinental Railroad. The nation's precarious financial situation contributed greatly to the government's cavalier attitude in breaking the Red Cloud Treaty of 1868 and the government's authorization of Custer's entry into the Black Hills to explore for gold. After Little Big Horn in 1876, Crazy Horse's murder, and Sitting Bull's retreat to exile in Canada in 1877, the US economy recovered briefly, but by the mid-1880s depression returned with renewed vigor. The government desperately needed to open up lands promised to Indians in order to stimulate financial growth. Consequently, the Dawes legislation intended to continue the US experiment initiated with the Five Civilized Tribes in the 1830s and use them again as a "test case" to reevaluate the entire procedure of allotting reservation lands. The more insidious objective of the legislation was that it was specifically designed to emphasize individual land allotment to Indians in order to chip away at what remained of tribal unity and accelerate the assimilation process. The legislation was also designed to coordinate with the actions of Indian agents responsible for dismantling fundamental tribal unity at the reservation level. Indian agents like Sitting Bull's warden, James McLaughlin, were assigned the task of undermining and discrediting the authority and ability of traditional religious, political, military, and social leaders, while emphasizing individual ownership, materialistic ambition, agriculture, and Christianity. The Dawes Act encouraged this overall process by allotting parcels of land to individual Indians based on the Homestead Act template, which required registration of community membership and documenting each person on official tribal rolls. While McLaughlin and other Indian agents persistently attacked the credibility and influence of leaders like Sitting Bull, these ancient divide-and-conquer tactics served their purpose, and cracks soon appeared in tribal unity.

Tensions between McLaughlin and Sitting Bull continued to mount with increasing intensity during the last half of the 1880s until fate once again drew Buffalo Bill and Sitting Bull together: concerned that Sitting Bull might be involved with the Ghost Dance or Messiah movement that was beginning to sweep across the Trans-Missouri, Commanding General of the Missouri Division of the US Army, son-in-law of General William T. Sherman, and long-time veteran of the Indian Wars, Nelson "Bearcoat" Miles asked his old friend Buffalo Bill to visit Sitting Bull's Grand River compound at Standing Rock and convince the chief to peacefully surrender to authorities in order to remove himself from the dangerous circumstances surrounding the messiah frenzy. Deeply chagrined when Cody arrived at his headquarters with official orders to arrest Sitting Bull, McLaughlin gave Buffalo Bill wrong directions to Sitting Bull's compound in order to buy himself time to react. While Cody was busy searching for Sitting Bull, the Indian agent sent a desperate wire to Washington pleading with President Benjamin Harrison to rescind General Miles's orders to arrest Sitting Bull. Successful in his appeal to President Harrison, McLaughlin instituted martial law and ordered the military to remove Cody from Standing Rock Reservation.

Cody obviously believed he had no reason to be concerned for his physical safety when he accepted General Miles's orders to remove Sitting Bull from the Ghost Dance frenzy. This could be considered a testament of Cody's courage, but more significantly it speaks silent volumes about his knowledge of Indian people, his genuine concern for them, and his friendship with Sitting Bull. With Cody out of the picture, however, McLaughlin immediately ordered his Indian police force to arrest Sitting Bull. McLaughlin certainly was aware that his decision to arrest the chief during the peak intensity of the Ghost Dance would very likely lead to Sitting Bull's murder, and this was perhaps his ulterior motive. Whatever McLaughlin's true reasoning for ordering Sitting Bull's arrest at that critical time, the result was the Lakota leader's death during the mangled attempt to take him prisoner on December 15, 1890. Sitting Bull's murder set events in motion that led to the Wounded Knee massacre fourteen days later.

By late summer 1890 the Ghost Dance religion had completely swept over all the Lakota reservations. Standing Rock, Pine Ridge, and Rosebud swelled with nightly dances summoning the ghosts of their lost relatives. Concerned Indian agents began to wire authorities in Washington that the Ghost Dance was at the verge of exploding into a new, far-reaching Plains Indian rebellion. By December, when McLaughlin sent his Indian police force to arrest Sitting Bull, the Ghost Dance movement had reached fever pitch. Now convinced that the Ghost Dance movement was the beginning of another major armed Plains Indian insurrection, the US military had increased its presence on the reservations in parallel with the mounting intensity of the Messiah movement. Of course this military presence escalated when, expecting trouble, Indian agents ordered Lakota chiefs and sub-chiefs to surrender their various bands to authorities for "military protection."[8]

Since Little Big Horn, anytime there was any mention of a Plains Indian rebellion it was immediately assumed to be led by Sitting Bull. But as Sitting Bull biographer Stanley Vestal suggests, a belief in a second messiah implies belief in a *first* one, and the old medicine man most certainly was not a Christian. As the Ghost Dance movement spread to his compound on Grand River on Standing Rock Reservation, it is more likely that Sitting Bull allowed his followers to participate simply as another way to defy McLaughlin—and because he believed his followers should be free to dance.

Immediately following Sitting Bull's murder, the Lakota assumed the mass killing of the tribes they had long feared had finally begun. Desperate, they began to flee to Pine Ridge and the only surviving leader they hoped might be able to save them through diplomacy: Red Cloud.

The chief of the Minneconjou bands of Lakota was known as *Sitanka*, or Big Foot. Certain the government annihilation of the Sioux had begun, Big Foot led his ragged band of followers through the night en route to Pine Ridge and Red Cloud's protection. The old chief was suffering from pneumonia as the Minneconjou crept through the freezing winter night to avoid the military.

Led by several surviving officers from Custer's divided command at Little Big Horn and arriving in the Dakotas from Fort Riley, Kansas, the 7th Cavalry was ordered to begin a flanking maneuver from the south to prevent Big Foot's band from joining with fellow Minneconjou bands led by Kicking Bear and Short Bull. By December 25, however, a brutal winter storm froze the Great Plains and forced the Minneconjou to make camp.

By morning Big Foot's condition had worsened, and he began to hemorrhage. But the chief's critical condition allowed Oglala messengers to unite with their Minneconjou cousins to bring word from leaders at Pine Ridge that Kicking Bear and Short Bull had agreed to meet there December 29 to surrender. The Oglala also suggested to Big Foot that he should route his band far to the southwest to avoid 7th Cavalry troops, now camped along Wounded Knee Creek. Big Foot, now coughing up blood, decided to ignore that advice and take the most expedient path to Pine Ridge. That unfortunate decision led him straight into Major Samuel Whiteside's command.

Whiteside demanded and immediately received Big Foot's unconditional surrender. Within moments, the 7th Cavalry surrounded Big Foot's band and ordered them into camp on Wounded Knee Creek. Realizing Big Foot was critically ill, Major Whiteside compassionately offered the chief his ambulance and medical assistance, and the old man ordered the Minneconjou to do as the soldiers commanded. Once the Minneconjou were encamped, Whiteside made it absolutely clear to them that they were prisoners. Big Foot's band was surrounded by troops armed with two rapid-fire Hotchkiss cannons. Later on the evening of December 28, Colonel James W. Forsyth arrived and took command of the operation. Forsyth promptly deployed his troops with Whiteside's 7th Cavalry—remnants of Custer's old regiment—and added two additional Hotchkiss cannons to the artillery and soldiers now strategically encircling the unfortunate band of Lakota.

Oglala holy man Black Elk's cabin on Wounded Knee Creek was only a few miles west of where Big Foot's band was surrounded by Colonel Forsyth's forces. The medicine man had only recently returned to Pine Ridge from Paris as the Ghost Dance frenzy was reaching fever pitch among the Sioux. Upon hearing the gunfire, Black Elk prepared himself for battle and raced on horseback toward the sound of the shooting. Galloping to defend his kinsmen, Black Elk met other Lakota warriors along the way, and soon a band of twenty warriors arrived at the scene of the fighting and discovered cavalrymen riding along the hillsides shooting down into the ravines. Bullets buzzed past them as they raced into the fury. Black Elk and the other Lakota warriors ventured into the dry gulches and were shocked to discover that "dead and wounded women and children and little babies were scattered all along there where they had been trying to run away. The soldiers had followed along the gulch, as they ran, and murdered them in there. Sometimes they were in heaps because they had huddled together, and some were scattered all along. Sometimes bunches of them had been killed and torn to pieces where the wagon guns hit them. I saw a little baby trying to suck its mother, but she was bloody and dead."[9]

It is estimated more than three hundred Lakota men, women, and children perished at Wounded Knee Creek that horrible day. As if to freeze the memory of the tragedy into America's collective consciousness, a blizzard swept over the Great Plains even as mortally wounded women and children attempted to crawl away from the soldiers' bullets to die in peace. Their bodies were later discovered frozen in grotesque positions.

PART TWO

We risk being the first people in history to have been able to make their illusions so vivid, so persuasive, so 'realistic' that we can live in them.

—Daniel Boorstin, *The Image: A Guide to Pseudo-Events in America*

Chapter Eight
The Wizards and the Western

*I remembered how the spirits had taken me to the center of the earth
and shown me good things, and how my people should prosper. I
remembered how the Six Grandfathers had told me that through their
power I should make my people live and the holy tree should bloom.*[1]

—Black Elk

While Lakota men, women, and children were being murdered at
Wounded Knee, plans were already underway in Chicago to host
an international celebration of the four-hundredth anniversary of
Christopher Columbus's arrival in North America. In 1889 France
had thrown down the gauntlet when it opened the Exposition Universelle, a big, exotic, stunning world's fair punctuated by Alexan-
dre Gustave Eiffel's thousand-foot tower of iron and steel that many
viewed as evidence that the French had moved ahead of America
with technological engineering skills and architecture. Chagrined,
America immediately began planning a world's fair that would
surpass the Exposition Universelle. Having finally recovered from
the near total devastation of a catastrophic 1871 fire and famous
for the creation of skyscraper architecture, Chicago eventually won
the intense national competition to host the World's Columbian
Exposition, and in October 1892 construction began on a futuristic White City designed to audaciously showcase America's wealth
while also exhibiting the United States' technological advances and
emerging dominance on the world's industrial and cultural stage.
When it finally opened in May 1893, the Chicago World's Fair, as
the exposition quickly became known, would eventually attract 26
million people, prove the electronic era of the Industrial Revolution feasible, introduce the Ferris Wheel, Shredded Wheat cereal,
Crackerjacks, Juicy Fruit chewing gum, zippers, and, because of a
controversial paper delivered by a young historian named Frederick

Jackson Turner, poetically articulate the ambiguous transitional tensions permeating the age.

Presenting such exhibits as the electronic White City alongside Harvard professor and pioneer American paleontologist Frederick Ward Putnam's exhibition representing the Darwinian progression of the "stages of man," the organizers, architects, and designers of the World's Columbian Exposition wished to portray the future as their major theme. In reality, however, exactly the opposite was true: the exposition underscored America's lingering connections with the past. Columbus's "discovery" marked the beginning of the Euro American era, but 1890, Wounded Knee, and the end of the Indian wars were equally significant, as both the beginning and ending of the Columbian period were *defined* by contact with Indians. After Wounded Knee, however, the pervasive attitude of Americans was that Indian people would remain frozen in time, fading in history and representation with each successive generation, excluded from the new culture and political world emerging in North America, and eventually vanish.[2]

In fact, soon after Columbus's arrival the common belief of Euro Americans was that the frontier and its original inhabitants were doomed to disappear. Aside from the fundamentally inherent genocidal implications of the concept of Manifest Destiny, the perfect metaphor representing the general public's perception of the vanishing frontier was transparent in the nickname "Lo" that Euro Americans piously gave to American Indians; "Lo, the poor Indian" was a brutal indictment that reflected Euro Americans' idea that indigenous people would simultaneously vanish with the frontier.

Because of the desire of the World's Fair producers to project a futuristic theme, and the *Wild West*'s deep Indian connections to the recent past, Buffalo Bill and Nate Salsbury were denied permission to exhibit at the exposition. Undaunted, Cody and Salsbury simply rented space at the legal boundary at the entrance of the fairgrounds, and the *Wild West* proceeded to attract audiences larger than those attending the World's Fair; indeed, many attending the *Wild West* left assuming they *had* attended the World's Fair.[3]

Cody's struggle with the producers of the Chicago World's Fair paled, however, in comparison to the colossal battle that had recently been waged to determine who would demonstrate the potential of electrical power to the world and light the White City. During the early 1880s the preeminent visionary wizards of the electronic revolution—Thomas Edison and Nikola Tesla—had attempted to join forces, but by 1886 the temperamental pair had argued and parted ways. Aware that the man selected to light the White City would determine much of the electronic future of the world, sorcerers Edison and Tesla entered into a fierce bidding war and elevated their feud to an epic scale.[4]

Thomas Edison first appeared at the vanguard of American inventors in 1875 with the creation of a multiplex telegraph that allowed several signals to be sent simultaneously on a single wire. In March 1876, after he narrowly lost the race to patent the telephone to Scottish-Canadian Alexander Graham Bell, Edison's naturally competitive spirit quickly evolved into the prickly, protectionist armor that would characterize the rest of his long, creative life. Edison began his experiments with the "harmonic telegraph" much later than Bell and his competitor Elisha Gray and, stung by the loss of the patent to Bell, intensified his experiments and quickly roared back with the creation of the phonograph, a variation of the "harmonic telegraph." Next, in 1878, Edison invented the incandescent light bulb and firmly established his reputation as the preeminent American inventor of the age. Edison's light bulb simultaneously created the need for an electric distribution system as well as safe, controllable currents of electricity to allow the bulb to replace wicks and oil lighting. By 1882, armed with 110 mono-directional volts, Edison lit a ten-block area around his laboratories in Manhattan and switched on the world's first electrical power distribution center.[5]

Nikola Tesla provided Edison his only competition to light the White City. Often referred to as the father of modern physics, Tesla was a Romanian Serb who studied in Austria before going to work for an Edison subsidiary electric company in Eastern Europe. In 1882 Tesla relocated to Paris with the Edison Company and promptly attracted the attention of his boss, Charles Batchelor. Two years later Tesla arrived in New York practically penniless, armed only with a letter of recommendation to Edison from Batchelor. Impressed with Tesla's brilliance and his radical, visionary approach to the field of alternating currents, Edison immediately hired the electronic genius. The legend in the history of electricity is that Edison offered Tesla fifty thousand dollars if he could redesign and perfect the inefficient motors and generators his staff of engineers' previous experiments had yielded. Tesla took Edison for his word and worked day and night on solving the problems—all the while creating more patents for the Edison Company as his experiments progressed. Tesla eventually asked about the money he was promised and Edison replied that he apparently had "failed to understand American humor" and refused to pay him. Furious, Tesla resigned. In 1886 Tesla finally recovered financially and formed the Tesla Electric Light and Manufacturing Company.

Fortune finally blessed Tesla in 1888 when he met Pittsburgh inventor George Westinghouse. Westinghouse had created a rotary steam engine as well as an early form of internal combustion engine in 1865, and two years later he constructed a device to guide derailed trains back onto the tracks. But Westinghouse made his fortune in 1869 when he created a new braking system for trains using compressed air to simultaneously brake individual cars. Westinghouse listened to and appreciated Tesla's radical concepts of polyphase electrical systems allowing the transmission of alternating currents over vast distances, bought Tesla's patent, and the two became partners.

Threatened by Westinghouse and Tesla joining forces, and also realizing he would need vast amounts of capital to expand his electric empire and compete with his rivals, Edison immediately partnered with financier J. P. Morgan to create the General Electric Corporation. Much to General Electric's chagrin, however, Westinghouse won the World's Fair bid, denying Edison his dream of lighting the White City.[6]

To fully comprehend the connection of Edison's and Tesla's feud to the mythology legacy of the Trans-Missouri requires a brief return to the 1860s and the birth of modern telecommunication. As mentioned earlier, even as Pony Express riders were delivering information across the Great Plains and Rocky Mountains at record speeds, the infrastructure for electronic telegraph lines was simultaneously racing across the continent to link the coasts with Morse code. During this period a Bostonian named William Barton Rogers realized the Industrial Revolution was giving birth to multiple innovations at such a rapid pace that the United States needed a university to prepare its citizens to harness, focus, and channel these increasingly powerful technological energies. In 1861 Rogers founded Boston Technological University—destined to be rechristened in 1916 as the Massachusetts Institute of Technology—and the university quickly became the center of American technological research. After the Civil War and the completion of the Transcontinental Railroad, a generation of men born during the infancy of the Industrial Revolution began flocking to Boston Tech. Teenage "geeks" of the 1840s and 1850s, many of these young men proudly nicknamed themselves lightning slingers or brass-pounders. It is easy to compare the act of these lightning slingers learning Morse code to students training in the sciences of computer code today; their intimate knowledge of the birth, infrastructure, and "headline" language of the new form of electronic communication linked these young men together in the mid-nineteenth century as surely as e-mail permits society to instantly and easily communicate globally in the twenty-first century. Bonding via the magnetic telegraph in an embryonic version of today's Internet allowed these young men to nourish their fascination with the power and future of electricity and continue their education until they began to gather around the exciting experiments in electronic communications taking place in Boston in the late 1860s.[7]

It is no coincidence that the lightning slingers began flocking to Boston in 1868, because that year also marked the completion of the Transcontinental Railroad. The Transcontinental Telegraph had established the first lines of its infrastructure the year Boston Tech was founded in 1861, but eight years, a Civil War, and a presidential assassination later, the government had also completed a multi-line telegraph system running alongside the railroad line spanning the continent. The Industrial Revolution—specifically the Transcontinental Railroad and Telegraph—had ushered in a golden age for communications and inventors.

One of the lightning slingers who arrived in Boston around this time was Thomas Alva Edison. Born in Ohio in 1846—the same year as William F. Cody—Edison had difficulty in school because he was nearly deaf in his left ear, but also because of his never-ending questions, which his abusive teacher determined to be self-centered. But Edison was blessed with a mother who realized her son was highly intelligent and who elected instead to home-school him. A voracious reader, Edison quickly outpaced his parents as teachers, and soon they were forced to hire tutors for their precocious son. By age twelve Edison was reading the classics in literature as well as science. Yet Edison's adolescent ambitions also led him to seek employment on the railroad lines as a butch-boy, as the young men who sold newspapers and snacks on the passenger cars were then called. Butch-boy Edison created his own newspaper, sold subscriptions to regular passengers, and was doing quite well with his enterprise until a twist of fate changed his life when he saved a railroad stationmaster's young son who had wandered onto the tracks of an oncoming train. As a token of his appreciation for young Edison's heroism, the stationmaster taught him Morse code, and Edison became a lightning slinger during the formative years of the telegraph in America.

Edison spent much of his youth as what was known as a tramp operator, traveling from town to town seeking work on the railroad and telegraph lines. His frequent extracurricular employment and numerous failed experiments—often with disastrous results—led to his being fired from many jobs, and because of a lifetime of alienation from normal social structures, he also found it difficult to work in the classical European group experiments that were the standard at Boston Tech. As a result, Edison abandoned school and made his way to Manhattan, where after enjoying financial success by inventing a stock-ticker that he sold to railroad entrepreneur Jay Cooke's Wall Street brokerage, he began to hire electrical engineers and chemical scientists from all over the world and put them to work experimenting in his laboratory in Menlo Park, in Orange, New Jersey. The Edison companies, of course, would soon become a gusher of innovations that would herald the arrival of the electronic age, and Edison would become renowned as the "Wizard of Menlo Park." Even though Edison and J. P. Morgan's General Electric Corporation lost the bid to light the Chicago World's Fair, the company they created remains today one of the most important corporate entities in modern global electronics and communications.[8]

Yet in 1893, even though the promoters, wizards, and captains of capitalism wished to emphasize the future and technology, the American History Association's convention was also being held at the World's Columbian Exposition. A young historian named Frederick Jackson Turner delivered a speech to the convention that was initially greeted with somewhat tepid response, yet soon began to inspire intense arguments that continue to this day. Titled "The Significance of the Frontier in American History," Turner's speech emphatically heralded dramatic change in America's future. It is important to note that the core of Turner's thesis was heavily influenced by Theodore Roosevelt's four-volume *The Winning of the West: History of the Frontier*, in which the future president argued that conditions on the American frontier were creating a "new race." Roosevelt believed it was destiny that Americans had replaced the "scattered savage tribes, whose life was but a few degrees less meaningless, squalid, and ferocious than that of the wild beasts." Roosevelt also believed that war against the "savage" was noble and that it was thus the fate of the indigenous peoples of the world to be trampled under the boot of western civilization.[9]

"In Theodore Roosevelt's *Winning of the West* (1885–1894), Buffalo Bill's *Wild West*, and a number of other writings, images, and performances," Philip J. Deloria notes, "American history took shape, not as a frontiersman's struggle with wild lands, but as one long Indian war, a violent contest in which Americans were shaped by constant struggle with a dangerous and challenging adversary."[10]

Keeping with the theme commemorating the four-hundredth anniversary of European presence in North America, Turner elaborated on Roosevelt's thesis and suggested that the first colonists in the New World naturally thought and acted like Europeans. The historian argued that the process of "Americanization" occurred at the precise moment in time and space of the passing of the savagery of the wilderness into the settlement of civilization. Turner thus concluded that Americans had defined their unique national identity balanced on the very razor's edge of the frontier as it trekked across the continent.

Turner's speech remains controversial today because, as historian Patricia Limerick's *The Legacy of Conquest: The Unbroken Past of the American West* observes, its thesis ignores women and minorities and only represents the male Caucasian role in the creation of the American mythological psyche. Moreover, as previously noted, the frontier did not move in a consistent, fluid progression across the continent; instead, it hopscotched and zigzagged from the North to the South, from Tennessee to Texas to Iowa and then back down to the Southwest, and so forth. In 1893, however, even though Turner's speech was largely ignored by the general public, it had terrific resonance among dominant—Anglo-Saxon, Protestant—individuals, institutions, and organizations throughout the nation because it finally explained why and how the unique American personality had developed in ways so remarkably different from the other nations of the world.

Census demographers in 1890 had nevertheless concluded to great fanfare only recently before the opening of the Chicago World's Fair that the American frontier had vanished. When coupled with Turner's thesis and a series of economic failures in the mid-1890s that had the nation teetering at the brink of a major financial depression, speculation ricocheted among movers and shakers from Wall Street and Washington to the halls of academia debating the direction the nation would take next in order to continue the great American experiment without its frontier laboratory. Complicating matters, in spite of periodic economic recessions and depressions, the continued flowering of the Industrial Revolution throughout the world had simultaneously introduced multiple new eras, and American ingenuity was introducing the majority of the technological innovations. Articulating the American personality consequently became a much more complex psychology by 1893. In the early decades of the Industrial Revolution, the slower pace of the nation had allowed time for psychological reflection and intellectual adjustment with the advent of most major technological innovations. By the turn of the twentieth century, however, scientific and technological advances were occurring at such an astonishing pace that no one had time to properly contemplate and process the changes. Adding to this continual tumultuous state of national psychological instability, America was suddenly flooded with more immigrants than ever before. Moreover, by 1893 most of these immigrants were no longer working class WASPS, Irish Catholics, or blue-eyed, blond Teutonic farmers arriving from western and northern Europe. The majority of America's new immigrants were now arriving from southern and eastern Europe: Italians, Serbs, Hungarians, Greeks, Ukrainians, Russians, and Jews. These new Americans turned Roosevelt's and Turner's WASP thesis of the American immigrant nation and its Manifest Destiny on its ear.

Aside from the pejorative, idiosyncratic definition of the term *savage*, Roosevelt and Turner of course also conveniently neglected to mention that western civilization's "frontier" was the American Indian's *home*. Sadly, at the end of the nineteenth century most agreed with Roosevelt's and Turner's definition of savage and perceived the massacre at Wounded Knee as simply a bloody exclamation point ending yet another Darwinian survival-of-the-fittest chapter in the eternal march of civilization; all that mattered was that the rich bounty of North America's natural resources was now theirs. As the Industrial Revolution increasingly begat technological progeny such as instant telecommunications and swifter, safer, more convenient transcontinental travel, the precept that the frontier and its original inhabitants were vanishing at an astonishing rate became only more deeply entrenched as an inevitable reality. As previously discussed, Buffalo Bill's profound love of the Trans-Missouri and his subsequent explosive global fame—made possible because of the rapid development of telecommunications—led him to the depressing epiphany that the public's perception was that he was personally responsible for the demise of the "wild" West. The need to reconcile his love of the Trans-Missouri with the ill-perceived public impression of his leading role in the ultimate downfall of the frontier became William Cody's primary motivation to present and somehow preserve the region and era at the very moment of its passing.

This desire certainly inspired the first cave painting; it is apparently fundamental human nature to defy the ephemeral nature of our existence by recording our experience while in this realm. Yet the Decalogue's Second Commandment to the Israelites, "Thou shall not make unto thee any craven image, any likeness of anything that is in heaven above, or that is in the earth beneath, or that is in the water beneath the earth" is obviously in direct conflict with this primal human yearning. Thus, throughout the development of western civilization, various religions and ascetic sects, profoundly aware of the inherent mythological authority in the act of documenting human history with illustrations, have forbidden the creation of "craven" images. Through physical fear and spiritual manipulation, the Catholic Church forced gifted artists to restrict their painting and sculpture to didactic, dogmatic, biblical themes. Most Protestant denominations simply followed suit, ultimately resulting in blond, Anglophonic depictions of the swarthy, Semitic Christ.

The actual ability to capture and record a moment in time most certainly began its rise to prominence in secular, global mythologizing with Louis Daguerre's creation of the daguerreotype photographic procedure in 1837—the same year Samuel Morse's renowned code first appeared. Later, Matthew Brady's daguerreotypes captured images of loved ones departing to fight in the Civil War, as well as grim scenes of the death and destruction the conflict produced, and popularized photography. Daniel Boorstin coined the phrase "graphic revolution" to describe the quarter century between the 1837 creation of the telegraph and photograph and the Civil War because the creation of photography also introduced fundamental change into the iconic environment as printmaking, posters, and advertising each elaborated and expanded upon the singular, literary, print-oriented culture of previous generations.

The Civil War also produced the need for an affordable camera and film that the general public could easily learn to use and transport. George Eastman was the first person to manufacture dry glass photographic plates in 1878 and within a decade Eastman would also develop a paper roll sensitized with photographic emulsion. Eastman's paper roll had perforated edges that allowed a person to take a photograph and then, using a tiny hand crank, roll the paper with the captured image forward through a small, square box—his landmark, portable Kodak camera. Underscoring Boorstin's definition of the graphic revolution and the impact of advertising born fifty years earlier, when Eastman introduced his Kodak camera in 1888 he spent twenty-five thousand dollars advertising and establishing it. Next, in 1889, Eastman created modern film technology with his invention of a synthetic, plastic strip with perforated edges that he named celluloid.[11]

Finally freed from dogmatic religious control of style and subject matter with the innovation of the daguerreotype, painters and sculptors immediately began to venture into new, more expressive mythological realms such as Impressionism, Surrealism, Constructivism, and Cubism, while other, more technically oriented visionaries continued experimenting with the camera. Even though most people today consider Edison to be the person who invented the motion picture camera, the groundwork for the creation of the device was in fact laid by other men. In Palo Alto, California, in 1878 Eadweard Muybridge—funded by the same Leland Stanford who financed the Central Pacific section of the Transcontinental Railroad—conducted what he called a chronophotography experiment using multiple cameras to record a galloping horse. Muybridge later edited the individual images into a chronological ribbon and exhibited the animated strip of the galloping horse in a box he called a praxinoscope. Viewers were astonished to realize for the first time that a running horse's hooves were indeed at various times completely off the ground. By 1879 Muybridge's praxinoscope had evolved into what he called a zoopraxiscope, or the "wheel of life," but because of Muybridge's original experiment, silent movie pioneers such as Mack Sennett often referred to their line of work as "galloping tintypes."[12]

While Muybridge—an English immigrant—was photographing multiple individual images to exhibit the movement of a galloping horse, a Frenchman named Etienne-Jules Marey was experimenting with simultaneously recording multiple images of pelicans in flight. Using fellow Frenchman and astrologer Pierre Jules Cesar Janssen's revolutionary concept of a revolving photographic plate, Marey constructed a camera "gun" capable of capturing twelve photographs per second—which, like Muybridge, he dubbed chronophotography. Unlike Muybridge's individual images, however, Marey's camera-gun was able to "shoot" multiple images on a single plate. His first multiple exposures were done on glass plates, but Marey also began to experiment with strips of sensitized paper. Soon another Frenchman, Louis Aimé Augustin Le Prince, began to experiment with long rolls of paper coated with photographic emulsion, and the stage was set for a dramatic change in heroic global mythmaking.[13]

Aware of Muybridge's and Marey's breakthrough experiments with motion picture cameras, Edison brought Englishman William Kennedy Laurie Dickson to Menlo Park and assigned him the twin purposes of constructing a mechanism to record movement on film and a complementary device for viewing the mechanism's recording. In November 1890 Dickson produced a crude, motor-driven motion-picture apparatus he called a kinetograph. Dickson's new form of the camera was a synchronized shutter and sprocket system with an electric motor that could move film forward. Dickson's camera was essentially the same as the state-of-the-art variety used today, but the electric motor of Dickson's camera initially proved impractical because its size rendered it unwieldy and it required electricity. The result was that pioneer filmmakers rejected it in favor of more nimble, hand-cranked cameras.

By early 1891, based on his breakthrough with the kinetograph, Dickson unveiled the kinetescope and also presented a trial film—regarded to be the first movie made in America—he called *Monkeyshines One*. Edison immediately applied for a patent for both devices, and on May 20, 1891, the first demonstration of the invention was offered at the Edison laboratories for the Federations of Women's Clubs of Manhattan. Dickson's new film featured him bowling and taking his hat on and off.

In February 1893 Edison engineers constructed a small tar-paper shed with an interior turntable to enable them to rotate the structure and follow the available light entering through a hinged sun roof. They dubbed their crude motion picture studio "Black Maria." Soon Edison began applying to the Library of Congress for copyrights for his films—some of the earliest of which featured cast members from Buffalo Bill's *Wild West*. By May 1893 the Edison Company offered the first public demonstration of the kinetescope/kinetograph system and, because of Edison's obsession with the phonograph, immediately began experiments with adding sound to film. On April 14, 1894, Edison licensed the first commercial operation of the kinetescope with a coin-operated box when the Holland Brothers opened a kinetescope parlor in New York City and began exhibiting films in their arcade. The film was essentially a peep show designed for a single customer and featured images on a continuously looped belt that rotated in front of a shutter and electric lamp. Then, on May 20, 1895, a film of a popular prize fight made by Woodville Latham and his sons Otway and Grey attracted an audience of more than five hundred people, and the age of commercial movies officially began. After the patent for Dickson's inventions was finally issued to the Edison Company in August 1897, the kinetescope quickly became popular at carnivals, sideshows, and arcade parlors.[14]

The most important piece of this new form of mythmaking fell into place as moving pictures when Edwin S. Porter, an inventor and former projectionist, patented an enhanced projector with a steadier stream of film and a brighter image. Naturally, Porter's projector quickly attracted Edison's attention. Born in 1870 in Pennsylvania, Porter had been a plumber, exhibition skater, sign painter, custom tailor, and telegraph operator—all before his eighteenth birthday. After a three-year tour in the navy, Porter's natural aptitude with electronics led him to New York and the fledgling motion picture industry. After a brief experience exhibiting films in the British West Indies and Central America, Porter returned to the United States and began using moving picture cameras to record news events before becoming a resident kinetescope operator at the Edison Manufacturing Company in 1899. When the length of moving pictures began to expand, Porter started making short narrative films about everyday life. Porter's breakthrough occurred with the 1903 film *The Life of an American Fireman*, in which he introduced innovations in film structure that remain in use today. For example, Porter was the first filmmaker to shoot scenes out of sequence and later edit them together in a chronological narrative sequence with parallel storylines. He also created the dissolve—a gradual fade out of one scene into a gradual fade into another—cross-lighting, and balloons indicating actors' thoughts. Immediately after his *Fireman* film, Porter directed and released *The Great Train Robbery*, considered to be the first Western and, even more importantly, the very first film to demonstrate the narrative storytelling possibilities of the new medium.

Aside from expanding the storytelling possibilities of the art form, Porter exhibited strong commercial instincts in his selection of subject matter. He had worked as a projectionist in the exhibition side of the business and the experience taught him what early movie audiences wanted and appreciated. He was also well-aware that the American public was familiar with the subject of *The Great Train Robbery*. The story was based on a recent Wyoming train robbery by Butch Cassidy's Hole in the Wall Gang, in which the mob uncoupled a car from a train, blew it up, and made off with five thousand dollars. The robbery had been adapted to the stage and produced as a melodrama around the country, and it was a natural for film.[15]

While *The Great Train Robbery* proved moving pictures to be a commercially viable and intriguing new form of storytelling, it also introduced the phenomenon of the Western movie "star." A Jewish actor from Little Rock, Arkansas, named Max Aaronson changed his name to Gilbert Anderson and, with an obvious respectful bow—and a heroic commercial wink—to the famous alliteration of "Buffalo Bill," took on the galloping tintype persona Bronco Billy, and the age of the Western celluloid hero officially began. Anderson quickly partnered with Chicago film pioneer George K. Spoor to form Essannay Studios, and over the next few years the pair produced 376 Bronco Billy Westerns. Essannay, named by creating a combination of Spoor's and Anderson's initials, moved its base of operations from Chicago to California in 1913 and a year later lured the British comedian and rising global movie phenomenon Charlie Chaplin away from Mack Sennett's Keystone Studios.[16]

Also based in Chicago, Essannay Studios' major competitor was a man who had worked as a magician in the minstrel show business before getting into moving pictures. William Selig founded the Selig Polyscope Company in 1896 with equipment purchased illegally from European manufacturers pirating Edison's patents. Consequently, the Selig Polyscope Company was the first film studio to flee Chicago, relocating to Edendale, California, to get as far away as it could from Edison's legal hounds. Selig was strongly encouraged to make the move by native Californian Francis Boggs, a veteran stage actor who had toured extensively throughout the Southwest before settling into the theater scene in Chicago. Boggs met Selig in Chicago and became the director of the Selig Polyscope Company. In 1908 Boggs experimented with *The Fairylogue and Radio Plays*, which featured South Dakota shopkeeper-turned-writer L. Frank Baum narrating a combination slide and film presentation of an early incarnation of his *Wizard of Oz* story. In March 1909 Boggs returned to California to make *In the Sultan's Power*, recognized as the very first feature film made completely on the West Coast. In 1910 Boggs cast real-life cowboys Hoot Gibson and Tom Mix to star in the film *Pride of the Range*. The pair returned with *The Two Brothers* in 1911, but shortly after the film was completed both Boggs and Selig were shot by a berserk Japanese caretaker. Selig lived, but Boggs did not. Suddenly out of work, in 1912 Hoot Gibson returned to the rodeo circuit and won both the "Best-all-around cowboy" award at the famous Pendleton Round-Up in Oregon and the steer-roping championship of the Calvary Stampede in Alberta, Canada. Gibson's career as a Western hero was further sidetracked by his service in World War I, but he began working again in films with director John Ford in 1921 and was a star of Westerns until well into the 1940s.[17]

Boggs's other discovery, Tom Mix, had served in the army during the war with Spain in 1898 but went AWOL to get married. Mix apparently redeemed himself with the authorities, however, because in 1905 he rode in President Theodore Roosevelt's inaugural parade alongside legendary Deadwood, South Dakota lawman Seth Bullock. After Roosevelt's inauguration Mix became a star with the famous Miller Brothers 101 Ranch Productions, physically connecting him with both the era of arena reenactments of Cody's *Wild West* and the genesis of the motion picture industry. After signing with Selig in 1910, Mix made more than one hundred Westerns for the company before eventually signing with producer William Fox. At William Fox's studio Mix made nearly two hundred more two-reelers in which the classic "good versus evil/black hat-white hat" theme of the Western became firmly established in his heroic tales. Soon audiences everywhere recognized the cut of Mix's ten-gallon Stetson hat and his flamboyant style of Western apparel, and *everyone* knew the name of his horse, Tony. It is important to note that future Western film stars and conservative icons John Wayne and Ronald Reagan were imprinted as children during Tom Mix's heyday, and as adults both recalled being heavily influenced by the cowboy star's Western morality plays.[18]

In contrast to Mix's flamboyant costume pieces, perhaps the most realistic of the early Western film stars of moving pictures was William S. Hart. A trained Shakespearean, Hart was forty-nine years old with decades of experience in the theater before his fascination with the Old West inspired him to embark upon a film career in 1914. Hart was obsessed with realism and noted for fretting over minute details of his costumes and befriending such Western legends as Wyatt Earp, Bat Masterson, and Montana painter Charlie Russell, hiring them as consultants for his pictures. Hart reveled in his 1870s boyhood on the Great Plains where, much like Buffalo Bill, his playmates had been Lakota children. As a result of this childhood, Hart was acquainted with the language and culture of the Sioux and incorporated this knowledge into his film stories.[19]

In 1915 Hart was paired with director Thomas Ince, the man considered the master of the two-reel Westerns. Ince pioneered such fundamentals to filmmaking as shooting scripts that contained specific information about scenes, such as interior and exterior shots. Ince was also the first director to use a screenwriter and film editor rather than doing it all himself as most early directors had.[20] Ince began his career in 1910 working as a director for the Independent Moving Pictures Company, an organization founded in 1909 by Carl Laemmle, a German Jew who immigrated to the United States in 1884. Laemmle labored for twenty years as a bookkeeper before he began buying nickelodeons and expanding into film distribution. In 1912 Laemmle brokered a legendary partnership with Patrick Powers, Joseph Schubert, Harry Aitken, William Fox, Adolph Zukor, and other pioneer independent filmmakers, distributors, and exhibitors to relocate to Southern California and form what would eventually become known as Universal Studios. The group complained that because of Edison's restrictive patent controls they were increasingly forced to use French motion picture equipment and market their films in Europe to survive. In 1908 the Motion Picture Patents Company negotiated a settlement between the maverick producers and the Edison Trust, the motion picture camera and projection manufacturing company American Pathe, and also with celluloid film manufacturer George Eastman. This landmark settlement allowed the United States film industry to finally blossom in a more free and independent marketplace. The immediate result of this flowering was that by 1910 the intersection of Sunset Boulevard and Gower Street in Los Angeles was so crowded with cowboy and American Indian actors seeking—and finding—work in motion pictures that it became known as Gower's Gulch. Slapstick comedy surely brought in cash at the box office, but the Western already represented America's collective mythological narrative in the early twentieth century.

Sitting Bull's discovery of celebrity as a survival tactic and vehicle for subtly shaping non-Indian mythology was also flowering. Fifteen years of experience in the *Wild West* had taught Plains Indians that most political and legal confrontation with non-Indians was now directly connected to images and perceptions that non-Indians had constructed around them. By entering the fledgling motion picture business, Indians sought to continue their struggle on the cultural front—specifically through all the emerging forms of mass media that promised to reach vast audiences with mythological metaphors. Sitting Bull's fame and success in the *Wild West* show provided Plains Indians their first opportunity to explore the world of the *washichu* for themselves, but also to have both large and small effects on how non-Indians portrayed them and their culture. Now motion pictures offered even more opportunities for depictions of Indians and their culture to be subtly shaped *by Indians themselves.*[21]

Lakota author Luther Standing Bear was one of the first Indian warriors on the mythological front hustling work in motion pictures at Gower's Gulch during this period in Hollywood's history. Born as Plenty Kill in 1868 and reared as a traditional Lakota during the first decade of his life, Standing Bear became one of the first Lakota children to be sent to Carlisle Indian Industrial Institute in Pennsylvania. Standing Bear was also destined to become one of the first published American Indian authors. In his *Land of the Spotted Eagle,* published in 1928, Standing Bear lamented the fact that the warrior culture of the Lakota had passed when he reached young manhood. When Standing Bear went east to Carlisle School he left believing he was going there to die. When his father asked if he wanted to go away with the white people, he bravely answered "yes" because he could think of no reason for white people wanting little Lakota children other than to kill them. So young Standing Bear thought going to Carlisle was his opportunity to prove that he was prepared to die with courage; he went to Carlisle to prove to his father and his people that he was brave and willing to offer his life for them. "I was destined, however, to return to my people," Standing Bear wrote, "though half of my companions remained in the east in their graves. The changes in environment, food, and clothing were too sudden and drastic for even staunch bravery to overcome."[22]

Standing Bear's thoughts and reminiscences in *Land of the Spotted Eagle* and *My People the Sioux* were destined to become early definitive literature concerning Lakota religion, culture, and philosophy. Standing Bear's recollections of his childhood at Carlisle were among the first to shed light on methods used by teachers to assimilate young Indian children into Euro American culture. For example, Standing Bear's remarks concerning the changing of children's names to those in common use in the English language poignantly suggest that even more important intercultural possibilities were tragically lost by non-Indians employing such short-sighted and prejudicial tactics: "Instead of translating our names into English and calling Zinkcarziwin, Yellow Bird, and Wanbli K'leska, Spotted Eagle, which in itself would have been educational, we were just John, Henry, or Maggie, as the case might be. I was told to take a pointer and select a name for myself from a list written on the blackboard. I did, and since one was just as good as another, and as I could not distinguish any difference in them, I placed the pointer on the name Luther."[23]

Standing Bear returned to Rosebud Reservation in 1884 after graduating from Carlisle Indian School. He taught school for several years on the reservation and, though present as the Ghost Dance intensified on Rosebud Reservation, somehow avoided being drawn into the movement. After the massacre at Wounded Knee, Standing Bear managed a dry goods store on the reservation until he learned in 1898 that Buffalo Bill was seeking an interpreter to travel to England with the *Wild West* show. He traveled with Cody for two seasons before nearly being killed in a horrible wreck of the *Wild West* train that left him with multiple injuries that prevented any future intense traveling. Today Standing Bear's recollections of his relationship with Buffalo Bill perhaps offer the most perceptive insight into Cody's unique bond with the Indian performers in his *Wild West* and the old scout's associations with Indians in general.

After recuperating from the train wreck, Standing Bear returned to the reservation, married, and had a son. He was given his allotment of land according to the Dawes Act and settled into quiet family life. Unfortunately, the injuries Standing Bear sustained in the *Wild West* train wreck left him susceptible to illness, and he was advised by a doctor to seek a milder climate. So Standing Bear contacted *Wild West* competitors the Miller Brothers 101 Ranch Productions in Oklahoma and worked with them for a while. In 1912, having heard about the splendid climate in Southern California, Standing Bear wrote to film director Thomas Ince seeking work in the movie business. Ince sent money, and Standing Bear headed to Hollywood.

Standing Bear immediately went to work in films starring William S. Hart and Douglas Fairbanks and eventually became so close with Ince that the director used him as an interpreter in much the same way Cody had in the *Wild West*. Ince hired Lakota people regularly, but most of them would stay only a while before becoming homesick and returning to their families and the reservation. So Ince put Standing Bear under contract at sixty dollars a week to help novice Sioux actors make the transition from the reservation to Hollywood. Standing Bear worked in the movie business for the next twenty-seven years. He died in 1939 on the set of the Cecil B. DeMille classic *Union Pacific*.

In 1912 Buffalo Bill also decided to try his hand as a filmmaker. Early in the creation of the medium Cody had entertained an offer to get into motion pictures but, deciding he could do better on his own, turned it down. Still, the idea intrigued the aging star. He thought he might be able to extend his old formula into the new medium and convince men who had participated in actual historical events to reunite and recreate them before the camera. Unfortunately, Cody was deep in debt to Denver former bartender Harry Tammen when he reached this decision. Tammen had been a bartender at the famous Palmer House Hotel in Chicago and it was most likely there that he met Essannay Studios owner George K. Spoor. Tammen relocated to Denver as the head bartender at the Windsor Hotel and later opened a free museum and curio shop. On a return visit to Chicago Tammen met a man named Fred Bonfils who had come into a large sum of money in an illegal lottery in Louisiana. Bonfils and Tammen formed a partnership, purchased the *Evening Post* in Denver, and promptly changed its name to the *Denver Post*. The pair quickly became noted for printing scandalous headlines at the *Denver Post*, but also for their third-rate Sells-Floto Circus, which they had created by hiring a dog-and-pony act with the last name Sells to make the public believe they were somehow aligned with the famous Sells Brothers Circus.

Tammen thought the last name of the Italian sports writer who worked for his newspaper sounded like a circus and merely added the name Floto to the title of the venture. Bonfils and Tammen also drove a legal and financial wedge between Buffalo Bill and his old friend, impresario, and partner, Major William "Pawnee Bill" Lillie, and in doing so succeeded in bringing Cody totally under their financial control and obligating him to work in their circus. When the ink dried Cody had even signed over the rights to his famous sobriquet to the pair.

Similarly, George K. Spoor and Essannay Studios had a definite link to Denver. Soon after Spoor and Anderson created Essannay Studios in Chicago, an exhibitor from Denver contacted them and asked if he could supply a film a day. Spoor naturally contacted Tammen to verify that the film business indeed held such a promising future in Denver. Soon thereafter Denver became one of the first hubs of Essannay's operation. In 1912 Tammen quickly brokered a deal with Essannay to create The Col. W. F. Cody (Buffalo Bill) Historical Pictures Company.

Revitalized with the possible new direction for his career, the old scout decided to entitle his film debut *The Indian Wars* and recreate historical events in which he had participated, such as the Battle of Summits Springs and the controversial duel with Yellow Hand and the "first scalp for Custer." Cody made the worst judgment of his career, however, when he decided to recreate the "battle" at Wounded Knee. To be fair, the massacre at Wounded Knee was the most recent major historical event in the West, and Cody always attempted to recreate topical pivotal events as quickly as possible with as many of the actual participants as he could reassemble. But he was *not* present at Wounded Knee, and, equally significantly, he had publicly denounced the incident as an atrocity. Cody was thus embarking into territory that was out of his mode of operations morally and thematically, while simultaneously venturing into a strange new medium of expression. Finally, as years of alcohol abuse were certainly by then taking their toll on his mental abilities, it is more likely that Cody was motivated by the fact that he was an old man in ill health, deeply in debt, and desperate to cling to his former glory.[24]

Philip Deloria notes that whereas the massacre at Wounded Knee was a milestone marking America's pacification of Indian violence, Buffalo Bill's foray into motion pictures with *The Indian Wars* reveals a "similarly pivotal moment of change and cultural negotiation. On one side of this pivotal moment lay the nineteenth-century *Wild West* show, a dramatic life performance that successfully engaged the tensions surrounding violent conflict. On the other side stood the twentieth-century Hollywood film, its technologies of mass production reaching audiences differently and engaging them for a different set of expectations. Films, of course, never repudiated the sensibility of Indian violence found in the Wild West. Indeed, they were the shifting of Indian violence from nineteenth-century *possibility* to twentieth-century titillation and *metaphor*."[25] (Italics Added)

Cody went to his friend General Nelson Miles and arranged with the government to supply troops and equipment for the historical reenactment. The decision nearly destroyed the pair's long friendship, as General Miles demanded strict details according to government records of the event, all of which gobbled up thousands of expensive feet of film. Even though they believed it was disrespectful for Cody to return to the actual location—consecrated with the blood of their women and children—to film the massacre, out of loyalty from the old *Wild West* days a few disgruntled Lakota agreed to appear in the film. Even so, rumors circulated among the crew that some of the Lakota warriors intended to use live rounds of ammunition instead of blanks when the massacre was filmed. Complicating an already disastrous situation, Cody was not a skilled film director and quickly lost control of both General Miles and the Indian people in his cast. In the end it was a miracle they were able to shoot any footage at all. The sad final result was that Cody estranged himself from Indians and the military, the two groups he had spent most of his life honoring. As might be expected, the project also proved to be a financial disaster. Cody had hoped to use the footage as illustration for a speaking tour, but for the first time in his long career Cody's impeccable instincts for historical timing were off target, and the entire project shamed Buffalo Bill among his old Lakota friends.

Since the 1820s the creative blurring of reality and fiction by political heroes like Andrew Jackson, sensationalist newspaper pioneers like James Gordon Bennett, and broadside rabble-rousers like Ned Buntline had fused with the natural evolution of American entertainment and the buckskin heroic role model developing on the frontier to create the first true *global* celebrity: Buffalo Bill. The technological inventions of Morse, Daguerre, Eastman, Edison, and Tesla and advancement in the electronic communication of images had simultaneously expanded through the efforts of pioneer film technologists such as Eadweard Muybridge, Etienne-Jules Marey, Pierre Jules Cesar Janssen, William Kennedy Laurie Dickson, and Edwin S. Porter to inspire spellbinding new ways for us to perceive ourselves and chronicle our historical narrative of who and what we are. By the end of the nineteenth century, pioneer visual storytellers such as Porter, Francis Boggs, and Thomas Ince had begun to develop narrative screenplays and employ actors like William S. Hart and Tom Mix—and Luther Standing Bear—to bring the heroic archetype of the American story, and mythmaking, into a new realm of human expression. Yet even as these apparently diverse technologies, people, and events appeared to be serendipitously falling into place to create this new form of storytelling, the men who would eventually create the brilliant organizational structure of this mythological puzzle were only just beginning to arrive from eastern Europe.

Chapter Nine
The Dream Factory and a New Red Scare

Under the tree that never bloomed I stood and cried because it had withered away. With tears on my face I asked the Great Spirit to give it life and leaves and singing birds as in my vision.[1]

—Black Elk

After nearly two decades of humiliating defeats such as the Connor expedition, the Fetterman Massacre, the Battle on the Rosebud, and the Battle of Little Big Horn—a period during which the US military never clearly *won* an open fight with Plains Indians—Sitting Bull's peaceful surrender in 1882 only signified a hollow victory for the War Department. Perhaps because of the embarrassing failure to reconcile such defeats militarily, the United States refused to refer to what happened at Wounded Knee as a massacre until well into the second half of the twentieth century. Preferring instead to classify the atrocities as a "battle," authorities in the War Department handed out Medals of Honor and intentionally interpreted the massacre through the media as the "end of armed Indian resistance" in North America. Philip Deloria has, of course, noted that the "end of armed resistance" is more accurately defined as *pacification* and that pacification ideology served as a bridge between the two dominant assumptions of the eighteenth and nineteenth centuries—that Indians were violent and that they were disappearing—and various forms of primitivism emerging in the twentieth. While conveniently rationalizing the theft of Indian property, pacification also reinforced the continuing Euro Americans notion that the Indian was naturally disappearing with the advance of civilization. "Indians might not vanish," Deloria notes, "but they would become *invisible*, as the very characteristic that once defined them—the potential for violence—was eradicated."[2]

British naturalist Charles Darwin's landmark 1859 book, *On

the Origin of Species, originated in England, but very specific aspects of his theories took root and blossomed in the United States, particularly interpretations that became known as social Darwinism and the implications of "survival of the fittest" when applied to unbridled capitalism, corporate greed, and the effort to subdue North America's original inhabitants. Pacification of the American Indian provided politicians and corporate powerbrokers with the opportunity to devote their attention to other policies based on interpretations of cultural and economic implications gleaned from Darwinism in order to introduce yet another dramatic socioeconomic experiment—one that would rapidly supply the labor force industry needed for growth.

The allotment era created by the Dawes Act—the legislation that Sitting Bull fought until his last breath—coincided with a period known as the "open door era" of US immigration policies. Since the 1840s the flow of immigrants into the United States had been steadily increasing, and until the National Origins Act of 1924 imposed quotas on the numbers of people allowed entry into the country, literally millions of immigrants came to America. Twenty-three million immigrants entered the United States between 1890 and 1920, and more than a million immigrants would enter America between 1920 and 1921 alone. During this era a massive influx of immigrants from southern and eastern Europe introduced an unprecedented infusion of incongruity into the predominantly white, Anglo-Saxon, Protestant nation. Even as poets, preachers, and politicians praised small towns, farms, and pristine majestic landscapes as the sentimental definition of American identity, massive numbers of immigrants swarmed into the nation's cities, creating overcrowded, menacing slums and ghettos filled with foreign accents and dialects.[3] Agrarian America had changed into an industrial nation virtually overnight; her rural culture had transformed into an urban society, and her homogenous population had become heterogeneous.

In spite of the Statue of Liberty's sentimental call for "huddled masses," many Old World prejudices continued to prevail in America. With Indians safely sequestered on reservations, Jews were the one ethnic group aside from blacks most frequently denied entry into mainstream WASP society in America. Other than menial factory labor, the furniture business, rag and junk collection, and the garment industry, anti-Semitism excluded immigrant Jews from most jobs in America. After centuries of persecution in Europe, Jews were accustomed to being considered outsiders, and because they were themselves recent immigrants, they were blessed with a comprehensive understanding of the recreational needs of those new to America. The genesis of the penny arcade business in America at the turn of the century thus provided many Jews a way to make money by providing inexpensive entertainment for the staggering numbers of immigrants arriving daily in the eastern population centers of the United States. Like the majority of the Jews such as Samuel Goldfish (later "Goldwyn"), Louis B. Mayer, Harry Cohn, and Carl Laemmle—men destined to invent the Hollywood studio system and create the motion picture industry—Adolph Zukor emigrated from eastern Europe. Zukor was born in the tiny farming community of Risce, Hungary, and his father died when Adolph was an infant. Zukor's mother remarried but also died seven years later. Now orphans, Zukor and his brother were taken in by an Orthodox Jewish uncle who demanded that both boys become rabbinical students. After studying the Talmud for years, Zukor gathered the courage to inform his uncle that he did not want to become a rabbi, and the uncle promptly arranged an apprenticeship for him with a family in a nearby community. The children in this foster family were fans of dime novels, and reading the adventures of Buffalo Bill offered Zukor his first glimpse of America and inspired him to immigrate. Zukor appealed to the Hungarian Orphans Board for assistance and departed for America at age sixteen with the forty dollars the board granted him sewn into his vest.

Like many eastern European Jews, immediately upon arrival in New York Zukor obsessively devoted himself to shedding his Jewish past and assimilating into his new life in America. The industrious young Zukor quickly discovered the path that would lead him to great wealth and power. Working with a furrier in the garment industry and learning the basics of the trade, by age nineteen Zukor had started his own business purchasing scraps of fur and then designing, sewing, and selling the garments himself as a contract furrier. Soon he had money in the bank. With his earnings as an independent furrier, in 1893 Zukor treated himself to a trip to Chicago to attend the World's Columbian Exposition, and there he met Max Scholsberg, another Hungarian Jew who was also prospering in the fur business. Zukor decided his prospects were better in Chicago than in New York and entered into a partnership with Scholsberg that quickly started to bring in large profits. Unfortunately, Scholsberg returned to Hungary for a brief visit and was conscripted into the military, and Zukor suddenly found himself without a partner. Young and overwhelmed with responsibilities, Zukor made several bad decisions that reversed his fortunes, and he nearly went bankrupt. Zukor had nevertheless impressed another Chicago furrier named Morris Kohn—also a Hungarian Jew—who, having begun his career trading with the Lakota on the Great Plains, knew the fur business from the ground up. Soon Kohn proposed another partnership: he would provide capital and sales, and Zukor would be responsible for design and manufacture of garments. The new venture opened in December 1896, and when Zukor married Kohn's niece Lottie Kaufman a few months later, Kohn and Company truly became a family business. By 1899 Kohn and Company opened a New York branch that also prospered, and soon they relocated the business headquarters to Manhattan to be closer to the heart of the fashion industry. In 1902 Zukor correctly predicted that red fox would become the most desired fur of the fashion season, and the company's earnings shot through the roof. Zukor was hardly thirty years old, and his profits from his successful speculation were between one hundred thousand and two hundred thousand dollars.

In 1903 a cousin of Zukor's returned from the Pan-American Exposition in Buffalo, New York and approached him for a loan. Max Goldstein had been introduced to an arcade impresario named Mitchell Mark, who was Thomas Edison's Buffalo sales representative and operated Edsonia Hall, a penny arcade featuring Edison's electronic wonders: phonographs, peep shows, and moving pictures. Mark offered Goldstein a partnership in the opening of a new arcade on 125th Street in Manhattan for three thousand dollars. Goldstein didn't have the cash, so he asked his wealthy cousin to lend him the money. Zukor loaned Goldstein the money knowing absolutely nothing about the penny arcades, but he was so intrigued by his cousin's description of this new form of entertainment that he soon visited the arcade and realized he could make a lot of money in this line of work as a sideline to the fur business. Zukor convinced Morris Kohn that they should open an arcade of their own on 14th Street in New York, where large crowds of immigrants prowled the dance halls and saloons seeking cheap thrills to escape the boredom and estrangement of their new reality in America. Zukor and Kohn rented an abandoned restaurant, installed more than one hundred peep machines, named their arcade Automatic Vaudeville, and the coins immediately began rolling in. Although Zukor and Kohn initially considered their new venture as peripheral, both soon began to lose interest in their fur business as they became ever more enchanted with the arcade. Their interest was certainly stimulated by the fact that the arcade was soon bringing in up to seven hundred dollars a day and earned more than one hundred thousand dollars in its first year of operation. The success of Automatic Vaudeville encouraged Zukor and Kohn to open similar arcades in Newark, Philadelphia, and Boston, and at the end of the first year the partners decided to liquidate their fur company in order to devote their full attention to the arcade business.

Kohn had met Marcus Loew in Minneapolis when both were working as traveling salesman for clothing companies. Born in 1870 in lower Manhattan, Loew had been a small, sickly child who rose from deep poverty by selling curios on the streets. Like Zukor and Kohn, Loew had worked seven years in the fashion industry at a wholesale fur company. Along the way Loew met the famous stage actor David Warfield, and the pair became close friends, speculating in real estate together. Soon after Kohn and Company relocated from Chicago to New York, Zukor was introduced to Loew, and when Zukor and Kohn began expanding their arcade business to cities other than New York, Loew persuaded the pair to let him and Warfield invest in the operation and split a single share of stock. At the time that Loew and Warfield invested in the expansion, however, Zukor had already decided to sell his shares in the new arcades and hold interest only in the original Automatic Vaudeville on 14th Street in Manhattan. Loew and Warfield eventually sold out of the Automatic Vaudeville chain of arcades, but the experience had only whetted their appetite. In 1904 they formed the People's Vaudeville Company and opened four other arcades in New York and a fifth in Cincinnati that they dubbed the Penny Hippodrome.

While in Cincinnati, Loew learned there was a "movie" theater across the Ohio River in Covington, Kentucky. Curious, Loew visited the movie theater and was instantly smitten. He returned to Cincinnati, installed a 110-seat theater above the Hippodrome arcade, and drew an audience of five thousand for his first Sunday feature. Soon Loew remodeled all his arcades in Manhattan and within six months returned his investors' money.

Inspired by Marcus Loew's success with movie theaters, in 1906 Adolph Zukor decided to convert the top floor of Automatic Vaudeville from an arcade into a movie theater. He called his theater the Crystal Hall because of the glass staircase he created to get patrons to the top floor. Like Zukor's Automatic Vaudeville arcade, the Crystal Hall movie theater prospered. Flush with the success of the Crystal Hall, Zukor rented a vacant store next to Automatic Vaudeville and opened his first theater devoted purely to movies.

During the next year Zukor partnered with a former prize-fighter and vaudeville promoter named William Brady who had secured the New York City rights to a new experiment called Hales Tours. The Hales Tours concept was to remodel a theater to make it look like a train car and show travelogues to create the illusion of movement. The novelty of the concept worked like a charm, attracting audiences large enough to convince Zukor and Brady they should expand to Philadelphia, Pittsburgh, Boston, Newark, and Coney Island. The Hales Tours idea worked equally well in those cities for about six weeks. But the gimmick served only to suck Zukor and Brady in deeper, and once the freshness of the concept faded, audiences waned. In desperation Zukor and Brady managed to lease a copy of *The Great Train Robbery*, and screening that film kept their theaters up and running, but in a year's time the partners had lost nearly two hundred thousand dollars and Zukor was once again facing bankruptcy. Instead of pulling up stakes and folding his tent, however, Zukor went back to square one, tearing out the illusion of train cars in his theaters and reconverting them to movie theaters. He kept the theaters open every evening from nine to midnight, and at the end of two years he had paid his debts and began to turn a profit.

Modern audiences have readily accepted the storytelling and mythological implications of motion pictures now for over a century, but during the genesis of the industry the people responsible for the creation and dissemination of the technology, as well as men like Zukor and Loew, who were busy structuring the distribution and exhibition system for the new amusement, considered the motion picture business to be a novelty—and a rather unsavory one at best. The experience with Hales Tours had nevertheless opened Zukor's eyes about movies in general. He had the epiphany that as long as motion pictures were treated as novelties, the public would continue to consider them as such; like motion picture projectionist Edwin Porter before him, Zukor had glimpsed that the future for movies was visual storytelling. By 1908 Zukor had concluded that, like the Hales Tours, the short one reeler films were not destined to last. Moreover, he had realized that motion pictures could not survive by appealing merely to the poor working classes that gave them initial success; in order to survive and prosper as an art form, movies had to attract the middle-class audience. Equally significantly, Zukor also realized that if motion pictures were to endure as an art form they had to imitate the preferred art forms of the middle class—the novel and legitimate theater—and to accomplish this required that film expand its undeveloped narrative potential.[4]

Convinced that audiences would sit for longer films, Zukor paid forty thousand dollars for the rights to exhibit a ninety-minute movie of the *Passion Play*, filmed on location in Germany, where the drama had been performed for nearly three hundred years. Everyone predicted Zukor would lose a fortune when he opened *Passion Play* in New York, but the film earned a profit and verified his instincts that audiences would sit for movies the same as they did for stage plays.

While Zukor was exploring ways to enhance the storytelling aspect of the new form, his old friend Marcus Loew was busy amassing a sizable chain of movie theaters. Realizing they shared a common desire to attract middle-class audiences to their projects, the pair entered into a new partnership, with Zukor focusing on improving the quality of motion pictures themselves and Loew concentrating on enhancing their theaters. Loew continued accumulating theaters and the partnership profited while Zukor traveled all over Europe in search of films and filmmakers, even cornering Carl Laemmle in 1910 in an attempt to convince the producer-distributor to start making feature films. Laemmle was not interested, but a year later he introduced Zukor to Edwin S. Porter, the director of *The Great Train Robbery*. Porter informed Zukor that another producer had just purchased the rights to a French film called *Queen Elizabeth*, starring the famous American stage actress Sarah Bernhardt. Zukor called his competitor and without even negotiating, bought the rights from him for thirty-five thousand dollars. Having discovered the formula of signing renowned stage actors to appear in filmed versions of well-known plays, Zukor titled his company Famous Players in Famous Plays.[5]

Zukor and Loew were of course in the process of creating the foundation of Paramount Pictures and what would become the first phenomenally successful, vertically integrated infrastructure of the Hollywood studio system and motion picture industry. Yet even as Zukor, Loew, and the other eastern European immigrant Jews were envisioning and engineering the organizational framework for a bold new form of creating and propagating mythology, the older version, Buffalo Bill's *Wild West*, was still attracting record-breaking crowds on both continents.

Whereas immigrant Jews struggled with bigotry and attempted to shed their European past to assimilate into the dominant

Anglo-Saxon culture in America, in the years immediately after the massacre at Wounded Knee, with the distinct exception of appearing in Buffalo Bill's *Wild West*, American Indians had become virtually invisible. It is important to note here that many of the Indian men appearing in Buffalo Bill's show—Sitting Bull and Black Elk, for example—were religious, military, political, or social leaders of the Lakota-Cheyenne-Arapaho confederacy of insurgents. It is also important to note that, when asked, most of the Indian performers confessed that even though it was pretense, they enjoyed the opportunity to put on war paint and ride, chase, and shoot at white men one last time. Nevertheless, because the leaders of that alliance were now prisoners of war, Buffalo Bill had to officially request permission from the government to "exhibit" them. Yet even while officials in Washington made Cody and his organization jump through multiple bureaucratic hoops in order to employ American Indians, the *Wild West* also fit their assimilation programs perfectly; Indian people remaining on the reservation could be more easily manipulated with a significant portion of their leadership absent into performing in the *Wild West*, and efforts to break down traditional bonds of communal unity stood a much better chance of success. While US military and religious powers were aggressively attempting to forcefully stamp out any remaining vestige of the "savage" in order to replace tribal people with reconstructed, individualistic, materialistic, Christian farmers, the American Indian performers in the *Wild West* were being introduced to regally refined European monarchs, learning about the non-Indian's history, religion, and culture, and simultaneously being taught such fundamental necessities as how to be paid with money, as well as how to spend and save the money they earned. Furthermore, Buffalo Bill encouraged Indian performers to set up a tipi village wherever the *Wild West* performed, and their "sideshow" quickly became as popular as the main event itself. For over three decades curiosity seekers from all over the world visited the Indian villages of the *Wild West* for a firsthand glimpse, albeit brief and superficial, into the culture of the American Indian. And the Indian performers returned to the reservation with the personal experience to teach their relatives more about the non-Indian. Most significantly, even as Cody drew absolute mythological power from the visual, unspoken reality of Indian performers in his show, Indian leaders in the *Wild West*—trained through timeless generations of traditional, *theatrical* ceremonies and pageantry created to emphasize, underscore, and depict events related in their oral history—were completely aware of the cultural and mythological impact of Buffalo Bill's creation and their evolving role in its success; after all, Indians represented the "wild" part of Cody's famous creation. Blessed with this insight, Indian performers were quietly yet indelibly fusing the mystical strength of their values, culture, and religion into Cody's unique and evolving form of storytelling as a means to provide for their own mythology an ironic circumstance in the *Wild West* in which it could somehow survive until future generations could resurrect it. Even though early show business demanded Indians to be depicted as savages, their instinctive understanding of the impact of visual storytelling, dance, and theatrical ceremony on history certainly allowed them to realize that the future would perceive them as something quite different from "savage." Thus, by following Sitting Bull's example and entering show business, Plains Indians were paradoxically preserving their way of life by exhibiting it before a worldwide audience while simultaneously providing medicine men, leaders, and relatives remaining on the reservation vital time to protect and preserve sacred ceremony and mythology by obscuring it in secrecy.

Even as Plains Indians struggled to preserve the most precious aspects of their religious traditions and culture in clandestine ceremony while simultaneously adjusting psychologically to their evolving new identity both on and off the reservation, non-Indian primitivists—convinced after Wounded Knee that violent resistance had finally been eliminated—suddenly became fascinated with romantically incorporating Indians into the American experience. With tragically poignant irony, Indian people were being forced at gunpoint to renounce *everything* about their identities while the non-Indian American public had not been so obsessed with assuming a romantic Indian identity since the era of James

Fenimore Cooper in the 1820s and 1830s that culminated with the publication of Henry Wadsworth Longfellow's *Song of Hiawatha* in 1855. Now that Indians were pacified within the boundaries of a rapidly shrinking reservation system, it was finally safe for Americans to idealistically explore the imprint of the indigenous culture upon the immigrant nation.

Philip Deloria suggests the reason for this change is that the non-Indian assumptions that accompanied pacification shifted dramatically at the end of the Indian wars. Deloria notes that prior to 1890 non-Indians had good reason to expect violence if they encountered Indian warriors in the forest or on the prairies. After 1890, however, "the masculine aspect of Indian violence" had been fundamentally tamed and the opposite assumption prevailed; Indians were now considered completely safe, and "the dangerous warriors no longer counterbalanced open-armed princesses." Perceived as docile, incongruous figures beyond the borders of their reservations after the end of the Indian wars, Indian men and women alike were now rendered vulnerable to new methods of non-Indian violence.[6]

One needs only to recall the tobacco store's "wooden Indian" to begin to realize how these new non-Indian hostilities first revealed themselves in the marketplace. But the enormous sales of patent medicines at the turn of the twentieth century are an indication that Americans of the wooden Indian/medicine show era were already buying goods with the hope that they would be transformed by them. This suggests that the anticipated transformation was not limited to appearances, but was also a matter of changing how one felt about oneself. The era of the wooden Indian and the medicine show also implies that by the early twentieth century a correlation between personal transformation, entertainment, and consumption had occurred and rendered these three aspects of American culture virtually indistinguishable.[7]

The fusion of consumption, entertainment, identity, and democracy is perfectly embodied in the father of the American department store and super patriot John Wanamaker, a businessman who became infatuated with Indians during this bewildering—yet definitive—period in US history. President William Howard Taft

spoke at the dedication of the new Wanamaker store in Philadelphia in 1911 and referred to the venture as "one of the most important instrumentalities in modern life for the promotion of comfort
among the people," thus prompting historian Alan Trachtenberg
to ask two obvious questions: What did the opening of a futuristic
department store have to do with Indians, "the most impoverished
and allegedly backward of the diverse peoples of the United States?
And what did Indians have to do with America herself?"[8]

The tobacco store's wooden Indian essentially answers
Trachtenberg's important questions. Advertising was most certainly the most extroverted prodigy of the wedding of entertainment, consumption, and electronic media in American culture.
Of course, merchants have always realized that entertainment was
among the most effective ways of luring customers. In early nineteenth-century America, barkers at fairs and bazaars often used
entertainers to attract crowds as entertainment, and the selling of
goods has been a central feature of the American socioeconomic
dynamic since the nation's infancy. Wanamaker's prototype for the
department stores that arrived late in the nineteenth century was
considered by him and other merchants as a "stage on which the
play is enacted." The theme of that play was consumption.[9]

Born in 1838, John Wanamaker conceived his store as the "epit-
ome of the nation and a model of the future," and he was right on target with his both his conception and its projection. The store began
in 1861 as a men's shop in Philadelphia, expanded to New York in
1904 (complete with a two-thousand-seat auditorium), and by 1911
had become the preeminent American shopping palace—the template for the intertwining of entertainment and retail that would
evolve into the amusement park–scale shopping malls popularized
throughout what self-proclaimed "peripheral visionary" and Grate-
ful Dead lyricist John Perry Barlow defined in the late twentieth
century as the "United States of Generica." A Republican politician,
Wanamaker served as postmaster general throughout the 1889–1893
administration of President Benjamin Harrison. While serving in
Harrison's cabinet, Wanamaker introduced rural free delivery and
parcel post to the nation, a noteworthy effort that aligned the eastern

base of the American commercial distribution system with a viable network into the rural South and remote West.

In 1906 Wanamaker's son Rodman hired former preacher and sometimes writer Joseph Dixon as a publicist at the Philadelphia store. Born in 1856 in upstate New York, Dixon held theological degrees in both New York and Pennsylvania but lost his wife and church after he was caught committing adultery. At the turn of the century he worked as a lecturer for the Eastman Kodak company before being hired by Rodman Wanamaker. Dixon had by 1908 become educational director of both of the Wanamaker department stores and initiated a program that would span eighteen years and entail numerous expeditions into Indian Country "with a small crew of photographers led by Dixon himself that produced, in addition to illustrated lectures, brochures, press releases, interviews, and countless ephemera, three editions of *The Vanishing Race* (1913, 1914, 1925), many thousands of still photographs, a number of motion pictures, including *The Song of Hiawatha*, and *The Romance of a Vanishing Race*, edited from some fifty miles of raw footage, and an unexecuted plan for a National American Indian Memorial in New York harbor."[10]

Underneath all the sentimental American Indian patina, the Wanamaker organization's ultimate intention was to divide its patrons into two distinct classes: buyers and sellers. Trachtenberg reveals that Wanamaker created his store as a prototype to encourage the smooth functioning of American business as well as a capitalistic solution to the class anger and labor union violence that had rocked America in the 1880s with aftershocks continuing well into the 1890s. Wanamaker's answer to the intensifying class struggle was first to transform "worker" into "buyer." This accomplished, Wanamaker's concept department store would provide accessible goods to *all* classes of Americans. To ensure accessibility, Wanamaker nourished the notion of instant gratification and provided accessibility of goods by becoming one of the first American merchants to introduce the charge account.[11]

Still, Trachtenberg's two important questions remain unanswered: What did a big city department store have to do with

Indians? And what did Indians have to do with America herself? Aside from being the romantic pet project of wealthy "merchant prince" Rodman Wanamaker and his minion, Joseph Dixon, according to Trachtenberg, "*made merchandising seem the enactment of American destiny. The* store imagined itself…a palace of consumption, the store was also a machine for acculturation and Americanizing the foreign-born not yet Americans. For Wanamaker's *sold not just merchandise but also a look, the appearance of belonging to America.*"[12] (Italics added)

While at the dawning of the nineteenth century John "Appleseed" Chapman was paving the route for settlers into Indian Country with apple orchards and alcoholic cider along the Ohio River, through creative and romantic marketing and advertising ploys such as those created by the Wanamaker department stores, the militant "vanishing" Indian of the nineteenth century gradually became perceived by non-Indians as the proud, now pacified "first American" of the twentieth century. Similarly, by skillfully developing and marketing the romantic image of the *inclusion* of the first American, such tactics could subliminally ease the twentieth-century immigrant's assimilation into the theatrically consumptive society US businessmen were creating.

A few exceptional Indian men such as Charles Eastman and Luther Standing Bear were able to successfully take advantage of this romantic window opening and enter the world of the non-Indian; indeed, when he left Carlisle Institute the first job Luther Standing Bear had in the non-Indian world—as did most Carlisle graduates—was working at Wanamaker's department store in Philadelphia.

Charles Eastman, meanwhile, was born in 1858 to the Dakota Many Lightnings and his mixed-blood wife Mary Nancy Eastman, and his non-Indian grandfather was the noted American painter Seth Eastman. Named Ohiyesa at birth and raised as a traditional woodlands Dakota until age fifteen, Eastman was sent to mission schools as a teenager. Eastman's intelligence was soon recognized by missionary teachers, who made it possible for him to attend eastern prep schools. Eastman graduated from Dartmouth University in 1887 and, after receiving financial assistance from a wealthy Boston social activist, graduated from Boston University in 1889 as the first American Indian medical doctor. Dr. Charles Eastman returned to the Dakotas to begin his first assignment at the Indian Health Center at Pine Ridge Reservation, where he met and fell in love with non-Indian Christian welfare activist Elaine Goodale and converted to her faith. A published poet and teacher, Goodale had also held the position of superintendent of all the Indian boarding schools in South Dakota since 1885. Eastman and Goodale were the medical team responsible for the care of survivors of the massacre at Wounded Knee in December 1890. The pair took a wagon out to the site of the atrocities, loaded up the few women and children they could find, and brought them back to a church at Pine Ridge for treatment. After he and Goodale married in 1891, Eastman quarreled with non-Indian authorities at Pine Ridge and left the Indian Health Center, relocating to Wisconsin with hopes of setting up a private medical practice. Predictably, no one would believe an Indian could possibly be a doctor, and after enduring spurious charges of practicing medicine without a license, Eastman was forced into different lines of work and other forms of social activism. Consequently, from 1894 to 1897 Eastman established scores of Indian chapters of the Young Men's Christian Association throughout Indian Country, while he also recruited students to attend the Carlisle Indian Industrial Institute in Pennsylvania. Eastman took his wife's advice and began writing, and beginning with *My Indian Boyhood* in 1902 he became the first published American Indian author as well as the first Indian medical doctor. Eastman eventually published eleven books, two of which, *The Soul of the Indian* and *My Indian Boyhood*, are now considered classics. In 1903 President Theodore Roosevelt recruited Eastman to assist with revising the disastrous allotment policies of the Dawes Act of 1887, and in 1910 pioneer primitivist Ernest Thompson Seton asked him to help with the creation of the Boy Scouts of America. Eastman's fundamental contributions to the Boy Scouts program continue even today to be a passageway for many non-Indian youths to enter into an exploration of Indian culture. Eastman continued his efforts to assist Indian assimilation and served during the Coolidge administration from 1923 to 1925 as an agent to inspect the proper implementation of the government's Indian policies.[13]

Charles Eastman's and Luther Standing Bear's assimilation into the world of the non-Indian is especially significant considering that they accomplished this while the United States itself was in a dangerous transitional state. Because of the nation's rapid growth as a military and industrial power during the latter half of the nineteenth century, it was inevitable that the United States would seize a dominant role on the world's stage in the twentieth century. Historian Frederick Jackson Turner's articulation of emigrant America's unique personal relationship with a vanished frontier served to psychologically confuse an already nebulous national identity and most certainly contributed subliminally, if not openly, to the United States asserting its military might with Spain in an attempt to create new frontiers and heroic archetypes. Still, having brilliantly articulated WASP leadership in the march of civilization for over a decade, it is no coincidence that men like William Randolph Hearst and Theodore Roosevelt ascended to power during this period in the history of the United States.

If the rise of Theodore Roosevelt had not contributed to America's impulse to test her military might against Spain, newspaper magnate William Randolph Hearst would most certainly have fulfilled the role. There is substantial evidence that his sensationalistic newspaper syndicate fanned the flames that forced President William McKinley to declare war on Spain in 1898. When Evangelina Cosio y Cisneros, the seventeen-year-old grandniece of the president of the insurrectionist Cuban government, was imprisoned for allegedly luring a political foe of her uncle into a trap to be captured, Hearst sent a *New York Journal* reporter to Cuba to literally pry open Cisneros's prison bars and rescue her. The Cisneros affair vividly explains Hearst's impact on the United States' war with Spain because the episode provided the newspaper tycoon with a reason to begin printing xenophobic editorials and rabble-rousing headlines agitating for a declaration of war against Spain. On assignment from Hearst to cover Cuban civil unrest, the famous western artist Frederic Remington wired his boss that the country was not politically enflamed, but was instead quiet. Hearst supposedly wired him back: "You furnish the pictures and I will furnish the war."[14]

The Trans-Missouri origin of William Randolph Hearst's fortune and media empire was in the heart of Lakota country—the Black Hills, to be precise. It could be argued that Hearst's father, George, was the most successful veteran of the California gold rush of 1849. Born in Missouri in 1820, by the end of his adolescence George Hearst had learned the mining arts from a local doctor in order to support his widowed mother and siblings. Arriving in the California goldfields in 1849 he quickly prospered and entered into a partnership with fellow miners Lloyd Tevis and James Haggin, and the trio began buying claims around the West—the famous Comstock Lode in Nevada among them. By 1869 more than $150 million in silver and gold had been extracted from the Comstock Lode; by 1890 that total had expanded to $340 million.

In April 1876—two months before the Battle of Little Big Horn—Hearst and his partners learned about the discovery of a gold deposit in the Black Hills that piqued their curiosity. They bought the claim in 1877 and named it the Homestake Mine, and Hearst personally took charge of operations. In 1879 the partnership sold shares in the mine and listed it on the New York Stock Exchange, where it became the second-longest listing in Wall Street history, eventually producing more than $1 billion in gold.[15]

Expelled from Harvard because of a practical joke and later readmitted only to flunk out, young William Randolph Hearst reviewed his father's vast holdings and decided that he would try the newspaper business. Hearst took control of his father's *San Francisco Examiner* and immediately launched a campaign against safety violations committed by the Southern Pacific Railroad, employing the techniques of his predecessors, Benjamin Day and James Gordon Bennett, to create sensational news in order to dramatically increase his paper's circulation. More significantly, however, Hearst learned he could satisfy his desire to shape public opinion with newspapers. Hearst boasted that he also learned he could "ruin a man" with his newspapers—something that specifically inspired him to want even more power. In 1895 he bought the *New York Journal* and declared war on Joseph Pulitzer's *New York World*. The ensuing war of words naturally created massive increases in circulation for both newspapers.

Though he was initially a liberal Democrat, Hearst's desires to shape American opinion to fit his increasingly conservative political philosophy drove him to create such a formidable press empire that by 1920 he owned twelve daily newspapers in eight cities throughout the country. By its peak years during the 1930s the Hearst Newspaper Syndicate consisted of twenty-six newspapers in eighteen cities with a total circulation of approximately 5 million. In the early 1930s, during the most brutal years of the Great Depression when unemployment soared to 33 percent of the population, Hearst newspapers represented 12 percent of total daily circulation in America and 21 percent of Sunday circulation.[16]

The Hearst Newspaper Syndicate most certainly sold thousands of newspapers on January 10, 1917, when Buffalo Bill died in Denver. Six months later, when the ground high atop Lookout Mountain near Denver finally thawed, Cody was buried there. Aside from metaphorically punctuating the end of the frontier era in American history, Cody's passing also marked the beginning of a historic new epoch on the world's stage; in March 1917, two months after Cody's death, the Russian Revolution began in St. Petersburg. Angry Bolsheviks began a series of social upheavals and civil war raging throughout Russia that would end the reign of Nicholas II and his family of czars, who had ruled the country for generations. By 1919 Vladimir Lenin and his Bolsheviks had seized leadership and created the world's first industrialized communist nation.

By 1918 the world was also in the midst of an unprecedented worldwide plague that by some estimates eventually killed nearly 100 million people. The Spanish flu attacked people between the ages of twenty and forty with such ferocity that its victims would often be healthy in the evening and dead by morning. By the time medicine eventually vanquished the virus in the early summer of 1920, nearly seven hundred thousand Americans and over a third of the population of Europe had perished. Medical experts have suggested the flu spread so rapidly because of the new type of war being waged in Europe. The conflict was largely fought in filthy trenches, and such close unsanitary contact naturally contributed to the spread of the disease, but the Great War also introduced chemical warfare to the world. Soldiers' immune systems were either damaged or weakened by the constant bombarding of chemicals, malnutrition, and filth, which provided the virus a fertile opportunity to take root in humans and spread. With social and economic revolution altering everyday life with such great speed and a global plague cutting a grim swath of death, paranoia spread just as surely and quickly as the flu virus between 1914 and 1920.[17]

The United States' entry into World War I in Europe in 1917, a global pandemic, the labor revolution, and the rise of communism in Russia struck corporate America with unprecedented political terror. Already profoundly affected psychologically by the dramatically rapid industrial and technological advances arriving regularly throughout the last quarter of the nineteenth century, with the distinct exception of the brutal oppression of czars, the United States had been struggling with the same social, political, and cultural problems that sparked the Russian Revolution and set in motion the international escalation of communism. Nevertheless, America was certainly no stranger to revolutionary political movements and violent activists advocating social and political change; as recently as September 1901 America had experienced the assassination of President William McKinley by anarchist Leon Czolgosz, who subsequently became one of the first to be executed in Thomas Edison's electric chair.

Throughout the second half of the nineteenth century, the anarchist movement had grown exponentially in America as the labor forces expanded with the increasing numbers of European immigrants, the accelerated growth of industry, and the spread of poverty-riddled urban ghettos. As the nation's industrial classes swelled, political leadership and capitalist profiteers faced frequent strikes and increasingly louder, more violent calls for unionization. Complicating matters, during the peak years of the Industrial

Revolution, in defiance of the rise of labor unions, many American capitalists and politicians embraced social Darwinism. Whereas the interpretation of Darwin's theory of evolution as "survival of the fittest" was perceived by many leading powerbrokers as a rationale for unregulated greed and power, such behavior was anathema to pioneer union organizers such as Eugene Debs. Debs began organizing firemen in his hometown of Terre Haute, Indiana, in 1875. After years of grassroots political organization of unions in the Midwest, Debs was elected president of the American Railway Union at the onset the economic Panic of 1873. Debs organized the famous Pullman boycott and strike against the Great Northern Pacific Railroad and completely shut the company down. The union organizers were promptly incarcerated, and Debs spent his time in jail reading the works of Karl Marx. Upon release from jail in 1900, Debs decided to enter politics and, because he had become convinced the plight of the worker is essentially a class struggle, founded the American Socialist Party. Debs ran for president on the Socialist ticket in 1900, losing to Republican William McKinley. After McKinley was assassinated in 1901, Vice President Theodore Roosevelt immediately ascended to the Oval Office. Only forty-two at the time, "Teddy" became the youngest president in United States history.

In 1904 Debs campaigned against Roosevelt with a stronger organization and fared much better. He lost the election, however, returned to union organization, and, with radical William "Big Bill" Haywood, founded the Industrial Workers of the World (IWW) in 1905. When the IWW quickly became radicalized and violent, Debs parted ways with the notorious Haywood and the union.

Anarchism and socialism continued to expand exponentially as the power struggle between workers and capitalism throughout the industrial United States intensified. Responding to this, Americans of a more diplomatic persuasion began gathering together to form a movement seeking a more peaceful approach to the problem. The progressive movement eventually absorbed both Eugene Debs's Socialist Party *and* Theodore Roosevelt's maverick Republicans, but the anarchist movement continued to become increasingly violent through the outbreak of World War I in Europe in 1914, the Russian Revolution, and the United States' declaration of war against Germany in 1917.

As the powerbrokers of government and industry were increasingly threatened by anarchists, Socialists, and Communists and joined forces against them, many Americans were reacting much differently to the dramatic changes that were sweeping the nation. Radical intellectuals and artists—the children of the era Mark Twain dubbed the "Gilded Age"—had come to believe the 150-year-old tradition of encouraging individualism in America had led only to rampant materialism and the downward spiraling loss of a spiritual sense of community. While the anarchist movement took an increasingly violent position to counter this trend, Eugene Debs was aware that progressive Americans were against such aggressive action and consequently directed the Socialist movement toward the more peaceful political mainstream. In the tradition of Emerson, Thoreau, Melville, Hawthorne, Harriet Beecher Stowe, and Mark Twain, many young thinkers and writers such as Upton Sinclair and Jack London began using their literary talents to expose inequalities and injustices in industrial America and depict the circumstances that created the need for unions and civil disobedience in the first place. Debs's political campaign influenced Jack London, Upton Sinclair, Clarence Darrow, and Florence Kelley to create the Intercollegiate Socialist Society in 1905, and in 1906 Sinclair published *The Jungle*, his blistering exposé of the US meatpacking industry. The book created such a public outcry that Congress passed the Pure Food and Drug Act before the year ended; it also inspired Teddy Roosevelt to coin the term *muckraker* to describe Sinclair's reportage approach to literature. The prolific Sinclair continued publishing a steady stream of novels that revealed the underbelly of American industries from coal to oil, and when in 1918 the government used the Espionage Act of 1917 and Sedition Act of 1918 to imprison Eugene Debs, Upton Sinclair took up leadership of the Socialist cause. Sinclair founded the first chapter of the American Civil Liberties Union in California in 1920 and in 1926 ran for governor of California on the Socialist ticket.[18]

Even as activists Debs and Sinclair sought to change America's ideological and political direction, the nation's mythological consciousness was beginning to shift to a completely different social and artistic perspective. The woman destined to lead this movement away from the dark mythological underbelly of America's Gilded Age, Mabel Ganson, was born into a wealthy Buffalo, New York banking family in 1879. Strategically located on the eastern shore of Lake Erie in territory originally claimed by the Iroquois and Seneca, Buffalo prospered in the early nineteenth century when it became the western terminus of the Erie Canal. Thus many of the titans of American capitalism and culture lived in Buffalo; indeed, one of the Ganson's neighbors was Mark Twain. The street in Buffalo that Mabel Ganson played on as a child was often visited by presidents, dating back to Millard Fillmore and Abraham Lincoln. In 1901, after being shot by the anarchist Leon Czolgosz after his speech in Buffalo at the Pan-American Exposition, President William McKinley was taken to a mansion near the Ganson home to recuperate. When McKinley died, Theodore Roosevelt was sworn in as president on the steps of a house across the street from Mabel's home.

Set apart from the urban sprawl of Manhattan, the tightly knit, Anglo-Saxon community of Buffalo was without doubt one of the power centers of the Gilded Age. As a result, young Mabel witnessed firsthand the negative impact of money and power on the family fabric; often shuffled out of the way as child, Mabel believed her parents showed more affection to their expensive thoroughbred dogs than to her. A sensitive, lonely child, Mabel recognized at a tender age that her mother and father needed love, but that neither of them knew how to give or receive it.

In 1900, nineteen-year-old Mabel married into even greater wealth. Mabel and shipping magnate Carl Evans had a son before Carl was killed in a hunting accident, leaving Mabel an extremely wealthy young widow. In 1903 Evans married wealthy architect Edwin Dodge, and the couple, along with Mabel's son, John, moved to Florence, Italy, and bought a palatial villa. There Mabel discovered her direction in life when she began absorbing the history of the Renaissance in Florence and reinterpreting it for her era by holding regular salons for European intelligentsia and wealthy American expatriates such as Leo and Gertrude Stein and Gertrude's companion Alice B. Toklas. In 1912 Mabel convinced her understanding husband, Edwin, to return to America, where she continued hosting her artistic gatherings with weekly salon sessions in her Greenwich Village home. In 1913 she helped organize the International Exhibition of Modern Art in Manhattan. The Armory Show, as the exhibition quickly became known, was destined to shape the direction of global culture and mythology from that point forward with its introduction of abstract art and the works of visionary artists such as Pablo Picasso and Marchel DuChamp to America; as a paradoxical heir and counterpart to Hall Jackson Kelley's empirical concept of Manifest Destiny, the Armory Show announced that the center of the art world had shifted from Florence and Paris to Manhattan and, doing so, also audaciously proclaimed that the modern creative perception of civilization had relocated from Europe to America.

Soon after the Armory Show, Mabel Dodge began a romantic affair with John Reed, an American radical journalist who was also a close friend of union activist Emma Goldman. Acting on Mabel's inspiration, the pair united William "Big Bill" Haywood's International Workers of the World with philanthropists, Marxists, socialists, anarchists, and painters to produce a most unlikely pageant in Madison Square Garden: the depiction of a labor strike in Paterson, New Jersey. Dodge's affair with Reed continued until the journalist's 1916 departure for Russia at the eve of the Bolshevik Revolution. Reed died in Moscow and is—famously to some, infamously to others—the only American buried in the Kremlin.

In 1916 Mabel divorced Edwin Dodge and married the painter Maurice Sterne. By 1916 she had also begun intense therapy sessions with A. A. Brill in New York. Abraham Brill was an Austrian psychiatrist who was the first practicing psychoanalyst in America and the leading figure in the embryonic American psychoanalytic movement. Brill was also the first person to translate Sigmund Freud's works, such as *The Interpretation of Dreams*, into English and introduce them in America. Brill's association with Mabel

Dodge led him to frequent her Greenwich Village salons, where he met the leading radicals, avant-garde artists, and intellectuals of the era and introduced many of them to psychoanalysis; indeed, in the early twentieth century Mabel Dodge's Greenwich Village salons created the most fertile environment in America to introduce new and different thinking like Freudian psychotherapy into American consciousness. In Dodge's salons every taboo subject from free love to feminism and birth control was enthusiastically broached by the leading radical and progressive thinkers of the day. Mabel made certain that noted thinkers of opposing perspectives were present to discuss controversial topics and thus intentionally cross-pollinated provocative ideas and concepts. She also became the foremost primitivist of the early twentieth century.

Through her salons and her therapy sessions Mabel Dodge became increasingly convinced that western civilization was racing toward apocalypse and that its only salvation was to embrace the art and culture of the American Indian. In 1919 she and Sterne, along with the anthropologist, socialist-folklorist, and pioneer feminist Elsie Clews Parsons, moved to Taos, New Mexico, to establish a bohemian literary colony of freethinkers. Soon after the trio's arrival in Taos, a Pueblo Indian named Tony Lujan greeted them and suggested a house and piece of property that they eventually purchased. Once Dodge, Sterne, and Parsons moved in, Lujan set up a tipi outside their house, began drumming, and continued doing so until Mabel relented to his proposal of love, came out of her house, and moved into the tipi with him. Naturally, Sterne fumed and threatened to shoot Lujan, but he eventually surrendered to fate when Mabel demanded that he return to New York. Mabel Dodge and Tony Lujan married in 1923, and soon alternative thinkers, artists like Alfred Stieglitz and Georgia O'Keefe, and writers like D. H. Lawrence and his wife, Frieda, began arriving in Taos regularly to visit Mabel and Tony. A center for philosophic change in America had taken root.[19]

Elsie Clews Parsons was definitely influenced by her new life in Taos. In 1922 the anthropologist edited a "literal fiction" about *being* Indian. Parsons's *Life by Several of Its Students* was a collection of twenty-seven brief essays by several of America's most prominent ethnologists in which the editor assigned her "students" the task of writing an account of some minute aspect of the culture he or she studied from the perspective of an indigenous member of that culture. Parsons's intention was to disregard "the white man's traditions about Indians" in order to write from the viewpoint of the indigenous culture and mentality. Parsons remarked that "'few, if any of us, succeeded in describing another culture, or ridding ourselves of our own cultural bias or the habits of mind. Much of our anthropological work, to quote a letter from Spinden, 'is not so much definitive science as it is immunity from the dream of "being Indian" *in place of learning from natives other ways of being American.*'"[20] (Italics added)

As an antidote to the psychological wounds inflicted by obsessive-compulsive capitalism and cultural imperialism, Mabel Dodge Luhan sought to create a new mythological consciousness based on America's indigenous culture. While America was also rapidly becoming intoxicated with celebrity during the 1920s, conservative WASP Americans were quick to note that the increasingly popular entertainment industry—particularly the motion picture industry—was dominated by immigrant Jews; indeed, many believed Hollywood to be the source rather than the reflection of the dramatic changes in morals and values that were beginning to reveal themselves throughout the country. Drug and sex scandals such as the infamous Roscoe "Fatty" Arbuckle rape case in 1921 had jolted the film community and shocked the world. Themes of Hollywood films were, of course, merely reflecting the irreverent attitudes of the Jazz Era of the Roaring Twenties, and, as such, were challenging the moral values of mainstream Victorian-American culture. Hectoring from church and religious groups concerning the increasingly degenerate morals reflected in Hollywood and its films resulted in censorship laws governing films varying from state to state. This cumbersome system required films to be edited according to individual state prerogatives; the procedure also often slashed any semblance of continuity from a picture's narrative. So Hollywood and Washington DC joined together for the first time and hired career government employee William Hays to create and head a new department. The chairman of the Republican National Committee from 1918 to 1921, Hays had been appointed by President Warren Harding to serve in his administration as postmaster general. In January 1922 Hays resigned his cabinet position and became the first president of the Motion Picture Producers and Distributors of America (MPPDA), a position he would hold until 1945. Hays created the first standard censorship code, or moral standard that Hollywood agreed to abide by when creating and distributing motion pictures. Films became more morally sanitized after the Motion Pictures Production Code (also called the Hays Code), but the personal lives of the filmmakers and the glittering entourages they attracted became only more skilled at keeping their peccadilloes hidden from the public, thus creating tabloid journalists such as Walter Winchell, a former vaudeville performer turned "keyhole-gossipmonger" to tantalize and reveal them. Yet even as politics had exerted power and control over Hollywood, the film colony was about to do the same thing to politics.[21]

Destined for an important future as a historian and early Indian rights activist, Alvin Josephy Jr. arrived in Hollywood in 1934 to take what was essentially a nepotistic position as a screenwriter at MGM studios. That year had been perhaps the cruelest of the Great Depression, and young Josephy had been forced to drop out of Harvard University because of the financial strain on his family. The nephew of American publishing mogul Alfred A. Knopf, Josephy nevertheless grew up on the fringe of privilege in Manhattan in a world populated by distinguished characters such as one of his early mentors, cultural satirist H. L. Mencken. In his autobiography, *A Walk Toward Oregon: A Memoir*, Josephy offers insight into powerbrokers Louis B. Mayer and William Randolph Hearst and, doing so, describes the very first time a movie studio and corporate America joined forces to destroy a political campaign.

Even as he embarked upon his screenwriting career in Hollywood, young Josephy was already a dedicated political activist with a quick, discriminate eye for social injustice. At Harvard

Josephy had become an early supporter of Franklin D. Roosevelt's New Deal policies, and this encouraged him to lead a nationwide student campaign against populist Democratic Louisiana senator Huey P. Long's emergence to power from what Josephy considered the dangerous extreme left wing of American politics. By the time of Josephy's arrival in Hollywood, he had developed a clear, discerning political perspective of the serious socioeconomic problems California and the nation faced.

"Some of the 'cure-all' panaceas were advanced by quacks and promoters," Josephy writes, describing California at the time of the Great Depression, "and others by well-meaning reformers, the most popular of whom was Upton Sinclair, a mild-mannered fifty-six-year-old Socialist and muckracking author of the early part of the century."[22]

Sinclair had written a runaway best-seller book entitled *I, Governor of California, and How I Ended Poverty* and in 1933 had registered as a Democrat in California and announced that he would seek the Democratic nomination for governor. Sinclair's book quickly became the rallying point for the millions of unemployed Americans flocking to California seeking a better life, and almost one thousand EPIC—End Poverty in California—clubs sprang up almost overnight. Sinclair's campaign promised to create two different economic systems in California. The existing private-enterprise system would continue to produce for profit, while a new state-run alternative system would put the unemployed to work producing for use rather than for profit in a system of cooperative farms and factories acquired by eminent domain or with tax monies. Sinclair's message reached hundreds of thousands of Californians suffering through the Great Depression, and soon volunteers were working zealously throughout the state for his election.[23]

When Sinclair won the Democratic primary by a landslide over eight opponents, California politicians and corporate powerbrokers panicked. Concerned that Sinclair's policies would devastate them financially, they initiated a massive public relations campaign to destroy him. The effort was conceived, implemented, and supervised by the media empire of William Randolph Hearst and by the head of MGM, Louis B. Mayer, who could commandeer and direct the creative talent required to accomplish mythological character assasination.[24]

Immigration officials had misplaced Louis B. Mayer's birth records when he entered Canada with his family from Russia as a three-year-old child. Mayer was so super-patriotic that the bureaucratic mistake only gave him an excuse to claim the Fourth of July as his birthday. Mayer ran the studio that bore his name—Metro-Goldwyn-Mayer—like a nineteenth-century European patriarch. Generally recognized as the "Tiffany" Hollywood studio of the 1930s and 1940s because its stable of stars sparkled brighter than any others, the studio's motion pictures also reflected America's highest moral standards.

Mayer's journey to America was not unlike Adolph Zukor's, except that Mayer's father emigrated from Russia to Nova Scotia. In 1903, at age nineteen, Mayer departed Canada for a new life in Boston. Soon after arriving Mayer fell in love, married his sweetheart, and became the father of two girls. A Jew, Mayer's opportunities for employment were limited, and he supported his family as a scrap metal collector while also working at scores of other odd jobs. Mayer got into the business of exhibiting movies when he opened a 650-seat theater fifty miles north of Boston in Haverhill, Massachusetts. A series of successes quickly vaulted Mayer from his theater and distribution connections in New England to the pinnacle of control at Hollywood's major studio.[25]

Because of their similar conservative political opinions, William Randolph Hearst and Louis B. Mayer were close friends and collaborators. MGM distributed the films of Hearst's mistress, Marion Davies, and she was the studio's highest paid star. Immediately before the political campaign of Upton Sinclair ignited, however, Hearst and Mayer argued and parted ways. Even while Hollywood tongues wagged that Hearst had caught Davies in a compromising position with a famous actor in her bungalow on the MGM lot, Josephy explains the real reason for Hearst and Mayer's feud was actually professional jealousy: Louis B. Mayer had offered two plum film roles to another actress. Infuriated, Hearst moved

Davies, her lavish bungalow, and his Cosmopolitan Pictures from MGM to Warner Bros. Sinclair's phenomenal political rise, however, gave Mayer and Hearst reason to put their differences aside and join forces to destroy him.

Hearst unleashed his papers' full force against Sinclair, printing negative features about him while Mayer attacked with "publicity and advertising experts, directors, writers, actors, and extras to produce false and scurrilous newspaper and billboard ads, radio spots, fake newsreels, and anti-Sinclair posters and flyers, depicting Sinclair as a dangerous imbecile, an unwashed, bearded, bomb-throwing anarchist, and atheistic Communist, an enemy of religion, a crazed vegetarian, and a supporter of free love."[26]

Mayer and Hearst were methodical if nothing else. Mayer announced that if Sinclair won, MGM would leave the state of California, and he demanded every MGM actor and employee making over one hundred dollars a week donate a day's salary to the campaign to ruin Sinclair. He even barred newsboys from selling Sinclair's newspaper, *Epic News*, in front of the studio. Mayer ordered the so-called prince of Hollywood, Irving Thalberg, to create newsreels that MGM exhibitors in California added to their normal programs.

Soon Thalberg's newsreels depicted hordes of deranged bums filmed on their way to California from other parts of the country, announcing to the camera that Upton Sinclair had promised to take care of them if they helped him get elected. The "bums," of course, were film extras hired to be part of Mayer and Hearst's campaign of intentional lies and manipulative distortions that was delivered in every medium of communication. Josephy very succinctly described the Hearst-Mayer-Thalberg creation as "an ugly forerunner of the wholesale use of hired public-relations and advertising experts to help candidates smear opponents, a practice that would become familiar in 'negative' American political campaigning in the future."[27]

Hearst and Mayer's misguided "patriotic" behavior had much broader repercussions than the mere derailing of a threatening political campaign by a powerful American Socialist. The invention of the aggressive Hearst-Mayer-Thalberg corporate multimedia template for confronting alternative political perspectives and socio-economic dilemmas leaves little doubt why the poor Oklahoma migrants depicted in John Steinbeck's American masterpiece *The Grapes of Wrath* were greeted so inhumanely by the good people of California. After the despotic creation of such a cynical fairytale by a pair of paranoid megalomaniacs, the citizens of the Golden State—and the United States—must have certainly believed all "Okies" were the first waves of Eugene Debs's and Upton Sinclair's hordes of invading Reds.

Mayer and Hearst had nevertheless discovered a new "red savage" to vanquish. Hollywood and corporate mass media had united to create prototypical technological propaganda to battle this "subversive" new enemy with mythological hegemony. The tumultuous political climate, the precarious financial condition of the world, and the dramatic technological advances of motion pictures had merged with the art of storytelling and the will to invent mythology as propaganda. All these circumstances converged to set the stage for the flowering of a variation of the heroic American role model that had proved to be the lifeblood of the early motion picture industry: the cowboy. Though the early template for the American Adam was based on the frontiersman model born in the primordial forests of eastern North America and was first personified by Boone, Jackson, and Crockett, once the American population began to migrate onto the Great Plains and into the Rocky Mountains, Buffalo Bill Cody adapted the formula and introduced the role of the plainsman as the evolution of the archetype. As Cody's star faded with the rise of motion pictures, however, a new adaptation appeared as if out of nowhere, just in time to flicker across the silver screen. Having already earned his spurs during the genesis of the galloping tin-types, the American cowboy had charmed the world and contributed greatly to the expansion of the storytelling power of film. Now as the centerpiece of the new form of visual storytelling, the cowboy was poised like a knight on his white steed, prepared to bravely ride to the rescue in the darkest hours of the Great Depression to boldly claim his singular heroic birthright.

Chapter Ten
A WASP in the Wilderness

*The Voice spoke like someone weeping, and it said: 'Look there upon
your nation.'…and they were thin, their faces sharp, for they were
starving. Their ponies were only hide and bones, and the holy tree
was gone.*[1]

—Black Elk

So how did the cowboy—an anonymous late-nineteenth-century
hired hand who drifted from ranch to ranch seeking occasional
work—become the heroic archetype of twentieth-century America? As noted, Hollywood's silver screen cowboy merely personified
a mythic archetype of American identity that had been evolving
in the United States for 125 years—particularly during the latter half of the nineteenth century. Yet the renowned playwright
of *Man of La Mancha*, Dale Wasserman, has observed that one
of two situations initiate *every* theatrical plot: "a man goes on a
quest," or, "a stranger comes to town."[2] The nameless, wandering
ranch hand certainly rides effortlessly out of history's shadows on
the trail of either of Wasserman's dramatic plot devices; indeed, as
legendary characters from Daniel Boone to Huck Finn and from
Woody Guthrie to Jack Kerouac reveal, the archetypical *American*
is a dislocated traveler, a wanderer. Consequently, the ambiguous
trail rider's very anonymous mobility allowed pioneer Hollywood
screenwriters to easily wed mysticism and morality into the cowboy's otherwise historically vacant personality, thus creating a
twentieth-century mythological adaptation of Buffalo Bill's nineteenth-century plainsman prototype as the hero of the Western.

  In the first two decades of the twentieth century, the everyman-
cowboy archetype worked brilliantly in moving pictures because,
as with Charlie Chaplin's *Little Tramp* of the same period, the form
of the Western easily adapted into a visual morality play depicting

the anonymous individual's brave struggle against an increasingly impersonal, industrialized, materialistic society. Chaplin embodied the tough little guy—the immigrant—and his witty survival on the city's mean streets, but Shakespearean William S. Hart's stone-faced, moralistic cowboy personified American values and courage roaming over the majestic vistas of the frontier. Whereas English-man Chaplin's tramp was an immigrant everyman hero of the urban East, the hero as portrayed by Hart and other pioneer silent film cowboys were, like Buffalo Bill before them, western Ameri-can personalities. Unlike Cody, who united Plains Indian and Euro American culture into what was essentially a new American "tribe" in order to stage and exhibit reenactments of historical events, how-ever, the cowboy Hart and others portrayed in films was a singu-lar character, a lonesome drifter—either a tarnished knight with a mysterious past on a noble quest, or a "common man" trapped in an ethical dilemma that would ultimately require his true heroic nature to rise to the occasion, triggering a moral metamorphosis while simultaneously revealing his unique "American" approach to prob-lem-solving. This iconic version of the hero resonates with Perceval's quest for the Holy Grail in the Arthurian legends of England as well as countless other mythic global archetypes. Remaining focused on playwright Wasserman's theory of two simple plot devices, however, we also return to the quintessential "drifter on a quest" and the "stranger who comes to town," Don Quixote, as envisioned in the mid-sixteenth century by the man of La Mancha himself, Spaniard Miguel de Cervantes. Applying Wasserman's "quixotic" plot theory to Hollywood cowboy heroes we discover that virtually all classic Westerns begin with one, or sometimes both, of the master play-wright's devices; indeed, as evidenced in the classic *Shane* and many other Westerns, the man on a quest is also the stranger who comes to town. This wedding of plot devices also conveniently brings the narrative of the lonesome hero into intimate interaction with the community's narrative, an indication of how dramatically suitable the historically ambiguous drifting cowboy became as a mythologi-cal representation of the American personality at the turn of the twentieth century when motion pictures were gaining popularity.

As discussed earlier, it is no coincidence that this period also marks the United States' sharp turn toward imperialism with the rise of Theodore Roosevelt's political career. As a law student at Columbia University, Roosevelt enrolled in political theorist John W. Burgess's classes and was inspired by the professor's notions that the Teutonic and Anglo-Saxon people were the best "adapted" to lead the march of civilization. Burgess's radical racial premise was based on his attempts to wed Darwinian concepts of natural science to political science and jurisprudence. From this dangerous perspective, Burgess reasoned that political competence was a talent not equally bestowed on all nations. Burgess thus concluded that the Aryan and Anglo-Saxon races had consistently proven themselves in singular possession of the political gifts of unification required for leadership.

Later, as secretary of the navy, Theodore Roosevelt combined Burgess's political theories of race competence with the military concepts of Captain Alfred Thayer Mahan and his 1890 book, *The Influence of Sea Power on History*. Powerfully aided by newspaper tycoons William Randolph Hearst and Joseph Pulitzer and their cheerleading from the sidelines for a war with Spain, Roosevelt began to put his theories of military power and civilization into practice on the global stage.[3]

In a speech titled "Expansion and Peace," delivered at the twilight of the nineteenth century and reflecting the pervasive attitude of his constituency, Roosevelt boasted, "It is only the warlike power of a civilized people that can give peace to the world...due solely to the power of the mighty civilized races which have not lost the fighting instinct, and which by their expansion are gradually bringing peace to the red wastes where barbarian peoples of this world have held sway."[4] Sadly, in spite of Roosevelt's very impressive talents as a historian, when reading his *The Winning of the West* it becomes impossible not to be profoundly shocked by his repeated shameful conclusions that it is the destiny of the red, brown, copper, and black people of the world to fall under the relentless march of Anglo-Saxon civilization. Roosevelt was indeed so unapologetically racist and imperialistic that his imprint on the image of the

Western heroic role model of the twentieth century is blatant—
especially when it comes to "fightin' injuns." Because of his belief
that it was the Manifest Destiny of the Anglo-Saxon race to envi-
sion and control the course of global civilization, and because of his
love-affair with the Dakota Territory of the Trans-Missouri, Roosevelt championed the western frontier as the mythological proving
ground for Americans and the cowboy as the heroic prototype.
Or, as Garry Wills so cleverly observes, "He [the cowboy] is the
unwitting heir to the long tradition of anti-intellectualism created
precisely by American intellectuals."[5]

Thus, the heroic cowboy archetype of the Western was conceived in the East; indeed, the characterization of the valiant
American cowboy was invented at the dawning of the twentieth
century by three New England Brahmins: Theodore Roosevelt,
painter Frederic Remington, and author Owen Wister—all eastern
Ivy League establishment figures—reinvented western experience
in image, story, and history to resonate with their own manipulative needs for a heroic national past (and future) controlled by
Anglo-Saxon dominance.

Only slightly less transparent in its inherent racial motivations,
Wister's *The Virginian*—dedicated, incidentally, to Theodore Roosevelt—is considered by most Western historians as the singular
template that created the cowboy as a heroic role model in literature and later in film. *The Virginian*, according to Elliot West,
also "took its modern shape from the yearnings and stresses of late
nineteenth-century America *east of the Missouri, those regions that
would provide the most of the demand and financial sustenance for the
commercialized myth*."[6] (Italics added)

The eastern invention of the nineteenth-century western vagabond ranch hand as the twentieth century's American Adam actually had much more to with power than with "yearnings" or even
the "financial sustenance for the commercialized myth." Robert G.
Athearn explains that the men who created the myth of the cowboy
were in fact "sons of the old-stock families, appalled at the waves
of new immigrants that were washing up on the Atlantic coast.
[When] Harvard graduate Owen Wister created *The Virginian*, he

made his cowboy a hero of yesterday's America, a square-jawed and blue-eyed cultural sentinel who opposed the oncoming hordes of non-Nordic newcomers. And Frederic Remington, another Ivy Leaguer, who became the most famous illustrator of the disappearing West, was quite specific on his views on the situation. The Italians, Chinese, 'Huns,' 'Injuns,' and eastern European Jews were 'the rubbish of the earth...the rinsins, the scourins, the Devil's lavings,' he wrote. 'I've got some Winchesters and when the massacring begins I can get my share.'"[7]

The success of *The Virginian*, published in 1906, quickly stimulated a literary movement focused on a return to a less materialistic time and an exploration of the great outdoors—once again—"before it vanished." Jack London and poet Robert Service heard the call of the wild and headed north to Alaska, while other "adventure" writers followed Wister's lead and headed due west. Adding to the popularity of the movement, virile outdoor magazines, illustrated by Remington, Charlie Russell, Nathaniel Wyeth, or one of their many imitators, began to sprout like dandelions. During World War 1 and shortly thereafter, Zane Grey's books became enormously popular by taking Americans back to a time when life was simpler. Between 1917 and 1924 Grey's novels were consistently in the top ten of the best-sellers. When actual working cowboys were asked to compare Owen Wister's and Zane Grey's cowboys, however, most commented that *The Virginian* was a "cowboy novel without cows," but Zane Grey's characters "actually herded cattle...sweated, grew saddlesore and bone weary aboard uncomfortable range ponies, occasionally got drunk in town, and even offered readers a mild cuss word now and then."[8]

Even though Zane Grey's characters were defined by working cowboys as more realistic than Wister's "Virginian," Robert Athearn recalls a fellow historian's observation to emphasize the theory that the archetypal twentieth-century hero of the American West was invented by eastern powerbrokers in order to maintain Anglo-Saxon dominance over the United States' mythological consciousness: "Leslie Fiedler once remarked that in archetypal form the Western was a fiction that involved the reactions of a transplanted WASP in wilderness conditions. In many ways Zane Grey's protagonists fit this description in that the standard plot depicted the eastern 'pilgrim' who countered the rigors of western life by adapting to the environment and thereby experienced a cultural and physical metamorphosis in the untamed part of America. In this Darwinian laboratory, Grey's heroes survived weaker men, while at the same time they offered moral, social, and even political lessons to less-fortunate brothers in the east. Perhaps unconsciously, he was offering the reading masses Turner's thesis on a fictional platter."[9]

It is important to note here that this eastern invention of the romantic cowboy hero as envisioned by Roosevelt, Remington, Wister, Grey, and pioneer Hollywood filmmakers is post-frontier and post-Buffalo Bill; indeed, in the early 1880s William F. Cody was the first person to use the cowboy term *roundup* to describe gathering cattle when he was forced to explain the word to eastern journalists before they could continue writing their stories. Cody was in fact already fast becoming an international legend *before* the golden decade of the cowboy began in the mid-1870s with the great cattle drives, and he remained a star for nearly two decades past the cowboy's original heyday. It is equally important to note that those legendary cattle drives that initially brought the cowboy recognition occurred primarily because the US government was legally bound by treaties to supply Indian tribes with beef to replace the buffalo the tribes were unable to hunt since the government demanded that Indians surrender their weapons. Consequently, the cowboy was essentially performing for wealthy western cattlemen the same function an urban factory worker performed for an eastern corporate industrialist and thus was originally a mere footnote in a much larger national mythological narrative. Pioneer Hollywood mythmakers such as Edwin Porter, Thomas Ince, and D. W. Griffith elaborated on the simplistic cowboy prototype invented and brilliantly acted out from the stage of his "bully pulpit" by Roosevelt, gloriously painted in narrative imagery by Remington, and, particularly, rendered in elegant prose by Wister and later, as pulp-fiction working hand in glove as stories adapted to movie scripts, by Zane Grey. Conversely, Buffalo Bill's plainsman archetype emanated from the intimate reality and combination of Indian and Euro American frontier existence in the Tran-Missouri and the epic, mythic period in American history spanning the emigration and Indian war eras.

After dominating the first twenty years of the motion picture industry, however, the popularity of the Western cinematic cowboy that William S. Hart, Tom Mix, Colonel Tim McCoy, Harry Carey, Hoot Gibson, Ken Maynard, and a host of other silent film stars adapted from the Wister/Grey template was rapidly fading into cliché by the 1920s. As film technology and visual storytelling were advancing rapidly, the public's fascination with silent screen cowboys was diminishing. It is therefore significant that Hollywood returned to the original form of the Western and the heroic epic mythology of the Trans-Missouri to interpret and celebrate America's "national narrative" when the first motion picture cowboy archetype faded.

The 1923 New York premiere of *The Covered Wagon* heralded the debut of a technological innovation known as Deforest Phonofilm, or sound on film. Regardless, *The Covered Wagon* was eventually distributed nationally without sound and thus recognized by film historians as the first epic-scale Western of the silent era. Based on Emerson Hough's novel of the same title, *The Covered Wagon* was an instant critical and commercial success. The film celebrated pioneer spirit on the frontier, but cynically depicted one of the emigration era's most important personalities as a drunk; its inaccurate characterization of Jim Bridger in his first portrayal in a motion picture took the mountain man's actual historical reputation decades to overcome.[10] *The Covered Wagon* became a major critical and box office hit, but William S. Hart, the old Shakespearean stickler for realistic Westerns, defended Jim Bridger when historians and uninformed film critics of the day would not. Hart, with a characteristic sprinkling of self-righteousness typical of his bristly personality, summed up *The Covered Wagon* as "a good picture to those who do not know…But to those who know or have studied the frontier days, it is a sad affair…Jim Bridger made a senile, undersized old bum, when at that time he was forty-four years old."[11] When debating anything about the American West the old curmudgeon cowboy, who also spoke Lakota, never minced words. To be fair, however, critics commented that *The Covered Wagon* director, James Cruze, made brilliant symbolic use of the pioneer's plow throughout his film, cinematically depicting the simple V-shaped farming tool as a powerful twin-bladed metaphor, simultaneously representing death to Plains Indians and civilization to emigrant pioneers.[12]

In spite of all the fanfare about sound associated with the premiere of *The Covered Wagon*, controversial inventor Lee Deforest was often embroiled in patent and copyright disputes, and his Phonofilm process for synchronizing sound with film—as well as Thomas Edison's and all other early explorations to wed sound and film—failed to catch on. Even so, tongues wagged throughout the film colony that pictures would soon talk as well as move; everyone in Hollywood knew it was inevitable that the film industry would be forced to incorporate the technological innovation.

Four brothers from Pennsylvania would lead Hollywood into the era of sound and film synchronization. By 1925 upstart Warner Bros. Studio was beginning to compete with Marcus Loew's and Louis B. Mayer's MGM Studios, Adolf Zukor's Paramount Pictures, Carl Laemmle's Universal Studios, Harry Cohn's Columbia Studios, and William Fox's Fox Studios. The sons of immigrant Polish Jews, the four Warner brothers—Harry, Albert, Sam, and Jack—began their careers as arcade owners and film exhibitors in Pennsylvania and Ohio. By 1918 Sam and Jack had opened production offices on Sunset Boulevard in Hollywood while Harry and Albert ran the business end of the family operations in New York. The fledgling company had its first major success with a rescued shell-shocked German Shepard named Rin Tin Tin that survived World War I in France to become a star of silent films. The 1923 Rin Tin Tin film *Where the North Begins* established Warner Brothers as the major independent studio in Hollywood and launched the career of noted pioneer film producer and future head of Twentieth Century Fox Film Corporation, Darryl F. Zanuck.

After Zanuck signed noted Broadway actor John Barrymore to star in the film *Beau Brummell*, Warner Bros. Studios was able to secure the financial backing of Wall Street investment firm Goldman, Sachs and Company and several other eastern banks.

The Warner brothers primarily considered synchronized sound on film as a way to eliminate the expensive fees they were paying orchestras to accompany their films in large theaters, but they also believed merging sound with film would provide moviegoers in the hinterland the "movie palace" experience the major population centers enjoyed, thereby enabling them to compete with MGM/Loew's and Zukor's Paramount theater chains. In 1925 Warner Bros partnered with Western Electric Company to form the Vitaphone Corporation specifically for the purpose of uniting sound and film. Warner Bros. first found success experimenting with preludes, or short films such as one showing the president of the Motion Picture Producers and Distributors Association, Will Hays, congratulating Vitaphone for its efforts with sound. Darryl F. Zanuck rose to head of production at Warner Bros. in 1927 and hired popular vaudeville performer Al Jolson to star in *The Jazz Singer*. When the comedian uttered the words, "Wait a minute, you ain't heard nothing yet," in that film, the era of silent movies officially ended.[13]

Still, it took a mouse to prove the synchronization of sound and film would work economically. Of equal cinematic significance to Zanuck adding sound to film—especially in the age of computer-generated animation that would come to dominate the motion picture industry by the late twentieth century—upon seeing *The Jazz Singer*, struggling animation pioneer Walt Disney was inspired to add sound to his cartoons. Disney and his team of artists set up a bed sheet screen in his backyard and projected footage from their silent cartoon *Steamboat Willie* through the animator's bedroom window in order to prevent the noise of the projector from interfering with their crude experiment to add sound to film. While the film rolled, the Disney animation team added harmonica music and sound effects including whistles, bangs, slaps, and crashes and were amazed to discover their cartoon performing on a completely new level; the sounds appeared to be part of the footage. Disney was now convinced that sound synchronization as well as animation were the future of movies, and, even mortgaging his house, anted up everything he owned to prove it. After Walt's brother Roy secured the major funding for the venture, the Disneys hired recording engineers who were as innovative as the brilliant team of animators they had assembled to create cartoons. Now working as a unit, the recording engineers and animators worked day and night to create a recording studio complete with a stage that would allow them to isolate sound and thereby control and manipulate the recording and eventual merging of musical scores with animation. Disney called his musical cartoons "Silly Symphonies." They may have been silly, but the musical cartoons proved sound and film could be economically synchronized.

"Just as *The Jazz Singer* had sent shock waves through the film industry a year earlier," Disney biographer Neal Gabler writes, "rival animation studios immediately recognized that *Willie* had wrought a revolution in their art...Other studios raced to catch up, but Disney had a head start now as well as his special synchronizing system, and it would be a year before competitors were making musical cartoons of their own with anything like the fusion of *Willie*. Some never could catch up. *Felix the Cat* animator Hal Walker lamented that 'Disney put us out of business with his sound.'"[14]

Having outlasted Bronco Billy, William S. Hart, and all other Western celluloid heroes, the reigning king of serial Westerns, Tom Mix had a more serious problem than talkies; Mix's simplistic, "white hat versus black hat" formula serials had simply reached the end of the trail. Whereas pioneer film directors such as James Cruze and John Ford returned to the Trans-Missouri and epic mythological scale in the early 1920s with *The Covered Wagon* and *The Iron Horse*, the era of Tom Mix's serial Western peaked around the same time and began a long, steady decline into B-movie status. Once recognized as Gower's Gulch because of the cowboys and Indians who gathered there seeking employment in the Westerns being filmed during the infancy of the motion picture industry, by 1929 Sunset Boulevard and Gower Street became known throughout

Hollywood as Poverty Row. Because of its shrinking fan base, however, the serial Western, or chapter-plays as they were becoming known in Hollywood, continued to earn healthy profits for Tom Mix, Hoot Gibson, Colonel Tim McCoy, and others throughout the 1920s and 1930s; even as their numbers diminished, the fans who remained loyal to the early form of the genre were increasingly intensely devoted. The chapter-play format of B Westerns would thus prove itself able to adapt to changing times as it evolved into singing cowboy horse operas by the 1940s and 1950s.

Legendary director John Ford began his career with silent Westerns, so it was natural that he would repeatedly return to the form during his long reign in Hollywood and be recognized as a master of the genre by the mid-twentieth century. Arriving in Hollywood in 1914, Ford followed his older brother, Francis, to the film colony. A vaudeville veteran, Francis had initially found success in motion pictures as an actor, but by the time of his kid brother John's arrival, he had become an accomplished screenwriter and director and the head of his own production company, Bison 101, at Universal Studios.

Francis hired John for bit parts in films that taught his brother the basics of the film business. Along the way the younger Ford met and befriended one of Hollywood's leading cowboy stars, Harry Carey. In 1917, at the urging of Carey, Universal's founder, Carl Laemmle, offered John Ford his directorial break with *The Tornado*. From 1917 to 1928 Ford directed more than sixty one-, two-, and three-reel silent Westerns starring Harry Carey, Hoot Gibson, and other cowboy stars for Universal and for William Fox Studios.

Inspired by *The Covered Wagon*'s critical and commercial success, John Ford was also profoundly impacted by the film's artistic celebration of the transplanted Anglo-Saxon mythology as it was expressed in James Cruze's depiction of the American spirit confronting the frontier in the Trans-Missouri. Ford's 1924 breakthrough directorial film, *The Iron Horse*, explored the same themes as *The Covered Wagon* and examined the unique American personality born in confrontation with the Great Plains frontier landscape during the construction of the Transcontinental Railroad. Ford was so obsessed with the concept of the American personality as envisioned by Theodore Roosevelt and Frederick Jackson Turner that he incorporated folk songs like "Red River Valley" and Stephen Foster's "Oh Susanna" into the musical score of his films to accentuate, connect, and define these sentimental traits in his characters and landscapes. Irishman Ford would continue to select frontier stories portraying similar characterizations and subject matter and score his films with adapted Americana music for the rest of his long career, often going so far as to hire musicians to play traditional music on the sets of his films to inspire actors' performances. Nevertheless, even though he loved and respected the genre, when *Stagecoach* was released in 1939 the Western had fallen so far out of favor in Hollywood that Ford had not directed one since *Three Bad Men* in 1926.[15]

Attending a movie allowed one to escape reality for a few hours, and as the Great Depression deepened, movie palaces provided a perfect environment to forget one's troubles. Consequently, Hollywood studios—especially Mayer's MGM studios—increasingly produced films with positive, uplifting themes that encouraged the nation to hold fast to the sentimental mythology of the American Dream. Even though the Great Depression continued well into the late 1930s, Ford's *Stagecoach* was released as a general feeling of optimism was finally beginning to return to America. Reflecting this positive mood, in 1939 Hollywood released a bumper crop of films such as *Gunga Din*, *Wuthering Heights*, *The Wizard of Oz*, and *Gone with the Wind*, all destined to become classics. Cecil B. DeMille's *Union Pacific* was also released in 1939; indeed, it was DeMille who had directed Hollywood's return to the form of the epic mythological Western in 1936 with *The Plainsman*, in which he cobbled together a story loosely based on the friendship of Buffalo Bill and Wild Bill Hickok. This said, it is important to note here that *Stagecoach* is not technically an "epic" Western at all; some critics of the day referred to it instead as "a romantic melodrama on rolling wheels made briefly exciting by an Indian attack." And when asked to comment on the "realism" of the Indian attack, the reliable and ever pragmatic old critic William S. Hart tartly observed that the iconic stagecoach chase scene Ford and legendary film stuntman Yakima Canutt staged was unrealistic because Indians would have had the gumption in the beginning to simply shoot the horses and quickly put an end to any chase.[16]

Although he lived and breathed the American West and genuinely attempted to create realistic portraits of the cowboys and region he so adored, by 1939 Hart had already been an anachronism for twenty years. After two decades in the industry honing his skills as a storyteller and director of films, Ford, on the other hand, instinctively understood that humans are visual creatures and that motion pictures are all about visual storytelling; one glance of Monument Valley in *Stagecoach* imparted more information about the story Ford wanted to tell than twenty pages of scripted dialogue. Most significantly, Ford also realized that the landscape of the American West gave birth to her heroes, and by visually incorporating Monument Valley into *Stagecoach*, he introduced the majestic scale of the American West as the heroic stage upon which epic film mythologizing occurs. In a John Ford film the landscape thus became as important as a character in the script. Yet after nearly a quarter of a century of directing motion pictures, Ford was also a master of creating illusion; most of *Stagecoach* was actually filmed in a Hollywood studio. Because of the region's irregular rock patterns, in 1939 there were few roads in Monument Valley over which a rider could gallop a horse—or where a technical crew could film a stagecoach rolling at full speed. Thus scenics had to be filmed in the valley and later edited into the final cut of the film in Hollywood. Even the unforgettable visual introduction of John Wayne as the Ringo Kid, often referred to as one of the most stunning entrances in cinematic history, was shot on a set in a Hollywood studio. The stagecoach rolls through Monument Valley and a shot rings out as Ford's camera rapidly zooms in on John Wayne standing alone against a mesa, saddle in one hand, simultaneously twirling and cocking his Winchester with the other. Even though he had labored in B Westerns on Poverty Row for a decade, this dramatic entrance in *Stagecoach* launched the career of John Wayne. In meeting the Ringo Kid, America was introduced to John Ford's cinematic version of Teddy Roosevelt's heroic WASP archetype interacting with the epic visual scale of the American West while preparing to battle its last indigenous warrior, Geronimo. All that was missing was Ford draping John Wayne in an American flag.[17]

The location of *Stagecoach* in the great Southwest at the eve of an attack by Geronimo subliminally underscored the mythological significance of John Wayne's introduction. *Stagecoach* also offers vivid evidence of Philip Deloria's observations of Indian pacification; even in the twenty-first century the very mention of Geronimo's name still shatters thoughts of peaceful conciliation, and with America at the brink of a world war in 1939, the old Apache warrior offered the perfect metaphorical foil to define Ford's new cinematic hero.

Like Geronimo, Crazy Horse's name also triggers images of the pre-pacification era, yet neither of the great Lakota leader's two boyhood nicknames, Curly or Worm, would have sent chills up the spines of brave men. Likewise, few would have fled in terror of a man named Slow, the nickname first given to the precociously ponderous child who would grow into the mighty Sitting Bull. Correspondingly, a man with the androgynous name Marion seemingly could *never* have become the heroic American male role model of Western films for over half of the twentieth century. Nevertheless, the man the world now recognizes as John Wayne was named Marion Robert Morrison when he was born in Iowa in 1907. When a brother was born a few years later, young Marion's mother decided she preferred her first-born son's middle name for his sibling and simply changed young Marion Robert's name to Marion Mitchell. From that day forward Marion had trouble with his mother—and women in general. After the Morrison family relocated from Iowa to Southern California in 1911, the legend is that a Glendale, California fireman dubbed young Marion "Little Duke" because the kid's constant companion was a huge Airedale dog named Duke that dwarfed the youngster. Preferring Duke to Marion, the boy readily adapted to his more masculine nickname.

In *John Wayne's America: The Politics of Celebrity*, Garry Wills makes the significant connection that both John Wayne and Ronald Reagan were from Iowa. Adding nuance to Robert G.

Athearn's, Leslie Fiedler's, and other Western historians' observations of the creation of the mystical cowboy film archetype as
well as the future political cowboy archetype, Wills observes that
while Reagan maintained connections with his Midwestern past,
"Wayne forgot Iowa and Iowa forgot him." Wills believes this was
because it served Reagan to be an ordinary, unaffected Iowan,
but John Wayne had nothing to gain from being from Iowa. He
believes it is significant that Reagan lost his nickname (Dutch) in
California and reclaimed his real name (Ronald), whereas John
Wayne abandoned his first name in the Golden State, gained a
nickname (Duke), and then traded his family name for a stage
name. Emphasizing the implication of the anonymous drifter to
the continuing evolution of the heroic cowboy in motion pictures,
Wills concludes: "If Wayne was not quite Sergio Leone's 'Man with
No Name', he was at least a man from nowhere. That nowhere was
Winterset, Iowa."[18]

In California, however, young "Duke" Morrison was fascinated
with movies, grew up watching William S. Hart and Tom Mix
Westerns, and later attended the University of Southern California
(USC) as a law major. A large, graceful, athletically gifted young
man, Morrison quickly won a position on the school's championship football team. The Hollywood legend of the beginning of
Marion Morrison's metamorphosis into John Wayne is that Tom
Mix wanted his own personal box at the USC coliseum. Seats at
USC home games were the hottest-selling tickets in Los Angeles,
however, so Mix had someone on his staff approach USC football
coach Howard Jones, whereupon Jones offered a counterproposal:
if Mix would arrange to hire some USC football players at the
Fox Studios during the summer, he would in turn arrange for Mix
to have his own personal cluster of box seats. Mix immediately
agreed, and in June 1926 Jones arranged for Duke Morrison to
get one of the plum summer jobs at the Fox Studios for thirty-five
dollars a week.[19]

After a surfing injury ended young Morrison's football career,
he continued working at Fox Studios in the props department, a
job Wayne himself later described as essentially being a "glorified

furniture mover." Soon, however, the young props master started to get offered bit parts in films, along the way becoming friends with director John Ford in 1926.

There are multiple versions of the actual meeting of Ford and Wayne, but they all center on the theme that one day John Ford noticed Morrison working on a set and called out to him condescendingly, "You one of Howard Jones's bright boys?" Morrison answered, "Yes," and then Ford ordered him to get down in a football stance. Young Morrison had barely gotten into a three-point stance before Ford kicked the youngster's hand out from under him and sprawled the boy on his face in the dirt. Already a Hollywood legend for a nasty streak that frequently expressed itself as blatant cruelty, Ford laughed and said, "And you call yourself a football player. I'll bet you couldn't even take me out." Morrison rose and lunged at Ford, drove his leg into the director's chest, and sent him sprawling on his hind side. The various stories continue that the set went absolutely quiet as Ford sailed to the ground and that everyone waited with hushed breath for Ford to explode in anger and banish this upstart kid from Hollywood forever. Instead Ford burst out laughing, instantly adoring the youngster who would not be intimidated.[20]

The legend continues that Ford soon became a mentor for Morrison as the young man began to win larger roles in films. In reality, however, a rift occurred between the two after Morrison accepted his first starring role in 1930's *The Big Trail*, directed by Raoul Walsh. *The Big Trail* had what was for 1930 an astonishing $2 million budget and was promoted by William Fox Studios as the "first outdoor spectacle" of the sound era. Walsh, who had lost an eye in a freak accident filming *In Old Arizona* when a frightened jackrabbit jumped through the windshield of his car, had noticed Morrison moving furniture on a set and was impressed with his size, graceful movement, and masculine good looks. Walsh wanted Tom Mix or Gary Cooper for his lead, but both actors were already committed to other films, and young Morrison looked good and was available. Duke Morrison was screen-tested, hired, and sent to various instructors to learn to ride a horse, handle a gun, and speak on camera. As the Hollywood publicity machines began to roll, American history buff Walsh wanted originally to change Morrison's name to that of Revolutionary war hero Anthony Wayne. When it was suggested that "Tony" sounded Italian, Walsh changed Duke Morrison's name to the more Americanized, twin-masculine John Wayne.

Soon after Wayne completed filming *The Big Trail*, however, Ford started giving his young protégé the cold shoulder. John Wayne biographers Randy Roberts and James S. Olson explain: "Understanding Ford's motives for doing anything was a difficult calculus. A man of deep insecurities, and sensitive to slights real and imagined, something or other was always getting under his skin. Perhaps he was upset that Duke had left his small stock company to work for other directors. Perhaps he misinterpreted a remark or action by Duke. Perhaps he heard a rumor that set him on edge. Perhaps nothing at all happened and Ford was just being mean and ornery."[21]

Garry Wills believes Ford's true motivation for shunning young John Wayne was fierce jealousy of Raoul Walsh, and he supports his premise revealing that the discovery of John Wayne was only one of several instances in which Ford attempted to appropriate Walsh's accomplishments. Wills points out that Ford claimed he worked as a cowboy out West before arriving in Hollywood, whereas his rival Walsh had in fact driven herds with vaqueros in Mexico. Wills also notes that Ford claimed to have acted (behind a Klan mask) in his idol D. W. Griffith's *The Birth of a Nation*, whereas Walsh played John Wilkes Booth in Griffith's landmark film—"with his face fully exposed"; indeed, Walsh was so close with D. W. Griffith that the director sent him to negotiate film rights for a Griffith production with Pancho Villa during the Mexican Revolution.[22]

Wills also looks behind the Hollywood illusion of the legendary introduction of Ford and Wayne and exposes the fable establishing their lifelong partnership: "Ford is supposed to have said, 'So you're the football player?' and asked him to prove his prowess: Can Wayne stop him?" Wills explains that in one version of the story Wayne sets himself in lineman's stance and Ford kicks both Wayne's hands out from under him with one sweep of his foot, whereas in other versions of their first meeting, Ford is a runner and breaks away from Wayne's attempt to tackle him. In all variations of the theme, however, Wayne proves his mettle in the end and sends Ford sprawling, and two men become fast friends ever after. Wills sums up the legend of Ford and Wayne's meeting with the astute observation that the scenario "sounds like any number of male bonding scenes in Ford movies. Ford plays [Victor] McLaglen [a Ford stock-company actor] to Wayne's 'quiet man' [referring to *The Quiet Man*, Ford and Wayne's classic film about an American boxer and his pugilistic brother-in-law]. Blows make them buddies and they stagger off to a bar to celebrate."[23]

Scott Eyman offers another explanation for Ford's erratic loyalty toward his protégé regarding *The Big Trail* with the suggestion that the director's habitual binge drinking had severely damaged his strict contractual relationship with Fox Studios during this time and was the probable source of his jealousy about John Wayne working on a major Western film with his chief rival at the studio. Yet perhaps the entire matter was based on the fact that Ford's finely tuned Hollywood shrewdness merely sensed imminent disaster concerning *The Big Trail*. William Fox had lost most of his fortune in the 1929 crash of the stock market, and his Fox Studios were already wobbling as a result. Moreover, the late 1920s witnessed a dramatic shift away from Westerns toward films reflecting the unstable, turbulent—and increasingly violent—social and political climate of the Jazz Age, Prohibition, and the Great Depression. Rather than buckskinned, horseback heroes in big Stetsons, movies began to celebrate anarchistic themes featuring the "café society" of the Roaring Twenties and the unprecedented proliferation of celebrity itself that exploded throughout America during this period. As technology and modern media increasingly connected the nation with print, radio, and film, Americans increasingly succumbed to the sirens of fame; people were now becoming famous simply for being famous—or infamous. Of course outlaws such as Frank and Jesse James and Butch Cassidy had become famous for being infamous in the nineteenth century, but in the 1930s cinema stars such as James Cagney, Edward G. Robinson, George Raft, Humphrey Bogart, Marlene Dietrich, Barbara Stanwyck, Joan Crawford, and Bette Davis reflected and glorified the escapades of famous real-life outlaws, fedora-topped gangsters, gun molls, con artists, and petty thieves like Al Capone, John Dillinger, Babyface Nelson, and their girlfriends. Even comedy reflected the cynical national personality of the early days of the Great Depression as W. C. Fields ridiculed pseudo-independence, while the Marx Brothers' revolutionary mayhem and wordplay created hilarious chaos out of stodgy, pseudo-aristocratic order.[24]

In spite of all the hoopla and having opened to good reviews, *The Big Trail* was a commercial flop, and, aside from contributing greatly to the final collapse of William Fox's studio and his eventual bankruptcy, it derailed the epic-scale Western for a decade. The film's failure demoted the career of the newly christened John Wayne to Poverty Row Western serials, where he remained throughout the 1930s. Banished by John Ford and unable to find work after *The Big Trail* flopped, Wayne signed with agent Al Kingston, who put him under contract to Nat Levine, the head of tiny Mascot Studios. Levine had started his career working as an office boy for Marcus Loew and had risen to become Loew's personal secretary. After departing Loew's empire and relocating to Kansas City, Levine learned film distribution with the *Fritz the Cat* cartoon franchise and eventually began to develop chapter-plays into "action serials" in the 1920s. Levine's incredible volume of inexpensive productions allowed him to survive and even prosper during the market collapse of 1929. Consequently, John Wayne could not have been in a better place to learn his craft as a cowboy action star than with Levine at Mascot Studios.

During this period Wayne met a cowboy-stuntman from the state of Washington named Edward "Yakima" Canutt. Canutt would eventually become as important to Wayne's career as John Ford. The stuntman picked up his nickname when he dominated the rodeo circuit from 1917 to 1924. Like many cowboys of that period, Canutt discovered he could continue his rodeo career while also making money as a stunt man in Hollywood during the off-season. Canutt was considered the top stuntman in Hollywood when Nat Levine hired him in 1928 to coordinate all Mascot Studio stunts and direct second-unit crews. Along with playing all the heavies in Mascot productions, Canutt would become John Wayne's double for the rest of his career, often substituting for the star in dangerous scenes. Later, while working for Monogram Studios on Poverty Row, Wayne and Canutt choreographed a style for fighting in films that would revolutionize stylized fist fighting throughout the film industry. In the silent era actors and stuntmen tossed stylized punches at each other's chest and shoulders, resulting in fight scenes that appeared awkward and phony. The "pass system" that Wayne and Canutt created, however, featured the pair swinging haymaker punches at each other's jaw with powerful follow-through energy from both fighters. The blows were of course choreographed to just miss their mark, but from the camera's different perspectives, the punches appeared to connect. When sound effects were added later to the fight scene, the blows looked like direct hits.[25]

Between 1930 and his 1939 breakthrough in *Stagecoach*, John Wayne made numerous B Westerns for tiny Mascot and Republic Pictures, as well as other independent producers. Even though he nearly had a decade of serials under his belt, the Ringo Kid character in *Stagecoach* would prove to be his breakthrough role and truly introduce him to the world.

John Wayne biographers Roberts and Olson maintain that much of his screen persona was based on John Ford's friend and star of his early movies, Harry Carey. Harry Carey represented to John Ford "the embodiment of American manhood—democratic, dignified, quiet, dependable, and at ease with himself." Carey was without doubt the most no-nonsense cowboy of the silent era. Unlike Tom Mix, Hoot Gibson, or Bob Steele, Carey developed a commanding movie charisma—a plain-dressed sincerity down to the pistol tucked into his pants rather than in a silver-inlayed, hand-tooled leather holster belt. In an age of theatrically broad pantomime, Carey's technique emphasized subtlety. In such films as *Straight Shooting* (1917), *The Phantom Riders* (1918), and *Desperate Trails* (1921), Ford and Carey refined and developed Carey's screen image, one that in Roberts and Olson's opinion "would be transferred whole to John Wayne. 'Duke,' Ford later told a young John Wayne, 'take a look over at Harry Carey and watch him work. Stand like he does, if you can, and play your roles so that people can look upon you as a friend.'"[26]

When Ford and Wayne reunited to make *Stagecoach*, the template for a new vision of the epic Western was in place. After *Stagecoach*, however, it would take nearly another decade for the pair to finally discover the combined power of their talents as a cinematic team. While the Ford-Wayne collaboration would be responsible for countless hours of splendid mainstream entertainment over the decades of their reign as the leading purveyors of the Western cinematic art form, those same decades would prove disastrous for Indian performers as well as Indians in general. After finding employment in Hollywood since the very beginning of the industry, Indian performers were more dramatically affected by economic changes than technological ones. Whereas pioneer film studios and early directors such as Thomas Ince and D. W. Griffith hired Indian actors like *Wild West* veteran Luther Standing Bear in an attempt to capture authenticity, by 1930 it was more economically feasible to hire Hispanic or Italian actors, put them in buckskins and feathers, and have them grunt in Pidgin English. By the time John Wayne started making Westerns in the late 1920s, the number of Indians working in Hollywood was already rapidly dwindling. After the Great Depression, Indian actors in Hollywood became a rarity.

Still, Indian actors continued to make their way in the film industry during the World War II years in Hollywood and the rise of Ford and Wayne. It should be noted also that, as with his stock company of non-Indian actors, even though they might be depicting Plains Indians and wearing feathered war bonnets, to his credit Ford repeatedly hired the same Navajo Indians in the Monument Valley region when he returned there to make motion pictures. Because he had already been so skillfully portraying Indians both in real life and in motion pictures for decades, and also because he had assembled a vast and impressive collection of American Indian costumes, artifacts, props, and other paraphernalia, Iron Eyes Cody was often hired as an advisor or technical director on John Ford films as well as the productions of other Hollywood directors during this era. Nevertheless, as studios abandoned the *Wild West* tradition of building large, diverse theatrical companies, the ranks of Indian actors in movies rapidly diminished. While the number of Indian performers in movies declined, the number of films depicting savage Indian opponents increased, especially in the twentieth century's middle decades. Whereas movies at the turn of the century depicted the uncertainty of Indian transitions into WASP culture, Depression- and World War II–era Hollywood chose instead to return to broad nineteenth-century stereotypes of Indians. Consequently, even as the majority of twentieth-century Americans believed that Indian people had been pacified, they also expected to see images of Indian violence in movies depicting nineteenth-century themes. Philip Deloria notes, "When these expectations functioned simultaneously, the effect was devastating. Contemporary Indian people seemed like pathetic anachronisms— anachronisms because they appeared as primitive and savage as Indians on-screen; and worse, pathetic because as pacified people, they lacked even the screen Indians' determination to resist white conquest. And thus, the often-repeated assertion among Indian people that, growing up at mid-century, they had identified with the cowboys rather than the Indians."[27]

Chapter Eleven
The Indian "New Deal"

*As I sit here, I can feel in this man beside me a strong desire to know
the things of the Other World. He has been sent to learn what I
know, and I will teach him.*[1]

—Black Elk

When John Ford and John Wayne took the reins of the cinematic
Western in the late 1930s, many Americans were becoming aware
of a powerful spiritual bond between Indians and non-Indians.
For many this change in perception began during World War I,
when American Indian men volunteered, bled, and died in Europe,
fighting alongside non-Indian US soldiers. Non-Indian awareness
of this ironic allegiance during the so-called "war to end all wars"
combined with the growing post–Wounded Knee romantic primitivism movement and led many to believe the original Americans
deserved United States citizenship. Complicating this notion, however, the United States had by the 1920s been inextricably bound
with American Indian nations by complex treaties and assimilation
policies throughout the history of the relationship. From the very
beginning this unique bond created a profoundly intricate situation often requiring legal interpretations and appeals to be resolved
by the US Supreme Court. Still, because of mounting public sentiment calling for American Indian assimilation, the American
Indian Citizenship Act was enacted in 1924 during the administration of President Calvin Coolidge.[2]

It was also during Coolidge's administration that a non-Indian
sociologist named John Collier ascended in political prominence by
suggesting radical changes in US Indian policy. Born in Atlanta,
Georgia, in 1884, Collier became concerned about the rise of individualism and materialism in American society while he was a student at Columbia University in Manhattan. Collier's reputation as

a pioneering social worker and reformer began to gather momentum as he actively sought a counterbalance to the negative effects of America's widespread obsession with greed and individualism in the family and the workplace. His efforts with such causes as unionization, tenement and factory reform, and better educational opportunities for immigrants made him an early champion of the working class.

Collier had known Mabel Dodge since her salon days in Greenwich Village and in December 1920 was invited to join the growing number of artists, writers, anthropologists, social workers, and intellectual activists gathering around Mabel and Tony Lujan's art colony in Taos, New Mexico. Because of her famous salons in Europe and Manhattan, and especially after helping organize the historic 1913 Armory Show in New York that dramatically shifted the global focus of modern art from Europe to America, Mabel Dodge—now Mabel Dodge Luhan—and her cultural experiment in Taos had become a magnet for artists, intellectuals, and alternative thinkers. Soon after relocating to the Southwest, Mabel started attracting painters like Georgia O'Keefe, Leon Gaspard, and Nicolai Fechin and literary mavericks like D. H. Lawrence to Taos. Mabel's marriage to Pueblo Indian Tony Lujan was essentially a metaphorical wedding of Mabel's growing flock of artists, writers, and social scientists with the wisdom of Tony's ancient indigenous culture of the Taos Pueblo. Through Mabel Dodge Luhan's conscientious efforts, Taos had become a place where the ancient, the modern, the visionary, and the bohemian could contemplate a different version of the future of "western civilization."[3]

A longtime resident of Taos, author Frank Waters was a close friend of Mabel and Tony's. Waters has often been referred to as one of the most distinguished Western writers of the twentieth century. His *The Man Who Killed the Deer*, published in 1942, is recognized as a classic on Pueblo life and has never been out of print; indeed, seventeen of Frank Waters's twenty-five books, written over a period of fifty-four years, remain in print. His nonfiction studies *Masked Gods, Navajo and Pueblo Ceremonialism*, and *Book of the Hopi* are used today as primary source books. *Mexico Mystique: The*

Coming of the Sixth World of Consciousness is considered the comprehensive study of the pre-Columbian culture and religion of the Toltecs, Aztecs, and Maya in Mexico and Guatemala.

Frank Waters described Mabel and Tony's intentions in Taos from an intimate perspective in his memoir, *Of Time and Change*: "Knowing herself incompetent to interpret Indian life, Mabel drew others to Taos. With them she hoped to instigate here a rebirth of the dying western civilization from the body of Indian culture. Among them of course was D. H. Lawrence, in Mabel's view the greatest living writer. He and his wife Frieda lived for short periods on a mountain ranch that Mabel gave him. Lawrence savagely resented Mabel's will to dominate him and, ill with tuberculosis, fled to Mexico. Although he admitted that neither he nor any white man could identify himself with Indian consciousness, he predicted that the cosmic religion of the pueblos, although temporarily beaten down by Anglo materialism, would see a resurgence and 'the genuine America, the America of New Mexico' would resume its course."[4]

Focusing on the American psyche in his *Studies in Classic American Literature*, D. H. Lawrence concluded in 1924 that American consciousness was incomplete. After examining the literature of James Fenimore Cooper, Nathaniel Hawthorne, Henry David Thoreau, Herman Melville, and Walt Whitman, Lawrence proclaimed the American Indian to be the source of the nation's incomplete awareness. Lawrence believed that the Euro American's rational mind imprisoned him in an authoritarian social structure, whereas Indians represented pure instinct and freedom and the true spirit of North America. Classic American literature revealed to Lawrence that the Euro American desperately desired the American Indian's sense of spirit, place, and freedom, yet he invariably failed to embrace aboriginal America and thus *become complete*. Lawrence believed white Americans needed either to destroy Indians or to assimilate them into a white world to resolve the crisis. Philip Deloria points out, however, that both of Lawrence's solutions were "aimed at making Indians vanish from the landscape. But losing this unexpressed 'spirit' required a difficult, collective, and absolute decision: extermination or inclusion. It is a decision that the American polity has been unable to make or, on the few occasions when either policy has been relatively clear, to implement."[5]

Arriving in Taos and encountering thinkers such as Lawrence, John Collier immersed himself in the Pueblo world and was profoundly moved experiencing tribal people clinging to the very family values that were, lamentably, vanishing from his own culture. In his memoir, *From Every Zenith*, Collier described the moment of his cultural epiphany watching Pueblo Indians perform the Red Deer Dance as part of their Christmas celebration: "the discovery came to me there, in that tiny group of a few hundred Indians, was of personality-forming institutions, even now unweakened, which had survived repeated and immense historical shocks, and which were going right on in the production of states of mind, attitudes of mind, earth-loyalties and human loyalties, amid a context of beauty which suffused all the life of the group. What I observed and experienced was a power of art—of the life-making art—greater in kind than anything I had known in my own world before."[6]

Collier departed Taos in 1921 and headed for San Francisco. A changed man, he now totally rejected the assimilation policies the United States imposed on Indians and began to call for programs encouraging cultural pluralism and a repeal of the Dawes Act. Collier maintained that because of the long history of unscrupulous management in the Bureau of Indian Affairs (BIA), the organization had focused negative attention on corrupt non-Indian leadership rather than concentrating on reforming the debilitating official policies of the US government that were systematically destroying American Indian culture.

By 1922 Collier emerged as the leading non-Indian American Indian activist. His appearance on the national political scene also marks a major turning point in the relationship between Indians and non-Indians in America. After Collier became director of the American Indian Defense Association, his political efforts to reform official government policies toward American Indians began to bear fruit. In June 1926 Collier convinced Secretary of the Interior Hubert Work to authorize the Brookings Institution in Washington, DC, to hire an acknowledged expert on the federal government's administrative policies and procedures, Lewis Meriam, to conduct a comprehensive study titled *The Problem of Indian Administration*. Published in 1928, the *Meriam Report*, as the study became known, exposed the numerous breakdowns of the government's Indian policies and how such failures greatly contributed to subsequent problems with education, health, and poverty. *The Meriam Report* intensified interest in Indian affairs, and President Herbert Hoover appropriated the funding to implement the suggested important changes, but congressional foot-dragging and the stock market crash of 1929 derailed the efforts. When Franklin D. Roosevelt took office in 1932, however, he appointed John Collier commissioner of Indian affairs, an office the sociologist was to hold until 1945. Collier united Indian rights with Roosevelt's New Deal programs and championed the Indian Reorganization Act of 1934 (IRA).

When the Dawes Act was signed into law in 1888, American Indian lands totaled 138 million acres; by the 1934 IRA repeal of the legislation, Indian ownership had dwindled to 48 million acres. Aside from terminating the Dawes Act, the IRA (or the Wheeler-Howard Act, as it is also known) extended limits on the sale of American Indian lands. Moreover, the IRA also addressed this important issue by authorizing the secretary of the interior to purchase additional lands or to proclaim new reservations for Indian people throughout America.

The Meriam Report—and subsequent congressional investigations—verified that the Dawes Act had permitted land speculators to gobble up Indian land and, even worse, the legislation had wreaked havoc on ancient tribal traditions. The IRA consequently sought to resurrect American Indian culture, restore limited tribal sovereignty, and generally signal a significant attitudinal change toward Indians and tribal governments. Throughout the legal relationship between Euro Americans and Indians, the legislative and executive branches of the federal government had failed miserably to define the proper relationship that existed between the Department of Interior and the Bureau of Indian Affairs in their trustee capacity, and the IRA created the opportunity to finally articulate an appropriate legal relationship and regenerate tribal governments in the process.[7]

As an additional benefit to the termination of the insidious allotment system of the Dawes Act, the IRA provided tribes with the opportunity to organize in their general interest in order to adopt written constitutions that would grant them status as federally chartered corporations that would later be formally approved by the secretary of the interior. It is also important to note that an equally significant provision of the IRA—"special education for Indians"—reached beyond Lewis Meriam's recommendations and was enacted during a time when it was not popular to accept the validity of Indian culture or traditions. Under this important provision the US government's educational policy would no longer demean and degrade Indian culture; instead, positive values of Indian culture would be *emphasized*. Under the IRA, government Indian schools would be required to develop curricula materials from tribal traditions and folklore, thereby bringing to Indian people an affirmative sense of their immediate past and the positive principles inherent in their unique way of life. The "special education" section of the IRA even made provisions for a scholarship fund for formal education of Indians of academic ability.[8]

The IRA also offered tribes the option to vote on whether or not they wished to accept the changes the legislation would bring. Tribes were given a two-year grace period to decide, but the language of the legislation was specific that the vote was a *one-time* opportunity; if the tribe voted against accepting the provisions of the legislation, it could not be reconsidered in the future. The IRA also allowed tribes to employ legal counsel to help them consider and decide such important matters and established a special fund from which the secretary of interior could make loans for tribal economic development.

A feature that would in the future undermine Collier's vision more than any other section of the IRA, however, was the stipulation that no longer permitted inheritance of lands by individual Indians. Any individual claiming a part of a plot of land held by multiple owners would receive only a certificate indicating he or she owned a percentage of interest in tribal lands. Rather than unifying, this aspect of the IRA was destined to create dissention among various tribes in the decades to come.

Founder of the Institute for the Development of Indian Law Vine Deloria Jr. observes, "The last title of the bill was a half century ahead of its time. It provided for a Court of Indian Affairs. The court was to consist of seven justices appointed by the President with the consent of the Senate. It would have authority over all legal controversies affecting Indian tribes. The justices of this special court would have ten-year terms, thus avoiding any one administration's packing the court either against or in favor of the Indians (although it was doubtful if any President would consider packing the court in favor of Indians). The court would have eliminated the perennial problems of the tribes having to litigate their treaty rights in state courts with appeal to the federal system."[9]

As might be expected, Collier's vision immediately became slowed by the inherent bureaucracy of government procedure, while being greeted with fierce opposition from conservative non-Indian *and* Indian quarters. While some were quick to support the educational aspects of the IRA, Christian missionaries in particular bristled at the notion of non-Christian people being granted religious freedom. Church leaders accused Collier of attempting to revive paganism and undermining a century of missionary effort. They voiced their strongest objections to the proposal that tribes would be granted full power to reinstitute ancient religious ceremonies that they deemed heathen.

While Christian leaders protested, many career government employees were enthusiastic about the shift toward self-government in Indian Country. Trapped in the middle, government agents had been the targets of the reform movement's barbs coming from one side, and on the other side, apprehensive Indian people who refused to cooperate with them. Most government workers consequently viewed the legislation as long overdue in placing the responsibility of conditions in Indian Country on the tribal governments, thereby absolving themselves of blame.[10]

As the IRA met with increasing opposition in non-Indian and Indian camps, Collier took bold action that caught all factions by surprise and called for a series of gatherings throughout Indian Country to consult with Indians personally about the legislation. The first of Collier's congresses held March 2, 1934, in Rapid City, South Dakota, attracted representatives from most of the tribes of the northern Great Plains. Many of the Lakota attending Collier's conference were concerned with losing treaty rights, but Sioux full-bloods also vehemently opposed mixed-bloods who had sold their lands dominating any proposed tribal programs. As mixed-bloods with no lands in twentieth-century America were known as "hangs-around-the-agency" Indians, this triggered an issue that had divided the Oglala since Red Cloud seized leadership of the "hangs-around-the-fort" (Fort Laramie) Oglala in the 1850s. The old problem had become only more aggravated and divisive over time and reared its head yet again during the Collier gathering. So while Collier addressed this internal political issue, he was also forced to deal with other plains tribes that had sent missionary-coached Christian Indian representatives to the gatherings to protest reverting back to the old pagan ways. In spite of the turbulent beginning, Collier was able to eventually win the support of the assembled Indian delegates in Rapid City and convince them that he would suggest amendments concerning the issues they protested. After losing the vital support of the largest tribe in the country, the Navajo, however, a crestfallen Collier returned to Washington only to discover his congressional support also retreating and the heart and soul of his visionary legislation severely diluted by amendments. Various senators and congressmen had so significantly altered the bill that the legislation and many of the good reforms of Collier's proposal were lost. The ban on inheritances was gone, and, sadly, the Court of Indian Affairs was dropped completely. As a final insult, Collier was attacked personally, accused of subversively attempting to institute soviet-style collectivism under the guise of restoring American Indians to a position of political stability.[11]

Ultimately the IRA set in motion the first revitalization movement in Indian Country, but unfortunately the promise of Collier's New Deal reform legislation was never fully realized. The Dawes Act and other, more legally refined legislative variations of its fundamental design to seize Indian lands, destroy their culture, and force assimilation had extracted a heavy toll from the tribes' collective psyche. Many of the old customs and traditions that the IRA sought to restore had vanished during the four decades since the tribes had entered the reservation era and been forced to accept the culturally destructive allotment policies of the Dawes Act. Several generations of children had been removed from their families and communities to be educated by Christian missionaries in government schools and, as a result of the proselytizing, had lost their language as well as the customs and traditions of their people. Simply, forty years of reservation oppression and assimilation policies had subdued and trained Indian people to be insecure and bewildered about their past, present, and future. Leaders needed time and the circumstances to retrieve and revitalize the old ways and figure out how to apply them to the twentieth century. Self-government according to Indian traditions proved even more problematic, however, because the newly designed constitutions were similar to the traditions of some tribes but completely unfamiliar to others. When counselors tried to help, traditionalists became skeptical because the new constitutions were based upon agrarian districts that had been created when the allotment policy dictated that Indians would be taught to farm by area "bosses." Worse, during this transitional period, familiar tribal methods of selecting leadership had surrendered to the institutions of the dominant culture, and the constitutions were designed largely according to the Anglo-American political system. This naturally further alienated traditional Indians, who viewed this as simply another legal trick to manipulate them.

World War II brought an end to what was left of efforts to restore traditional culture to politics in Indian Country. In order to support the war effort, budgets were dramatically slashed for domestic government programs, leaving many agencies either operating on a shoestring or closed. During this period many Indian people also left the reservation to work in the city in industries supporting the war effort or to serve in the armed forces. Under constant attack by critics who charged him with attempting to institute socialism in America on the reservations, John Collier resigned as commissioner of Indian affairs in 1945. He had served twelve years, longer than any other person in history, and even though he had come to believe his personality attracted as much opposition as his programs, his accomplishments were numerous. Most significantly, Collier initiated radical change in the official policies of the United States toward Indians. At a minimum, he forced the government to admit that Indian religion, culture, and tradition were essential to the success of any future efforts or policies in Indian Country.[12]

Even while John Collier attempted to radically reform the United States' policies toward American Indians, however, a new wave of farmers swept out onto the Great Plains. Irrigation had brought water to the region, and high prices for grain crops—especially for wheat during the World War I years—had encouraged even more Americans to try their luck with dry-land farming. Since the founding of the Jamestown colony in 1607, American farmers had by 1870 occupied 407 million acres over the 263-year period. In the barely thirty years between 1870 and 1900, however, non-Indians had opened more land to the plow than their ancestors had during the previous two and a half centuries. By 1930 non-Indians occupied an additional 430 million acres as the farming, cattle, and ranching industry expanded north from Texas into Colorado, Wyoming, Montana, and the Dakotas.[13]

Specifically reflecting the dramatic impact of the Dawes Act on the Lakota Nation, the population of western South Dakota quadrupled during the first decade of the twentieth century. Several counties in the western half of the state reported a 200-percent increase in population during these years. In the twenty years since Wounded Knee, over 26 million acres were taken by homesteaders in the Dakotas. By 1920 land values had increased steadily, the production of grain crops rose dramatically, and millions of new acres had been put into production. Since the turn of the century, a subtle yet significant change had taken place in the West. In the coming years this transformation would indeed become much more obvious, but during this era the rising number of farmers had not grown in scale with the dramatic increase in new acreage opened to the plow, thus implying that the average size of individual farms was growing, but that absentee ownership was also proliferating and corporate ownership of farms and ranches was becoming more common.[14]

World War I hastened this shift toward corporate agribusiness that intensified throughout the 1920s on the Great Plains. During that decade and continuing into the early 1930s, the region experienced a period of apparent prosperity as food grains—wheat in particular—steadily rose in price. Increasingly, labor-saving machinery began to attract even more speculators who merely rented the land and hired others to farm it for them. Eventually tiny farming communities sprouted even deeper in the Trans-Missouri, and in those years over 5 million acres of prairie grassland were converted to wheat land.

It is important to note that most of these farmers were not wasteful or careless. Most were descendants of farmers and had learned the art of farming the hard way and by living on the land had probed deeper into the heartland. By the 1930s, however, everything in their education and experience was about to change. As early as 1933, farmers in southwestern Kansas experienced unusual dust storms so immense that their tractors were buried in the drifts left in the wake. Soon thereafter the biblical swarms of grasshoppers arrived and stripped the fields that survived the heat and drought.[15]

The first enormous clouds of dust followed the grasshopper plague. Soon, from a region spanning over 100 million acres of the Great Plains, wave upon wave of colossal dust storms—some over two hundred miles wide and five miles high—swept across North America like rolling, mountainous sand dunes, enveloping the Western Hemisphere from the Rocky Mountains to the middle of the Atlantic Ocean. Over three hundred thousand tons of topsoil darkened the sun at noon. At times people could not see their hand in front of their face. Dangerous static electricity sparkled and slashed eerily in the atmosphere created by the clouds of swirling earth. Families tied themselves together with ropes to prevent becoming lost in the dust storms. Americans had never experienced anything like this before; fine dirt particles filled their lungs and created a disease known as dust pneumonia; often families that remained on the plains literally coughed up bloody mud for days before dying of suffocation. By April 14, 1935—a day that became known as Black Sunday—the phenomenon that was now being called the Dust Bowl was an unmistakable indictment that Abraham Lincoln's Homestead Act of 1862 had been a miscalculated undertaking to forcefully transplant an agrarian society upon a landscape for which it was absolutely unsuited. The technological advances and industrial farming that arrived on the Great Plains in the later part of the nineteenth century exacerbated the situation with massive overproduction. Marketed as the "world's breadbasket," the region had instead harvested environmental catastrophe. When the dust storms finally ceased, more than a quarter-million people had fled the Great Plains, contributing greatly to the dramatic decrease in population that demographic scientists had already begun observing at the turn of the twentieth century; the human population of the Great Plains had begun to flee the region almost as quickly as it was settled along railroad lines only thirty years earlier. By 1936 the region of the old Louisiana Purchase would be home to 2 million American farmers subsisting on public assistance.

Already tattered and torn by the cruel winds of the Great Depression, the American Dream became a ghostly nightmare that haunted non-Indians' history in North America. As the dark clouds rose from the Trans-Missouri it was as if the Indian/non-Indian mythologies that clashed there in the nineteenth century were somehow physically manifesting again in the twentieth century as a phenomenal environmental catastrophe. As destructive as it was, the Dust Bowl proved that the technological violence the United States had unleashed on the Trans-Missouri in the nineteenth century was ultimately no match for the landscape itself; indeed, the very landscape rose as the dust in defense against the non-Indian's invasion.

The Trans-Missouri depopulated all but the hardiest of non-Indians in the twentieth century almost as quickly as it was populated by them in the nineteenth century. Yet even as the non-Indian populations fled, the Dawes Act had eaten away at the fringes of what remained of Indian lands as surely as the grasshopper plagues that descended on the region to announce the arrival of the great dust clouds. Even while the Dust Bowl refugees fled the region, however, the West maintained its magnetic mythological influence on the latest version of the American heroic archetype as the powerful cinematic storytelling team of John Wayne and John Ford found its footing in Hollywood. Yet even as Ford and Wayne rode out of Monument Valley in their *Stagecoach*, the thunderheads of war were gathering in Europe and Asia. Soon, Indians and non-Indians would be called upon again to join together to fight and die alongside one another defending America.

Chapter Twelve
A Clarion Call for Heroes

This is a good day to die. Think of the helpless ones at home! Then we all cried "Hoka Hey!"[1]

—Black Elk

The Japanese attack on Pearl Harbor on Sunday, December 7, 1941, was instantly followed by an unprecedented surge of Americans rallying to defend their country. This was especially the case in California, where everyone feared the attack in Hawaii was only the beginning of an imminent Japanese invasion of America's West Coast. By mid-December fierce patriotism replaced preliminary invasion panic, and the film industry rapidly responded to America's urgent call for volunteers. Top Hollywood actors Gene Autry, Henry Fonda, Clark Gable, Sterling Hayden, William Holden, Burgess Meredith, Robert Montgomery, Tyrone Power, Jimmy Stewart, Ronald Reagan, and Gilbert Roland joined with famous producers Harold Roach, Jack Warner, Darryl Zanuck, renowned directors John Ford, Frank Capra, John Huston, William Keighley, and William Wyler, noted screenwriters Garson Kanin and Budd Schulberg, and scores of cameramen, technicians, stagehands, and other members of the film industry who eventually enlisted in the military. Randy Roberts and James S. Olson note: "By October 1942 more than 2,700 people—or 12 percent—of the men and women in the film industry had entered the armed forces. Some like Fonda and Stewart enlisted quietly and without fanfare. Others, like Reagan, Zanuck, and Gable, made the process of enlistment and service an act of public theater. But they all served."[2]

Washington immediately took control of the steel and automotive industries as well as any other business interests vital to American security, and President Franklin D. Roosevelt's advisors urged him to also take control of the film industry. But the president believed the film industry would function better if the studio heads remained in charge of operations. Only weeks after December 7, Roosevelt remarked, "The American motion picture is one of our most effective media in informing and entertaining our citizens. The motion picture must remain free in so far as national security will permit." Hollywood moguls interpreted the commander in chief's remarks to mean that the government was going to allow them to continue to make money if they combined entertainment with propaganda dedicated to serving the war effort.[3]

Since the inception of the motion picture industry, America's extreme right had spit venom accusing Hollywood of being a bed of Communists controlled by immigrant Jews. Consequently, most of the Jewish studio heads in Hollywood walked on eggshells as Hitler and the Nazis rose in power in Europe. Even before the war officially began, Jewish producers like Samuel Goldwyn had joined with humanitarian aid groups to raise millions of dollars in relief funds for European refugees. War, however, was ironically "peace" for Hollywood's Jewish film moguls; once the United States entered the conflict in Europe as well as the Pacific, Washington finally acknowledged and *sanctified* the sentimental Americana message immigrant Jewish producers such as Goldwyn, Zukor, and Louis B. Mayer had been encoding in their films since the genesis of the industry in a sincere effort to shed their "outsider" status. Washington's similar desire to infuse society with frontier mythological themes of can-do Yankee ingenuity, sentimental Americana, and fierce patriotism was clearly emphasized in June 1942 when the newly appointed chief of the US Office of War Information's Bureau of Motion Pictures, Lowell Mellett, reiterated Roosevelt's remarks that Hollywood's greatest contribution to the war effort would be to maintain normal production of quality films, only adapted now to subjects reflecting the impact of the war on America and her people. A former editor of the *Washington Daily News*, Mellett believed Hollywood could "render a priceless service" by making motion pictures that were entertaining yet that also interpreted the war for Americans and people around the world. Mellett emphasized that the government would like to see films produced that "dramatize the underlying causes of the war and the reason why we fight," stressing that "unless the public understands these, the war may be useless." Finally, Mellett accentuated, "We would like to see more and more true pictures of America…You know it is true and you know also, I am sure, that the real America is a better sort of place and real Americans are perhaps a little better people than their average in the pictures that foreigners see."[4]

Hollywood had anticipated Mellett and Washington's request for patriotic films with the 1941 release of *They Died with Their Boots On*, featuring swashbuckling Australian actor Errol Flynn as General George Armstrong Custer. Flynn had traded tights and sword-fights for pistol duels in 1939 in *Dodge City* before filming *Virginia City* and *Santa Fe Trail* back-to-back in 1940. It is curious to note that just a few months before Flynn's feisty characterization of the impetuous general, Custer was first portrayed in moving pictures by Ronald Reagan in *Santa Fe Trail*, and the future president depicted the impetuous general as a "quiet, sincere, and dedicated soldier."[5]

By the 1940s most Hollywood actors like Errol Flynn and Ronald Reagan had to train with professionals to learn to ride horses and handle firearms before attempting to portray historical Western characters. Of course, during the early days of Hollywood and the glory days of Gower's Gulch, most actors portraying cowboys were in fact *real* cowboys; they were westerners like Frank Cooper, who actually knew how to ride and shoot. Born in Helena, Montana, in 1901, Frank had grown up on a ranch, the son of a Montana Supreme Court justice. While in college he had worked as a guide in Yellowstone National Park, but in 1924 his father became the administrator of the estates of two cousins in California, resigned his judicial position, and moved the family to Los Angeles. There, Frank reconnected with Montana cowboy friends who were scouting Gower's Gulch looking for film work. Six-foot-two and a lean and muscular 180 pounds, Frank caught the eye of Samuel Goldwyn's secretary, and she began introducing him to the right people in the film colony. Because Frank Cooper was such a common name, the young man eventually settled instead on Gary Cooper as a pseudonym. Soon thereafter, Samuel Goldwyn was visiting a set and, spying from behind a curtain, watched as the film's director singled out Cooper from a crowd of cowboy extras watching a scene. Unaware the boss was spying on them, the director asked the green young cowboy to attempt an impromptu, non-speaking bit part, and, impressed with Cooper's instant grasp of acting, naturalistic style, and rugged good looks in the spontaneous scene, Goldwyn immediately cast him in the lead of the 1927 silent Western *Open Range*. Cooper did so well in *Open Range* that in 1929 Goldwyn cast him in his first talking film—poetically, *The Virginian*. By 1936 and Cooper's portrayal of Wild Bill Hickok in Cecil B. DeMille's *The Plainsman*, it is obvious that as the Great Depression deepened and the rise of the Nazis in Europe intensified, Gary Cooper had firmly established himself as Hollywood's Western heroic archetype long before *Stagecoach* premiered in 1939. Despite the Hollywood legend that John Ford cast John Wayne in *Stagecoach* in order to create a fresh, new hero for his films, Garry Wills offers evidence that one need only examine the next three films Ford directed, *Young Mister Lincoln* and *Drums Along the Mohawk* in 1939 and *The Grapes of Wrath* in 1940, to discover that this was not the case; rather than Wayne, Ford cast Henry Fonda in the lead in all three of those films. When Ford hired Wayne again in 1940 it was in Eugene O'Neill's *The Long Voyage Home*—like *Stagecoach*, an ensemble piece. Since the part required Wayne to use a Swedish accent, Wills believes that Ford considered Wayne as more of a character actor than a leading man during this period in their relationship. After directing five feature films over a two-year period, as soon as *The Long Voyage Home* was completed, forty-six-year-old John Ford immediately went off to the war in the Pacific.[6]

John Wayne, meanwhile, contemplated the effect enlisting in the military would have on his blossoming—but still not meteoric—career. Although he continued to get work in films after *The Long Voyage Home*, Wayne had not become an instant star following his breakthrough role in *Stagecoach*. He was also still legally bound to Poverty Row because of his long-term contract to Republic Pictures. Capitalizing on Wayne's outstanding reviews in *Stagecoach*, Republic immediately released four films in his *Three*

Mesquiteers series and cast him in *Dark Command* in 1940. In a sense he had traveled full circle, as *Dark Command* was directed by Raoul Walsh, the man who a decade earlier had cast him in his first feature role and renamed him in *The Big Trail*. *The Long Voyage Home* flopped at the box office but still won Academy Award nominations for best picture, screenplay, and black-and-white cinematography, eventually losing in those and three other categories. Ford still owned the evening, however, because he won the Academy Award for best director for his iconic film adaptation of John Steinbeck's *The Grapes of Wrath*.[7]

Meanwhile, as John Ford filmed the war in the South Pacific, Wayne began a trio of films—and a romantic affair—with the German actress Marlene Dietrich. Dietrich had become an international star in *Morocco* in 1930, but her most famous role in *The Blue Angel*, while a critical success, was actually the first of a decade-long series of major financial bombs at the box office. By the time *Stagecoach* jump-started John Wayne's career at the eve of 1940, film distributors had proclaimed Dietrich box office poison and the actress had retreated to the French Riviera to recover from the critics' slings and arrows and contemplate her next career move. Complicating matters for the actress, as Hitler's war machine began running rampant over Europe, Dietrich's German heritage left her few options for plum roles.

Dietrich and John Wayne shared the same agent, Charles K. Feldman, a Los Angeles attorney who in the early 1930s formed the Famous Artists Corporation, one of the leading talent agencies in Hollywood. During the 1930s Feldman had earned fortunes for many of Hollywood's leading stars, Marlene Dietrich among them. Feldman was an early advocate of the "package deal," and it was this casting concept that brought his two clients together professionally and romantically.[8]

Feldman had to somehow reinvent Dietrich and decided the old "fish-out-of-water" routine just might work; he decided to remove the sex goddess from her normal high-fashion locations and costumes and displace her in a gritty story set in the American West. Feldman then convinced producer Joe Pasternak to cast Dietrich with ever-popular James Stewart in the Western *Destry Rides Again*, which premiered in 1939. In the film the actress would portray a dance hall girl deemed by the bigoted community as unworthy of Jimmy Stewart's character but ultimately good enough to sacrifice her life for the man she loves. *Destry Rides Again* was a hit with critics and audiences alike, and Dietrich's career was revitalized.[9]

Having eliminated European affectations and formality from Dietrich's screen persona in the *Destry* role, her management—in typical Hollywood fashion—decided to repeat the formula. *Destry Rides Again* was followed by *Seven Sinners*, in which Dietrich was cast as a vagabond barfly, drifting from island to island throughout the South Seas. This time around Dietrich's character sacrificed herself for an American hero by abandoning her love to prevent the destruction of his naval career.[10]

In 1941, after removing several leading men from consideration, Dietrich's management cast John Wayne as the diva's leading man in *Seven Sinners*, a role he reprised in *The Spoilers* in 1942 and in *Pittsburgh* the same year. Decades later Dietrich claimed she had tried to teach Wayne how to act but that he had failed to learn anything from her. The German temptress was, of course, legendary for her real-life sexual escapades with many of Hollywood's leading men—and women. Although married with four children at the time, John Wayne quickly became another notch on her bedpost.

Marlene Dietrich may have failed to impart any of her acting talents to John Wayne, but he was learning something from her that was much more important to him at the time. While his mentor John Ford was not only willing but eager to put his country first and hurry to defend America in combat with his talents, in Marlene Dietrich, John Wayne discovered the consummate example of someone obsessed with career. Following the example of the German diva's single-minded devotion to self, Wayne would summon forth the discipline to focus solely on getting to the top in Hollywood.[11]

In 1941 John Wayne was thirty-four years old, at his physical peak, and the demand for actors in his age bracket was increasing exponentially as more young men volunteered or were drafted daily to serve in the war. *The Big Trail* had given him a taste of stardom, but destiny had instead taken him to Poverty Row, where he had spent a decade of his youth making fifty-nine serial B Westerns. Now fate had teased him with fame again with *Stagecoach*, only to desert him to face alone the moral dilemma of whether to enlist in the military or capitalize on his blossoming career in Hollywood. When the war began Wayne was classified 3-A, meaning having a wife and family deferred him from conscription. Still, as the demand for troops grew, draft boards required young men to come in and officially register in order to apply for and receive deferments. John Wayne did not personally apply for the November 17, 1943, continuation of his original deferment, but most film historians believe Republic Pictures executive Herbert J. Yates made sure Wayne received the extension. Yates had suddenly lost his biggest star at Republic when Gene Autry enlisted, and after that setback the studio executive had every reason to keep John Wayne under contract, in the saddle, and out of uniform. By April 1944 the war had reached its peak, however, and Wayne was reclassified 2-A, or deferred from service because of "support of health, safety, or national interest." Nevertheless, as the war in Europe became critical a month later, Wayne was notified he was 1-A, or "available for service." This initiated a flurry of deferment pleas, until May 5, 1945, when Wayne was again classified 2-A. By the conclusion of the war, his age earned him a 4-A draft status.[12]

Wayne also realized that if he enlisted and served and was fortunate enough to return from combat alive and physically intact, he would nevertheless have lost an equally significant battle for an actor: the struggle with age. He would certainly be passed over by the aspiring hordes of younger actors that would be invading Hollywood when the war ended. Wayne could not use the excuses of age or family, however, because even though he was thirty-four, married, and had children, bigger stars such as Henry Fonda, Clark Gable, Tyrone Power, and James Stewart were all older than Wayne and with broods of their own and still had volunteered for service.[13]

While all this ambivalence concerning military service was occurring, Wayne was learning at Dietrich's knee. He watched

Dietrich expertly exert control over every minute aspect of her career while also skillfully manipulating the people who could further her goals. Wayne applied Dietrich's self-centered approach to his dilemma about the war and his career as he chose to maintain his momentum in film rather than enlist. The biggest problem with his decision was how to explain it to his super-patriotic friend John Ford. Having bonded with the director, Wayne certainly realized that his failure to enlist in the military would create a problem between them that would ricochet throughout Hollywood; as a member of Pappy Ford's stock ensemble of film actors, Wayne was surrounded by the director's network of patriotic professional friends and colleagues. As time passed and he continued to accept roles in films, Wayne began writing to Ford regularly, expressing his intentions to enlist after the completion of whatever movie he happened to working on at the time. Upon accepting each new film part, Wayne offered a variety of lame excuses explaining why he had not enlisted. He usually claimed that Herbert Yates threatened to sue him if he enlisted; having separated from his family after the Dietrich affair, he also claimed his ex-wife refused to allow him access to important personal documents that he needed to enlist. Of course when none of these explanations held any water, he finally—indeed, logically—expressed the reasoning that he could wield a more positive influence on the war effort as a movie star than as a buck private.[14]

Many people in Hollywood supported Wayne's "positive influence" defense. There were indeed other men and women who strictly followed Lowell Mellett's advice and continued to work in the wartime production of films rather than enlisting. In March 1942, following the world premiere of his film *Reap the Wild Wind*—staring John Wayne, incidentally—Cecil B. DeMille delivered a speech to the Associated Motion Picture Advertisers in which he reiterated the president's and the chief of the Bureau of Motion Picture's opinion concerning the matter, maintaining: "The job of motion pictures is to help bring home a full realization of the crisis and of the deadly peril that lurks in internal squabbles. Ours is the task of holding high and ever visible the values that everyone is fighting for. I don't mean flag waving, but giving the embattled world sharp glimpses of the life that we've got to hang on to in spite of everything."[15]

With the absence of leading men in Hollywood, John Wayne was quickly becoming the poster boy for the motion picture image of the fighting American that President Franklin Roosevelt's Bureau of Motion Pictures—and the Office of War Information—wished to project to the country and the world. Critics point out, however, that many of John Wayne's films during this period contributed little to the war effort even though his star continued to rise while the conflict raged on. Garry Wills observes, "[Wayne's] real breakthrough was still ahead of him; but he was making it clear that if single-minded careerism would get him there, he was bound to make it. This cost him the chance to serve his country at its time of greatest unity against worldwide foes. Some in Hollywood never forgave him for that. Part of John Ford never forgave him. A few even claim that Wayne did not forgive himself—that the compensatory super-patriotism of later years, when he urged the country to wars in Korea and Vietnam, was a form of explanation. If so, it was not enough. This is a man who called on other generations to sacrifice their lives, and called them 'soft' if they refused."[16]

So how *did* an actor who avoided military service during World War II become *the* twentieth-century archetype for American super-patriotism? Wayne's appearance in *Stagecoach* introduced him to mainstream American movie audiences, but the steel-willed, fiercely inflexible American most have come to identify with John Wayne's defiant personality both on and off the screen was created when director-producer Howard Hawks convinced the actor to portray an older man in a darker, more complex role than he had ever attempted before. Filmed in 1946 and released in 1948, *Red River* and the character of British immigrant Tom Dunson became John Wayne's true breakthrough role; his portrayal of Dunson vividly established the very first example of the on-screen personality that would characterize all of Wayne's roles for the rest of his career and eventually overwhelm his off-screen reality as well. That said, it is also important to note that, in essence, Tom Dunson is an anti-hero, and, as the prototypical "John Wayne" role that would ultimately define Marion Morrison as a hero both in film and life, the character demands examination.

Nearly forty in 1946, Wayne was no longer the willowy, rosy-cheeked ingénue in *The Big Trail*, nor was he still the lean, mysterious Ringo Kid in *Stagecoach*. Without using a hint of a British accent in the creation of the screen personality of Tom Dunson, however, John Wayne brilliantly transformed himself into a powerful authority figure, a cruel, unbending, often ruthless character who disguises any appearance of vulnerability. There is no gray in Tom Dunson's life; he perceives everything as black or white. He expresses little affection for anything but principles; he is a man with unique, defiant courage and the resolve to stand alone against any odds. Skillfully making use of sentimental little personality traits, characteristics, and behavior patterns theatrically played subtly by Wayne and professionally staged, directed, filmed, and edited by Howard Hawks to be recognized vicariously by the audience, Dunson's character frequently reveals that underneath his gruff exterior beats the heart of a proud, sentimental, archetypical American. As Hawks's plot of *Red River* unfolds, Dunson also represents an alpha-male leader for younger men to fear yet emulate.

In an opening written by Hawks in his trademark sexist style and obviously intended to emphasize his leading man's determined pioneer personality, Dunson prepares to depart a wagon train and abandon an adorable young woman who so worships him that she practically melts in his arms. A lesser man could not resist the charms of this delicious creature, but this is the first indication that Dunson is not a man who easily reveals his emotions, and he coolly announces he has a ranching empire to build before considering a wife and family. He pushes the brokenhearted damsel away and informs her that after he's established his empire he'll send for her. In a farewell gesture, Dunson gives the young woman a cherished bracelet left to him by his late, beloved mother in England, and then, with his devoted Sancho Panza—Walter Brennan as Nadine Groot—and a prize bull with which to begin his cattle empire, he departs the wagon trail and heads south.

After traveling only a few hours, Dunson and Groot see smoke on the horizon in the region of the wagon train. The obstinate character the world would recognize forever thereafter as "John Wayne" is revealed here in Dunson's matter-of-fact decision that because of the distance between them and the ambushed wagon train, there is nothing they can do; everyone—including Dunson's sweetheart—has certainly perished. Without offering a prayer, shedding a tear, or even once considering whether they might be able to save any possible survivors—including the sweetheart—Dunson and Groot simply resume their journey. Very soon after the pair re-embark upon their trek, however, a young boy and a cow, shell-shocked survivors of the wagon trail attack, suddenly appear. Here, the old Western realist William S. Hart would have most certainly pointed out to writer-director Hawks that if Dunson and Groot did not have time to return to the train to save any possible survivors, how on earth did a traumatized adolescent boy and his cow manage to make it to them so quickly after the massacre? Even worse, the boy's appearance does not immediately convince the blasé Dunson and Groot that there might be other survivors. Instead, Dunson slaps the kid out of his confused mental state and back to reality— a trademark "cowboy psychological technique" that Wayne would perform for countless shell-shocked, or cowardly, young actors for decades to come. (His favorite psychological therapy for spirited, defiant women of course was to turn them over his knee for a good spanking.) To his credit, the feisty young version of Mitch Garth—who over the course of his film debut in *Red River* would mature into Broadway actor Montgomery Clift—thanks Dunson for the ritual male initiation slap but, telegraphing the motion picture's plot, warns Dunson never to slap him again. As Dunson, Groot, the bull, and now the boy and his cow resume the journey, however, they are promptly attacked by an Indian war party. An Indian Dunson kills is wearing the bracelet he left with his beloved damsel on the wagon train, thereby conveniently confirming his earlier pragmatic prediction of her fate. In typical Howard Hawks fashion, the bracelet continues to make appearances throughout *Red River* as a metaphorical representation of Dunson's sentimental link to his mother and the "old country" and the family he secretly longs to establish on this frontier.

Soon, Dunson, Groot, boy, bull, and cow cross the Red River of the film's title and pass into the mythical land of Texas. As if personally commissioned by the original papal doctrine of discovery, Dunson immediately claims everything south of the Red River with a speech that either Teddy Roosevelt or Frederick Jackson Turner could have written if Howard Hawks hadn't done it for them. Within moments of the speech two Mexican vaqueros straight out of central casting appear promptly on cue. The vaqueros greet Dunson and Groot and inform them they are trespassing on their employers' land and must leave pronto. Dunson rudely orders one Mexican guard to return to his employer and notify him that this land now belongs to him. Foolishly, the vaquero reaches for his gun, and Dunson kills him on the spot. He then orders the surviving vaquero to return to Mexico to inform his employer that everything south of the Red River now belongs to Tom Dunson. As the vaquero departs, Wayne assures him he will bury his compadre and "read some words over him"—a chore that will be repeated frequently as Dunson regularly murders people throughout the film.

According to Wayne biographers Roberts and Olson, *Red River* reveals itself to be equal parts *Mutiny on the Bounty*, with Tom Dunson as Captain William Bligh and Mitch Garth as Fletcher Christian; *Moby Dick*, with Dunson as Captain Ahab and Garth as the first mate Starbuck; and *Exodus*, with Dunson as Moses and Garth as Joshua. Roberts and Olson suggest, "Duke had never breathed so much life into the character; he had never transformed the type into such a believable person." Vitally significant, Wayne realized that Dunson was a formula character he could portray *repeatedly*, a part that did not require the young, creaseless face and lean body of a romantic lead. Wayne rightly figured that if movie magic could make him look like he was in his fifties to play Dunson, then when he was actually *in* his fifties, and older, he could still play that character.[17]

John Ford realized the same thing. One of the reasons he had cast Wayne in *Stagecoach* was because of his imposing physique;

Wayne was large enough to match the majestic scale Ford wished to capture in Monument Valley and graceful enough to move over that rugged landscape with ease. When Howard Hawks asked Ford to help edit *Red River*, however, and the director saw Wayne's performance, he realized that Wayne had matured and his acting skill now finally matched his size and physical grace. While editing *Red River*, Ford told Hawks, "I never knew the big son of a bitch could act."[18]

While John Wayne was avoiding military service, learning to act in films and building his career in Hollywood as World War II raged in Europe and the Pacific, Navajo code talkers and thousands of other brave American Indian warriors in the military were paradoxically defending *two* nations—the United States as well as their own—in the conflict. After surviving one of the bloodiest battles of World War II at Iwo Jima in 1945, Pima Indian Ira Hayes participated in Joseph Rosenthal's iconic photo of victorious US Marines raising the American flag atop Mount Suribachi.

Alvin Josephy Jr. was also a veteran of the Battle of Iwo Jima. Disgusted with the motion picture industry after his youthful adventures as a scriptwriter under the tyranny of Louis B. Mayer at MGM, Josephy had returned to New York in the mid-1930s with hopes of continuing his career as a writer. After knocking around Manhattan unable to make ends meet as an author, journalist, or playwright, Josephy drifted into broadcasting at WOR Radio in Manhattan around the time Hitler's war machine began invading countries throughout Europe.

Almost twenty-seven and married with a child on the way, Josephy was deferred from service because of being employed in communications that were "essential to the war effort." Josephy nevertheless believed he could better serve the country in uniform, and he applied for an officers training program in the navy only to be rejected because of asthma and poor eyesight. Soon, however, he received a telegram inviting him to Washington to interview for a position in the Radio Bureau of the Office of Facts and Figures (OFF), an organization Josephy described as "a wretchedly named but very high-powered, proactive government war propaganda agency, which was led by Archibald MacLeish, the distinguished American poet and the head of the Library of Congress, and staffed by many well-known writers, editors, and leading figures in radio and other creative fields."[19]

One can only imagine the communication logjams that followed December 7 as the various members of Roosevelt's administration rapidly sorted out defensive and offensive responses to the Japanese attack. Roosevelt obviously felt it was vital for the left hand to know the intention of the right, and by mid-June of 1942 the Radio Bureau of the Office of Facts and Figures that Alvin Josephy had joined was consolidated under the very same Office of War Information umbrella as Lowell Mellett's Bureau of Motion Pictures. Even though he was now more directly involved in the war effort as a communications professional, Josephy still believed it was his patriotic duty to get himself on the front lines to physically fight for the things he believed in. One day he was expressing his desire to see action and a friend suggested a combat correspondent unit in the Marine Corps that might interest him. When Josephy mentioned his eyesight, the friend suggested he take along an extra pair of glasses.

The next day Josephy met World War I veteran Brigadier General Robert L. Denig at the Marine Corps headquarters in Arlington, Virginia. After Pearl Harbor, Denig had ended his retirement to head the Marine Corps Division of Public Relations and create a company composed of several hundred combat correspondents. Three months after meeting General Denig, Josephy completed Marine Corps boot camp at Parris Island in South Carolina with the rank of sergeant, and by November 1942 he received orders assigning him to the Third Marine Division, which was then engaged with the Japanese in the Solomon Islands in the South Pacific. Aware of his background in radio, however, General Denig called Sergeant Josephy into his office to inform him that he wanted him to carry recording equipment as well as a typewriter into combat. Denig explained that "some music man" from the Library of Congress wanted authentic recordings of the songs of World War II for the nation's archives. A military man, Denig had no interest in what songs the fighting men were singing; he did, however, want recordings of marines in combat. So before departing for the South Pacific, Alvin Josephy visited Harold Spivacke, head of the music division in the Library of Congress, for training. Spivacke was the man who had initiated and archived the famous field recording efforts of folklorists John and Alan Lomax, and he was now assigned to teach a young marine journalist how to operate field recording equipment. Only now, rather than in southern prison cells and the porches of cabins in Appalachian hollows, the equipment would be used where bullets would be flying and men would be dying. The recording equipment weighed over fifty pounds but was neatly packed into a secure carrying case that also contained a heavy twelve-volt battery and a converter for the combat conditions in the South Pacific. After a few sessions with Spivacke, Josephy was trained to make battlefield recordings.

Sergeant Josephy said goodbye to his wife and family the first week of January 1944 and left to join the Third Marine Division at Guadalcanal. Josephy had no sooner arrived at Guadalcanal, however, before the Third Division shipped out for the Marshall Islands. By the time Josephy's division reached the Marshall Islands, news arrived that Allied forces had stormed the beaches of Normandy and the invasion of Europe had begun. In July 1944 marines launched a violent, amphibious ship-to-shore invasion of Guam with Sergeant Josephy lugging his recording equipment along the beachhead. As withering gunfire slashed the air and splashed around him in bloody water, Josephy captured the very first audio recordings intimately describing deadly combat; two-thirds of the marines who crossed the reef in the amphibious gondola with Josephy were dead when the fighting ended. Weeks later Josephy got a letter from General Denig informing him that his hour-long recording of the marine assault of Guam was "unprecedented and was the best of the war so far and that all the networks had played it."[20]

Horrible as the fighting was, Guam nevertheless paled alongside what Josephy and his marine comrades were destined to encounter at Iwo Jima. The tiny, barren, volcanic island was situated within Japan's internal circle of defenses roughly 750 miles north of Guam, and thus it was vital to both Japan's offensive and defensive strategies. The entire island was only five miles long and two and a half miles wide at its broadest section. Every square inch of the island was covered with huge artillery, 320mm mortars, anti-tank and antiaircraft guns, and rocket bombs, all situated to target any invasion in a lethal crossfire. The Japanese had two airfields in operation there with a third under construction, but for over two months the island had been subjected to a near-continuous air and naval bombardment by US forces, so it was assumed that much of the island's defenses and thirteen-thousand-man force had been severely diminished. If American forces controlled Guam, the United States not only could prevent further Japanese attacks from their base at Iwo Jima, but could use their airfields to coordinate air assaults on Tokyo and other vital Japanese targets.

The marines were unaware, however, that the entire island was honeycombed with caves interconnected with underground tunnels and protected by heavy layers of steel and concrete. The Japanese had also doubled their force there and had merely hidden in their bunkers during the air and naval bombardments to await the imminent invasion.

The US Marine Corps invasion of the island began in late February 1945. The Japanese commander's strategy was to allow the first marines to come ashore before ambushing them in deadly crossfire while heavy artillery prevented reinforcements from landing to assist them. Reports estimated that as many as 35 percent of the first marines to go ashore on Iwo Jima were killed.[21]

Meanwhile, the 21st Marines landed on the island. "In two days of nightmarish fighting," Josephy wrote in his memoir, "the two battalions of the 21st suffered huge causalities, trying unsuccessfully to drive north through an inferno of artillery, mortar, and rocket fire coming from a network of Japanese positions concealed in a desert of precipitous black sand dunes, scraggly bushes, and torn banyan trees."

On February 23, the 28th Marines of the Fifth Division captured Mount Suribachi, a 546-foot-high volcano at the southern tip of the island. The first patrol to reach the mountaintop raised an American flag on the summit. The patrol was accompanied by Staff Sergeant Louis R. Lowery, a marine with *Leatherneck* magazine who photographed the event. The flag raised by the first patrol and photographed by Lowery, however, was believed to be too small to be seen by those on the beach below. Consequently, a second patrol, accompanied by Associated Press photographer Joe Rosenthal, raised a much larger flag that could be seen from all over the island. Rosenthal's picture of the six men in the act of raising that second flag became the most famous photograph of World War II.[22]

A series of events surrounding the pair of flag-raising photographs on Iwo Jima immediately arose that substantiate media historian Daniel Boorstin's conclusion that "we risk being the first people in history to have been able to make their illusions so vivid, so persuasive, so 'realistic' that we can live in them."[23] Aside from the dramatic overall pose he captured of the raising of the flag, the Rosenthal photograph communicated the *communal* heroic statement of victory; none of the faces of the marines actually appeared in the image that was so powerful that it already suggested the colossal-scale sculpture it was destined to become. Controversy arose, however, when the photograph quickly became the most famous image of the war. Reacting to William Randolph Hearst's syndicated newspaper criticism of the Battle of Iwo Jima as a waste of American lives and money to win an insignificant island, Marine Corps brass began to use the famous photograph in their propaganda campaign. Eventually, however, the marines began to promote the *individuals* who raised the flag Rosenthal had photographed—such as Pima Indian Ira Hayes—as heroes. At this point the flag-raising debate intensified as some believed the real heroes were the marines who mounted the first, smaller flag, whereas the members of the group that posed for the Rosenthal shot just happened to be in the right place at the right time.

The argument continued after the war and had divided into two cults by the time Republic Pictures produced *Sands of Iwo Jima*, staring John Wayne, in 1949. Strapped for cash, tiny

Republic Pictures approached the Marine Corps for assistance with the production of the film. The Marine Corps responded with great enthusiasm, offering the use of base locales, military equipment, uniforms, and extras—all under the condition that the raising of the flag on Mount Suribachi would figure dominantly in the film. Next, the Marine Corps confirmed Daniel Boorstin's theory when—trapped in a delicate situation of image manipulation—the military *invited* Hollywood to tamper with reality: as neither of the flag-raisings had actually involved combat per se, the marine corps could not tarnish their beloved Rosenthal image, and yet they also could not diminish the image of fighting, victorious men the Marine Corps wished to project. Consequently, as a tough sergeant named Stryker in *Sands of Iwo Jima*, John Wayne would lead marines in battle to the top of Mount Suribachi and in 1949 would win his first Academy Award nomination for best actor. Author Garry Wills notes that the Stryker character was "closely modeled on the one Hawks had fashioned for the actor in *Red River*," that after the *Sands of Iwo Jima* "Strykerisms" like "Saddle up" and "Lock and load" became part of the US military lexicon, and that Wayne's portrayal of the character would also "enter the mythology of right-wing America."[24]

By the end of World War II and the release of *Sands of Iwo Jima*, John Wayne's heroic persona was complete; image had become life and life had become image. Wills concludes that "Wayne's later war movies would succeed to the degree that they rode on the effect Sergeant Stryker had on audiences. The movie merged the legend of the Marines and the legend of John Wayne. From now on the man who evaded World War II service would be the symbolic man who *won* World War II."[25]

As John Wayne's patriotic metamorphosis was occurring, an actual veteran of Iwo Jima, unable to cope with what he considered his unworthy heroic status and the marines capitalizing on his celebrity for recruiting and fund-raising propaganda, and certainly suffering from what is now recognized as post-traumatic stress disorder, alcoholic Ira Hayes drowned in his own vomit at age thirty-two. Also a veteran of Iwo Jima, Alvin M. Josephy Jr. returned safe and sound to his family and a decade later would become one of the most important non-Indian voices of the twentieth century.

During the years of the Great Depression and World War II, America needed a hero who could adapt to the rapidly evolving technological and mythological power of motion pictures. Like Buffalo Bill before him, John Wayne was a creature born in the entertainment arts. Both men artistically erased the lines between truth and fantasy, but Cody's heroic status was much more deeply rooted in reality than Wayne's. Although skillfully embellished, Buffalo Bill's skyrocket to international heroic status seventy years prior to John Wayne was based on actual events. Conversely, Wayne's heroic experience was absolutely synthetic. Both heroes were an accurate reflection of major military events of their times; Cody's "duel" with Yellow Hair was a mythological coda to America's most traumatic single military event of the nineteenth century, Little Big Horn, whereas the Battle of Iwo Jima heralded nothing less than the imminent conclusion of World War II. John Wayne's rise to heroic status was ultimately more significant than Cody's, however, because it proved that western civilization's Hollywood dream factory was now capable of creating technological illusions so persuasive that people could live in them.

Chapter Thirteen
When Johnny Comes Marching Home

*It is hard to follow one great vision in this world of darkness and of
many changing shadows. Among those shadows men get lost.*[1]

—Black Elk

Physicist J. Robert Oppenheimer fell in love with northern New
Mexico for many of the same reasons as Mabel Dodge Luhan.
Oppenheimer had frequently visited the Land of Enchantment
since the 1930s, even purchasing a cabin in the Jemez Mountains
near Santa Fe. While Mabel Dodge Luhan envisioned in Taos a
colony of artists, authors, social scientists, political activists, and
reformers acting as midwives attending a rebirth of western civilization based on American Indian culture, Oppenheimer visualized
something entirely different only seventy miles southwest in Los
Alamos. There he hoped to create a utopian scientific colony where
physicists could gather together to share theories and conduct
experiments. Oppenheimer's dream was realized when he was able
to convince Washington to base its top-secret Manhattan Project
in Los Alamos.

A longtime resident of Taos, Frank Waters would by the 1950s
become recognized as a leading authority on the indigenous cultures of the Southwest, Mexico, and Central America. In the
1940s, however, Waters was still an emerging writer who supported
himself by occasionally working at Oppenheimer's scientific colony
in Los Alamos during its beginnings, and the paradox of the prox-
imity of such dissimilar visions did not escape his piercing insight.
Waters observed in *Masked Gods*, "Perhaps in no other comparable
area on earth are condensed so many contradictions, or manifested
so clearly the opposite polarities of all life. The oldest forms of life
discovered in this hemisphere, the newest agent of mass death. The
oldest cities in North America and the newest. The Sun Temple

of Mesa Verde and the nuclear fission laboratories of the Pajarito Plateau. The Indian drum and the atom smasher."[2]

Waters further advances this polarized synchronicity in *Masked Gods* with a description of a summer picnic in the mountains outside of Taos with Mabel; D. H. Lawrence's wife, Frieda; British painter Dorothy Brett; Mabel's husband, Tony; and some Pueblo Indian friends. Once their steaks were properly sizzling over an open fire, the group placed blankets on the ground and continued their ongoing conversation. Accustomed to his wife's loquaciousness, Tony began to tap on a drum, inspiring one of the young Indian men to sing an eagle song. Soon thereafter, an eagle appeared soaring on thermals in the clear, blue New Mexico sky: "When suddenly the eagle screeches and shoots out of sight like an arrow. Just as a tremor shakes the mountains." Waters continues, "The peaks seemed jarred out of their sockets. The brown plain below ripples like a blanket. The whole earth and we upon it, the moaning trees, the weeping stream, the crying stones, shudder with a nameless fear, a black foreboding. It is over instantly. An hallucination. Nothing has happened. Yet something has. It is July 16, 1945. The first atomic bomb has been detonated on the desolate White Sands to the south. It is the end of thick twenty-five-cent T-Bone steaks. It is the end of our picnics. It is the end of an era. The Four Corners, America, the whole world has been set on the threshold of the Atomic Age."[3]

The bombing of Hiroshima twenty-two days later marked the world's entry into the age of nuclear warfare. A second bomb dropped on Nagasaki on August 9, 1945, ended World War II and, according to President Harry S. Truman and his advisors, prevented the deaths of the estimated one million US soldiers whose lives would have been required to successfully invade the island of Japan. The shocking visual image of mushroom clouds also emphatically announced to the world that the United States was now the most powerful military nation on the planet.

Experiencing the very instant of the first atomic detonation and, less than a month later, witnessing the horrific destruction of two Japanese cities, Mabel Dodge Luhan certainly must have believed that her early twentieth-century prophecy of western civilization's chaotic sprint to self-annihilation was rapidly coming true. As Waters poetically implies, in 1945 Mabel was also sixty-six years old and experiencing the end of multiple eras and relationships in her life. Only six months prior to Hiroshima and Nagasaki, Mabel's former friend John Collier had resigned as commissioner of Indian affairs. Mabel and Tony had held high expectations for Collier's reform movements in Indian Country, but the trio quarreled soon after FDR appointed Collier as commissioner of Indian affairs in 1933. The trouble began when they differed over irrigation rights on property Mabel controlled, but their quarrel escalated into a serious power struggle two years later when Collier consolidated the administration of all the southwestern Pueblos into the single United Pueblo Agency and appointed a female superintendent named Sophie Aberle to head the office. Chagrined, Mabel began writing increasingly antagonistic letters to Collier, complaining of Aberle's mismanagement of the twenty-two tribes under her jurisdiction. The feud erupted in 1936 when—claiming sovereign tribal rights—Taos Pueblo leaders arrested members of the Native American Church for using peyote as a sacrament in their religious ceremonies. Mabel and Tony supported the actions of the Taos Pueblo leadership; Collier, however, had only recently fought—and won—monumental battles in Congress to return religious ceremony rights to all tribes. Thus the behavior of the Taos Pueblo leaders and, consequently that of Mabel and Tony, flew in the face of Collier's very difficult struggles with right-wing opponents and his efforts to promote revolutionary policies of religious tolerance for *all* American Indians.[4]

Collier's difficult feud with his mentor, as already discussed, was only one of many passionate struggles he would be forced to enter into during his controversial twelve-year term as commissioner of Indian affairs. His bold attempts to revolutionize the United States' destructive American Indian policies frequently found him under attack from all sides. Throughout the New Deal period he not only had to defend himself and the Indian Reorganization Act against congressional opponents, but he also had to fend off attacks from dissident Indian groups as well. The most outspoken of these Indian protest groups was the American Indian Federation (AIF), led by Joseph Bruner. The AIF relentlessly attacked Collier and his policies as being communistic and anti-Christian, while a mixed-blood attorney from Oregon named Elwood A. Towner toured throughout the West slandering Collier as a "Jew-loving Pink Red." (Towner even went so far as to accuse President Roosevelt of being a Jew whose real name was Rosenfelt.) Anti-Roosevelt Senators Burton K. Wheeler and Elmer Thomas of course welcomed the inflammatory involvement of Bruner, Towner, and the AIF because it created the illusion of legitimacy by allowing assimilated Indians to testify at congressional hearings and provided them with yet another weapon to attack the Indian Reorganization Act and embarrass President Roosevelt.[5]

In 1944 conservatives launched their final attempt to repeal the Indian Reorganization Act during Collier's administration and Roosevelt's fourth, and certainly last, term. The Senate Committee on Indian Affairs was strongly opposed to Roosevelt, the New Deal, and Collier and issued a very critical report of the IRA and its operations that concluded by recommending that the IRA be repealed.

Collier's March 1945 resignation from the commissionership was prompted by his belief that he had become the lightning rod for the controversy surrounding the concept of Indian self-government, and the notion itself had become secondary in the complaints of both Indians and congressmen because the focus was all on him. Understanding this, Collier decided instead to fall on his own sword, and he resigned.[6]

The anti–New Deal contingency in Congress wasted little time in launching an assault on Collier's reform programs after his resignation. Once again Indians were attacked with bureaucratic policies, and authors Vine Deloria Jr. and David Wilkins lay responsibility squarely at the feet of President Harry Truman and the passage of the Indian Delegation Act in 1946: "One of the most pernicious transfers of authority within the executive branch," Deloria and Wilkins write, "was the Indian Delegation Act which authorized the secretary of the interior to delegate some of his power to the commissioner of Indian Affairs and for the commissioner to do likewise until power to make decisions was reduced to a much lower level." The immediate negative impact of the Indian Delegation Act was that every decision the bureau made was reviewed by someone higher up the bureaucratic chain of command. The result, of course, was massive bureaucratic logjams concerning important decisions that immediately affected Indian lives and property. Perhaps worse, blame for the confusion could be attributed to so many different offices and personnel that no one could be held accountable.[7]

It was inevitable that Collier's efforts to reform the United States' relationship with American Indians would attract accusations of socialism as conservatives hurled such blanket indictments at everyone and everything associated with Roosevelt and the New Deal. Jew-and Red-baiting had proliferated throughout America since the early days of union organizers in the late nineteenth century, but the innovative legislation and work programs Roosevelt created to counter the social and economic impact of the Great Depression profoundly threatened right-wing Americans and launched an anti–New Deal movement that continues to this day. Immediately upon entering the Nuclear Age and a so-called cold war with the Soviet Union after Roosevelt's death in April 1945 and the official end of World War II the following September, the political tactics of the far right-wing were about to be elevated to a veritable art form. America was about to have an inquisition.

The House Un-American Activities Committee, or HUAC, actually began its work in the early 1930s, but only blossomed when US Representative Martin Dies appeared on the national political stage in the late 1930s. A Texas Democrat, Dies was originally a supporter of Roosevelt's policies, but when his Dies Committee began investigating "Communists, crackpots, and Socialists" in 1937 the legislator quickly joined the vanguard of anti–New Deal sentiment rising from within Roosevelt's own political party. Because of his committee's congressional immunity, Dies did not need to provide evidence to substantiate any wild charges, and the fiery inquisitor was thus able to label individuals as "un-American"

or brand certain organizations as a Communist front without fear
of reprisal. Dies openly accused labor unions of shielding communists and even attacked members of President Roosevelt's administration, calling them Communist sympathizers.[8]

By 1939 the Dies Committee had morphed into the House Un-
American Activities Committee. Still chaired by Dies, the committee traveled to Hollywood to investigate Communist activity in
the film colony. Humphrey Bogart, Frederick March, James Cagney, and other top film stars were summoned and appeared before
the Dies Committee to state they were not "secret" Communists.[9]

World War II took focus away from Hollywood Red-baiting, but union organizing continued in Hollywood, and picket
lines and strikes increased as the Great Depression era continued
into the first years of the global conflict. Dies and his colleagues
returned to their investigations as soon as the war ended, however, and the circumstances that gave birth to the cold war era
first appeared on the horizon. In 1947 Hollywood conservatives,
most likely directed from behind the scenes by William Randolph
Hearst, formed the Motion Picture Alliance for the Preservation
of American Ideals. Rumors circulated that Martin Dies intended
to resign his congressional position and become chairman of the
organization, but Hearst minion Sam Wood was eventually elected
chairman. Wood evidently passed Hearst's strict fidelity test and
had directed two films starring Hearst's mistress, Marion Davies.
Having also directed the Marx Brothers classic films *A Night at
the Opera* and *A Day at the Races*, as well as *Madame X*, Wood was
a talented director who believed Hollywood's secret Communists
had manipulated voting to prevent his winning repeated Academy
Award nominations. By the end of the 1930s Wood had acquired a
profound hatred of President Roosevelt and his New Deal policies
and also was especially embittered over the loss of the Academy
Award for 1939's *Goodbye Mr. Chips*. Under Wood's leadership
Walt Disney, Robert Taylor, Gary Cooper, Adolphe Menjou,
Charles Coburn, Ward Bond, Hedda Hopper, and other Hollywood conservatives pledged themselves "to fight, with every means
at our organized command, any effort of any group or individual,

to divert the loyalty of the screen from the free America that gave it birth."[10]

After years of prolonged fighting and stalled negotiations during the late 1930s, Hollywood labor unions finally organized a strike that shut down Walt Disney's studios in 1941, enraging America's beloved animator. After the vicious donnybrook, Disney, much like Sam Wood, believed Communists had infiltrated Hollywood and were intent on using the power of movie mythology to bring down the country. There is, of course, substantial proof that many Communists and Communist sympathizers had indeed been working in the film industry since its inception. Richard Hofstadter suggests in *Anti-Intellectualism in American Life*, however, that the actual purpose of the "Great Inquisition" of the late 1940s and 1950s had little to do with exposing and catching spies or preventing espionage, but was instead the skillful manipulation of ambitious conservative Washington politicians and was intended primarily to vent "resentments and frustrations." Republicans had been out of power for nearly two decades; Congress nevertheless came under their control with the elections of 1946. After Roosevelt's three terms, Republicans believed Harry Truman was vulnerable and the climate was finally perfect to seize the presidency and regain power. Moreover, many extreme right-wing Americans blamed Jews for creating the war and wanted to punish them for it. It is thus no coincidence that one of the first targets of their campaign would be the nation's powerful myth-making machinery, as the very title of film historian Neal Gabler's definitive 1989 biography of the world's film capital, *An Empire of Their Own: How the Jews Invented Hollywood*, makes clear. Samuel Goldwyn biographer A. Scott Berg believes the Dies committee had a very specific goal in mind indeed and quotes Rabbi Edgar Magnin—known as the "rabbi to the stars"—to prove his point: "'Anti-communism' may have been on their tongues," Magnin said, "but anti-Semitism was on many of their minds. To give impetus to their cause, they turned not to that industry most riddled with Communists, but to one almost exclusively dominated by Jews, one guaranteed to draw headlines."[11]

Soon after the formation of the vigilante Motion Picture Alliance for the Preservation of American Ideals, William Randolph Hearst published an editorial in his *Los Angeles Examiner* in which he accused a "subversive minority" in the film industry of "contriving" to "glorify Russia" and "invent virtues for it that never existed."[12]

Backed by the power of Hearst's nationally syndicated newspaper chain, the Motion Picture Alliance confidently escalated the battle, writing a letter to North Carolina senator Robert Reynolds in which the group accused Hollywood of harboring Communists. The fact that the beloved Walt Disney—an animator of children's fairytales—had to fight off a Communist attempt to destroy his studios was offered as proof that the Motion Picture Alliance needed congressional attention on the matter. Prior to Disney's entering the squabble there had been a lot of in-fighting between the left and right in Hollywood, but with the Reynolds letter the alliance was no longer simply attacking Communists; they were assailing their own industry.[13]

By the autumn of 1947 more than forty members of the Hollywood community were subpoenaed to Washington to answer questions from the House Un-American Activities Committee, now chaired by New Jersey representative J. Parnell Thomas, whose most enthusiastic associate was freshman representative Richard M. Nixon of California.[14] Of the numbers receiving subpoenas, half were actually members of the Motion Picture Alliance. The majority of the remaining nineteen were well-known "leftist" Jews. The committee also summoned a few industry giants like Samuel Goldwyn, whose presence would serve to underscore the seriousness of the proceedings.[15]

Hollywood's liberal community promptly rose to defend its own, and directors William Wyler and John Huston joined with Ira Gershwin, Judy Garland, Edward G. Robinson and others to form the Committee for the First Amendment. The group circulated a petition that quickly gathered the signatures of more than five hundred Hollywood stars. Huston, Gershwin, Danny Kaye, Katharine Hepburn, Humphrey Bogart, Lauren Bacall, and several others were selected to deliver the petition to the committee in Washington.

The committee divided those subpoenaed into two categories: those who cooperated with the committee were deemed "friendly" witnesses, while nineteen were deemed "un-friendly" witnesses. Ten of the nineteen witnesses designated as unfriendly were called to Washington to testify in 1947 and became famous as the Hollywood Ten. The committee demanded that witnesses answer only one question: "Are you now or have you ever been a member of the Communist Party of the United States?" As the friendly witnesses had been allowed to read introductory statements, the first unfriendly witness called, screenwriter John Howard Lawson, who was indeed a Communist, assumed he would be granted the same privilege. When Lawson attempted to read his statement, however, Chairman Thomas insisted he simply answer the one and only question. Lawson ignored Chairman Thomas and continued to attempt to read his statement until Thomas interrupted him by loudly pounding his gavel. Lawson continued to read his statement over Thomas's repeated gavel pounding, and the conflict escalated until Thomas called for Capitol police and had Lawson removed from the premises.[16]

The members of the Hollywood Ten watched Lawson's physical removal from the chambers in shock, while the financial core of the motion picture industry in Manhattan immediately went into full-scale meltdown. All of the Hollywood studio executives were headquartered in New York and they called a hasty summit conference at the Waldorf-Astoria on November 24, 1947. The group unanimously voted to fire anyone who defied a congressional committee by refusing to define their history, if any, with the Communist party. The infamous era of the blacklist had officially begun.[17]

Several members of the Infamous Ten were sentenced to jail, while others such as Dalton Trumbo and Ring Lardner were essentially banned from working under the studio system in Hollywood. The conservative inquisition quickly spread throughout the film industry and from there to every other aspect of entertainment, ultimately affecting a generation of film, radio, and television programming and an entire generation of Americans. Even worse, the conservative inquisition drew a deep cynical line in the sand, dividing the nation's solidarity that had been won with blood, suffering, and sacrifice during World War II, and thus begat much of the bipartisan obstinacy that continues to have a profoundly disruptive effect on American mythological identity and unity today. Truman's advisor Clark Clifford later admitted that even though he abhorred the idea, the president had surrendered to pressures exerted by FBI director J. Edgar Hoover and US Attorney General Tom Clark and had deliberately exaggerated the threat of communism in order to counter the Republican attacks and win the election in 1948. Attorney General Clark gave Senator Joseph McCarthy the government list of subversive organizations, security clearances, and other classified information that allowed the witch hunts to rapidly intensify.[18]

This paranoid, jingoistic environment was of course the perfect setting for the blossoming of the WASP American heroic role model as envisioned a half-century earlier by Theodore Roosevelt, Frederic Remington, Owen Wister, and Zane Grey. "In that whole period, from 1939 to 1947," Garry Wills asserts, "[John] Wayne's name does not appear on any side of the struggle. A noncombatant during the physical shooting of World War II, he was also a noncombatant in the ideological war. The same careerism that kept him from wearing a uniform kept him from taking a stand. His role, finally, was to emerge after the battle and shoot the wounded. He became 'outspoken' only after the Waldorf conference had ended the war and the industry was voicing *only* one side."[19]

While John Wayne's starring role in the first skirmishes of the cold war was "shooting the wounded" survivors of the ideological witch hunts, it is equally important to examine John "Pappy" Ford's activities before and after World War II: An avid sailor, in 1934 Ford purchased a 110-foot ketch called the *Faith*, completely refit her at considerable expense, and rechristened her *Araner* after his mother's homeland. Soon after refitting *Araner*, Ford also enlisted in the Naval Reserve, receiving the commission of lieutenant commander. Anticipating a Japanese attack in the years leading up to World War II, Ford virtually converted his beloved *Araner* into a proxy US Navy vessel and, reporting his findings to his superior officers, began reconnaissance expeditions along the Pacific coast from the tip of Baja to Northern California. By 1939 Ford had also begun recruiting the best and brightest cinematic technicians in Hollywood and training them to film the war against the Japanese that he believed was inevitable. Even though Ford's wife, Mary, described her husband's warriors as "over-age and rich, people who never would have been drafted," Ford started putting his Hollywood navy of film experts through military drills. But the director was not simply playing warrior on his days off; in fact Ford and his wife and daughter were in Alexandria, Virginia, having dinner at the home of a high-ranking navy admiral and his wife on December 7, 1941, when the admiral was one of the first men informed of the Japanese attack on Pearl Harbor. Ford's elite film corps was immediately inducted into the US Navy with the rather pretentious title, the Eleventh Naval District Motion Picture and Still Photographic Group.

Ford's superior officer throughout the war was William "Wild Bill" Donovan. Donovan had won a Congressional Medal of Honor during World War I and was the head of a prestigious Wall Street law firm before being drawn back into military service after the Japanese attack. Donovan had become the head of intelligence of the Office of Strategic Services (OSS), and he accepted Ford's unit of specialists as the photographic element of his own elite organization. Ford consequently took orders *only* from Donovan, and Donovan took orders only from President Roosevelt. Donovan and Ford became very close, as "Wild Bill" was responsible for securing clearance and special military treatment for Ford to film such things as the aftermath of Pearl Harbor and the Battle of Midway. Ford nevertheless was only one of an ensemble of "bluebloods and brilliant amateurs" Donovan hand picked for his elite wartime unit. Veterans of Donovan's OSS included noted diplomat David Bruce; professional baseball catcher Moe Berg; Harvard University president James B. Conant; future Secretary of Health, Education, and Welfare and Common Cause founder John W. Gardner; future Supreme Court justice and ambassador to the United Nations Arthur Goldberg; noted historian Arthur Schlesinger Jr.;

and future heads of the Central Intelligence Agency (CIA) Allen Dulles (and of future Watergate infamy) Richard Helms.[20]

Donovan skillfully trained this eccentrically talented collection into a tightly bonded team of specialists with power, influence, and privilege. After the war, members of Donovan's team returned to Wall Street investment firms, Ivy League faculties, law partnerships, or, in Ford's case, Hollywood. Donovan had instilled in each and every one of his disciples the belief that they returned to civilian life with special knowledge and patriotic purpose.

Donovan's team had been the military's most informed special unit during the war, and as America emerged from the conflict as the mightiest military power on earth, the OSS alumni were destined for an even greater role. Donovan and his elite corps believed America would continue to need their proficiency in mythological manipulation if the nation was to remain dominant in peacetime. Moreover, if the United States hoped to restore order in the war's immediate aftermath while also coping with the powerful and surreptitious Russian and Chinese Communists, the OSS leaders and veterans considered themselves the only group capable of the task of allocating resources with "theoretical and technological expertise."[21]

Donovan's OSS alumni and their protégés thus had a profound impact on the United States' post–World War II direction. The nation's top universities and humanitarian and philanthropic organizations were eager to have graduates of Donovan's elite OSS team become part of, or return to, their boards and faculties. The OSS would soon transform itself into the Central Intelligence Agency (CIA), and shortly thereafter recruiters began to appear on college campuses, enlisting the best and brightest young Americans into the organization.

As the OSS morphed into the CIA after World War II, America promptly returned to her mythological history on the western frontier for inspiration and future direction. Even as Donovan's team of specialists were becoming ensconced in the upper echelons of American power and subterfuge after the war, historian and *Harper's* magazine columnist Bernard DeVoto's *Across the Wide Missouri* (1947) and *The Course of Empire* (1952) appeared on the best-seller lists. The success of *Across the Wide Missouri* as well as the post–World War II mission assigned to the OSS veterans probably contributed to John Ford's decision to direct four allegorical Westerns between 1948 and 1950, starting with *Fort Apache* in 1948, in which Ford attempted a personal interpretation of the Battle of Little Big Horn; *She Wore a Yellow Ribbon* in 1949, in which Ford evoked President Washington in the persona of a cavalry officer; and *Rio Grande* in 1949, in which Ford—to his credit—depicted a team of greedy politicians and Indian agents taking advantage of their position to abuse Indians for profit. *Fort Apache, She Wore a Yellow Ribbon*, and *Rio Grande* all starred John Wayne, and all three were written by James Warner Bellah, a xenophobic screenwriter who Garry Wills succinctly describes as a "rebellious authoritarian." In the last film in his quartet of late 1940s Westerns, *The Wagonmaster*, Ford returned to his roots in the silent era, and the result is often referred to by film historians as the most "poetic" Western ever made.[22]

Like John Ford, Alvin M. Josephy Jr. had served as a propaganda specialist during World War II. After the Battle of Iwo Jima, however, Josephy was ordered by General Robert L. Denig and Marine Corps brass to return to Washington. As discussed earlier, William Randolph Hearst launched a series of editorial attacks on the Marine Corps immediately after Iwo Jima in which he questioned whether the loss of so many lives and so much money had been worth the effort to win such a tiny island.[23] The Marine Corps responded by bringing some of its best correspondents home to articulate their side of the battle. The corps wanted Josephy and other war correspondents to go on bond-selling tours and do some speaking and writing to explain to the American public why it had been so important to destroy the Japanese air force's ability to launch bombing missions from the island and to make the additional point that under US control the island also provided the US Air Force the capability to launch attacks on Japan from closer bases. This, of course, also helped explain why the island was so well fortified and defended in the first place, and why such an extravagant price had to be paid to win it.

Josephy quickly collaborated with four other marine war correspondents to write *The U.S. Marines on Iwo Jima*, in which the authors detailed the battle and its causes. Josephy had, of course, been thrilled to reunite with his wife, Roz, and to meet his toddler daughter, Diane, for the first time upon his return from the Pacific. But the family barely had time to become acquainted because the Marine Corps war-bonds tour began even as *The U.S. Marines on Iwo Jima* was being hurried to publication by Dial Press. While on the tour Josephy met Ira Hayes and personally witnessed the pressure and phoniness the Pima Indian found so difficult that it eventually killed him. The tragic situation aroused great empathy in Josephy that is apparent in his poignant description of Ira Hayes: "his conscience and feeling of self-worth were assaulted by a demoralizing combination of lionization as a hero, which he felt he was not, since all he had done was help to raise a flag; patronization as an Indian curio from dignitaries and crowds who knew nothing about Indians and who had no interest in their problems; and discrimination and prejudice from anti-Indian racists who insulted him and hurt him even as they pretended to honor him."[24]

Of course much of Alvin Josephy's description of Ira Hayes in 1945 would have fit *any* Indian in twentieth-century America, as his circumstance truly reflected the lives of most Indians. After being "pacified" in the nineteenth century, Indians had been used by men like John Wanamaker to metaphorically "raise the flag" when they were reincorporated into the American identity and "pseudo-lionized" as "first Americans" at the turn of the century as the nation fell under the enchanting spell of "post-modern romantic primitivism." Ironically granted citizenship in the 1920s, Indians had been offered confusing hopes of the government actually recognizing their legal sovereignty during the Collier attempts at reformation during the Roosevelt New Deal, only to have those dreams cruelly snatched away just as they were beginning to materialize. Unfortunately, Ira Hayes was no exception in Indian Country; *every* American Indian understood what it felt like to be treated as a curio by a dominant culture that considered them invisible sub-humans one moment and national monuments the next. The resignation of Commissioner of Indian Affairs John Collier in March 1945 marked the end of the reform period of the New Deal; President Roosevelt's death a month later dealt the final blow. As the United States entered the infamous era of witch hunts and blacklisting, and the conservative element sought to regain complete and total control of the American mythmaking machinery, the rise of the right-wing element in national politics after World War II brought new destructive concepts to the halls of Congress concerning American Indians. The Republican success with General Dwight D. Eisenhower's election to the Oval Office in 1952 suddenly posed the most dangerous threat yet to Indian nations in the twentieth century.

Initially discussed during the final years of the Truman administration, the policy of termination was conceived to dissolve all legal treaties, eliminate reservations, and assimilate Indians into mainstream non-Indian social and economic systems. Initiated by the Eisenhower administration, termination was a essentially an updated version of the Dawes Act and its concept of allotments, as the policy proposed to divide tribal assets on a per capita basis and then demand that the individual tribal members forfeit all their federal rights to services and supervision. As in the actual physical enactment of the Dawes Act, the Bureau of Indian Affairs determined the tribes to be terminated and supervised the selling of tribal lands.[25]

As the Eisenhower administration sought ways to terminate the government's relationship with American Indians, John Ford and John Wayne began creating films with super-patriotic subtexts written by a jingoistic "rebellious authoritarian." Thus in the 1950s, any Indians still in the movie business assumed their corresponding role as "noble savages" to be subdued and pacified while simultaneously defining metaphorical WASP American heroes on the silver screen. Now, however, Indians were increasingly allegorical stand-ins for the real enemies, Red Communists. Conquering these new red savages required furthering the mythology of the march of western civilization beyond the twentieth century.

Chapter Fourteen
The Oracle of the Hearth

Behold, the living center of a nation I shall give you, and with it many you shall save.[1]

—Black Elk

Soon after returning to America from the Pacific war zone, Alvin Josephy received a letter from the head of MGM's story department, Kenneth MacKenna. The letter informed Josephy that MGM wanted to negotiate an option to develop a film based on a story he had written for *Look* magazine in which he described the death of a career marine during the invasion of Guam. MacKenna also offered Josephy a job as a staff writer at MGM as soon as he was discharged from the marines. Josephy suspected his cousin was behind the job offer and upon investigation learned that Eddie Knopf had a copy of his recording of the invasion of Guam and had indeed been playing it for studio executives. While flattered, Josephy had no desire to return to Louis B. Mayer's dictatorship of MGM Studios. Upon more careful consideration of his situation, however, Josephy decided that perhaps the climate had changed in Hollywood and that he might actually be able to create a screenplay of real substance in the new environment. After convincing his wife to relocate to Los Angeles, Josephy used his discharge pay to buy a used Packard and, with his cousin Billy Josephy as a traveling companion, headed west.

Like many veterans returning from World War II, Alvin Josephy soon discovered the transition back into civilian life was not as smooth as he had hoped. After arriving in Los Angeles he spent nearly three months sleeping on his cousin's couch and searching for housing for his wife and child to join him on the West Coast. Frustrated with his struggle to find a suitable, affordable place, Josephy turned to the Santa Monica chapter of the American Veterans

Committee (AVC), where he discovered many other young veterans who were also having difficulty finding housing. The group's frustration soon blossomed into a full-blown protest movement involving the AVC and Los Angeles chapters of the Veterans of Foreign Wars (VFW). As the movement gathered momentum with demonstrations in public parks in downtown Los Angeles, Josephy discovered the source of the housing problem was that the lifting of wartime controls had created instant chaos throughout the entire American housing industry. Ruthless builders and contractors were purchasing goods on the black market to quickly construct homes and apartments, and these unscrupulous men had no interest in building low-cost housing that returning veterans could actually afford.

Josephy was politically inclined by nature, and his involvement with the AVC housing movement turned him into an activist. He became the chairman of the Santa Monica AVC chapter, as well as a member of the executive committee of the AVC's Los Angeles Area Council, and eventually rose to become vice chairman of the AVC in California. Along the way, he continued his careers in literature and journalism, writing both a syndicated column called "We Won a War But...," and a novel he could not get published.

After months of searching, Josephy finally found a decent house that he could afford and sent for his wife and daughter to join him in Santa Monica. Again, like many returning veterans, Josephy sadly discovered that the strain of the separation during the war years had been too great and his marriage had broken under the pressure; after only a few weeks in Los Angeles, Josephy's wife asked him for a divorce. The couple parted amicably, and Josephy's estranged wife and their young daughter returned to New York.

Josephy's woes were only beginning. Like everyone else in the country, he was being drawn into the "cold war" and the ramifications of the McCarthy inquisitions reverberating throughout America's entertainment culture. Starting in the East, arguments about Communists and Socialists quickly permeated the AVC from coast to coast, leading to broad dissention and, ultimately, the resignation of most of the organization's membership, including Josephy. The fact that McCarthyism could destroy a veterans' organization with dissension perhaps best demonstrates the extent to which the inquisition had spread throughout mainstream American fabric at the eve of the 1950s.

By 1950, assisted by the GI Bill, many veterans began tackling problems for themselves, finding friendship and assistance in the VFW, the Disabled American Veterans, and the American Legion. The GI Bill was in full operation at this point as well, and this helped veterans afford their own homes *and* get a college education. The former servicemen and women of World War II were now well on their way to creating what Josephy defined as "the largest and most stable middle class that any nation had ever known."[2]

In the late 1940s thousands of Americans from all classes had discovered Bernard DeVoto's *The Year of Decision* 1846 (published in 1943) and *Across the Wide Missouri*, both books harbingers of change in the fundamental form of the Western movie. DeVoto's books also had a major impact on Alvin Josephy's life. As evidenced by the title of his autobiography *A Walk Toward Oregon: A Memoir*, Josephy had been enchanted with Oregon since childhood; indeed, Josephy's life had essentially been a series of failed attempts to migrate to the Pacific Northwest. Around the time DeVoto's books began to top the best-sellers chart Josephy's ex-wife returned his belongings as part of their divorce settlement. Among the materials was a very important package that contained Josephy's lifelong collection of nineteenth-century diaries, journals, and personal accounts of America's western migration to Oregon. The confusing readjustment from mortal combat to postwar America, the devastating emotional experience of divorce, separation, and loneliness, and DeVoto's books all combined with the return of his collection of western expansion memorabilia to rekindle Josephy's love affair with the American West into a white-hot flame. And yet the impact of Bernard DeVoto was only beginning to affect Josephy.

Born in Utah in 1897 to a Catholic father and Mormon mother, Bernard Augustine DeVoto, like Josephy, postponed his education at Harvard University to serve in the military. Unlike Josephy, however, after service in World War I, Lieutenant DeVoto returned to his studies at Harvard in 1920, eventually becoming a professor at the university. By the late 1920s DeVoto was the curator and editor of Mark Twain's papers, and the publication of *Mark Twain's America* in 1932 secured his role as the preeminent Twain authority and earned him wide-ranging acceptance as the scholar who brought the great writer's work to the forefront of American literature. In 1935 DeVoto began writing a regular column for *Harper's* magazine titled "The Easy Chair," and he would contribute essays to the magazine for the rest of his life. For the brief period from 1936 to 1938, DeVoto left New England and lived in Manhattan, where he was the editor of the *Saturday Review of Literature*. He returned to Harvard soon after resigning that editorial position and by the mid-1940s began publishing his books chronicling expansion in the American West.[3]

Robert Athearn explains that in the late 1920s, Bernard DeVoto had become the first to challenge the "purity of the pioneers" legend. Moreover, DeVoto's historical depiction of the pioneers was starkly different from the Theodore Roosevelt template and more closely related Francis Parkman's eyewitness description of actual emigrants around St. Joseph and Independence in 1846 in *The Oregon Trail*. Athearn notes that various mining rushes, such as the one of 1849, were anomalies because they were unnatural circumstances that tended to attract unstable characters, but that DeVoto believed the Great Migration of the nineteenth century was made up of three classes. The first group was composed of "restless, unadjusted people such as old soldiers, rivermen, and roustabouts." The second group was composed of people running from the law. The third—and this is DeVoto's largest class—were those who were forced by competition to leave.[4]

Concerned that DeVoto's generalizations of the pioneers were too broad to be considered accurate in all cases, Athearn further delineates the discrepancies between the three classes of DeVoto's pilgrims and the pioneers as described by Theodore Roosevelt and Frederick Jackson Turner. Doing this, Athearn perfectly underscores the how the mythological "American" that Roosevelt and Turner projected on the nation has worked so well for so long while simultaneously revealing an archetype audiences have seen dramatically presented in hundreds of B Westerns and war movies—one that also supports the anti-intellectual underbelly of America's self-image: "One aspect of the American legend is that, in general, these western settlers were highly individualistic people, given to personal solutions of problems, and that it was their ability to innovate that got them out of trouble where ordinary mortals failed." Athearn continues, "Over the years this notion was appropriated by the general public and was applied to Americans at large. One sees the myth running all through our military history, where the Yank, falling back upon his *native inventive qualities*, invariably confounds the enemy, who has to rely blindly on 'book training' and cannot think for himself."[5] (Italics added)

It is equally important to add to Athearn's insight here that since the days of Daniel Boone and Natty Bumppo, "falling back upon his native inventive qualities" in American folklore, literature, and films has often meant romantically recalling one's time spent living among American Indians and learning pragmatic survival skills and wisdoms of guerilla warfare.

The broad spectrum of the collective personality of legendary American pioneers suggested by historians DeVoto and Athearn blended perfectly into the paranoid political climate of the cold war/McCarthy era and suggested challenging new approaches to historical fiction and screenplays with multiple levels of social, psychological, and mythological interpretation. DeVoto's more realistic depictions of American pioneer stock surely combined with a more wizened American returning from the trauma and uncertainties of war and contributed to the beginning of the era of the anti-hero in American films. Yet before exploring anti-heroes and new villains, Hollywood first sought to explore its newfound, postwar moral awareness.

As Alvin Josephy suspected, returning World War II veterans were determined to create socially conscious art, literature, and movies, and this brought a new era to the Western. Far less socially controversial than addressing the potentially explosive African American question in 1950, it is not surprising that Hollywood first chose American Indians to explore its new social awareness. Since

the turn of the twentieth-century Indians had been rendered impotent as military foes, and, set apart from society on reservations for
sixty years, they were a "safe" and romantic concern, as well as one
intrinsically wedded into the subconscious of our national character.

In 1950 one of America's most beloved silver screen personalities, James "Jimmy" Stewart, starred in *Broken Arrow*, a film often
recognized by historians as the first of the modern era to present
a sympathetic portrait of American Indian humanity and culture.
Broken Arrow centers on a love story between Stewart's character
and a lovely Indian woman portrayed by non-Indian Debra Paget,
and much was made of the interracial romance depicted in the film
in 1950. Yet Philip Deloria's research reveals that as early as 1906
Indian actors and producers James Young Deer and Lillian St. Cyr
(a.k.a. "Princess Red Wing") were making films depicting interracial "white man/Indian woman" relationships and even more
controversial "Indian man/white woman" narratives in their films.[6]
Nevertheless, in 1950 the producers of *Broken Arrow* were brave to
bring the miscegenation taboo forward and present it in new technologies and scenic locations to mainstream American audiences.
Moreover, the historical context of *Broken Arrow* was also a fairly
accurate depiction of the Apache resistance of the period and the
power struggle between Cochise and Geronimo for leadership, and
the film certainly stimulated deeper exploration of their history by
the general American public.[7]

While Hollywood mythmakers were romantically examining social and historical issues in Technicolor fiction, however,
the reality of America by 1952 was that Julius and Ethel Rosen-
berg were executed for selling military secrets to the Soviets, and
the American public had been whipped into a state of frenzy over
Communist subversion. HUAC had successfully blacklisted most
of the New Deal reformers; right-wing conservatives launched
bureaucratic suppression in earnest, throwing radical activists out
of public housing and civil service and barring suspected organizations from public meeting rooms and from receiving critical tax
exemptions, and the Eisenhower Administration was attempting
the termination of the Indian nations. The political climate in 1952

is perhaps best reflected in the film often rated as the best Western of all time, *High Noon*, starring Gary Cooper. Shot in symbolic black and white, *High Noon* brilliantly encapsulated the anxiety of McCarthyism and the issue of the individual within the community's collective moral responsibility when facing mortal danger. Still, the film remains true to the heroic cowboy archetype as the tale of an aging but principled man bravely standing alone against a gang of killers bent on his destruction. Even Cooper's Quaker fiancée, played by Grace Kelly (metaphorically standing in for conscientious objectors), is drawn into the violence and is forced to kill when everyone else in his community cowardly "forsakes" him.[8]

The next year, *Shane* was released and, in those above-mentioned "best Western" lists it consistently appears in the top five.[9] Starring Alan Ladd and featuring Wyoming's majestic Grand Tetons as a backdrop, Shane is the quintessential Western film that represents *both* of Dale Wasserman's plot devices as it begins with the lone, single-name drifter with a mysterious gunfighter past arriving in a western farming community on the fringes of civilization. The gunfighter Shane is also on a noble quest to transform himself and settle into a new life as a hired hand for a loving family in a homestead community that is struggling to survive the lethal combination of the elements and a ruthless family of cattle barons who hate farmers and the change they represent. Within this complex context, director George Stevens managed to artistically weave a delicate 1950s romantic tension among Shane, his settler/partner, and the settler's wife, all the while developing a tender relationship with the couple's son, Joey, that is one of the most enduring in film history.

Although *High Noon* was shot on a Hollywood soundstage in black and white, both *Broken Arrow* and *Shane* were produced by the studios as vehicles to advertise and promote the technological advances of Technicolor and Cinemascope and the majestic locations of Arizona and Wyoming being "seen as never before." In fact most genres of motion pictures in the 1950s featured exotic locations and were filmed using the latest spectacular technological innovations in order to compete with a new medium that had been entering American homes in increasingly large numbers since its appearance in the mid-forties. Barely surviving the divisiveness of the McCarthy witchhunts, Hollywood faced perhaps an even greater challenge in the early 1950s.

Marshall McLuhan's famous aphorism "the medium is the message" arrived with the cultural impact of television. Linking the new medium to its nineteenth-century progenitors, media theorist Neil Postman best sums up what happened when it arrived: "Television gave the epistemological biases of the telegraph and photograph their most potent expression, raising the interplay of image and instancy to an exquisite and dangerous perfection. And it brought it into the home."[10]

Whereas the Industrial Revolution brought the Transcontinental Railroad into the pristine heart of nineteenth-century North America, the Electronic Revolution born in the same era came full circle with the arrival of television and aimed it directly at the mythological hearth of twentieth-century America. By 1946 six thousand television sets had been manufactured in America. These six thousand sets received broadcasts from only thirty stations around the country. From its "snowy," test-pattern beginning, arguments concerning the cultural impact of this new electronic gadget ran the gambit from academia to Congress, from church pews to barber shops, and finally to America's sacred dining room table. By 1951 more than 5 million television sets had been manufactured and more than 10 million households owned one, receiving broadcasting from more than one hundred stations. By the mid-1960s Americans owned 200 million televisions, more than half the total of the sets in the world.[11]

With decades of corporate and artistic experience in electronic image manipulation, studio executives in Hollywood were the first to recognize and understand the cultural impact of the oracle of the hearth. Hollywood's problems, however, were much deeper than fighting off the commercial onslaught of television. Immediately following the HUAC trials, the US Justice Department claimed that the chains of theaters the Hollywood studios owned constituted a monopoly. The courts consequently ruled in 1950 that the studios could no longer own and operate the theaters that exhibited their films. Film attendance plunged from a record high of 90 million tickets a week in 1949 to half that in 1952. More than six thousand movie theaters closed their doors in 1952. Threatened to their very core by the double-whammy of the commercial impact of television and the stunning loss of customers the new medium and the government ruling created, studios promptly capitalized on television's limitation to black-and-white broadcasting and began experimenting with advances in film technology such as Technicolor, Cinemascope, and 3-D. The studios also dramatically expanded budgets for directors and crews to travel to romantic and exotic locations to use these new technologies to enhance the visual impact that could not be captured on a small, snowy, black-and-white screen in someone's home. Of course, Hollywood had filmed the American West since the days of William S. Hart. But the West had never been seen on 35mm film in glorious Technicolor and Cinemascope before. Even though masters of the silent film era such as John Ford and James Cruze had composed visual poetry in silent black-and-white movies, these technological innovations in the late 1940s and early 1950s truly elevated the landscape of the American West to an even more significant visual mythological position. Simultaneously, Walt Disney and Mutual of Omaha created the genre of the "nature show" on television and began to introduce American families to the national parks and the animals that inhabited them. Through television and movies, millions of Americans were now visually experiencing and discovering their country for the first time.

Technological advances in filmmaking combined with fierce competition between the movie studios and upstart television networks and resulted in what many film historians consider the golden age of the Western. Through the diplomacy of accounting, movie studios and television networks found common ground and the studios began producing weekly series for the television networks. As is usually the case, commercial considerations also spawned this explosion of Westerns on television throughout the 1950s and early 1960s; the studios had decades of stock black-and-white footage of scenic locations from old Westerns, and the black-and-white broadcasts of early television provided them opportunity to shoot feature scenes cheaply on a sound stage in Hollywood with scenic stock footage later edited into the film to add visual realism. Consequently, from October 1958 through April 1959 seven of the ten most-watched weekly television series were Westerns. Both the motion picture and television industries nourished the Western during this period because it was a proven formula for storytelling and, most importantly, one that would be readily accepted into mainstream America's living rooms via the newfangled gadget of television. This development required more scripts than ever before, and the result was that the period developed the classic storytelling form of the Western to its highest standard with such films as *Broken Arrow, High Noon*, and *Shane* and television programs such as *Gunsmoke, Bonanza, Wagon Train, Wanted: Dead or Alive, Rawhide, Death Valley Days*, and *Have Gun, Will Travel*. During this era Warner Bros. Studios created an amazing stable of handsome, virile leading men and future Western stars such as James Garner, Hugh O'Brian, Jack Kelly, Clint Walker, Chuck Connors, James Drury, Steve McQueen, Clint Eastwood, and others with such series as *Cheyenne, Maverick, The Virginian, Bat Masterson, Wyatt Earp, The Rifleman*, and *Johnny Yuma*. Meanwhile, as the youngsters lined up for a shot at becoming the new Western hero in films, conservatives John Wayne and Walt Disney plunged headlong into American folklore, including Davy Crockett and the Alamo, to promote their conservative brand of patriotism during the uncertain times. When Tennessee's Senator Estes Kefauver wore a coonskin cap in the halls of Congress promoting Disney's and Wayne's forays into folklore with "the king of the Wild Frontier," the Davy Crockett craze officially swept the country, with everyone singing the Disney tune that most baby-boomer Americans can still remember; indeed, most baby-boomer Americans recall vivid details of all those heroic cowboy adventures from the 1950s and 1960s that entered our consciousness via the one-eyed oracle of the hearth.

Bernard DeVoto's books and the public's post–World War II appetite for Westerns also inspired Alvin Josephy to create an outline for a novel based on a band of veterans of the War of 1812 who head west. MGM optioned it, but as with the previous scripts Josephy developed and wrote for MGM, the studio failed to produce it as a film. While Josephy was courting Betty Peet, the woman who would become his second wife, and also working on his script about the War of 1812 vets, the anti-Communist hysteria in Hollywood reached fever pitch. One day two veteran MGM writers with whom Josephy had been friendly invited him into their offices and, "looking conspiratorial," locked the door. The pair invited Josephy to join them and other studio people, including Mr. Mayer himself, in "getting rid of all the Reds at MGM." The two screenwriters began naming the people they intended to expose as Communists, and Josephy recognized the people the pair targeted as peaceable New Deal Democrats like himself and "by no stretch of the imagination a threat or danger to the country." Faced with choosing high or low ground, Josephy—a courageous patriot who had gone to war to defend his country—knew there was only one choice. He laughed and declined their invitation to join their efforts. Josephy wrote in his autobiography that to his way of thinking, "right-wing extremists were no different or better than left-wing extremists."[12]

Even though one of Josephy's screenplays, *The Captive City*, directed by future renowned director Robert Wise and starring John Forsythe in one of his first feature roles, was eventually produced, by 1951 Josephy's days as a Hollywood screenwriter were numbered. One night at a dinner party he met a tall fellow in his early fifties named Dana Tasker. As they chatted Josephy learned Tasker had been an English teacher at Amherst before becoming the managing editor in charge of *Time* magazine's illustrations and weekly covers. Tasker asked Josephy to call him the next time he was in New York because he had a project he wanted him to consider.

Prior to 1951 *Time* had been printed totally in black and white, and publisher Henry Luce had directed Tasker to begin to include occasional color covers. Luce also instructed Tasker to create a new section for the magazine featuring a spread of exceptional black-and-white topical photography called "News in Pictures." Luce specifically ordered Tasker not to use photographers from the *Life* magazine staff or to use writers from the *Time* staff, but instead to find someone outside of the organization who could write and also recognize a good photograph when he saw one. Tasker offered the job to Alvin Josephy.

Eighteen months after Josephy arrived at *Time*, Dana Tasker left to join *Look* magazine, but Josephy had been promoted to associate editor and remained on the magazine's staff for the entire decade of the 1950s, supervising more than two hundred color projects covering a wide range of subjects. Occasionally, if a subject interested Luce, the publisher would watch over Josephy's shoulder, and in 1955 Luce assigned him a project that aimed Josephy's path toward the Northwest yet again: an eight-page spread of color photographs of the Lewis and Clark trail to observe the 150th anniversary of the expedition. After an extensive study of Bernard DeVoto's 1953 publication of *The Journals of Lewis and Clark* and traveling to the locations the explorers described themselves, Josephy wrote a shooting script and assigned *Time* staff photographer Bradley Smith the job of traveling the entire route of the voyage of discovery, shooting photographs of the rivers, mountain ranges, and wilderness areas Lewis and Clark had documented. Josephy printed excerpts from the explorers' journals beneath Bradley Smith's striking images, describing scenes that were essentially unchanged since 1805. Although the concept would become a cliché a generation later, Josephy clearly was the pioneer of this unprecedented approach of linking visual images of "sacred" American historical landscapes with the words of the first Euro Americans to see them.

As Josephy was being drawn deeper into the lives, history, and culture of indigenous America, however, his boss, Henry Luce, was openly hostile toward Indians. Luce's opinions were so strong that there was an unspoken blanket prohibition concerning any story about American Indians in *Time* magazine. "Luce simply did not like them," Josephy explains, "and called them 'phonies' because they refused to give up their reservations and live like everyone else, making their own way and paying taxes and stopping all their complaints and demands on the government."[13] Josephy continues to explain that Luce believed that "world history was a matter of someone conquering somebody else and that western Europeans had conquered Indians."[14]

Luce's survival-of-the-fittest perspective was, of course, misinterpreted Darwinism inherited from the Gilded Age, but it was a view shared by many powerful Americans in the 1950s. In fact, the opinion Luce and other conservative American powerbrokers of his era had about Indians contributed greatly to the termination policies initiated during the Eisenhower administration. Termination policies fraudulently proposed to "free" Indians by ending the reservation system and eliminating all government relations with the tribes. This tactic conveniently ignored the findings of the Meriam Report thirty years earlier, as well as a generation of reform initiated by John Collier. But even more significantly than these important precedents, termination policies did not take into account responsibilities for education, health, and other services *legally* guaranteed by treaties between Indian nations and the United States government. Still, the movement continued to gather steam until, one by one, several small tribes were terminated in spite of their resistance. Non-Indian entrepreneurs promptly swept in yet again, and Indians lost even more precious land and resources to bankers, ranchers, timber companies, and real estate speculators. Indian people who had known little life outside of the reservation were suddenly "relocated" to cities throughout the American West, cast out on their own unprepared to venture into the non-Indian's urban landscape.

Despite of the prejudice of his employer, Alvin Josephy had glimpsed his future. Next, he attempted to create a feature pictorial spread for *Time* on American Indian art that was promptly squelched by Luce. In spite of his resistance, Luce still had an ironic role to play in taking Alvin Josephy deeper into Indian Country.

Luce assigned Josephy a color project on Utah. Josephy was about to fly from Los Angeles to Salt Lake City to begin research when word arrived that Luce's plane had been forced to land in Boise, Idaho. During Luce's wait in Boise a local newspaperman took him on a tour that impressed the publisher greatly. Luce was so impressed, in fact, that he ordered Josephy to forget Utah and turn his attention to Idaho instead.

When Josephy flew to Idaho he immediately understood why Luce preferred that state to Utah. Even though he was smitten with the rugged landscape, Josephy was most attracted to the pragmatically creative, independent-minded people of Idaho. While touring the state with his guide from the Idaho Chamber of Commerce, Paul Nash, the entourage stopped at an airport near the Nez Perce Indian Reservation. There Josephy happened to meet a young Nez Perce Indian named Bill Stevens, and as they chatted Stevens voiced some of the tribe's problems and complaints. As Josephy was about to depart, Stevens said, "You know, the way things are going these days, if we had half a chance, you'd see the damndest Indian uprising that ever took place."[15]

When Josephy told his traveling companions what Stevens had said, a few of them laughed, but one man, Harry Hughes, who had served as a colonel on General Douglas MacArthur's staff during the war, asked Josephy if he knew anything about Nez Perce history. When Josephy replied that he knew next to nothing about the tribe, Hughes informed him that the Nez Perce had fought a war against the United States and had whipped the American army on several occasions.[16]

In that very moment Alvin Josephy's path synchronized with his lifelong dream of getting himself to Oregon. With his curiosity piqued about the Nez Perce, he was entering the phase of his journey that would finally take him there. It would also take him deep into twentieth-century Indian Territory for the rest of his life.

"Despite my interest in Ira Hayes," he writes, "I still knew very little about most American Indian tribes and nothing at all about the Nez Perces, whose name did not ring dramatically for me like those of the Sioux, Arapaho, Comanche, or any of the other great historic tribes and whose best-known leader, Chief Joseph, sounded like an uninteresting, mission-controlled Indian."[17]

Yet the deeper Josephy probed into Nez Perce history the more he realized that his ignorance of American Indian history was a reflection of many more Americans who, like himself, knew little if anything about Indian people. Soon he started to think that the story of the Nez Perce was a grand, epic theme just waiting for someone to tell it. Eventually, Josephy was able to visit the Nez Perce Reservation and meet with tribal people. He found the Nez

Perce to be very friendly and flattered that someone from *Time* would express such interest in them. Impressed with the knowledge of their tribe Josephy had gathered from books, his contacts introduced him to tribal chairman Angus Wilson and tribal historian Allen Slickpoo, as well as members of the tribe's governing executive committee and three surviving members of the 1877 conflict known as Chief Joseph's War.

Once he was introduced to the infrastructure of Nez Perce society, Josephy immediately recognized the deep chasm evangelicals and government policies had created within the tribe; one side was decidedly "Christian," while the other was considered "heathen." Most of the Christian contingency considered Chief Joseph to be a troublemaker who had brought bad times to the tribe; indeed, Joseph's relatives had been driven to a remote section of the reservation where they lived in virtual exile.

Josephy soon discovered the situation at the Nez Perce Reservation was not uncommon throughout reservation America. Leaders who resisted the invasion of their homeland were generally considered troublemakers by reservation survivors who had converted to Christianity and were seeking assimilation on whatever terms the white man granted or deemed appropriate. In spite of his writing commitments, Josephy was inspired by this paradoxical situation to begin research for a book based on this shameful treatment inflicted upon defeated Indian leaders by their own people *and* the dominant non-Indian culture.

While continuing work on the book about the history of the Nez Perce, Josephy also began writing essays and articles for *American Heritage* magazine. Josephy's association with *American Heritage* and with renowned historians such as Bruce Catton and David McCullough (who also wrote regularly for the magazine) established his reputation as one of America's leading authorities on contemporary American Indians, and in 1959 Josephy departed *Time* to become the editor of *American Heritage*. Yet even as Josephy assumed the editorial chair at *American Heritage* he continued work on the book based on the subject of American Indian "patriot chiefs" such as Chief Joseph, Red Cloud, Sitting Bull, and Geronimo, who were later shamed by confused generations of their own people. It was fundamentally important that American Indians now had a supporter as the editor of the nation's most prestigious historical magazine, but with the publication of *The Patriot Chiefs: A Chronicle of American Indian Resistance* in 1961, Alvin Josephy arrived as the most important non-Indian activist in America since the reformer John Collier. Chairman of the Crow tribe Edison Real Bird put Alvin Josephy's impact in Indian Country in perfect context with a single remark: "This is the first time that anyone has ever referred to us Indians as patriots."[18]

Alvin Josephy's rise as a nationally recognized historian coincided with the golden age of the Western and the arrival of television as the technological oracle of the American hearth. In earlier times people sat around a glowing fire to listen to stories, but by the mid-1950s the nation's s mythological narrative continued as American families gathered around the glow of a television set to watch the Western as "historical fiction." By 1955 the world also recognized John Ford and John Wayne as the most important team in Hollywood producing Westerns as feature films. In 1956 the pair released a Western that would herald a return to the oldest form of entertainment in the New World.

Chapter Fifteen

The Searchers and the Captivity Narrative

Maybe if I could see the great world of the Wasichu, I could under-
stand how to bring the sacred hoop together and make the tree to
bloom again at the center of it.[1]

—Black Elk

The popularity of the captivity narrative during the mid-nineteenth century convinced poor Fanny Kelly that if the Sioux warriors who kidnapped her on the Wyoming prairie got their hands on her infant daughter, they would murder the child. The thought so terrified Fanny that when the war party swept her away on horseback she purposely dropped her precious baby on the prairie with only a hysterical mother's hopeless prayer for her survival. Several days after her capture Fanny recognized a familiar piece of fabric and a blonde scalp on a warrior's belt and assumed that in spite of her desperate act to save her baby, little Mary was dead.[2]

In 1864 Fanny Kelly obviously had good reason to fear for her baby's life. Instances of violence, brutality, torture, and rape in the Trans-Missouri were indeed the unjustified acts of individual sadistic Indians, but also extreme tactics used by war parties to make non-Indian invaders think twice about remaining in Indian Country. Most acts of violence and kidnapping were, however, retaliatory; indeed, *non-Indian* savagery had initiated the Indian wars only a few weeks before Fanny Kelly was taken captive when Colonel J. M. Chivington's militia attacked and murdered a large band of Cheyenne Indians under a flag of truce at Sand Creek and sexually mutilated the corpses of the men, women, and children after the massacre. Shocked, the warrior-oriented Plains Indians had never experienced such savagery at the hands of any of their traditional enemies, nor had they ever inflicted such depravity on any of their foes; Lakota, Cheyenne, and Arapaho warriors vowed that Chivington's barbaric behavior would be returned tenfold.

It becomes important to emphasize the obvious here: when Indians raided white homesteads they promptly killed the males and, for reasons of horseback expediency, infants. Women and young children were taken as captives. Women were frequently sexually abused. The captivity narrative thus succinctly encapsulates the miscegenation fears inherent in the Indian/non-Indian relationship while also vividly expressing the viciousness and sadism both cultures proved themselves capable of committing against one another. To relate a tale of captivity, however, it is germane that one *survives*. Moreover, after surviving, one must return to one's original culture to relate the captivity to family and community. From the non-Indian perspective, the return of women and children—sometimes half-breed children—thus becomes the relevant theme of the captivity narrative.[3] On the other hand, when either civilians or the US military raided Indian villages, not only were Indian men, women, infants, and children summarily murdered, but often their horse herds were slaughtered and all their possessions burned. So, in the majority of cases, Indians raiding homesteaders and taking captives was almost always specifically retaliatory; non-Indian women and children were taken to replace Indian women and children killed by whites. Yet it is equally true that having lost so many members of their families to wanton, racially motivated violence by barbarians like Chivington, many of the Indian men who put on war paint during that era were indeed insane with rage, obsessed with vengeance, and highly skilled in many perverse forms of torture. In short, the captivity narrative is nothing less than a dark passageway both into and perhaps *out of* the core dilemma of the Indian/non-Indian relationship.

Frederick Turner (not to be confused with late-nineteenth-century historian Frederick Jackson Turner) informs us that soon after Euro Americans arrived in North America, the captivity narrative became the *first* form of popular entertainment in the "New World." Moreover, Turner reveals that the captivity narrative developed the capacity to alter its fundamental details in order to conform to the nuance of the settlers' changing situation with western expansion, all the while maintaining the resonance of its traditional, recognizable theme in order to evoke a primal emotional response. Turner explains that until the end of the eighteenth century the captivity narrative served to "demonstrate that the hand of God could penetrate the darkest and most tangled interiors to rescue His children from the hands of the savages." Turner explains that returning from captivity represented for women and children the "opportunity" to praise God for having granted them the "privilege" of such righteous suffering. Surviving Indian captivity thereby represented God's infinite mercy and offered captives who returned to civilized society the possibility of becoming better Christians for having endured the temptation and barbarism of the savage. Entering into the nebulous territory of "incomplete Euro American consciousness" that D. H. Lawrence explored in his *Studies in Classic American Literature*, Turner thus describes the captivity narrative as "the perfect scripture for a civilization's sense of its encounter with the wilderness, for in the redemption that rounded it out there was victory. The happy ending was a triumph, an ultimate mastering of everything the wilderness and its natives could throw up in the way of opposition and temptation." Turner concludes that the non-Indian interpretation of the captivity narrative is classic Christian "fear of becoming possessed by the wild peoples...but also, more profoundly, by the wilderness and its spirits. We might say it is *the fear of going native*."[4] (Italics added)

Turner's razor-sharp insight further reveals that fear of losing oneself in the wilderness—or, becoming indigenous—is deeply embedded in Judo-Greek-Christian mythology. Even as Moses descended Mount Sinai with the tablets containing the Ten Commandments in his arms, the children of Israel, having "lost themselves in the wilderness," had become possessed by paganism, forging a golden calf as a surrogate deity to idolize and celebrate in dance, thus already breaking the first and second commandments. History makes it unquestionably clear that the fear of "going native" that Turner suggests haunted pioneers was indeed quite real. Very little is recorded of the non-Indians who fled their own society and culture to live with Indians; they simply vanished. Nevertheless, in instances not shaded in testimony by pejorative Christian opinion, many women and children taken by Indians and later returned to civilization preferred instead to remain with their Indian families. Perhaps this is because most men considered captive women "tarnished" from sexual abuse by the Indians and refused to take their wives back when they were rescued and women knew they would be ostracized upon returning to white culture.

By desiring to remain with Indian captives, however, aside from shunning the opportunity to praise God for her salvation, white woman triggered the deepest sexual fears of the non-Indian male with the inherent implication that she *preferred* the sexual favors of her captor. Thus Turner's analysis of the captivity narrative as frontier scripture must be considered strictly as brilliant insight into the *non-Indian*, Christian interpretation of the phenomenon, whereas the legendary Cynthia Ann Parker's actual history as a returned non-Indian captive better presents the *Indian* perspective of the captivity narrative; rather than praising God when Texas Rangers finally rescued Cynthia Ann twenty-four years after she was taken by the Comanche war party in 1836, she had to be locked in a room to prevent her repeated attempts to escape and return to her Comanche husband and their three children. Modern psychology suggests that Parker's story and other captivity stories like hers corroborate the so-called Stockholm syndrome, in which a kidnap victim bonds with the kidnapper. In the first days and weeks of her captivity, Cynthia Ann's bonding with her Comanche captors was probably related to this strange psychological quirk specifically associated with kidnapping. But over time she *became* a Comanche, as evidenced by the fact that when she learned one of her Indian sons and her daughter were dead, she began to willfully grieve herself to death in 1870.[5]

The Cynthia Ann Parker story thus represents the polar opposite of the penitence scriptures Frederick Turner describes as the early settler's Christian rationalizations when reintroducing "violated" captives to civilization; Parker's explicit message was that there was *mystical deliverance in becoming indigenous*. Like so many other legends deeply embedded within the epic story of the

American experience suggesting Anglo-Saxon spiritual deliverance in Indian Country, the legend of Cynthia Ann Parker is as profound a part of Texas frontier history as the Alamo; schools, buildings, and streets throughout Texas are named after Parker. Hers is simply one of the most famous examples of the captivity narrative in American history.[6]

Because of the embedded notions of forbidden sexual adventures and mystical liberation in the wilderness inherent in the Cynthia Ann Parker legend and other captivity narratives, it is allegorically ironic that in 1956—at the peak of a right-wing political movement to illegally terminate *all* government relations with American Indians—the two foremost heroes and cinematic mythmakers of that very same politically conservative movement, John Ford and John Wayne, selected the captivity narrative as the subject for a film. Moreover, the film was financed by WASP aristocrat and heir to the Minnesota Mining and Manufacturing (3M) fortune, Cornelius Vanderbilt "Sonny" (sometimes, "Joc") Whitney, who was also a cofounder, and chairman of the board (1928–1941) of Pan-American Airlines. Because of Ford's history with the OSS and the creation of William "Wild Bill" Donovan's embryonic CIA, and because of Wayne's eventual rise to heroic right-wing ideological iconic status, it is practically inconceivable, yet of profound mythological significance, that they would select the captivity narrative as a subject to depict on the silver screen. Yet it is even more astonishing that they would approach the subject from a perspective of creative insight and awareness that openly addressed the taboo subject of miscegenation as the very source of the ancient conflict between Indians and non-Indians. *The Searchers* was thus a milestone indication that the Western had come full circle as a mythological genre; equally significant, the film's subject matter connected the preeminent icons of Western movie mythmaking of twentieth-century America—Ford and Wayne—to the nation's oldest entertainment form.

In his 1979 essay "The Searchers" in *New York* magazine, Stuart Byron suggests that these multiple historical dichotomies are perhaps what give strength to the film: "If the movie achieves epic status, it is because it says—with passionate and agonizing conviction—that the beliefs of both the conservatives and the liberals are equally valid: The American Dream is real and true, and yet America is a country founded on violence."[7]

Most of the violence that founded modern America occurred between Indians and non-Indians. Thus *The Searchers* also brought the captivity narrative forward into modern iconography as the source of profound inherent interracial implications and, accomplishing this, simultaneously implanted the subliminal afterthought into the awareness of post–World War II Indian and non-Indians that we have always been—and shall always remain—mythically bonded; ultimately, the captivity narrative reveals itself to Indians and non-Indians as a hierophantic mirror; one sees in the other what one loves –and hates- about oneself. The fact that *The Searchers* would become widely recognized as the pinnacle of both John Wayne's and John Ford's careers is merely an insinuation of poetic justice; the continually evolving international success and critical acclaim of *The Searchers*, however, suggests the film will last throughout the ages, and this aspect of longevity implies the film has historical and spiritual consequence. Hindus, of course, call this Karma.[8]

The Searchers was released in 1956 when the Western movie had reached its peak in popularity as an American art form. There is unmistakable historical symmetry to the fact that Wayne's career peaked in 1956. Wayne made thirty-eight more films before his death in 1979, but none of his roles came close to his brilliant performance as Ethan Edwards. Of course he finally won an Academy Award for his role in 1969 as Rooster Cogburn in *True Grit*. But most suspected that acknowledgment was sentimental and awarded for his vast body of work and contributions to cinema rather than for the actual role itself. After *The Searchers* he began to play "John Wayne" both on and off screen. He never again expressed the emotional range or surpassed the screen presence of Ethan Edwards.[9]

Garry Wills suggests that John Wayne and John Ford had already begun to reverse roles before filming *The Searchers*. Wills breaks down the Wayne/Ford career collaboration in detail and suggests that "over half Ford's best work was done with Wayne... put another way: the *only* great films Ford made from 1950 on were his four made with Wayne [*Rio Grande*, 1950; *The Quiet Man*, 1952; *The Searchers*, 1956; and *The Man Who Shot Liberty Valance*, 1962]. Wayne was carrying Ford by the end, where Ford had carried Wayne early on."[10]

Wills believes Ford "found in Wayne the combination of a man unconquerable yet paradoxically vulnerable...the range of characters has been unjustly dismissed, out of contempt for the Western or Wayne or both. But the real Ahab of our films is not the pallid Gregory Peck of John Huston's *Moby Dick*. It is, as rock critic Greil Marcus noted, Wayne's Ethan Edwards. In *The Searchers*, says Marcus, 'Wayne changes from a man with whom we are comfortable into a walking Judgment Day ready to destroy the world to save it from itself.'"[11]

The literary perspective of Alan Le May's novel *The Searchers* created the situation for this unusual metaphysical synchronization to occur within Ford's film adaptation. The surface plot of Le May's novel centered on the captivity narrative and is generally considered to be inspired by the Cynthia Ann Parker story.[12] Nevertheless, the subtext of Le May's novel focused on the bitter racism dividing the two cultures, and his story's resolution suggested pathways toward healing the divisiveness. The script John Ford and Frank Nugent adapted for *The Searchers* remained remarkably faithful to the Le May novel, in which the author cleverly reversed the traditional form of the captivity narrative and, rather than sensationally exposing the captive's suffering at the hands of "savages," presented instead the poignant emotional perspectives of the family of a kidnapped child. Of equal importance, Nugent and Ford chose to retain Le May's entire storyline, even keeping all the names of the characters from the novel—except one. The character of Amos Edwards was renamed Ethan, for fear it would be associated with Amos of *Amos 'n' Andy* radio fame.[13] Ford also added broad comic relief with the characters of Charlie McCorry (played by Ford's son-in-law, Ken Curtis) and Ward Bond's Reverend Samuel Clayton. The only other change from the novel to the screenplay was major because it focuses the miscegenation theme clearly and squarely at the heart of an otherwise heroically ambiguous film. In Le May's novel Martin Pawley is an eighteen-year-old *white* orphan who has been reared as part of the Edwards family. In Ford and Nugent's screen adaptation, Pawley becomes one-eighth Cherokee.

Ford and Wayne were indeed keenly aware that the Ethan Edwards character was an anti-hero and that the Martin Pawley character was the true moral compass of the story. Since *Red River,* however, both Wayne and Ford had witnessed the power of casting Wayne *against* heroic type while simultaneously remaining within his heroic Americana screen persona, and the pair knew they could create in Ethan a powerfully dramatic character. To accomplish this, the film's beginning scenes provide enormous amounts of visual information about the Edwards family, none more than Ethan. The audience meets him arriving on horseback at his brother's homestead with the weariness of a long ride through the desert etched into his sand-crusted, whisker-stubbled face. He is wearing a military cape and carrying a saber on his bedroll. Before we see the fury raging in him, however, we are first shown his tenderness. Without a word spoken, John Ford's skills as a director combined with Wayne's and Dorothy Jordan's acting talents to reveal that Ethan is in love with his brother Aaron's wife, Martha, and she is in love with him. We are also led nonverbally to believe that Ethan and Martha realize their affections must forever remain repressed, thus adding to the complexity of Ethan's character and his relationship to the family. When Ethan lovingly greets his little niece Debbie and sweeps her off the floor and into his arms to present her with a gold Mexican medallion, we get another glimpse of Ethan's gentleness and affection, yet his gift also reveals the darker side of his personality, as the medal is an indication that he has been a mercenary in the war in Mexico.

Soon after Ethan's arrival a posse of Texas Rangers appears under the leadership of his former Confederate comrade, Reverend Samuel Clayton. Reverend Clayton's Rangers are in pursuit of a herd of stolen cattle and are conscripting men to join their band.

To avoid leaving the Edwards family without men to protect them, Ethan and Martin Pawley agree to go with the group to retrieve the stolen cows. During the swearing-in ceremonies, the audience gets another glimpse into the complexity of Ethan's personality as he and Clayton promptly reengage in a long-running feud over matters of principles. Ethan agrees to join Clayton's posse in pursuit of cattle thieves, but when he refuses to take the Texas Rangers' oath we learn that he is an unreconstructed Confederate and probably sideways with the law as well. Consequently, in the first ten minutes of *The Searchers*, we are introduced to the most complex personality John Wayne would ever portray on film. In Ethan Edwards, Wayne creates a character both ruthless and righteous; indeed, Edwards is a bigot who believes a man can honor only one oath in a lifetime and therefore continues to fight a war for a losing cause. We also learn that Ethan Edwards is a loner, in love with his brother's wife, and possibly wanted by the law.

When the rustling proves to be a ruse by Comanche to lure the men away from the Edwards homestead, *The Searchers* ignites. Even as the story quickens, Ford and Wayne methodically unleash Ethan's rage in stages, first by presenting him as coolheaded in the face of foreboding horror when he suggests that they can only cover the distance between them and the homestead by pacing their horses. When they arrive at the scene of the slaughter and Ethan sees what the Comanche have done to his brother and his beloved Martha, he slips instantly into insanity and begins his monomaniacal quest for revenge. Realizing the Comanche have taken his nieces, fourteen-year-old Lucy and ten-year-old Debbie Edwards captive, however, Ethan has no time for grieving. Even at the funeral for the murdered family, Ethan has little patience with the proceedings of society or Christianity. As Reverend Clayton begins his sermon, Edwards exclaims, "Put an end to it! There's no more time. Amen!"

Even though Ethan is opposed to Pawley accompanying him as he races to retrieve Lucy and Debbie before the Comanche can rape, torture, and murder them, expediency forces him to let the boy and Lucy's young sweetheart, Brad Jorgensen, tag along. Soon after the trio departs, however, Ethan discovers Lucy's tortured body and tries to conceal knowledge of her rape and murder from the two young men. One night as they are camped very close to the Comanche war party, Lucy's sweetheart Brad (played by Harry Carey Jr.) senses Ethan knows something and demands to know what he's learned about the girls. Ethan's rage explodes to the surface and reveals that his madness has reached an even deeper level. He orders the young man to never, *ever* ask him again to describe what the Comanche did to Lucy. Suddenly understanding Lucy has been tortured, raped, and murdered, the young man loses his head and runs out into the desert and into the Comanche camp. The shots of the nearby Comanche warriors in the distance let us know he is dead.

Ethan then coolly informs Pawley that because of Debbie's tender age, the leader of the Comanche will most likely spare her life and make her one of his wives when she matures. This knowledge reveals that Ethan's insanity has suddenly taken a bone-chilling turn; now he reckons he will kill Debbie because she will surely have *become* Comanche by the time he can locate her; the little girl he loves and searches for thus becomes the object of his searing hatred.

In spite of his madness, Ethan still has Martin Pawley to deal with. Making his bigotry clear, Ethan has repeatedly referred to Pawley as a "blankethead," a racial slur alluding to his Cherokee heritage. The fact that Ethan is already brimming with fury makes it seem unlikely that Ford felt he needed to create more dramatic tension between his character and the Martin Pawley character. It seems instead more probable that Ford had a much different motivation: in Alan Le May's original story, Pawley accompanies Edwards on the quest to find their captive relative, but Ford took a decisive step deeper into the territory of miscegenation in the adaptation when he and Nugent made the Pawley character a mixed-blood Cherokee in their screenplay. Doing this, Ford and Nugent created the embodiment of the very thing the Ethan Edwards character despises, shadowing him throughout the quest. As the plot and subplot of *The Searchers* converge, Martin Pawley becomes the audience's surrogate for watching Ethan's obsessiveness and hatred drive him to insanity. Throughout the quest, Edwards's frequent response, "That'll be the day," is an invariable reminder to Pawley that the man he is shadowing will not stop until the Comanche Debbie is dead.[14] When ultimately it is Pawley who rescues Debbie from the Comanche, however, the film delivers the powerful subliminal impact that the true hero of *The Searchers* is the progeny of *interracial* union.

Even though Martin Pawley, not Ethan Edwards, is the hero of the film, John Ford biographer Scott Eyman suggests the director created an equally compelling moment for John Wayne when the inevitable moment arrives in Edwards's quest for him to murder his niece, Debbie. During the battle with the Comanche in which Pawley frees Debbie from her captors, Ethan and Debbie's eyes lock and she immediately glimpses his insanity and runs for her life. Ethan pursues and eventually corners the girl, and the story arrives at its moment of truth as the madman stands over his niece, prepared to kill the "Indian." Then, Eyman notes, Edwards suddenly "reaches down and hoists her over his head in one swooping movement, a gesture that repeats his greeting to the child Debbie in the beginning of the film. He brings her down into a cradle position and quietly murmurs, 'Let's go home, Debbie.' The murderous Ethan finally feels the tidal pull of family; humanity is affirmed over hate and destruction. In touching Debbie, he feels the human being rather than the abstractions of his racism...As performed by John Wayne, it's one of the great moments in movies—*balletique*, emotionally true, murder alchemically transmuted into the protective embrace of love, Ford insisting that we can only realize our truest selves when we can accept all of the many forms of humanity we meet.[15]

The Searchers was a moderate box office success during its theatrical release in 1956, yet after a decade of social upheaval, a new generation of Hollywood filmmakers and historians in the mid-1960s began to recognize *The Searchers* as a classic. Even in 1956, however, critics realized John Wayne's genocidal characterization of Ethan Edwards had taken the traditional Western hero to the very threshold of evil. Wayne biographers Roberts and Olson note another important accomplishment of Wayne's performance in *The Searchers*: "Gene Autry and Roy Rogers, now relegated to Saturday-morning television, were still singing melodies atop Champion and Trigger; Duke had entered another realm."[16]

Over the last fifteen years of his life John Wayne would enter yet another realm. By the mid-1960s the civil rights and counterculture movements began to coalesce and effect serious transformation in American society. By the 1964 presidential election, John Wayne's defiantly conservative on- and off-screen persona had evolved into such popular heroic significance among reactionary groups such as the John Birch Society that Republican candidate Barry Goldwater was inspired to don a cowboy hat and exploit this image in an effort to entrench the threatened WASP power establishment deeper into resistance of the growing public outcries for social change. Goldwater also correctly assumed that by welcoming the extreme Right into the mainstream he would simultaneously be welcoming and incorporating wayward southern conservative "Dixiecrats" into the Republican Party. Even though Lyndon Johnson soundly defeated Goldwater, the Arizona Republican's insight quickly bore fruit, and disenchanted southern Democrats—shell-shocked over Johnson's liberal Great Society program and historic civil rights legislation—immediately began to shift their alliances to the GOP. Richard Nixon certainly benefited from this successful political tactic and transference of philosophical alliances when he defeated Hubert Humphrey in 1968, but no one profited more from this reactionary shift in political parties than John Wayne's fellow Iowan, movie star, two-term Republican president, and revered godfather of the so-called neoconservative, anti–New Deal Republicans of the twenty-first century: Ronald Reagan.

Even as Wayne's iconic image rose as the grassroots poster boy of super-patriotism throughout conservative America and set the stage for Reagan's Republican renaissance, his heroic status as a genuine Western film star began to rapidly diminish in the 1960s. Of course he was now an old man by any standard, but that made no difference; the heroic Western archetype of his era had already been replaced in the mid-1960s by Hollywood's ultra-violent, quintessential man-with-no-name anti-hero, Clint Eastwood. By the end of the 1960s, when John Wayne made *The Green Berets*, most Americans under the age of thirty-five recognized him simply as an elderly, out-of-touch, right-wing pitchman.

The gradual descent of John Wayne's cinematic star marked yet another dramatic transformation of the American heroic archetype. It is no coincidence that Wayne's heroic status dimmed as the old studio heads attempted to follow the astonishing success of the much beloved MGM-style musical *The Sound of Music* with scores of follow-up musicals like *Hello, Dolly!*, *Paint Your Wagon*, *Dr. Dolittle*, and *Sweet Charity* that were very expensive box office failures. When coupled with the deaths of many of the old studio heads, the result was that by the mid-1960s, most of the major studios were sold to corporate entities: Gulf and Western bought Adolph Zukor's Paramount Pictures, Warner Bros. was merged with Seven Arts Productions, and United Artists was bought by the Transamerica Corporation. The baby-boomer generation was also reflected in the men who now assumed control of the newly corporate-managed studios; by 1967 many of the new studio heads were under the age of forty. When the violent gangster film *Bonnie and Clyde* appeared in that same year, the outdated heroic role model, advances in film technology, the new corporate system run by younger executives, the new ratings code, and counterculture movement announced a new day in Hollywood mythmaking. By the time Peter Fonda and Dennis Hopper reinterpreted the iconic Western genre and the lonesome drifter archetype yet again in 1969 with *Easy Rider* and their hippie characters were murdered by ignorant rednecks at the film's end, the lines between Roosevelt's, Wister's, and Wayne's WASP cowboy and the counterculture anti-hero were drawn. When Sam Peckinpah's choreographed blood-ballet *The Wild Bunch* appeared in 1969, allegorically depicting the wild West's bloody imperialistic transition into the twentieth century, it was clear that the Western genre was transforming itself yet again to reflect the Vietnam War and the violent clash of culture, identity, and power taking place in America.

PART THREE

This, finally, is the punch line of our two hundred years on the Great Plains: we trap out the beaver, subtract the Mandan, infect the Blackfeet and Hidatsa and the Assiniboin, overdose the Arikara; call the land a desert and hurry across it to get to California and Oregon; suck up the buffalo, bones and all; kill off nations of elk and wolves and cranes and prairie chickens and prairie dogs; dig up the gold and rebury it in vaults someplace else; ruin the Sioux and Cheyenne and Arapaho and Crow and Kiowa and Comanche; kill Crazy Horse, kill Sitting Bull; harvest wave after wave of immigrants' dreams and send the wised-up dreamers on their way; plow the topsoil until it blows to the ocean; ship out the wheat; ship out the cattle; dig up the earth and burn it in power plants and send the power down the line; dismiss the small farmers, empty little towns; drill the oil and natural gas and pipe it away; dry up the rivers and the springs, deep drill for irrigation water as the aquifer retreats. And in return we condense unimaginable amounts of treasure into weapons buried beneath the land which so much treasure came from—weapons for which our best hope might be that we will someday take them apart and throw them away, and for which our next best hope certainly is that they remain humming away under the prairie, absorbing fear and maintenance, unused, forever.

—Ian Frazier, *The Great Plains*

Chapter Sixteen

Custer Died for Your Sins

"With this pipe," the grandfather said, "you shall walk upon the earth, and whatever sickens, there you shall make well."[1]

—Black Elk

When *The Patriot Chiefs: A Chronicle of American Indian Resistance* was published in 1961, Alvin Josephy was discouraged by his book's disappointing initial sales. Defending his difficulty marketing the book, Josephy's agent explained that the general public perceived Indians as a broken people, sequestered on reservations, and of interest only to anthropologists, western historians, and missionaries. Therefore, the agent concluded, books about Indians were a difficult niche market.

Unconvinced his agent's opinion was accurate, Josephy visited several leading Manhattan bookstores and sadly discovered the explanation to be generally correct; books about Indians were shelved in the back of the stores alongside books about natural history, dinosaurs, plants, birds, and animals rather than being placed alongside biographies and histories of Americans, Europeans, Asians, Africans, and other great world cultures. Puzzled, Josephy began asking bookstore managers for a justification of this marketing tactic and was informed that Indian books had "just always been placed there." The longer he pondered booksellers' indifference toward Indians, the more annoyed Josephy became with the realization that bookstore marketing tactics were simply a reflection of the pervasive thinking throughout the United States in 1961: Americans believed Indians to be a vanished people. "Thinking about it made me angry," Josephy wrote in his autobiography, "and I vowed that someday, some way, I would do something about this ignorant insult."[2]

Despite Josephy's conviction to raise American awareness about Indian culture in the twentieth century, sales for *The Patriot*

Chiefs continued to falter until, by the mid-1960s, the book had practically disappeared from the marketplace. Then at a conference Josephy was surprised by a University of Texas professor who approached him with the news that *The Patriot Chiefs* had become "enormously popular" on the Austin campus; Josephy's professor friend wanted to know how he had known to write an "antiestablishment book" back in 1961. Josephy immediately contacted his publisher and was surprised to learn that sales for the book were indeed skyrocketing, apparently stimulated because "people believed that I was part of the flowering counterculture movement and had written the book to protest the side of America that had got us engulfed in the Vietnam War."[3] Of course Josephy had written and published the book before the rise of the counterculture movement and its resistance to the war in Vietnam. Nevertheless, as counterculture awareness of American Indians expanded, sales of *The Patriot Chiefs* grew exponentially until Josephy's book had risen to classic status by the decade's end.

With sales of *The Patriot Chiefs* soaring in the mid-1960s, Josephy intensified his exploration of the past, present, and future American West from his new position as editor of *American Heritage* magazine. Meanwhile, he developed stronger bonds with members of the Nez Perce tribe and continued working on a book about their history. Josephy's uncle Alfred A. Knopf offered him a contract when he finally completed his massive manuscript about the Nez Perce. Josephy initially accepted Knopf's offer but later declined when marketing considerations forced the publisher to insist upon drastic cuts to the manuscript. Knopf amiably released his nephew from the contract, and the next day Josephy ran into the director of the Yale University Press, who immediately offered to publish the manuscript without editing down its intended scope. To Josephy's delight, *The Nez Perce Indians and the Opening of the Northwest* became a main selection of the History Book Club and won many awards. Alvin Josephy was suddenly *the* non-Indian author shaping the new standards by which Indian histories should be written. "Hidden in the book, however, was an ingredient that had not been easy to acquire," Josephy writes. "By the time of publication,

Betty and I over a period of ten years had become familiar with the many problems facing contemporary Indians. During that time, we had become more than historians of the American Indian. We had become actively engaged in Indian affairs and were now advocates for them."[4]

The Josephys had in fact become much more than advocates. Success now allowed them to divide their time between their home in Greenwich, Connecticut, and a small ranch in Wallowa County in Oregon. Soon after purchasing the ranch, the Josephys established a summer camp there for Indian children, and with the election of John F. Kennedy and a new administration in Washington, Alvin made use of his multiple connections in publishing and politics to intensify his campaign for Indian rights—particularly with the young president's secretary of the interior, Stewart Udall.

By the 1960s American Indians needed all the advocates they could get. The Eisenhower administration's termination policies had cruelly attacked the very heart of Indian unity: the core family group. This divisive policy brought even deeper hardship and misery to a people already subjugated by moral indifference and Byzantine government programs to backbreaking poverty and social abandonment. The forced removal of children from their families had profoundly wounded several generations of Indian people, but the termination of tribes sharply divided Indian families even further into those preferring to stay on the reservation and those departing the reservation to seek employment and new lives in such cities as San Francisco, Denver, Minneapolis, Chicago, Omaha, Phoenix, Albuquerque, Rapid City, Tulsa, Oklahoma City, and Dallas.

As mentioned earlier, after John Collier resigned as commissioner of Indian affairs and the Roosevelt era ended, conservative congressmen intensified their push to terminate all federal services with Indian tribes until the notion took root in the Truman administration and blossomed during the Eisenhower era. In part to counter this growing conservative movement, a group of American Indians focused on contemporary indigenous concerns—a Pan-Indian collection of almost one hundred politically oriented tribes—met in Denver in 1944, founded the National Congress of American Indians (NCAI), and immediately elected an Oglala Lakota woman, Helen Peterson, as the body's first executive director. Throughout the various political administrations after Collier's resignation, the NCAI was able to provide an effective political counterforce to defend Indian rights. In spite of the growing unity of the NCAI, however, the Bureau of Indian Affairs still used termination to threaten uncooperative tribal leaders.[5]

Throughout the 1950s, proponents of the termination movement accused traditional Indian rights advocates like Alvin Josephy of being anti-assimilation and preferring that Indians be kept on a reservation like "zoo animals." The arrival of John F. Kennedy's New Frontier in 1960 did not bring much change from the termination programs of previous administrations; indeed, it has been argued that matters worsened when the Democrats gained control of Congress in 1955. With the Eisenhower termination policies still in effect, the theory arose among Democrats that if the concerns of Indians were merged with those of corporate America it would serve to buffer the conservatives' efforts to terminate federal services to the tribes. So in August of that year Congress passed legislation that amended existing laws concerning the leasing of Indian lands and allowed nonagricultural surface lands to be leased for general purposes for a period of twenty-five years, with an option to renew the lease for another twenty-five-year term—essentially a fifty-year lease of tribal and individual lands. Conservative congressional members specifically attacked Section 3 of the 1955 legislation, which prohibited entering into any lease whose terms might delay or prevent termination of federal services and supervision. Of course, everyone realized this entire legal exercise was ultimately another bipartisan political/corporate legal circus ultimately intended to gain further access to Indian property. More significantly, the NCAI and other American Indian activists realized the Kennedy administration needed to ensure passage of its conservation bills and could not politically afford to alienate itself from influential members of the Senate Interior Committee. Several important Democratic members of that powerful congressional committee were strong supporters of termination. Among them, Secretary of the Interior Stewart Udall supported termination of the tribes, so it became vitally important that an American Indian advocate of Alvin Josephy Jr.'s integrity and knowledge had gained his confidence.[6]

As Josephy's prestige rose with the success of *The Patriot Chiefs* and *The Nez Perce Indians and the Opening of the Northwest* and his editorial position at *American Heritage*, he was soon asked to become a representative of the Episcopal Church on the Council on Indian Affairs, a prominent interfaith organization of lobbyists composed of such august institutions as the Daughters of the American Revolution, the General Federation of Women's Clubs, Oliver La Farge's Association on American Indian Affairs, and the one-hundred-year-old Indian Rights Association of Philadelphia. The NCAI and other Indian lobbying organizations joined with the Council on Indian Affairs to meet occasionally with Secretary of Interior Udall and various senators and congressmen in a conference room in the Department of Interior Building in Washington. There, they would openly discuss Indian policies and programs, hear from tribal representatives about the conditions of their various reservations, and air the many complaints coming from Indian Country.

Udall was from Arizona and was thus aware of many Indian problems from firsthand experience. He eventually came around to Josephy's thinking about the termination issue, but his hands were tied to the Kennedy administration's broader political agenda, and there was only so much he could do. Josephy writes in his autobiography that he and Udall had many conversations and eventually became close friends. Most significantly, over the course of these talks Udall and Josephy discovered that they agreed on several of the fundamental conditions that would continue to make "the 'Indian problem'—really 'the white man's problem'—impossible to solve until they were ended." Udall and Josephy acknowledged that non-Indians spoke for Indians; non-Indians created and implemented government policies and programs for Indians; non-Indians essentially governed every aspect of the twentieth-century Indian's life. They concluded that without the rights of self-determination and sovereignty, Indians remained like "colonial subjects, ruled by other people's thinking and by decisions that were made for them." Vitally important, Josephy and Udall realized ultimately that *they* were making these observations as non-Indians.[7]

This highly significant observation of the absolute subservience of American Indian life to non-Indian authority and Washington policy wags in the mid-twentieth century was soon made painfully apparent to Josephy at the funeral of his good friend Oliver La Farge, the famous anthropologist and Pulitzer Prize–winning author of *Laughing Boy*. A non-Indian, La Farge was the president of the Association on American Indian Affairs (AAIA) and had personally invited Josephy to join the board of that organization. The AAIA was composed of many philanthropists who shared La Farge's sympathies for the plight of American Indians and worked to improve their desperate circumstances. The organization also shared La Farge's fundamental belief that Indians had to be assimilated, and this attitude of superiority led the organization to patronize Indians and treat them like children who needed non-Indians to oversee and handle their affairs. When La Farge died in 1963, Josephy was delegated to represent the AAIA at his funeral in Santa Fe and was dismayed when an elderly grand dame of the Santa Fe community and longtime contributor to the AAIA piously asked him what would become of all of the Indian people who depended upon La Farge "to do all their thinking for them."[8]

Josephy's perceptions of who should be speaking for Indian people had begun to change when he attended an "unprecedented" conference at the University of Chicago in June 1961. There he first realized the winds of change were blowing throughout Indian Country. The Council on Indian Affairs and more than four hundred leaders representing sixty-seven tribes assembled for the first time "to appeal to the federal government for the right merely to participate in the making of policies, programs, and budgets for their tribes."[9] Even though it was considered bold action in 1961, the statement did not assert legal rights as much as it played on non-Indian sympathy and underscored that Indians had been "great citizens." Their request was of course denied, but global events— including the rise of the civil rights movement in America—kept the issue alive. Young Indians attending the Chicago conference, however, were made vividly aware of the inconsistencies between the reality of life in Indian Country and the refined political language the council was forced to use when attempting to express that brutal realism to Washington. Inspired with the intention of restoring a sense of pride to Indian nations, immediately after the conference an intertribal collection of dissident, college-educated Indians, led by a Northern Paiute from Nevada, Melvin Thom, and Clyde Warrior, a Ponca from Oklahoma, decided to organize themselves and formed the National Indian Youth Council (NIYC). While the NCAI, the Council of Indian Affairs, and other tribal leaders and non-Indian activists like Alvin Josephy continued working through traditional routes and even met with President Kennedy at the White House in March 1963 to discuss Indian concerns, the NIYC sent a clear message that young Indians were no longer going to humbly obey the rules of the Bureau of Indian Affairs or behave in the manner the dominant non-Indian society expected of them. After President Kennedy's assassination, however, the issue of Indian rights was quickly drawn into the larger civil rights arena and shifted into the Johnson administration's "war on poverty" program and newly established Office of Economic Opportunity. This action by Washington tested the NIYC's militant resolve, while also it pushed the NCAI's diplomatic skills to the brink.

Fundamental human rights are, of course, the cornerstone of the United States Constitution. Civil rights are in fact considered so important to Americans that they were later elaborated upon in detail in our remarkable Bill of Rights. Vine Deloria Jr. and Clifford M. Lytle remind us, however, that "Indian tribal societies had no concept of civil rights because every member of the society was related, by blood or clan responsibilities, to every other member." Deloria and Lytle further observe, "The National Congress of American Indians went to extravagant lengths to distinguish Indians from blacks during the late 1950s so as to keep the issues clear. Whether the leadership did not like blacks or whether they saw the danger in supporting integration at a time when members of the Senate Interior Committee were busy trying to terminate the tribes, or whether they simply didn't understand the depth of revolt represented by the burgeoning movement in the South, the fact remains that the NCAI studiously avoided involvement in civil rights issues."[10]

This issue of Indians, blacks, and civil rights reveals a troubling, uniquely American paradox: whereas blacks were fiercely *denied entry* into the dominant white culture and society, the American Indian was instead *forced to assimilate*; whereas blacks sought *inclusion* in the dominant culture, American Indians preferred *exclusion* from it. Film historian Neal Gabler reminds us that there is yet another powerful factor in this unusual equation that must be considered when examining the fundamental issue of civil rights and the evolution of America's core mythological identity: as surely as racial bigotry shaped the degree of assimilation to which Indians and Africans were allowed entry in white, Anglo-Saxon America, anti-Semitism created the same level of inclusion or exclusion of the immigrant Jews who created the Hollywood film industry. Denied any hope of complete access to the so-called American Dream, immigrant Jews created their own "dream factory" in Hollywood, thereby obsequiously shaping much core American mythology of the early twentieth century around Theodore Roosevelt's WASP vision of the perfect American that they had encountered upon entering the country at the turn of the century. Gabler believes the Jews who created the entertainment industry "embarked on an assimilation process so ruthless and complete that they cut their lives to the pattern of American respectability as they interpreted it." For a Jew to be accepted as an American, however, was an impossible dream at the turn of the century when the dominant culture was so threatened by the phenomenal numbers of Jewish immigrants from eastern Europe and Russia. Thus Gabler concludes that "the same impulse that drove the Jews to assimilate drove the self-appointed defenders of America to prevent Jews from assimilating and, in their view, tainting the country."[11]

Once the HUAC witch hunts ended, Hollywood was morally invigorated to return to the cinematic exploration of American social inequalities and injustices. To truly accomplish this, the industry faced a new challenge: the introduction of sound synchronization to film in the 1920s and the rapid evolution of film technology itself had initiated increasingly rapid advances in the cinematic arts. Each technological development exposed sharp differences in stage and motion picture acting techniques, but the blinding pace of the growth of corporate media and network television in the 1950s was indeed a powerful motivation for Hollywood to create more a progressively more realistic portrayal of life itself in films. Audiences began to expect a more realistic experience watching motion pictures in a theater than at home sitting on their couch watching television. As discussed earlier, Hollywood first responded with technological advances such as Technicolor, Cinemascope, and 3-D, all essentially novelty and gimmicks. Yet the further film technology pushed the envelope of realism, such things as language and antiquated acting techniques were also revealed as dated. Consequently, by the late 1940s stage actors with hopes of working in movies had begun flocking around acting teachers Lee Strasberg and Stella Adler in New York to study the method style of natural acting that the pair had mastered (and "Americanized") based on Russian Konstantin Stanislavsky's breakthrough psychological techniques. Meanwhile, screenwriters, producers, directors, cinematographers, makeup specialists, stunt artists, and other film professionals continued pushing the "realism" of every aspect of the art form of film. As surely as the advent of sound ended the careers of many silent film actors, advancements in cinematic technology increasingly exposed dated acting styles and ended the careers of many romantic American film archetypes. Minimally, technology and the quest for ever more realism in film split the genres of motion pictures into several categories, and the Western was perhaps more affected than any of the other forms. This was especially true in the case of Western film heroes, as suggested earlier in the stark difference between a character like *The Searchers'* Ethan Edwards and the singing cowboys of the same era.

Because of these circumstances, the post–World War II years— especially as reflected in Hollywood Westerns—witnessed the rise of the mythological anti-heroic archetypes rebelling against the invisible, yet dominant, political and corporate powers that created and enforced such divisive racial and social pecking orders in American culture. By 1961 characters like Marlon Brando's "Kid" in *One-Eyed Jacks* revealed new Western American heroes who had emotional wounds and psychological flaws, but in spite of—and often because of—those handicaps, exposed deep emotional and social chasms in the dominant culture's moral integrity.[12] By the mid-1960s, two major events dramatically altered the course of Hollywood mythologizing: the final decline of the old Hollywood studio system and the 1967 replacement of the old Motion Picture Production Code—the Hays Code—with the Motion Picture Association of America (MPAA) rating system. Yet by the 1960s and the beginning of the rise of the counterculture, mythological American values had already been successfully marketed and promoted via Hollywood films and the corporate entertainment industry throughout the free world for six decades. As the first generation of post–World War II Americans approached adulthood, however, American popular culture began to reveal vast, sharply defined differences between younger and older generations that not only crossed all racial and ethnic groups, institutions, and organizations in the United States, but also struck deep at the fundamental archetypes that defined the nation's historical identity. Mythological change was sweeping over the world as well as the United States, and Indian Country was no exception.

By 1964 the National Indian Youth Council began to assume an increasingly militant stance toward the government institutions that had traditionally governed its affairs. The first assertion of the NIYC's new attitude was a series of "fish-ins," or demonstrations intended to call attention to the fact that the state of Washington was knowingly abusing Indian fishing rights legally guaranteed by treaty.[13] As traditional Indian religious ideology began to exert an influence on the Indian youth movement, it also gained momentum throughout Pan-Indian society, penetrating deeper into the urban ghettos and into prison cells. By 1964 the attraction of the more radical approach of the NIYC was also creating major problems for the older Indian leadership of the NCAI, and dissension spread through the organization.

Alvin Josephy Jr. arrived at the annual NCAI convention in Sheridan, Wyoming, in 1964 and discovered the organization was in crisis, sharply divided into opposing factions. Josephy's fellow-Episcopalian member of the Council on Indian Affairs, Reverend Clifford Samuelson, had arrived in Sheridan earlier as a "self-appointed, well-meaning mediator, advancing his own compromise candidate for the position, a youthful Indian intellectual named Vine Deloria Jr., the son of a prominent Sioux deacon in the Episcopal Church and the nephew of Ella Deloria, a much-respected Sioux anthropologist."[14]

Alvin and Betty Josephy had known Vine Deloria Jr. through their mutual friend Reverend Samuelson for several years, and they immediately understood the logic of Samuelson's strong support of the young Sioux. The reverend arranged a meeting with Vine and the Josephys in his hotel room soon after arriving in Sheridan. "In the room," Josephy wrote in his memoir, "Clifford was drumming up votes for Vine from a number of tribal delegates, promising to help keep the NCAI alive if they elected Vine. 'The NCAI is being torn apart,' Clifford confided in me. 'We've got to do everything possible to help save it. It's the only national voice the Indians have.'"[15]

Born March 26, 1933, in Martin, South Dakota, on the Pine Ridge Reservation, Vine was a member of the Standing Rock Sioux tribe. His father, Vine Deloria Sr., and his grandfather, Philip J. Deloria, were indeed respected Sioux Episcopalian ministers, and his anthropologist aunt, Ella Deloria, was a colleague of pioneer American anthropologist Franz Boas. Vine's great-grandfather was the Yankton Sioux medicine man Tipi Sapa, or Black Tipi. Vine served in the Marine Corps from 1954 to 1956 and graduated from Iowa State University in 1958 with a degree in general studies. He promptly entered the Lutheran School of Theology, from which he graduated in 1963, although he chose not to be ordained as a minister. With such experience and talent, Deloria was uniquely gifted to guide the NCAI through the turbulent mid-1960s. His election

as executive director of NCAI in 1964 dissolved the internal bick-
ering among the older, founding membership of the NCAI, united
younger Indian leaders with his leadership, and heralded a new day
in Indian Country. Vine immediately set about reconstructing the
fundamental intertribal political organizational structure of the
NCAI, while also cleverly negotiating the best and worst aspects
of the Great Society programs of the Johnson administration for
Indian people. According to Josephy, Vine also "spent a lot of time
writing brilliantly witty and perceptive articles for the NCAI publication *The Sentinel* that heaped scorn on non-Indian enemies and
exploiters of the Indians."[16]

Vine's writing targeted, ambushed, and exposed the multiple
convoluted hypocrisies inherent throughout government institutions and policies, but, even more fundamentally important, upon
reading Deloria's work, Indian people throughout America recognized they finally had powerful leadership and the representative
voice they needed. Deloria's writing was equally important to Pan-
Indian America spiritually because his words also reunited various
warring factions around a common purpose of self-determination
as an alternative to the government's divisive termination policies.

When his term as executive director ended in 1967, Deloria had
reached the conclusion that nearly all American Indian problems
stemmed from *legal* origins. So he enrolled in the University of Colorado's law school, from which he graduated in 1970. While still
in law school, he published *Custer Died for Your Sins*, and, smash-
ing through the bookstore marketing ignorance and prejudice that
Alvin M. Josephy had encountered with *The Patriot Chiefs* at the
beginning of the decade, the book began a meteoric climb to the
top of the national and international best-seller charts. But *Custer
Died for Your Sins* was only the beginning. Vine Deloria Jr.—like
no other Indian or non-Indian before him—was destined over his
prolific literary career to intelligently and articulately analyze and
address in his diverse body of work the profound underlying and
unifying context of the social, political, spiritual, metaphysical,
psychological, theological, and legal issues and concerns of America's indigenous nations. His incredible burst of books following

Custer Died for Your Sins is staggering by any publishing standards: *God Is Red* in 1972, *Behind the Trail of Broken Treaties* in 1974, *The Metaphysics of Modern Existence* in 1979, and the list goes on for over four decades and twenty books, countless essays, anthologies, and editorials surveying a dazzling array of subjects. By 1974 the editors of six prominent religious journals had proclaimed him a "theological superstar of the future," one of eleven "shapers and shakers of the Christian faith," which prompted old Gilded Age conservative Henry Luce's *Time* magazine to refer to Vine Deloria Jr. as one of the "ten most important religious thinkers of the twentieth century."[17]

The arrival of an important American Indian leader like Vine Deloria Jr., and the timing of *Custer Died for Your Sins*, perfectly articulated the growing intensity of the youth moment in Indian Country. But the synchronicity also suggests that events in Indian Country in the late 1960s had been affected by the same "dynamic spiritual pattern" John Neihardt described in his autobiography. But aside from Deloria's blossoming prestige in the field of religion, *Custer Died for Your Sins* also opened windows of milestone awareness in the non-Indian world through its ambush and relentless assault on such things as the rampant racial condescension in the field of anthropology. Equally significantly, *Custer Died for Your Sins* set the stage for the publication of a book by an unknown Arkansas librarian that would eloquently touch the hearts of the non-Indian world and awaken them to the mythological changes that were coming soon to America.

.

Chapter Seventeen
A Librarian's Notebook

It may be that some little root of the sacred tree still lives. Nourish it then, that it may leaf and bloom and fill with singing birds. Hear me, not for myself, but for my people; I am old. Hear me that they may once more go back into the sacred hoop and find the good red road, the shielding tree.[1]

—Black Elk

Whereas *Custer Died for Your Sins* became a declaration around which Indian people rallied and organized, Dee Brown's *Bury My Heart at Wounded Knee,* published in 1970, brought the United States' sad history with American Indians out of the shadows and placed it in the spotlight. A runaway best seller, the book sold more than 5 million hardback copies, was translated into multiple languages, and is credited with altering previously accepted concepts of America's frontier history. *Bury My Heart at Wounded Knee* also forced historians to revise mythological perceptions of the nineteenth-century triumph of Manifest Destiny and to reconsider what oppressed American Indian leaders had been saying since Euro Americans first began translating their speeches.

Ultimately, *Bury My Heart at Wounded Knee* was the result of Dee Brown's lifelong love affair with the power of the printed word; indeed, Brown's life at times calls to mind Neil Postman's observation that America was dominated by the printed word and an oratory based on the printed word from the colonial period until well into the nineteenth century.[2] Published when he was eighty-five, Brown's 1993 autobiography, *When the Century Was Young: A Writer's Notebook,* begins with a comment that reflects Postman's insight concerning the impact of print on the early shaping of America's personality: "The early part of this century was the golden age of print, and I was born into it. Newspapers, magazines, and books—in that order—were the major sources of information and entertainment. Radio and television came later as interloping marvels, but even to this day the electronic devices do not match the authority of print."[3]

Dee Brown was born in 1908 just outside of Shreveport in tiny Alberta, Louisiana. Mark Twain died when Dee was two, yet even as a child he was aware that Buffalo Bill Cody, Thomas Edison, Teddy Roosevelt, President Woodrow Wilson, Henry Ford, Kaiser Wilhelm of Germany, Mrs. George Armstrong Custer, and real cowboys and Indians, including Hollow Horn Bear, "the Sioux chief whose face appeared on a postage stamp after his death," were all still alive.[4]

Dee Brown's father died in 1912. The next year his mother, Lulu, accepted a postmistress position and moved the family a hundred miles north of Shreveport to Stephens, Arkansas. With money earned as a "special delivery" boy for his mother, Brown purchased a mail-order hand printing press and immediately launched into business printing holiday greeting cards and a local Boy Scout troop's newsletter. There is an old newspaper adage stating that once ink and newsprint get in your blood you are forever addicted, and this was never truer than in the life of Dee Brown. This youthful obsession with printing inevitably led the boy to the town's newspaper offices, where he became a "printer's devil" and was introduced to his first ancient Linotype at the *Stephens News*. Soon after Brown started working at the newspaper, southwestern Arkansas became the site of one of America's first major oil strikes, and the region was rapidly inundated with oil derricks, flamboyant fortune-hunters, and roustabouts. Brown's job at the *Stephens News* provided him the opportunity to encounter many of the colorful characters that followed oil boom towns across the Southwest; wildcatters, flimflammers, and oil-lease hounds regularly passed through the newspaper offices with various—always rushed—printing requests. The boy quickly learned there was a dollar to be made in a newspaper office aside from simply printing the daily news.

Lulu Brown moved her family to Little Rock when Dee was

sixteen. They traveled to the Arkansas capital in a rickety Model T Ford on primitive sand roads so deeply rutted that drivers could remove their hands from the steering wheel, accelerate, and the vehicle would steer itself. The downtown Little Rock Public Library quickly became a second home for the young man and furthered his literary journey on a path that would appear in hindsight as deeply rutted with his destiny as those sandy Arkansas roads. Even though he remained open to alternative courses, from the beginning of his love affair with the printed word, Dee Brown slowly accelerated his dreams, all the while surrendering his fate to the power of words to take him where they would. While he was continuing his extracurricular education in the Little Rock Public Library as a sixteen-year-old, however, a librarian suggested books that sent Dee exploring the history of the American West for the first time and began his career as a writer. Brown became enchanted with the archetypal situations and characters in the United States prototypical adventure into the North American West contained in the three-volume set *History of the Expedition under the Command of Captains Lewis and Clark*. Brown describes his discovery of the Lewis and Clark expedition in near-Homeric terms: "It has been said that the most enduring works of literature are stories of journeys in which the chief interest of the narrative centers around the adventures of the hero or heroine. If this be true, there is no greater adventure story in American history…a journey filled with danger, mystery, romance, and grueling suspense. Instead of one hero it contains several and one sterling heroine, the Shoshone woman, Sacajawea, without whose aid they might not have reached their destination."[5]

Perhaps Brown's most extraordinary ability as a writer was his gift of placing history, landscape, and personalities in precise context. In his prologue, "Writing Western," in *Best of Dee Brown's West: An Anthology*, Brown compares several of his favorite instances in which one historical context led to another. He begins noting that a twenty-one-year-old from upstate New York named Jedediah Strong Smith read what Lewis and Clark had written and vowed to see everything they had seen and more. So Jed headed west. An obsessive mapmaker, Jedediah Smith was destined to become a legendary mountain man and was eventually recognized as the first non-Indian to cross the continent by land. Brown also notes in his prologue that George Catlin risked life and limb to paint the various tribes of the Great Plains and Rocky Mountains. When Catlin returned to Boston to show his paintings, Francis Parkman was so overwhelmed by the exhibition that he embarked upon a western expedition himself, and his journey inspired him to write *The Oregon Trail*. Brown also notes that a young man named John Colter fell under the enchanting spell of the Yellowstone Country as the voyage of discovery first passed through the region. Colter became recognized as the first mountain man because on the return journey he requested permission to remain in the region as a trapper in the region and received Lewis and Clark's blessing. Colter thus returned to the West even before he reached home. Finally, Brown emphasizes the importance of context to history by observing that if the Nez Perce had not "shared smoked salmon and camas root with the starving members of the Lewis and Clark expedition, shown them a route to the sea, and taken care of their horses, the explorers might never have reached the Pacific or returned to St. Louis."[6]

Not all of Brown's boyhood was spent in newspaper offices or libraries. One of the most charming sections of his autobiography describes a bygone, pre–Little League era when minor-league baseball teams traveled the country as the sport was establishing itself as America's national pastime. The Browns' home in Little Rock was only two blocks from the Arkansas Travelers ballpark, and baseball quenched the neighborhood boys' thirst for adventure. Boys retrieving baseballs hit over ballpark fences would be admitted free to games, so Brown and his young companions would take their gloves to the Arkansas Travelers games and wait for baseballs to fly over the fence. During this time in Dee Brown's boyhood he met his first Indians. Several Indians had come from Oklahoma to work on the rigs during the oil boom in Stephens. A Creek boy became one of Dee's closest friends in school, and after his family returned to Oklahoma, Dee visited him in Muskogee one summer. Dee's young Indian friend liked to say that his people belonged to one of the Five Civilized Tribes and that meant he was not a "wild" Indian.[7]

Shortly after becoming friends with the young Creek boy, Dee was attracted to an Indian baseball player on the Arkansas Travelers minor-league team. Moses Yellowhorse fascinated Dee Brown from the first day he saw him. Being Osage or Pawnee—and not a member of one of the Five Civilized Tribes by Dee's young Creek friend's definition—Yellowhorse was a "wild" Indian, with a chiseled nose and face that he could make look ferocious at will.[8]

A pitcher, Yellowhorse had played in the big leagues. Because of a propensity to walk batters, however, he had been returned to the minor leagues, where he spent most of his time warming up as a relief pitcher in the bull pen. One day during a game, Brown noticed Yellowhorse watching him. Soon, the large Indian hailed Brown over to the bull pen, tossed the baseball over the protective fence to him, and told him to take the ball and see the game. Soon the routine became a daily ceremony between Yellowhorse and Brown and his pals.

"Yellowhorse delighted in our joy," Brown writes, "and we delighted in his Indian 'giveaways.'...As a teenager nearly seventy years ago, I learned from Moses Yellowhorse that American Indians, even fierce-looking ones, could be kind and generous and good-humored—and faithful friends. From that time, I scorned all the blood-and-thunder tales of frontier Indian savagery, and when I went to the Western movies on Saturday afternoons, I cheered the warriors who were always cast as villains."[9]

After graduation from Little Rock High School, Brown worked for a while as a reporter and printer in Harrison, Arkansas, and appeared poised to drift from one small-town newspaper to the next when his mother suddenly changed his pattern. Ever entrepreneurial, Lulu Brown moved from Little Rock to Conway so that Dee's sister, Corinne, could enroll in Arkansas State Teachers College. To finance Corinne's education, Mrs. Brown leased a large house near the campus that also provided her with the opportunity to rent rooms out to women students. After Corinne received her teaching certificate and accepted a teaching position, however, Mrs. Brown invited Dee to come to Conway to help convert the house into a boarding house for male students. He pounced on the opportunity to go to college.

Soon after beginning his college career in Conway, the printer's ink in Brown's blood began to pulse and he returned to his old habits and started writing and editing for the college newspaper. During this period he also began working as a student assistant in the college library and quickly realized his interest in print had led him to his life's profession: Dee Brown was a natural-born librarian. Yet even as his career as a librarian was only beginning, a providential event in Dee Brown's life soon occurred when he was introduced to history professor Dean McBrien. A Nebraskan with a penchant for traveling the West in a Model T Ford accompanied by several hand-picked students, McBrien, according to Brown, "more than any other mentor set me upon the course I was to take as a writer. He probably did not care very much for the historical novels I later published, but he could not help but like my way of writing history because I borrowed or stole the methods that he used in his classes to charm his students into listening attentively."[10]

During the summer months McBrien cranked up his Model T and drove students on exploratory pilgrimages over unpaved roads across rugged Trans-Missouri terrain little changed since the nineteenth century. Along the way McBrien's touring classroom sought out and encountered Indian and non-Indian inhabitants in tiny western towns and often engaged them in lengthy, detailed historical conversations about the region they were visiting.

Brown noted that perhaps because he was a Nebraskan, McBrien considered the Great Plains exceptional and, unlike most Americans, refused to hurry across them. From McBrien young Dee Brown learned to cherish the immense distances and "enormous sky that would swirl above us with the passage of the slow-moving car." McBrien was also a living encyclopedia of western information and according to Brown had probably read every diary and narrative then available concerning the great overland migration of the nineteenth century. One summer McBrien and his students followed the entire path of the migration and the professor would stop for hours to examine historic locations along the Oregon Trail to make certain his traveling classroom connected with the landscape. Brown recalls that McBrien's notion of history was that "the past consisted of stories, fascinating incidents, woven around incisive biographies of the persons involved in the happenings. He liked little dashes of scandal—if they could be documented—and he insisted firmly that everything had to be authenticated from the available sources. He had saturated himself in the history of the American West. Before I met him I was interested in the American West, but he converted me into a fanatic like himself."[11]

McBrien also introduced Brown to the *physical* impact of the Trans-Missouri landscape on the spiritual and mythical history of its inhabitants. Brown was on a summer history adventure with McBrien in 1929 when the professor drove his Model T up one of those primitive western roads to a monument of stones erected beside the old Bozeman Trail in Wyoming. The memorial was placed at the exact location of the Fetterman Massacre where only sixty-three years earlier Plains Indians had delivered the US Army the greatest battlefield defeat in its then ninety-year history. When Dean McBrien rolled his Model T classroom to a stop at the Fetterman Massacre memorial, Dee Brown experienced an enlightened moment that is possible when a seeker's knowledge of historical events and geographic location synchronize. The occasion would mark the rest of his life.

"When a person who is cognizant of a recorded incident of history first comes upon the place where it occurred, the impact can have the force of an exhilarating electrical surge," Brown recalls. "I remember a strange prickly sensation when, at twenty-one, I first saw the rude monument of stones beside the Bozeman Road in Wyoming." One of the first major western historians to call attention to the fact that the Fetterman Massacre in 1866 would loom much larger in the annals of the Indian wars if Custer's defeat at Little Big Horn had not overshadowed it a decade later, Dee Brown recalls that the very instant he saw the stone memorial to the Fetterman fight he realized something "shattering had occurred there and around the site of the vanished Fort Phil Kearney, along the rim of the deceptive ridges, to the brooding Bighorn range, misty and cloud-covered that day. The air was filled with courageous spirits of the past—red-man spirits, white-man spirits."[12]

This sense of a "sacred site" Dee Brown perceived as a young man certainly underscores Luther Standing Bear and Vine Deloria, Jr.'s theories of how a specific landscape is made "holy," and the indigenous awareness he sensed that day in the Big Horn Mountains of Wyoming surely followed him on subsequent pilgrimages with McBrien throughout the American West. Among many other historic locations, they visited the Custer Battlefield, Fort Wallace, and Beecher Island, eventually arriving at a lonely hillside by a meandering creek on the Great Sioux Reservation.

"In those useful years of searching," Brown remembers, "the most painful place we came upon was a mass grave with a few flowers struggling to live around it, in South Dakota, the Pine Ridge Reservation. A monument bore the name of some Indians, but most of those buried there were unrecorded and unknown—men, women, and children, killed at Wounded Knee. That grave remained like the scar of a wound imprinted forever upon me."[13]

Brown carried the memory of that wound forward from his first visit to the site of the Wounded Knee Massacre. After departing Arkansas to attend George Washington University in the early 1930s, he took a minor librarian position in the Department of Agriculture in Washington, DC, during the beginnings of Roosevelt's New Deal and married his sweetheart, Sally Stroud. He and Sally settled into married life in Washington and Brown began socializing with many young writers in the New Deal Federal Writers' Project. A short story he wrote during this period eventually attracted the attention of a New York literary agent. When she wrote to inquire if he had a novel, Brown immediately started one. His literary effort was promptly sidetracked, however, when he was promoted and transferred to the Beltsville Agricultural Research Center and ordered to build a library from the ground up. Nevertheless, in spite of the daunting responsibility of creating a library from scratch, he somehow managed to complete a satirical novel about Washington, DC, during the New Deal era. The New York agent promptly placed it with a small Philadelphia publisher, Macrae Smith, and the book was scheduled to be published in November 1941. Once again fate—and the Japanese—had another course in mind for Dee Brown.

On December 8, the day after Pearl Harbor, Brown received a call from his publisher to request a meeting in Washington. At the meeting Brown was informed that Macrae Smith would not publish his novel; since the country was suddenly at war, the publisher felt it might be considered unpatriotic to publish even an innocuous work satirizing the government. When the publisher asked if he had any plans for another novel—"perhaps something patriotic"—Brown lied and said he did.

Chagrined by the loss of his ill-fated contemporary novel, Brown decided to "retreat into the nineteenth century." Brown's maternal grandmother had told him stories about his great-grandfather hunting bears with Davy Crockett in Tennessee, so Brown decided to begin with those tales and write a biography on Davy Crockett, but he sensed there would not be time to properly research the effort. So in three months he wrote a historical novel, *Wave High the Banner*, and it was published by Macrae Smith.[14]

Once again fate intervened in Dee Brown's life; a few weeks after the publication of *Wave High the Banner* he was drafted into the US Army and began basic training with the 80th Infantry Division at Camp Forest, Tennessee. The military only furthered Dee Brown's career as a librarian; soon after he completed basic training the army sent Brown back to college as part of its prototype Army Specialized Training Program (ASTP). First Brown and fellow recruits in the program were shipped to Alabama to attend classes at Auburn University. After a few weeks in Alabama, however, Brown's outfit was ordered to Philadelphia to report for classes at the University of Pennsylvania. As in Alabama, after arriving in Philadelphia the ASTP recruits either attended regular university classes or were repeatedly tested and offered no explanation of the purpose of the examination. After nearly a year of this routine the recruits learned the army had misplaced their orders. Upon discovering the error, the government sent the ASTP recruits to the University of Iowa in Iowa City, Iowa. After more classes and more unexplained testing, Brown was finally reassigned to Army Ground Forces Headquarters and returned to Washington.

During this confusing period in his military career Brown

formed a lasting friendship with Martin Schmitt, a colleague who had also been a librarian in civilian life. Schmitt loved John Neihardt's *A Cycle of the West* and could recite stanzas from the work from memory. Through their mutual interest in Neihardt's poetry, Brown quickly discovered that Schmitt was also a fanatic of Western literature.[15]

The War Department devised a point system for ASTP members to phase out of the army after the war ended. As Brown's and Martin Schmitt's duties steadily declined, they awaited their discharge from the service, and to pass the time the pair began collecting historical photographs of the Old West. Several of their earlier assignments had introduced them to the War Department's collection of military photographs, where they discovered files from the Indian wars. Soon Brown and Schmitt became obsessed with collecting photographs from the Indian wars and expanded their search to the National Archives, the Library of Congress, and the Bureau of American Ethnology. Investing every spare penny of their meager soldier's pay to purchase eight-by-ten-inch prints of American Indians, Brown and Schmitt amassed an impressive collection of images.

The pair had given little thought to publishing their growing collection of photographs until an editor from Macmillan requested a meeting to explore that possibility. Brown went to New York to meet with editors, but, after fully considering the cost of reproducing the images, Macmillan decided to pass on the project.

Next, Brown and Schmitt submitted their collection to the University of Oklahoma Press. Again, the cost of faithfully reproducing the photographs proved daunting, and after failing to secure grants to assist with financing, the University of Oklahoma Press also passed on the project. Brown and Schmitt vowed to make one last effort to find a publisher.

This time fate was on their side. After he submitted the collection to Charles Scribner's, famous editor Maxwell Perkins summoned him to New York for a meeting. When Brown arrived he was pleasantly surprised to discover Perkins had sequenced all 270 photographs of the collection along his office's long, deep window sills, and, running out of room there, continued the progression on the edges of a long wood table. Perkins proceeded to lead Brown through his storyboard, occasionally changing the arrangement of photographs or asking questions about captions or text. After guiding Brown through his sequence of the photographs, Perkins looked Brown straight in the eye and demanded, "Where are the Navajos?" When Brown explained to Perkins they had not been able to find enough Navajos to fit the theme of the collection, a disappointed Perkins told him the Navajos were his favorite tribe. Brown recalls that "he shrugged, waved me out of his office, and turned toward his desk. 'We'll make a fine book,' he called after me." Brown and Schmitt's *The Fighting Indians of the West* was published in 1948 and remained in print for many years.[16]

After leaving the military Brown accepted a position at the army's Aberdeen Proving Ground in Maryland. At Aberdeen, the librarian was introduced to the era of the cold war when he quickly noticed an increasing number of documents boldly marked "secret" and "confidential." Brown also realized he might just as well be a locksmith at Aberdeen because of the unusual number of locked doors, desks, and file cabinets he was required to maintain and document. Worse, the locks and combinations were changed every few weeks to maintain security.

Brown stayed at Aberdeen as a military librarian throughout the first phase of the cold war, before accepting a position at the University of Illinois–Urbana as the librarian of the College of Agriculture. After his move to Illinois, Brown and Schmitt continued their collaboration long distance and produced two other collections of photographic history, *The Settlers' West* and *Trail Driving Days*, also published by Scribner's. During this period Brown also wrote "several formula Westerns" to supplement his librarian's salary. He remained a librarian until *Bury My Heart at Wounded Knee* skyrocketed to the top of the world's best-seller lists in 1970.

Brown's memoir closes with several suggestions for aspiring writers, and in doing so he explains why he wrote *Bury My Heart at Wounded Knee* and why the book spoke so eloquently to late-twentieth-century America. Urging young writers to keep journals,

Brown reveals that while earning a living as a librarian, he always kept a small notebook nearby in which he had been collecting the poetic and symbolic words of American Indians of the nineteenth century wherever he encountered them. Brown confesses that in the beginning he had no intention of developing them into a book. Instead, he noted that he collected the speeches "simply for what the words express—the human condition, the love of the earth and its beings and the sky, devotion to a supreme power, heartbreaks and admonitions—spoken in rhythmic languages, at times lyrical, at times elegiacal."[17]

Many of the speeches were so psychologically haunting and emotionally striking that Brown was at first skeptical of their authenticity. He initially believed the translators of the speeches were probably emulating romantic English poets. Intrigued, however, Brown put his librarian skills to work and spent hours searching for the identities of the official interpreters of the speeches. He eventually arrived at the conclusion that it rarely mattered who interpreted the Indian leader's speeches; their words translated into English "with the same eloquence, seasoned with inspired metaphors and similes of the natural world."[18]

Dee Brown ends his autobiography discussing the Hindu word *serendipity* that shaped his long life and that, when combined with his habit of keeping notebooks, eventually led to his writing *Bury My Heart at Wounded Knee*: "Serendipity has been surprisingly helpful in guiding me to the exact information I needed, or into unknown pathways that proved beneficial for me to follow. On numerous occasions, I would be searching in one direction in vain when suddenly serendipity would make an appearance and lead me directly to an unexpected but ideal solution that I was totally unaware of."[19]

Dee Brown died December 12, 2002, at the age of ninety-four. His long life is a testament that the pen is indeed mightier than the sword. Upon Dee Brown's death, a professor at the University of Arkansas, C. Fred Williams, noted perhaps the most significant aspect of this great book: "The effect of *Bury My Heart* was essentially to give voice to the American Indians. They were always an important part of the American West, usually as the indirect object. Dee Brown made them the direct object."[20]

Dee Brown's reference to serendipity at the end of his autobiography eloquently resonates with John Neihardt's words at the close of *his* autobiography, *Patterns and Coincidences*: "I have long thought and previously remarked in a wondering exploratory manner that somehow there are dynamic spiritual patterns in our cosmos, that destiny is a matter of being caught up in such a pattern, apparently by accident, and being compelled to strive for realization of the stubborn stuff of this world, be it for good or ill."[21]

Neihardt's mention of "dynamic spiritual patterns" at the close of his long life, and Dee Brown's comment about "serendipity" at the close of his equally long life, recall and underscore descriptions by Charles Eastman, Luther Standing Bear, Vine Deloria Jr., and Ron Goodman of American Indian medicine men's ability to divine spiritual knowledge from detailed observations of organic life. The serendipity of Dee Brown's having been originally inspired by Neihardt's poetry, followed decades later by the astonishing global success of Brown's *Bury My Heart at Wounded Knee* and that book's setting the stage to provide Neihardt an unprecedented ninety minute on a popular network television program to discuss the spiritual vision of a nineteenth-century mystic Plains Indian forty years after *Black Elk Speaks* was published, is a powerful affirmation of Neihardt's observation that "there are dynamic spiritual patterns in our cosmos and destiny is a matter of being caught up in such a pattern." In Jungian terms, these events precisely synchronized to create a peak moment in this dynamic spiritual pattern that precipitated the rise of *Black Elk Speaks* to prominence.

As previously noted, *Custer Died for Your Sins* preceded both *Bury My Heart at Wounded Knee* and *Black Elk Speaks* on the best-seller lists and initiated the cresting wave all three books rode that stimulated renewed political, social, and spiritual examination of American Indians. All three books were part of a dynamic spiritual pattern that began when Sitting Bull realized physical, military confrontation with the technological invasion that Plains Indians faced was futile and learned to use his ironic celebrity status as a tool for nonviolent resistance. While *Bury My Heart at Wounded Knee* introduced readers to the eloquence of American Indian leaders and the tragedy of their losses, *Black Elk Speaks* suggested the possibility of the ultimate union of Indian and non-Indian mythologies. All three books spoke powerfully to Indian and non-Indian communities, but *Custer Died for Your Sins* was *written by* an Indian and was exactly what its title claimed: at once a sardonic allusion to the aggressive history of militant evangelical Christianity and indigenous America while also a manifesto heralding the rise of the Indian youth movement. It was the destiny of that movement to capture the attention of the entire world once again in 1973.

Chapter Eighteen
The Trail of Broken Treaties

The Voice said: "Behold the circle of the nation's hoop, for it is holy, being endless, and thus all powers shall be one power in the people without end."[1]

—Black Elk

In February 1973, ten months after John Neihardt's appearance on *The Dick Cavett Show*, *Black Elk Speaks*, *Bury My Heart at Wounded Knee*, and *Custer Died for Your Sins* were all riding high atop global best-selling charts when an electrifying lightning bolt of déjà vu struck. American Indian activists seized a church near the site of the 1890 Wounded Knee Massacre to begin a standoff that would hold international media spellbound for seventy-one days and would soon become known as Wounded Knee II. Capricious daily newspaper editors responded on the front pages of newspapers around the world with incongruous twentieth-century headlines such as "Indians Seize Western Town" and "Circle the Wagons."

Even though copies of *Bury My Heart at Wounded Knee* and *Black Elk Speaks* were selling by the truckloads, the Indians depicted in Dee Brown's and John Neihardt's books were safe in America's romantic past. Conversely, *Custer Died for Your Sins* addressed contemporary Indian concerns, and modern mainstream America's collective aftershock following the American Indian Movement (AIM) seizure of the church at Wounded Knee was the sobering realization that Indians still existed. Worse, they were angry and had been forced to resort to violence.

Although mainstream Americans born in the beginning of the twentieth century had been taught to consider Indians as romantic relics, their children, the baby boomers, increasingly regarded indigenous people as relevant. Once again exemplifying Philip Deloria's "playing Indian" and "pacified" thesis, from the beginning of the counterculture movement in the mid-1960s, hippies had adapted American Indians' long braided hairstyle, beads, fringed leather clothing, and tipis. During the infamous trial of the Chicago Eight that began in April 1969 and ended in February 1970, hippie political activist Abbie Hoffman dubbed the counterculture movement the Woodstock Nation. When a lawyer asked Hoffman where he lived, the activist replied, "I live in the Woodstock Nation." The lawyer demanded, "Will you tell the Court and Jury where it is?" To which Hoffman replied, "Yes. It is a nation of alienated young people. We carry it around with us as a state of mind in the same way as the Sioux Indians carried the Sioux nation around with them."[2]

When Hoffman coined the phrase *Woodstock Nation* during his trial he had only recently returned from an unprecedented counterculture event in upstate New York. Over a half-million young people—the largest audience in history attending a musical event—had gathered in August 1969 near the art colony of Woodstock, New York. Hippies had actually started referring to themselves as neo-American Indian tribes, however, long before Hoffman's dubbing the youth movement as the Woodstock Nation. Many belonging to the back-to-nature faction of the counterculture "tribes" were defined in earnest with Joni Mitchell's metaphorical description of the musical event in her song "Woodstock" in which she sang, "We've got to get ourselves back to the garden." Of course Mitchell's anthem could have been describing European colonialists seeking the Age of Enlightenment's "New Eden" in North America, Daniel Boone leading pilgrims into Kentucky and Tennessee, or Jason Lee's flock of New Englanders settling in Oregon's Willamette Valley, as well as the back-to-the-garden hippies of the Woodstock Nation.

Dale Bell, the producer of the Academy Award–winning film *Woodstock*, notes several important characteristics of the phenomenal gathering that his team observed and incorporated into the film: "People were talking about going back to green. Going back to the environment. Going back to the garden. Getting away from the war. Coming together. ...I think today a lot of the music and lyrics really hearken back to the movement that initially began in California with John Muir in the 1800s. …Rachel Carson wrote *Silent Spring* in 1962. There was real talk about the environment and what we should do about it. Eliminating pesticides was step one in that process, but there were many other components of trying to go green. *Woodstock* embodied and gathered together a lot of those concepts. We know for sure the first Earth Day took place just one month after *Woodstock* opened."[3]

The 1969 Woodstock concert defined the counterculture movement and many of the changes coming to America just as surely as the 1894 World's Columbian Exposition had defined the transition from nineteenth-to-twentieth-century America and articulated a dramatic shift in the American personality seventy-five years earlier. Many of those particularly stubborn and hardy hippie tribes that Joni Mitchell sang about still exist today "off the grid" in the backwoods, deserts, swamps, and mountaintops of North America. Yet by the time of Wounded Knee II in 1973, an increasingly large percentage of the Woodstock Nation had become shorn and scrubbed-up versions of Timothy Leary's radical "turn on, tune in, and drop out" generation. Indeed, by 1973 the majority of the rapidly fragmenting counterculture was getting haircuts, replacing bell-bottom jeans and tie-dyes with suits, ties, and wingtips, reentering corporate America's pecking order, and generally *re-assimilating* into American society and popular culture. In four short years these reconstructed factions of the Woodstock tribes adapted Joni Mitchell's mystical and biblical reference of "stardust returning to the garden" and began singing along with John Denver's popular "Take Me Home, Country Roads" and "Rocky Mountain High" anthems, which of course heralded instead an upper-middle-class, plastic-rustic, "back-to-nature" movement to Aspen, Vail, Jackson Hole, and other exclusive and ultra-expensive resort areas of the American hinterlands. And even though the majority of contemporary cowboy singers, songwriters, and poets would rather be branded with the doggies at roundup than admit it, the return to popularity of cowboy music and poetry in the early 1980s can be directly linked to the counterculture and to hippies. While Marty Robbins's classic early 1960s *Gunfighter*

Ballads album, and his classic hit song "El Paso" heralded a return to a more literary approach to Western ballads and served to distinguish between "Western" and "country" in the genre, the singer's basic musical arrangements, vocal styling, and harmonies harkened back to the Gene Autry/Roy Rogers/Sons of the Pioneers period of the 1930s, '40s, and '50s. The cowboy singer-songwriter-poet era that exploded in popularity during the 1980s, however, can be directly traced to the success of Michael Martin Murphey and his so-called "Cosmic Cowboy" period that occurred in one of the last remaining American counterculture strongholds, Austin, Texas. In 1972, Murphey was living in Austin and broke through on the national level with his first hit song, "Geronimo's Cadillac" (co-written with New York hippie poet, Charles John Quarto). "Geronimo's Cadillac" referred to a famous turn-of-the-century photograph of the Apache chief driving a Cadillac, but Murphey's edgier rock vocals and musical arrangements spoke directly to Joni Mitchell's neo-Indian tribes of Woodstock in its return-to-the-land chorus with an incongruous twist provided by General Motors: "Hey boys take me back; I want to ride in Geronimo's Cadillac." Murphey expanded his cowboy fan base when his eerie musical ghost story, "Wildfire," followed "Geronimo's Cadillac" onto the charts and became a smash hit and modern Western classic. As "Wildfire" was racing up the charts, Murphey continued performing and eventually shifted his focus from pop to country to traditional cowboy music, departing Austin for ranching life in Colorado and New Mexico. Soon thereafter, imitator sagebrush songsters and poets began to proliferate like jackrabbits on the open range, and the era of "git along little doggerel" was born. Even though Murphy and several of the cowboy singer-songwriters and poets of this era have contributed genuine musical and literary masterpieces celebrating ranching and rodeo life in the American West at the dawning of the twenty-first century, the majority of modern purveyors of the genre have simply slipped on Zane Grey's boots and assumed the role that the novelist filled at the turn of the twentieth century, providing a sentimental return to a simpler time and a cherished WASP vision of the American Dream. Like the archetypical Western form itself for over a century, if you substitute an African

American, Jew, Italian, Russian, Gypsy, or *any* ethnic personality other than a WASP as the leading character of a contemporary cowboy song or poem, it becomes as instantly incongruous as Geronimo driving a Cadillac. It's the reason Mel Brooks's *Blazing Saddles* is so hilarious, and, of course, the converse—a cowboy with a nuclear warhead—is why Stanley Kubrick's *Dr. Strangelove* is so frightening.

Once the lines were drawn at Wounded Knee II, however, it was clear that many of the idealistic post–World War II generation of Americans, like their forefathers, had unsuccessfully attempted to culturally embrace indigenous America. This was reflected in the fact that the majority of the counterculture movement had *incorrectly* assumed that AIM was simply another of the many radical, militant, minority "power movements" that were flourishing throughout the United States at the time, rather than a grassroots movement to protect Indians and restore the sovereign nation status of indigenous America. Racially stereotyping AIM in the same category as the Black Panthers, most members of the baby boomer tribes of the Woodstock Nation offered Indian activists a symbolically sympathetic, "black-power" clinched-fist salute and promptly returned to the harried pace of abandoning idealism in the pursuit of happiness, drugs, and the disco club scene. Yet in May 1973, as AIM and the US government negotiated a truce to end the siege at Wounded Knee, even former members of the counterculture who were by the mid-1970s rapidly re-assimilating into "the system" were at least superficially aware of Indian culture and history through the increasing numbers of popular books and motion pictures.

Even though it was dramatically altered during the 1970s, most of the idealism of the great counterculture movement was not abandoned. It is important to remember that many of the most positive social changes in American history were initiated during the 1960s. History reveals that the previous 150 years of WASP control and mythological manipulation of the American Dream dramatically weakened and declined in the spiritual light of the great civil rights and counterculture movements of the 1960s. It is also no coincidence that Richard Nixon's Watergate scandal in the early 1970s punctuates the end of the Vietnam War and the loss of idealism of the post–World War II generation as well as the shattering effect of the cultural wars on the nation's identity. Perhaps John Denver was really singing "take me home, country 'fork-in-the-road'" in 1972.

As the nation's bicentennial in 1976 drew closer, it was obvious that Americans of all races, classes, genders, and ages were reconsidering many of the mythological "truths" about the United States that had been accepted for two hundred years. The impact of *Black Elk Speaks*, *The Patriot Chiefs*, *The Man Who Killed the Deer*, *House Made of Dawn*, *Book of the Hopi*, *Touch the Earth*, *Custer Died for Your Sins*, *Bury My Heart at Wounded Knee*, *God Is Red*, *Seven Arrows*, and the scores of books that followed those classics indicated that a significant change in thinking *had* occurred concerning indigenous America. In the midst of the ambiguous transitional period leading up to the nation's two-hundredth birthday, it is noteworthy that the motion pictures *Little Big Man* and *Soldier Blue* were released in 1970. Both films were perceived by most critics of the time as anti-Vietnam statements, and both depicted the beginnings of the Indian wars of the nineteenth century: the Sand Creek Massacre of Cheyenne by Chivington's militia and the Battle of Washita and the Battle of Little Big Horn led by George Armstrong Custer. Whereas *Soldier Blue* was more purely a Vietnam allegory, Arthur Penn's film of Thomas Berger's 1964 novel, *Little Big Man*, focused yet again on the captivity narrative, and, demonstrating Frederick Turner's theory of the genre's fluidity, in Berger's novel as well as Penn's film, the form maintained its unique ability to reflect both the current times and the continuing powerful connections of Indians to America's identity.

After being taken captive by the Cheyenne as a child and reared in their culture, *Little Big Man*'s protagonist, Jack Crabb, is rescued and returned to non-Indian Christian culture. Upon returning to the non-Indian world, Crabb discovers that his ordeal has paradoxically robbed him of his identity in both worlds while simultaneously providing him a unique identity in both worlds. His spiritual escort through this ambiguous terrain is the wonderful character Old Lodge Skins, played to absolute perfection by Chief

Dan George. Old Lodge Skins was a brilliant composite of Black Elk and Iron Eyes Cody's weeping Indian from the public service advertisements, and to a nation eager to know more about Indians, he was a pragmatic and humorous "uncle" who could guide hippies through similarly ambiguous times. At the point in the story when Old Lodge Skins decides he wants to die and then proceeds to his burial site to await death, *Little Big Man* captures the hippie era with Dan George's memorable line, "Sometimes the magic works, and sometimes it doesn't."

Unable to fit in either world, Crabb, at one particularly low point, has the epiphany that his entire life has been defined by either Indians or white men trying to kill him. Eventually realizing this as a blessing rather than a curse, Crabb is generally regarded with indifference in both worlds, and begins to freely wander between relationships in both the Indian and non-Indian cultures. Crabb threatens no one, thus enhancing his ability to become virtually invisible as he crosses paths with legendary characters and participates in historic events. With a boot (or moccasin) in either world, Jack Crabb becomes a heroic zeitgeist of the nineteenth-century West while also powerfully reflecting the late-twentieth-century counterculture's awareness of the karmic debt it was inheriting from America's blood-soaked past.

Crabb is also a metaphor for America's ambivalent desire to be part of both the Indian and non-Indian world during this tumultuous transitional post-Vietnam era. To refer to Black Elk's mythological terminology, the divisive Vietnam War had "broken the hoop" of the American nation, and now, like the Indian, non-Indians were seeking a reunification of the Great Hoop. Thus Wounded Knee II was ultimately a significant turning point in mending the five-hundred-year relationship between Indians and non-Indians.

The American Indian Movement would soon become recognized by most indigenous people as a contemporary version of a continuing struggle between the native people of North America and the invaders of their homeland. Founded in 1968 by young urban Indians Clyde and Vernon Bellecourt, Russell Means, and Dennis Banks and often later supported financially by the actor

Marlon Brando, the American Indian Movement was initially concerned with police brutality in the Minneapolis/St. Paul region. As the National Congress of American Indians and the National Indian Youth Council before them, however, AIM eventually began to address many broader contemporary Indian issues such as sovereignty, restoring and honoring treaties rights, and reclaiming language, religion, and culture. Soon, both traditional tribal people on the reservation and these young urban Indians began to realize that simply *being* Indian, they faced similar circumstances in modern America; indeed, the 1973 Wounded Knee incident occurred because the situation in Lakota territory was not much different from the conditions that led to the massacre there in 1890. In many ways the abject poverty, broken treaties, silent racial hostility reflected in Byzantine government policies, and overall moral indifference that were present in 1890 had only worsened in the ensuing eighty-three years. For example, Shannon County, the location of Pine Ridge Reservation in South Dakota, held the shameful distinction of being the poorest county in America. The average life span of a male Oglala Sioux on Pine Ridge Reservation was forty years. Still, with a per capita income lower than many so-called third world countries, the traditional Lakota secretly held together and drew strength from their spiritual values and, in spite of intense efforts to dismantle and destroy them, were somehow rejuvenating in the remote regions of the reservations. Mindful of Lakota holy man Black Elk's 1868 prophecy that the Sacred Hoop of the Lakota Nation would be broken but would nevertheless reunify after seven generations had passed, many modern traditional medicine men and chiefs such as Archie Fire, Frank Fools Crow, and Leonard Crow Dog were expecting the return of the young urban warriors and were prepared to instruct them in the old ways.

The 1973 incident at Wounded Knee was an appalling condemnation of how desperate life had become for Indian people throughout America. In spite of the widespread romantic recognition of the history of their culture and the struggle to maintain and preserve it in best-selling books and popular movies like *Little Big Man* and *Soldier Blue*, generations of physical and mythological manipulation had indeed rendered *real* Indian people and their very real concerns virtually invisible to the general American public. Hence, the bold symbolism of the seizure of that church ambushed modern electronic media's "global village" and, in McLuhanist symbolism, announced that Indians indeed had *not* vanished and were instead making their grievances known to the world.

Here it is also important to note that Wounded Knee II marked an ironic, violent shift in confrontations between the FBI—an organization created in the early twentieth century to thwart the terrorist movement of immigrant anarchists—and the continuing struggle of indigenous Americans to defend their nations from invaders. To put Wounded Knee II in perspective as the turning point from peaceful demonstration to violent confrontation, we must return briefly to the creation of the National Indian Youth Council in 1961. Young Indians had become increasingly political throughout Indian Country over the preceding decade, and the militant attitude that blossomed during Washington State's fish-ins had indicated that more aggressive tactics might also succeed with other issues. As the conservative congressional element in Washington, DC, and various western state capitols continued to press for termination of government services to tribes and resist any attempts at peaceful diplomacy, Indian youth were indeed forced to become more politically motivated and employ tactics of civil disobedience in order to prevent the intense efforts of the United States government to force Indians to abandon the very last vestiges of their heritage and assimilate. This movement to become more politically active soon led to a series of important Indian victories.

The most significant of these new triumphs occurred in 1966 when Secretary of the Interior Stewart Udall fired Commissioner of Indian Affairs Philleo Nash because of his outspoken position against the termination of the Colville tribe in eastern Washington State. After the firing, Udall arranged a secret meeting of Bureau of Indian Affairs (BIA) officials in Santa Fe to outline a new program for Indians. The National Congress of American Indians discovered that part of Udall's plan was to turn over community action funding from the Johnson administration's Great Society program and its "war on poverty" to the BIA, thereby disqualifying the tribes as sponsoring agencies with the Office of Economic Opportunity. Consequently, representatives from sixty tribes greeted Udall in Santa Fe to voice their opposition to his planned program. Stunned by the Indians' ambush and suddenly desperate, Udall sent newly appointed Commissioner of Indian Affairs Bob Bennett to the assembly of tribal representatives, literally to play piano and stall them while he and the rest of his team hurried to devise a plan to adjust to his vulnerable situation. While Udall stonewalled to quickly strategize, Indians were a couple of steps ahead of him with a plan of their own to march to an Episcopal church where important non-Indian representatives of Indian interest groups such as the Association on American Indian Affairs (AAIA) were holding meetings to discuss future Department of Interior policies. When Udall learned of the Indians' plans to demonstrate at the church, he realized he had been cleverly outmaneuvered and promptly agreed to meet with officers of the National Congress of American Indians (NCAI).

In the meeting Udall pleaded with Indian representatives to understand that he was under intense pressure from powerful legislators to support the total termination policy. Then, Udall astonished NCAI leaders when he promised five years of work toward reversing termination policies if the Indians would simply agree to abandon the effort to halt termination of the Agua Caliente band of California. Now furious with Udall's proposal, the NCAI vowed to fight *everything* the Department of Interior attempted until eventually the secretary was forced to completely abandon his termination position. The effort to terminate the Agua Caliente tribe was ended. The National Congress of American Indians had won.

When the meeting in Santa Fe ended with an NCAI victory, Secretary Udall promised to create an omnibus bill that would "incorporate all Indian problems into one major piece of legislation." The NCAI was offered a vague promise that they would be consulted about the promised bill, and everyone departed Santa Fe harboring suspicions of what the other might do next.

By the summer of 1966, rumors reached Indian Country that Udall had already begun drafting the legislation without consulting the tribes. The NCAI believed the secretary to be a fundamentally honest man and determined these rumors had been leaked in an attempt by Udall's powerful conservative foes to create discontent and derail cooperation from Indian Country. The NCAI nevertheless obtained a copy of the Department of Interior's legislation and began structuring plans for an autumn ambush of its own that would direct the entire matter away from government control and toward the Indians' strength. A dozen of the most influential tribal chairmen in America were summoned to a secret meeting with NCAI leaders in Denver. There it was decided that the executive director of the NCAI would follow Commissioner of Indian Affairs Bob Bennett as he traveled Indian Country to consult with the tribes concerning the proposed omnibus legislation; as Bennett made his presentation, the executive director of the NCAI would hand out mimeographed copies of the proposed legislation. By the time Commissioner Bennett arrived in Billings to meet with tribes from the upper Rockies and Great Plains, he was shocked to discover that the tribes had already met and passed a resolution against the omnibus bill. After this second major NCAI victory the Department of Interior and the BIA abandoned its consulting charade and simply asked tribal leaders for suggestions that tailored the legislation to their specific needs.

The election of Richard Nixon in 1968 was greeted with much skepticism throughout Indian Country. The previous Republican administration had introduced, developed, and enforced the disastrous termination policies, and Indian leaders naturally expected the worst from Nixon. They were pleasantly surprised to discover that the Nixon administration initially proved to be sincerely interested in addressing the injustices that had been done to Indian people and, echoing the Johnson Administration, preferred instead an Indian policy of self-determination to the termination policies of the Eisenhower era. Giving Indians even more reason for optimism, Nixon had restored the terminated Menominee to tribal status and also returned the sacred Blue Lake to the Pueblo tribe of Taos. Unfortunately, after the first year of Nixon's initial term, the old government bureaucratic patterns returned, and once again young Indians' political concerns were repeatedly pushed to the back burner in Washington.

In late October 1969 an organization of young Indians, American Indians United (AIU), met in San Francisco for its annual convention. The day after the convention ended, the San Francisco Indian Center burned, leaving Bay Area Indians no place to gather. In early November nineteen Indian students from Berkeley and San Francisco State landed on Alcatraz Island and spent the night eluding guards before being captured and removed from the island the next morning. Still, the event generated enough local news to serve as a rallying call to Bay Area Indians, and on November 19 nearly three hundred Indians landed on the island. Suddenly Indians were global news. Perhaps even more significant, the Indian occupation of Alcatraz lasted from November 1969 until June 1971 and became a national call to action for Indian people.[4]

Mohawk Richard Oakes, Grace Thorpe (daughter of the famous Indian athlete Jim Thorpe), and Tuscarora medicine man Mad Bear Anderson, representing the "Indians of All Tribes" occupying Alcatraz, issued a public statement loaded with symbolism:

Proclamation to the Great White Father and All His People,

We, the Native Americans, reclaim the land known as Alcatraz Island in the name of all American Indians by right of discovery...We feel that this so-called Alcatraz Island is more than suitable for an Indian Reservation, as determined by the white man's own standard. By this we mean that this place resembles most Indian reservations in that: 1. It is isolated from modern facilities, and without adequate means of transportation. 2. It has no fresh running water. 3. It has inadequate sanitation facilities. 4. There are no oil or mineral rights. 5. There is no industry, and so unemployment is very great. 6. There are no health facilities. 7. The soil is rocky and unproductive; and the land does not support game. 8. There are no educational facilities. 9. The population has always exceeded the land base. 10. The population has always been held as prisoners and kept dependent upon others. Further, it would be fitting and symbolic that ships from all over the world, entering the Golden Gate, would first see Indian land, and thus be reminded of the true history of this nation. This tiny island would be a symbol of the great lands once ruled by free and noble Indians.[5]

The ongoing Indian occupation of Alcatraz Island continued to attract sporadic international news coverage, but over the next year a sense of apprehension spread throughout Indian Country. Rather than sympathetically listening to and addressing Indian concerns, even as the Alcatraz Island occupation lingered on, the federal government instead funneled monies into urban Indian programs hoping that would appease dissenters and make them go away. Meanwhile, Washington continued to regulate tribal reservation governments and designate the Indian officials they wished to head its various programs. Worse, even though activists were gaining international attention and support for their efforts, the government ignored its promises as quickly as the demonstrations ended and the radicals departed.

Then, in January 1972, the Chippewa tribe of Minnesota won a lawsuit pertaining to their fishing rights within reservation boundaries. Wealthy non-Indian resort owners and outfitters in the region were not pleased with the decision, as they had poached the Chippewa's lakes for decades without paying the tribe a penny; the non-Indian fishing and resort industry throughout the region was suddenly turned on its ear.

The issue intensified when the American Indian Movement held a convention at Cass Lake, Minnesota, in the spring of 1972 and involved itself—and the issue of sovereignty—in the situation concerning the Chippewa tribe's fishing rights. Since its inception, the American Indian Movement stressed unity in the support of tribal sovereignty. But the deeper that AIM activists explored the theory of tribal sovereignty, the more the concept began to reveal itself as being politically multifaceted in its essence. This was especially the case in Minnesota, where tribal officials interpreted tribal sovereignty to be support for the decisions of tribal councils; the Chippewa in particular had lost most of their ancestral lands through the allotment programs implemented during the closing years of the nineteenth century. AIM activists regarded this as a situation requiring a more aggressive stance that would serve to frighten non-Indians away from the Chippewa's lakes. So, during their convention, AIM activists blocked the roads to the site and protected their boundaries with armed guards. Dangerous disputes were eventually settled amiably, but activists had shattered the notion of pacification and announced their apparent willingness to use arms to once again violently confront non-Indian aggression in Indian Territory.[6]

Even more ominous, the confrontations at Cass Lake exposed a rift between the older tribal leadership and the younger, more militant activists. AIM leaders now increasingly perceived the nontraditional, older tribal leaders as "Uncle Tomahawks" and "Apples" ("red on the outside, white on the inside") surrendering control of the tribes to the federal government. From the beginning, AIM leadership had looked to the traditional spiritual and military leaders of the nineteenth century and contemporary traditional religious leaders for inspiration. As a result they became increasingly disgusted by late-twentieth-century nontraditional tribal leadership's unwillingness to defend and protect the people at all costs. They felt abandoned by modern tribal leadership, and the result was that for AIM activists and their growing numbers, sovereignty began to take on more serious ideological implications. Yet even among many of those same Indian leaders who so infuriated the AIM activists, the desire for a return to a traditional form of Indian government was no longer merely a rhetorical notion, and the sovereignty movement began to profoundly resonate throughout Indian Country.[7]

By 1972 the sovereignty movement also gathered momentum because funding for many of the Johnson administration's Great Society programs was being slashed, and Indians were the first to feel the financial cuts. The result of feeling doubly betrayed by powerless Indian leaders and Washington was the flame that brought the situation from a simmer to a boil. All through the summer powwow season, Indian leaders held meetings to discuss the increasingly dangerous situation. Young and old alike were becoming motivated to find a way to bring their situation to the attention of the American public, but the divisions among those tribal members now perceived as "government Indians," those perceived as "traditional," and those considered "urban" had dramatically developed into multiple chasms.

On the Pine Ridge Reservation in South Dakota, the traditionalist's worst fears were realized in 1972 when a mixed-blood named Dick Wilson won a controversial election and became tribal president of the Oglala Nation. Wilson held the traditional tribal people in disdain and, with thinly veiled secrecy, was a dummy for the ventriloquist powerbrokers in corporate and political America who wanted access to natural resources on Pine Ridge. Soon after his election, Wilson created a large police force composed of his relatives and friends who called themselves "Guardians of the Oglala Nation." Traditional Oglala promptly, and appropriately, dubbed them goons.

Just weeks before Wilson's election, in February 1972 two white brothers had kidnapped an Oglala man named Raymond Yellow Thunder in Gordon, Nebraska. The brothers savagely beat Yellow Thunder, stripped him from the waist down, and crammed his battered body into the trunk of their car. After driving around the region for several hours drinking, they stopped at an American Legion Hall dance, dragged the severely injured man from their car, and forced him half-naked onto the dance floor. A few compassionate non-Indians offered to help Yellow Thunder. Profoundly humiliated, he refused assistance and stumbled through the freezing night to his home on the reservation in Porcupine. Yellow Thunder died the following morning from the brain hemorrhage his torturers inflicted, beating him senseless the night before.

Oglala Lakota AIM member Russell Means happened to be from Raymond Yellow Thunder's hometown of Porcupine. Even though he was born on the reservation, Means had been raised in Oakland, California, and trained as an accountant. Means had become the head of the Indian Center of Cleveland, Ohio, as well as the head of the AIM office there. When Means learned of Yellow Thunder's murder he immediately headed to Gordon, Nebraska, to investigate matters himself. Soon, traditional tribal leaders on Pine

Ridge asked other AIM leaders to join Means and come to the reservation to investigate Yellow Thunder's murder.[8]

Dick Wilson and his goons were extremely threatened by the intervention of AIM activists. The "outsiders'" investigations promptly began to expose the tribal president's shady political connections and corrupt police force. Soon after arriving on the Pine Ridge Reservation, Russell Means and local AIM activists organized a demonstration to protest Raymond Yellow Thunder's murder. The demonstrators left Pine Ridge in a large caravan and headed for Gordon, Nebraska. As soon as they arrived, they were greeted by a large force of state troopers, local police, and reporters. After decades of indifference, the media were now suddenly flocking to Indian Country.

Months before Raymond Yellow Thunder's murder and the demonstrations in Gordon, AIM leaders had met on the Rosebud Reservation to discuss plans to mount a demonstration in Washington patterned after the civil rights gatherings of the early 1960s. The concept was for a caravan to begin in the West and travel from reservation to reservation gathering numbers as it headed east to Washington. Finances had prevented the idea from advancing further than the planning stages until fate intervened in September 1972, when one of the leaders of the Alcatraz occupation, Richard Oakes, was shot and killed by a guard at a YMCA camp in California. Once again, Oakes inspired unity in Indian Country; his murder became a rallying cry, and the caravan effort began rolling toward Washington. Dennis Banks led a car caravan that departed San Francisco, and Mad Bear Anderson led another from Seattle with the intention of arriving in Washington, DC, during the final week of the 1972 presidential campaign.

The Trail of Broken Treaties Caravan arrived in Washington on Friday, November 3, 1972, before the Tuesday elections. In a peaceful procession stretching over four miles long, nearly a thousand Indians of all ages and from scores of different tribes came to the nation's capital to offer a Twenty Point Proposal to the Nixon administration.

"The Twenty Points presented a new framework for considering the status of Indian tribes and the nature of their federal relationship," Vine Deloria Jr. later wrote about the demonstration. "It harkened back to the days of freedom, when the United States courted the friendship of the tribes in its desperate battle to maintain its independence from Great Britain."[9]

Of singular importance, the points the Indian activists addressed concerning treaty rights were of enormous significance because they represented a very clear consensus of twentieth-century Pan-Indian American opinion. Indians of every nation had the long-held belief that their treaties were legal documents that had been ignored or misinterpreted. Focusing the thrust of the caravan on those "broken treaties" united them into one voice.

Consequently, to emphasize the sovereignty issue, the first of the Twenty Points dealt with a restoration of constitutional treaty-making authority by repealing the 1871 appropriations statute forbidding the United States from entering into further treaties with tribes. The Indian activists argued that the 1871 statute had taken constitutional power and responsibility from the president and Congress. Next, the Twenty Points proposed that a new treaty commission be established to regulate treaties on a national, regional, and local basis. Other points pertained to reviewing past and present treaty infringements and addressing chronic incidences of violations.

Essentially, the Twenty Points clearly indicated that AIM and other political Indian activists had initiated profound change. Most important, the traditional reservation elders and modern medicine men had a dramatic and lasting impact on the young AIM leaders. Lakota elders realized the young men raised in inner-city urban America knew little of traditional ceremony or ritual. The elders also knew these young Indian men were hungry for the spiritual knowledge of the past that they possessed and were eager to share. The reuniting of a major section of the Sacred Hoop of the Lakota Nation broken at Wounded Knee in 1890 was now complete.

Author Peter Matthiessen's interview with imprisoned AIM leader Leonard Peltier explains how the BIA's disrespect for the chiefs and elders who traveled in Washington to present the Twenty Points of broken treaties led to the riots in the bureau's offices. Peltier explained to Matthiessen that elderly chiefs including Frank

Fools Crow and Charlie Red Cloud and many others had traveled to Washington to present the Twenty Points. Lodging had been promised for the elders and chiefs, but when they arrived at the housing the government had arranged for them, they were shocked to discover their rooms were full of rats. Peltier, Dennis Banks, and other AIM leaders were outraged that the BIA would be so disrespectful of these chiefs of their nations, so they went to the bureau's offices to demand better housing. If denied, they intended to stage a sit-in until their demands were met. BIA officials repeatedly stalled the Indian activists until a riot squad arrived and started beating the doors down. At this point a full-fledged riot broke out.[10]

The Indians clearly had a more important agenda and had never intended to occupy the BIA's Washington offices. After they were forced to barricade the offices' doors to protect themselves from the riot squads, however, the media and government officials assumed that, as at Alcatraz Island, militant Indian activists had intended from the start to seize and ransack the offices. The young Ponca head of Oklahoma AIM, Carter Camp, informed the press that Washington officials had promised a polite reception upon the arrival of the Indian leadership, and if they had honored that promise of dignified treatment, the entire confrontation could have been avoided.[11]

Unfortunately, the Twenty Points the activists had come to Washington to propose to Congress and the president were a casualty of the riots. As Vine Deloria Jr. observes, the parallels between the proposals of John Collier's Indian Reorganization Act forty years earlier and the Twenty Points are "startling." Deloria suggests, "Some of the parallels are certainly the paths along which the future changes in federal policy must lie if it is to be effective. The Collier proposal to establish a Court of Indian Affairs, for example, is very similar to the suggestions by the Trail of Broken Treaties of encompassing all Indians within a federal treaty relationship and getting up a treaty commission to determine violations of the treaties. When a particular solution is advanced by diverse and unrelated groups a number of times over the period of a century, it would appear that the problem is one that must be taken seriously."[12]

The possibility of a Court of Indian Affairs and the proposal of the Twenty Points were sadly lost as the activists were dismissed and branded as malcontents and radicals. After five days a truce was negotiated, and the Indians surrendered the BIA offices in Washington, broke into small groups, and headed home.

Inspired by the attention AIM brought to the disgraceful treatment of Raymond Yellow Thunder, and the way AIM representatives quickly came to the assistance of other legal problems on the reservation, particularly with issues concerning the elderly, various members of the organization were increasingly asked to assist with problems on Pine Ridge Reservation. Russell Means returned to Pine Ridge to study religion and Lakota language from medicine men and other elders, started a food purchasing co-op in his hometown of Porcupine, and announced his intention to run for tribal chairman. Naturally, this enraged Dick Wilson, and his goons increased their brutal abuse of traditionalists and AIM activists on the reservation. By February 27, 1973, Chief Frank Fools Crow announced that elders and AIM activists had decided to create a symbolic confrontation between them and Wilson's small army. Lakota women suggested they all go down to the church at Wounded Knee and make a stand.

The stand lasted from February 28 until May 7, ultimately took the lives of Cherokee and Lakota AIM activists Frank Clearwater and Buddy Lamont, respectively, and crippled US Marshal Lloyd Grimm for life. When the smoke cleared the event had cost the United States $7 million. Yet the violent confrontations created by the civil war on the Pine Ridge Reservation would tragically continue well past the negotiations that ended Wounded Knee II.

After the election of former BIA superintendent Al Trimble as tribal council president during the winter of 1975, Dick Wilson informed everyone on Pine Ridge that he was not pleased that he had been voted out of office by a margin of three to one. Nevertheless, Wilson held the office until April and intended to continue to use his remaining time in power to intimidate the people who had opposed him. On January 17, 1975, Wilson specifically threatened Trimble's hometown of Wanblee for its strong opposition in the election, and he made good on his threat. On January 30, fifteen of Wilson's goons wearing bullet-proof vests and armed with machine guns drove into Wanblee in three cars. The next morning shots were fired into the home of Vietnam War veteran Guy Dull Knife, a descendant of the Cheyenne chief Dull Knife. Witnesses identified the shooters, but the BIA police failed to arrest them. Later on January 30, the same men who shot into Guy Dull Knife's home overtook his friend, holy man Black Elk's great-grandson Bryon DeSersa, in a high-speed chase and fired repeatedly into the left side of his car. DeSersa's left leg was nearly severed by the hail of bullets, and he lost control of the vehicle and rolled it into a ditch. DeSersa's terrified passengers crawled from the car and ran for their lives. One brave passenger, George Bettelyoun, remained with DeSersa to help him out of the car, but realizing DeSersa couldn't walk, he soon fled as well. As the murderers chased the fleeing passengers over the prairie, Black Elk's great-grandson bled to death by the side of the road. Later, Bettelyoun identified the shooters and gave descriptions of their vehicles to FBI agents, who promptly arrested Guy Dull Knife for disorderly conduct. Eventually a man named Charlie Winters confessed to shooting DeSersa, and he and a man named Dale Janis served two years in prison for the murder. Dick Wilson's son Billy and his son-in-law Chuck Richards were acquitted on grounds of self-defense.[13]

Activists continue to plea for the release of AIM activist Leonard Peltier well into the twenty-first century. In 1975 Peltier was involved in a firefight on the reservation in which an FBI agent was killed, and his subsequent conviction and sentencing for the murder of the agent have been embroiled in controversy now for over a quarter of a century. It appears that Peltier will remain in prison for the rest of his life.

Many precious Indian and non-Indian lives were shattered and lost as Indian activists were forced to resort to militant civil disobedience and actual violence to bring their issues before the world's court of opinion in the 1960s and 1970s. Yet after Wounded Knee II, the electronically connected global village would never again consider American Indians invisible. Whereas their grandfathers shouted "Hoka hey!" and rode ponies into battle, the brave warriors of the late twentieth century had realized the epiphany Sitting Bull experienced when he joined the *Wild West* in 1885: celebrity is the conduit to the dominant mythology of western civilization. After the takeover of the church at Wounded Knee in 1973, several important American Indian activists began to go into show business.

Chapter Nineteen
Dances with Wolves and *Avatar*

A good nation I will make live.
This the nation above has said.
They have given me the power to make over.[1]

—Black Elk

The Western Writers of America held their annual convention in Oklahoma City in June 2009. On the opening morning of the gathering, the Marriott Hotel's convention hall was filled to capacity with Western writers, publishers, literary agents, screenwriters, film producers, and aficionados eager to engage the all-Indian panel with questions concerning non-Indians "writing about Indians." Led by best-selling Lakota author-actor Joseph Marshall III, the panelists concluded their opening remarks and opened the discussion to questions, answers, and comments. This conversation immediately prompted one particular thing worth noting: Kevin Costner's Academy Award–winning motion picture *Dances with Wolves* had significantly influenced *every* person in the room. Aside from inspiring Hollywood, cable networks, and public television to launch a watershed of feature and documentary film projects employing American Indians, Costner's decision to have actors speak the Lakota language and use English subtitles throughout the film not only eliminated the threadbare stereotype of movie Indians communicating in Pidgin English, but also honored an equally important elevated appreciation of Indian language and culture while simultaneously offering a much more subtle, realistic interpretation of the horse-and-buffalo culture of the nineteenth-century American West. Of course, this book argues that, whenever possible, American Indians have been subtly affecting the evolution of the non-Indian mythological interpretation of their culture since European explorers arrived in North America.

But the effort by Indians to personally and peacefully interpret their culture in books, on stage, and on film particularly intensified *after* the *Wild West* era and again after the violent civil war era at Pine Ridge that was marked by AIM's 1973 seizure of the church at Wounded Knee. The series of lengthy trials and eventual exonerations of AIM activists Russell Means and Dennis Banks, as well as Leonard Peltier's numerous murder trials and appeals (in which he was repeated found guilty), the decades of failed petitions to secure a pardon for Peltier, and his lengthy imprisonment all convinced leaders in Indian Country that the time had come to resort to different tactics. Many modern Indian leaders wisely turned to the strategy pioneered by Sitting Bull in Cody's *Wild West* to create, develop, and project *their* role into mainstream mythological awareness; once again activist Indians entered the entertainment industry.

By the mid-1980s, Alcatraz AIM leader John Trudell had become a major poet/songwriter, recording artist, and film star, and in the early 1990s, even Russell Means began a new career as a film actor in *The Last of the Mohicans*. Means would eventually even become a voice actor in a Walt Disney cartoon of the Pocahontas version of the captivity narrative. But American Indian use of motion pictures to affect social and mythological consciousness truly blossomed one hundred years after Sitting Bull's death, and eighteen years after Wounded Knee II, with Michael Blake's 1990 book and screenplay, *Dances with Wolves*.

It is important to note that the tribe depicted in Michael Blake's novel is Comanche, and the book's story takes place in the panhandle regions of Oklahoma and Texas, whereas the tribe featured in the motion picture is Lakota and the location is South Dakota. The relevance of this change of tribes and locations and the subsequent astonishing international success of *Dances with Wolves* yet again underscores John Neihardt's theory of the dynamic spiritual pattern and the mythological significance of the Great Plains of the Trans-Missouri. Imperative to Blake's screenplay of his novel, modern-day South Dakota had large and healthy buffalo herds, whereas the Texas/Oklahoma panhandle regions depicted in the novel did not. The requirement of buffalo herds thus had decisive impact on the groundbreaking theme of language that is central to both the novel and the film versions of *Dances with Wolves*. Even though there are major ongoing efforts now, when *Dances with Wolves* was filmed little had been done to retrieve the Comanche language in comparison to the decades of focused efforts by the Lakota to retain their native tongue. By 1990 there were indeed numerous course syllabuses on the Lakota language. Consequently, when the film eventually set its location in their country, the Lakota were prepared with expert teachers to train non-Indian actors to speak Lakota and to use the language throughout the film.

Another fundamentally important aspect of both the book and the film that is rarely discussed is Michael Blake's clever presentation of the captivity narrative in his story. In both his novel and his screenplay, Blake focuses on polar extremes of the captivity narrative. One extreme is represented by the leading female character Stands With A Fist, who represents the non-Indian taken captive as a child and reared and married into Indian culture. She is introduced in both book and film as the grieving widow of a beloved warrior. At the other extreme is Lieutenant John Dunbar. As mentioned earlier, many non-Indians—such as the mountain men— made the willful, conscious decision to embrace the Indian way of life, and *Dances with Wolves* concentrates on Dunbar's instinctive attraction to the indigenous culture in which he can reinvent himself and achieve spiritual transcendence. Through language Dunbar slowly develops indigenous awareness of the spiritual interconnectedness of life, and doing so transforms himself from shell-shocked, by-the-book American military man into the Plains Indian Dances With Wolves. A defining moment in Dunbar's path to indigenous enlightenment is a scene depicting him and Lakota leader Kicking Bird standing in tall prairie grasses as they discuss the Lakota effort to raise their children into good *humans*. By the time the military arrives to relieve him of his wayward prairie post and the film approaches its conclusion, Dunbar has nearly completely vanished into the Lakota Dances With Wolves; according to Lakota perception, Dunbar has become human. Thus, when his non-Indian military rescuers exhibit the wanton brutality and environmental rapaciousness of the society and culture he once fought for, Dances With Wolves wants nothing more of it; indeed, he is now ready to fight *against* his native culture—and he does. Becoming human, he has become indigenous.

Many Indians believed the love affair between the two non-Indian characters in the film was contrived and guilty of forced Hollywood symmetry. This perspective ignores the fact that the union of the two non-Indians in his narrative provided Michael Blake the splendid opportunity to emphasize the language barrier the two cultures faced and the efforts of Dunbar, Kicking Bird, and Stands With A Fist to overcome it. Vitally important, this core aspect of Blake's novel and script is also what made the use of the Lakota language absolutely logical—and therefore central—to the fundamental story, thus inspiring the producers to use it throughout the film.

The captivity narrative within Blake's novel and screenplay also discreetly addresses the miscegenation issue—and nonverbally symbolizes the powerful bonds of Stands With A Fist's genuine Lakota union by presenting her in mourning for her dead Lakota husband when Dunbar first meets her. Blake then dignifies the entire romance between Stands With A Fist and Dunbar by having them surrender their passions to a proper Lakota traditional mourning period before beginning their courtship. This subtle and sensitive approach also allows an appropriate time for Dunbar's transition into Dances With Wolves and creates a more detailed presentation of the social and spiritual life of the Plains Indians of the 1860s. Even so, the race issue in the film ultimately remains troubling and underscores the problem many American Indians have with the ending of Blake's screenplay: having been romantically and spiritually healed and united by the Lakota, the non-Indian couple rides safely away even as the military are descending upon the last wild bands of the Sioux.

Whereas everyone in the audience at the Western Writers of America's "Writing about Indians" symposium panel was involved in one way or another with interpreting or reinterpreting the mythological form of the Western in the twenty-first century in literature and film, it was noteworthy that *Dances with Wolves* had clearly initiated an effort by contemporary writers of Western historical fiction and nonfiction to explore and discover a more sensitive and realistic depiction of the form of the genre from an indigenous perspective.

Yet throughout the discussions that morning, Joseph Marshall had sat quietly and listened intently as electric energies surged back and forth between the panel and the audience. Eventually someone in the audience reversed the theme of the symposium itself and asked Marshall directly what he thought about Indians writing about non-Indians. Marshall's response completely underscored the theme of this book when he gently reminded the audience about the reservation system and how that unique reality continues to force Indians to live in two worlds. "So," Marshall concluded, "we have lived in your world, but you *still* haven't lived in ours."

Nevertheless, as mentioned throughout this text, creative writers and filmmakers have frequently used the form of the Western in order to return to the past to explore controversial social or political issues that are too explosive to confront in the present. Similarly, authors and screenwriters use the genre of science fiction to project volatile present-day topics into the future for examination. In December 2009 —barely six months after Joseph Marshall's remark to the Western writers gathered in Oklahoma City—Hollywood and state-of-the-art digital technology fused the Western and science fiction genres and ventured into an imaginary indigenous tribal culture as a means of delving deep into the controversial concepts of western civilization's environmental capriciousness, corporate globalization, and interplanetary hegemony—all of which was creatively centered around a futuristic version of the captivity narrative, the notion of "becoming indigenous," and Black Elk's power vision.

Even as spellbound audiences were bedazzled by the technological wizardry of modern moviemaking, most recognized the plot of James Cameron's landmark film five minutes into the experience. *Avatar* was a Western! In spite of the stunning combination of actors seamlessly interacting with innovative computer-generated graphics, spectacular and creative new use of the old 3-D format, a futuristic science-fiction premise, and its setting on another planet, Cameron's story—as the director no doubt intended—was familiar to anyone who had attended a movie since *The Great Train Robbery* in 1903. Like *Dances with Wolves* twenty years earlier, however, *Avatar* was not a "traditional" Western. Both films were certainly important departures from the form, yet, as this book concludes, for the past century the archetypical American "cowboy" has progressively revealed his hegemonic WASP origins and intentions, and the mythological form of the Western itself is evolving in kind; the villains in both *Avatar* and *Dances with Wolves* represent what the global community now generally recognizes as the "imperialistic American cowboy." Therefore, even though both films essentially remain cowboys-and-Indians Westerns, they reflect a fundamental mythological change: over the past quarter-century of ambiguity concerning which is which, the archetypes of "hero" and "villain" have now reversed. Moreover, whereas the remarkable critical and popular success of *Dances with Wolves* at the close of the twentieth century finally created the environment to present a more conscious perception of the American Indian throughout mainstream corporate media—particularly within the old form of the Western—*Avatar* is ultimately the very first appearance of western civilization's use of technology fused with an interspecies variation of the mythological plot device of the captivity narrative in a truly significant attempt to finally embrace nature and escape the curse of Genesis.

In his last book, *C. G. Jung and the Sioux Tradition: Dreams, Visions, Nature, and the Primitive*, published posthumously and edited by his son, Philip, and Jungian psychologist Jerome Bernstein, Vine Deloria Jr. suggests, "Perhaps the most extravagant pretense of western civilization is its tenaciously held belief that only humans matter in the scheme of things. The origin of this unwarranted arrogance is unknown, but psychologically speaking it is western culture's greatest inflation. In this tradition, humans are created last after all other creatures and are given the privilege of naming, thereby gaining ascendancy over all other beings. This is a subtle but key point in understanding the root psychology and philosophy of western culture. With this claim to naming, something important has already happened to western man in relation to the rest of creation."[2]

Deloria concludes that this assumption of dominance in the hierarchy of life tragically institutionalizes and ultimately separates western man from nature. Deloria continues his contrast of creation mythologies and explains that the traditional Sioux *also* believe that man was created last of all the creatures. Yet, unlike biblical Genesis, the Lakota believe that because all other living things were created *first*, man is thereby the youngest, and is thus dependent upon the wisdom and experience of the older creations. Deloria's comparisons of the biblical Genesis of western civilization with Sioux creation mythology also recall Ron Goodman's research into Lakota stellar theology and the primal race in the Black Hills between the two-leggeds and four-leggeds to determine who would eat whom. The distinction between the creation mythologies that becomes immediately clear is the inclusion of animals by Indians as opposed to the assumption of dominance, and thereby exclusion, of animals in the biblical version. Deloria suggests by including animals, there is an inherent implication that plants, insects, and stones have equal importance in the "scheme of things." In contrast, however, according to traditional Judo-Greek-Christian doctrine, the inclusion of animals, plants, and inanimate objects in religious ceremonies is the very definition of paganism. Consequently, whether or not Western civilization literally begins at a pivotal moment with Adam, Eve, and a snake at Eden's Tree of Knowledge, the implication is that by assuming they were above the rest of creation, men and women forever separated themselves from nature. We have also noted in this text that this evolving theological and psychological separation between man and nature was powerfully reinforced by author Frederick Turner's observation that when Moses was away on Mount Sinai receiving the Ten Commandments, the Israelites immediately "lost" themselves in the wilderness, constructed a golden idol as a surrogate deity, and reverted to paganism, thereby implying that embracing nature immediately led to the breaking of God's fundamental laws. Of course, the not-so-subtle mythological subtext of Moses's angry denunciation of the Israelites upon delivery of the Decalogue further expanded and deepened the epistemological chasm between nature and spirituality, as this implication of God's chosen people falling prey to paganism hop-scotched from Judaism into Christianity and, joined at the hip with Western civilization in Rome, began its obsessive march to rid the world of indigenous idolaters.

Departing Exodus and the biblical Tree of Knowledge, it is important to note that the spiritual connection to the sacred Tree of Souls in *Avatar* suggests the prophecy of the reunification of *all* tribes around the sacred Tree of Life depicted in Black Elk's power vision. In the years to come, *Avatar* may become regarded merely as the landmark blockbuster that reintroduced the novelty of 3-D to the mainstream motion picture experience of the twenty-first century. Or, its luster may diminish simply to be regarded as a "sci-fi *Dances with Wolves*." Whatever *Avatar*'s ultimate critical destiny, Cameron's film will remain significant because it connected the mystical mythological insight of nineteenth-century Lakota holy man Black Elk and the indigenous peoples of the world with the mainstream technological—digital—world of the twenty-first century. Moreover, *Avatar* united the world around the concept of Black Elk's mythological Tree of Life as a metaphor representing the multiple environmental crises humans currently face. This is noteworthy because the Internet has truly united the planet in instant, constant, free, democratic communication for the first time and, doing so, created the opportunity to finally reach an interconnected global awareness. *Avatar*, of course, powerfully suggests this awareness will rise from the indigenous people of the planet; indeed, in Cameron's film the concept of the avatar itself is western technology's embracing—indeed, inhabiting, the indigenous mind and body. This central metaphor in *Avatar* clearly returns to the captivity narrative and the delicate relationship between the indigenous people of the world—nature—and technology.

Another of *Avatar*'s primary metaphors—the neurological queue worn by the composite aboriginal Na'vi tribe of the planet

Pandora—also suggests a very direct physical and spiritual "connection" to the propensity of indigenous tribal people of the world to wear their hair long and braided and the traditional connection of this practice to paganism; the Na'vi neuro-queue becomes their direct "link" to the spiritual life force of the animals and plants with which they bond. Similarly, the neuro-queue functions as a technological metaphor; just as surely as most audiences quickly recognized that *Avatar* was essentially a new version of an old-fashioned Western, having spent the past twenty years logged on to computers in the multiple and various rapidly evolving incarnations of the Internet era, audiences also instantly recognized *Avatar*'s neuro-queue as a technological conduit by which the Na'vi "logged" into a biological network. Consequently, Cameron's film is a myth depicting humanity's development of technology to such a degree that it can reinvent the captivity narrative as a metaphor that embraces the indigenous mind, body, and spirit of another species. Thus the neuro-queue—like everything else in the motion picture—represents a metaphysical union of the natural world with the technological world.

Moving forward here with a comparison of *Avatar* and *Black Elk Speaks*, however, we must remain mindful of the late media theorist Neil Postman's admonition not to confuse message with metaphor. Postman cautions that message indicates an "unambiguous statement," whereas modern media intentionally uses various forms of ambiguous metaphors to "enforce their special definition of reality." Nevertheless, if, as some theologians and psychologists argue, western civilization worships technology, then the neuro-queue mythology of *Avatar* also appears to reinterpret aboriginal notions of universal connectedness. For example, the Lakota definition of prayer is "to speak with one's ancestors," and prayers are usually concluded with the remark *mitakuye oyasin*, a phrase that states the Lakota belief that all life is interdependent and intertwined within the Great Mystery; *mitakuye oyasin* translates roughly as "all my relations," or "we are all related." Whereas the very notion of *mitakuye oyasin* implies a connection to a larger network of spiritual relationships with all life, logging onto the

Internet could be interpreted as a twenty-first-century *technological act of prayer.*

Even as *Avatar* ironically ventures into unexplored technological territory while simultaneously remaining within the familiar genre of the American Western, Cameron's film at its core is, by Postman's cautious definition, an "unambiguous statement," and as such is minimally a harbinger indicating unprecedented mythological shape-shifting; *Avatar*'s astonishing—and almost instant—global popularity boldly announced to the world that the fundamental iconography of western civilization is rapidly transforming itself. It is no coincidence that Cameron cleverly created a variation of the American Western to reflect this phenomenal transformation. *Avatar* celebrates the notion that the evolving mythological archetypes of the twenty-first century are naturally shedding the racism and bigotry of the nineteenth- and twentieth-century WASP archetypes that spearheaded the relentless march of western corporate industrial civilization and controlled and shaped the image—and thus the reality—of American identity since the nation's inception. As *Black Elk Speaks*, *Dances with Wolves*, and *Avatar* all prophecize that in order to survive, the industrialized nations of the world are slowly being forced to incorporate the environmental wisdom of the indigenous tribal cultures, western science also appears to be finally glimpsing what the Lakota and other indigenous tribal people of the world have known since time immemorial.

In the late 1960s, after studying the barren biosphere of Mars, a British scientist working for the National Aeronautical and Space Administration (NASA), concluded—to great suspicion and near-ridicule by many in the scientific community—that Earth's biosphere is a "combination of physical components integrated to form a complex interacting system that maintains and balances the conditions favorable to human life"—or simply, that the Earth is a single organism. James Lovelock named his theory the Gaia hypothesis to honor the Greek earth goddess.

By 1973, also meeting with sharp criticism from fellow scientists, Chilean biologists Humberto Maturana and Francisco Varela, expanded upon Lovelock's Gaia hypothesis when they compared the single cell's ability to repair and reinvent itself with Earth's environment. Next, the Chileans coined the term *autopoiesis*, or "self-creation," to describe Earth itself.[3] Yet even as academics proceed with technological and environmental unification theories, western civilization's dominant religions appear to encourage the ignorance and avarice that nourishes the never-ending quest for natural resources in order to feed the ever-widening maw of capitalism, while the indigenous peoples of the planet continue to spiritually "log on" to the biological network of *mitakuye oyasin* and "speak with their ancestors."

This book has explored several ways in which populist frontier anti-elitist politics gave birth to American entertainment and how entertainment and consumption became indistinguishable in America by the dawning of the twentieth century. This book also concludes that more than any other culture on the planet, Europeans first became enchanted with the notion of progress, and that when transplanted in the "New World," the Euro American came to so strongly associate progress with technology that these two concepts merged to also become synonymous with entertainment and consumption. Foreshadowing tragic environmental consequences, the non-Indian's powerful, ubiquitous technology continues to instill a pseudo-religious attitude of arrogance and superiority that confuses the clear visions that must be called forth now to cope with increasing ecological dilemmas.

Pioneer primitivist Mabel Dodge Luhan's insight into the negative pathological, psychological, and social impact of materialism in early-twentieth-century America inspired her efforts to unite western civilization with the wisdom of the culture of the American Indian and clearly instigated a fundamental shift in these destructive patterns. Yet throughout American history, environmentalists from Ralph Waldo Emerson, Henry David Thoreau, and Walt Whitman, to John Muir, Aldo Leopold, and Bob Marshall, to Rachel Carson and Edward Abbey, have predicted dire consequences if humankind fails to appreciate the interconnectedness of nature. Modern mythologists such as Joseph Campbell and Robert Bly have introduced such archetypes as the Wild Man into contemporary society as an antidote for our over-rationalized minds and underworked bodies.

Even as scientists, theologians, psychologists, and social activists quibble over mystical, legal, and empirical issues, the astounding global popularity of *Dances with Wolves* and *Avatar* reveals that modern culture is increasingly eager—indeed, hungry—to explore the mythological, spiritual, and environmental implications of *Black Elk Speaks* and *mitakuye oyasin* through what *Avatar* suggests is an emerging physical and virtual fusion of culture, technology, and nature.

The Dr. Grace Augustine character in *Avatar* is an eco-warrior. She is an obvious composite of environmental heroes from John Muir to Edward Abbey, and scientific heroes from biologists James Lovelock to Humberto Maturana, with a sprinkle of gorilla activist anthropologists Dame Jane Goodall and Dian Fossey tossed in for good measure. *Avatar*'s back story informs us that Grace Augustine wrote the book on Pandoran plant life in which she revealed the entire biosphere of the planet to be an intricately interconnected neurosystem. Exploiting Augustine's anthropological research, humans created avatars of the Na'vi aboriginals in order to inhabit their bodies and thereby function in the otherwise hostile environment of Pandora and harvest the planet's vital natural resources. Irascible Grace Augustine is openly hostile toward authority figures, including the character in charge of the corporation's mining operations, Parker Selfridge, and she becomes a major allegorical statement at the end of the film when she joins Jake Sully, warrior princess Neytiri, and the Na'vi to oppose the humans' effort to destroy the Tree of Souls and is mortally wounded in the final battle for the planet. Before Grace dies, the Na'vi, Neytiri, and Jake Sully attempt to transfer consciousness from her dying human body into her Na'vi avatar. To accomplish this, however, Neytiri informs us that Grace's consciousness must first "pass through the eye of Eywa"—a challenge the scientist unfortunately fails. Yet even as Grace's life fades, her consciousness—much like information uploaded from a flash drive to a hard drive—is transferred into the Pandoran planetary neurosystem and, once "uploaded"—a metaphor for the phenomenal explosion of social networking in modern culture—Grace's consciousness reveals to the entire tribal population, as well as all other forms of life on Pandora, that humans poisoned their own planet, thus explaining their insatiable need for another planet's resources.

Even as this archetypal transformation is occurring in the fundamental mythological structure of the American Western in movie palaces around the globe with *Avatar*, the world is also simultaneously witnessing a technological return to tribal consciousness through the unprecedented explosion of social networking on the World Wide Web. This astonishingly rapid development is connecting the planet's population in an around-the-clock conversation that has, in the virtual blinking of an eye, become arguably the most significant transformation in human communications since the Industrial Revolution. With blinding speed, social networking has turned the global population into an interconnected system of hubs and pods of cyberspace communities linked as digital tribes. As Vine Deloria Jr. predicted in *We Talk You Listen: New Tribes, New Turf* in 1970, these virtual global tribes are rapidly returning to oral tradition as an alternative to the various forms of corporate media that have dominated the dispersing and gathering of information and goods as well as spiritual, cultural, political, social, and personal direction since the genesis of the Industrial Revolution. Social networking and the new oral tradition played an unprecedented role in the 2008 presidential election and promise to have an increasingly important role in the future of global politics. This is an indication that we have only seen the beginning of ways the Internet and social networking are impacting all forms of authority at their very foundation. The life-or-death struggles of so many traditional structures such as copyright laws, American institutions such as the recording industry, and the wobbling newspaper and publishing industries in this new digital world are but a few of the first implications that—to use a consistent *Avatar* mythological metaphor—Pandora's Box has been opened as far as media, communications, and the general future of the planet are concerned. If medium is the message, then humankind has not simply entered another new era, we have entered an entirely new *realm*.

When considering the mythological impact of the traditional Western film in American iconographical history, both *Dances with Wolves* and *Avatar* are unmistakable indications that this new mythological realm we have entered is most certainly linked to Lakota holy man Black Elk's powerful vision and prophecy. Like Vine Deloria contemplating the influence of *Black Elk Speaks* on world religion in the late 1970s, however, we can only speculate how the mythological connections to *Black Elk Speaks* in the motion picture industry will reveal themselves in the years to come. Nevertheless, since John Neihardt's appearance on Dick Cavett's show in April 1971, it is obvious that *Black Elk Speaks* has risen steadily to the point of having a significant effect on the multiple disciplines of theology, psychology, and anthropology. Even more important, Black Elk spoke through non-Indian John Neihardt to multiple generations of Indians and non-Indian Americans alike, and united as a single voice, *Black Elk Speaks* becomes a powerful metaphor of hope for the future. Now, as the influence of *Black Elk Speaks* on *Dances with Wolves* and *Avatar* would indicate, the Lakota holy man's power vision is dramatically altering the very fundamental structure of America's core mythological narrative: the Western.

Less than a month after its Christmas 2009 release, *Avatar* became the first film to reach billion-dollar blockbuster status so rapidly. Only weeks later, the film was proclaimed the number-one box office movie of all time; indeed, *Avatar* has earned significantly more than twice that earned by its closest competitor in the all-time box office charts, Cameron's earlier film, *Titanic*. Reacting to the film's remarkable success, critics and political pundits were quick to point out *Avatar*'s multiple thinly veiled analogies to the late-twentieth-century notion of "post-history," "neoconservative" American imperialism, the American wars in Iraq and Afghanistan, corporate America's rampant greed for vanishing natural resources, and the inherent racism tragically embedded in western civilization's insidious metamorphosis of the nineteenth-century concept of Manifest Destiny into twenty-first-century "corporate globalization." In spite of *Avatar* boldly addressing such important issues as the clash of western civilization's worldwide net of corporate capitalism with the growing movement of global environmentalism, a single line of dialogue in the film struck with particular intensity and revealed the motion picture as a forerunner of the yet-to-be-realized important role of indigenous people in the future creation of America's evolving heroic archetype. Jake Sully's avatar and the film's "General Custer," Colonel Miles Quaritch, are locked in mortal combat during the explosive and emotional battle for the planet at the film's climax. Arriving at his Little Big Horn moment, Quaritch asks Sully the ironic question: "How does it feel to betray your own race?" At this defining moment in *Avatar*, both hero and anti-hero are metaphorical representatives of technology and the ultimate evolution of Manifest Destiny into corporate universalization on the planet Pandora. Encased in his deadly robotic superstructure, Quaritch represents western civilization stripped of all its religious origins and underpinnings and finally revealed as unbridled materialism gone mad with rapacious anti-environmentalism, whereas even though Sully has momentarily departed his avatar body to engage Quaritch in combat, he has *become indigenous* through a fusion of nature, technology, and spirituality. Thus when the Na'vi warrior-princess Neytiri's arrows strike Quaritch with the deadly answer to his final, defiant question, rather than "betraying his race," the audience understands that Sully is defending sentient, enlightened beings. Consequently, when Sully later departs his human form to permanently inhabit his Na'vi avatar at the end of the film, the audience vicariously joins him and, doing so, embraces the notion of technology as an ironic mystical conduit to becoming—as the Lakota might say—*mitakuye oyasin*; Sully now realizes he is part of everything. *Avatar* thus finally poses an intriguing mythological question: Has the creation of virtual reality expanded our fundamental notion of reality itself to the degree that we believe we will eventually merge nature and technology to facilitate humanity's spiritual evolution into enlightened beings?

Surely this degree of transformation can occur only if we are able to probe the depths of our subconscious to awaken a new collective global mythology of unity and environmental harmony as suggested by Black Elk. After visiting the Taos Pueblo early in the twentieth century, pioneer psychologist Carl Jung suggested a great strength of the Indian people lies in their intimate communion with the archetypal world of the collective unconsciousness. The Indian capacity to probe deep into the mystical realms of numinous powers might prove increasingly important if only a few of the dire environmental predictions of modern science become reality in the future. One of the most significant differences between the intuitive natural reality of the Indian and the scientific and technological reality of the modern non-Indian is the Indians' interior communion with the depths of their psychic being. Throughout his long professional life, Jung argued that the non-Indian so overdeveloped his ego and his rational processing to the point that centuries ago he lost most of the communion he had with the archetypal world of his own unconscious. Conversely, American Indian mythology, religion, culture, and ceremony contain all of the classic archetypes for exploration of the collective unconsciousness—specifically, but not exclusively, in relation to North America. The heroic personality and the symbolic journey, the vision quest, the recognition of the "center" as a Mandala (Medicine Wheel) representing the self—all strongly support Vine Deloria's 1979 declaration that *Black Elk Speaks* forms the central canon of a perception of reality clear and strong enough to stand alongside any other in the world.

Avatar, like *Dances with Wolves, Little Big Man*, and other motion pictures over the past forty years, suggest that both Indian and non-Indian Americans continue seeking mythological transcendence in the Trans-Missouri by means of our national narrative, the Western. Considering our rapidly expanding ability to create illusions so vivid that we can "virtually" live in them, and the idea that the projection of motion pictures promises to change yet again in the very near future to become lifelike holographic images, the mythological implications are staggering to contemplate. When motion pictures, television, and computer images are holographically transmitted, they will most certainly introduce entirely new dimensions to our fundamental perceptions of reality and the creation of archetypes to define our dreams. Therefore, if the medium is the message, it becomes most significant that Black Elk's power vision is central to the story of *Avatar* as the mythological medium of western civilization—the motion picture—transforms from a two-dimensional to a three-dimensional format. It is equally significant that American Indian actors and technicians are now actively participating in creative artistic and administrative roles in shaping the future direction of the medium and the genre of the Western as it transforms itself.

Aside from suggesting that the Trans-Missouri region of North America has consistently provided a vital mythological landscape for both the Indian and the non-Indian, this book has explored the Plains Indian stellar theology that inspired holy men such as Black Elk. This book has also surveyed the impact of Old Testament theology on Old World notions of progress, technology, consumption, and entertainment, shown these concepts to be the primary influences of Euro American tradition, and contrasted these core aspects of the non-Indian mythological narrative with the indigenous mythology of the Trans-Missouri; it has reviewed and connected the dramatic rise in emigrant populations in nineteenth-century North America with the growth of media, and noted the dramatic changes in society created with the inventions of new mediums such as telegraphy, photography, and the phonograph. This book has chronicled the synchronization of these various mediums into the art of making motion pictures and noted the impact of cinematic techniques on the evolution of mass telecommunications and social global networking. This book has explored the evolution of the heroic American archetype from the nation's European origins forward and chronicled the jingoistic, racist origins of the cowboy as the character that usurped the frontiersman to seize the metaphorical role of hero when motion pictures became our medium of mythologizing and Hollywood rose to become the world's "dream factory." This book has noted that James Cameron's landmark film *Avatar* is evidence that the roles of villain and hero have completely reversed and that Cameron's film introduces a highly evolved version of the European's oldest form of entertainment in the New

World, the captivity narrative, and, doing so, suggests a possible passageway through which to begin a journey toward transcending the seemingly incompatible realms of technology and nature. Finally, this book implies that the neuro-queue depicted in *Avatar* as a means of connecting an individual with an entire biological system, and the technological act of logging on to the Internet, are actions not unlike the Lakota act of prayer, or "speaking with one's relatives," in that Plains Indians consider communication with one's "relatives" to signify an interconnected biological web of all life.

Imbued with the mystical revelations and prophecies of *Black Elk Speaks* and other indigenous wisdom from around the planet, *Avatar* thus turns the captivity narrative inside out while simultaneously declaring a heretofore inconceivable mythological merging of nature and technology. *Avatar* also suggests this fusion of technology and nature as a possible route for Indians and non-Indians that could finally unite them with common goals and contribute to the resolution of their five-hundred-year estrangement in order to proceed into the new mythological realms we are entering as humans struggling to become enlightened beings.

Playing Indian

I had not attended a Western Writers of America (WWA) convention since the gathering in Cody in June 2006, but my script for the DVD release of my trilogy *A Ballad of the West* had been honored as a finalist for the organization's prestigious Silver Spur Award for best documentary film of 2009, so I drove to Oklahoma City to receive my certificate and to attend a couple of the lectures and symposiums being offered during the convention. Afterward, I planned to drive up to Miami, Oklahoma, to see my old friend J. R. Mathews and support his political campaign for assistant tribal chairman of the Quapaw tribe with a musical performance.

I was also looking forward to reconnecting with Lakota author Joseph Marshall III at the WWA convention. Marshall's novel *The Long Knives Are Crying* was a finalist for the organization's 2009 Silver Spur for best Western long novel. I had met Joseph Marshall in the spring of 2007 when we were both presenters for the 26th annual Neihardt Spring Conference at the Neihardt Center in Bancroft, Nebraska. The theme of the conference was "Neihardt's Heroes," so Marshall, James C. Work, John Mangun, and I focused our presentations on that stimulating subject. A relative of Crazy Horse, Marshall discussed Neihardt's celebrated sensitivity to Plains Indian history and culture, focusing specifically on Neihardt's historic poetry about the famous Oglala warrior-chief in *The Song of the Indian Wars*. Listening to Marshall speak about Neihardt's perspective of the death of Crazy Horse, I was deeply impressed that the poet's work was continuing to speak truthfully to Indians in the twenty-first century. But I was also moved by Marshall's inherently dignified, charismatic personality. Much like Vine Deloria Jr., Marshall was absolutely at ease interacting with a non-Indian audience; he carefully selected his words to articulate and highlight his points. Tall and lean, on occasion Marshall had also worked in films such as Steven Spielberg's award-winning mini-series *Into the*

West; watching him move as gracefully as he spoke that day at the Neihardt Center, I thought he could easily become one of America's foremost indigenous actors as well as one of Indian Country's most important literary voices during the early twenty-first century.

I reconnected briefly with Joseph and his wife, Connie, during the opening ceremonies of the 2009 WWA convention. The Marshalls both seemed as pleased to see me as I was to see them, but because of the large crowd and the festive circumstances it was difficult to engage in anything more than distracted chitchat, and soon we were swept up in the many introductions and dangling conversations that accompany such soirees. The following morning at the symposium panel, "Writing about Indians," that Marshall chaired, however, I experienced a catharsis upon hearing his closing remark to the non-Indian writers gathered there: "We have lived in your world," Marshall concluded, "but you *still* haven't lived in ours."

Marshall's insight reminded me why, as a non-Indian, I felt justified writing this book; I *have* lived in both Indian and non-Indian cultures for most of my adult life. Even though I still do not consider myself indigenous, my long periods of time spent in the company of Indians and "playing Indian" on stage have provided me the opportunity to explore the concept from a unique perspective. Driving into Tulsa's city limits brought my reasons for writing this book into even sharper focus because of the 1984 American Indian Theater Company (AITCO) production of *Black Elk Speaks*, and memories of how my relationship with Chris Sergel allowed me to participate in its creation. Even though my long friendship with Vine Deloria Jr. introduced me to a broad and richly textured spectrum of Indian history, religion, culture, and politics in twentieth-century America, my relationship with Chris and the AITCO finally enabled me to combine my career in entertainment with my personal efforts to embrace Indian life. Chris, his abiding love of Indian people, and his enduring devotion to *Black Elk Speaks* brought me to Tulsa for the first time and initiated my involvement with J. R. Mathews and the American Indian Theater Company.

Chris's company, Dramatic Publishing—established in Chicago in 1885 by his grandfather Charles Sergel—was arguably the oldest theatrical publishing house in America. In his youth Chris had sailed a schooner around the world writing features for *Sports Afield*, lived for a year in the African bush as a big game hunter, and, as a lieutenant commander, taught celestial navigation during World War II. When he rose to head his family's theatrical publishing company he adapted *To Kill a Mockingbird*, *Cheaper by the Dozen*, *Up the Down Staircase*, and many other classic books for the stage. *Black Elk Speaks* was the project that most personally motivated him.

When I was introduced to Chris Sergel at Neihardt Day in 1978 and he asked me to join the team he was assembling to produce *Black Elk Speaks*, I had no idea of the impact meeting him would have on my life and career. Three years after our meeting in Bancroft, Chris arranged a meeting between me and renowned Broadway playwright Dale Wasserman, author of *Man of La Mancha* and the stage adaptation of Ken Kesey's *One Flew Over the Cuckoo's Nest*. Chris's introduction subsequently led to a deep and abiding friendship with Dale, two years of intimate theatrical work with him creating the leading role of "the drifter" in his musical comedy *Shakespeare and the Indians*, and starring in more than 150 performances of the show. As the icing on the cake, Wasserman also took me to the United States' foremost theatrical laboratory, the Eugene O'Neill Theater Center in Waterford, Connecticut, where after attending a performance of my one-man show *Seekers of the Fleece*, the institution's founder, George C. White, named me the O'Neill's first—and heretofore, only—official Balladeer in Residence. All of these career highlights were ultimately training me for the theatrical production of *Black Elk Speaks*.

Shortly after being introduced in 1978, however, Chris and I sat on the porch of Neihardt's writing cabin and he informed me that he had originally tried to purchase the rights to *Bury My Heart at Wounded Knee*, not *Black Elk Speaks*. In 1973 Chris had traveled to Little Rock and met with Dee Brown in his home, and was surprised and disappointed to learn the book's rights were entangled in complicated legal squabbles that the author feared would go on for years. As they visited, however, Brown informed Chris that the theatrical and film rights to *Black Elk Speaks* were indeed available. Brown said that *Black Elk Speaks* was essential source material for *Bury My Heart at Wounded Knee* anyway, and he urged Chris to contact the Neihardt family and negotiate directly with them.

Immediately after securing the rights to *Black Elk Speaks*, Chris adapted Neihardt's book to the stage and produced a short run of his play in New York. The debut was very well-received but was never intended to run for more than a few weeks. By the time I met Chris in 1978, he had revised his original script several times and was ready to begin assembling a theatrical production team composed primarily of Indian performers. Chris informed me that he also intended to mount the play in a region of the country with a heavy Indian population—probably Denver or Rapid City—but he was also considering Flagstaff and Tulsa.

In 1981 I was in New York City promoting a recording I had produced, and I contacted Chris for an update on developments with *Black Elk Speaks*. When we met the next day Chris asked me to drive with him from Manhattan to his home in Connecticut to meet a young Indian man from Oklahoma who had convinced him to mount the production of *Black Elk Speaks* in Tulsa. In his late twenties, J. R. Mathews was a handsome, gregarious Quapaw Indian from Miami, Oklahoma. From the beginning of our friendship, I have preferred J. R.'s Quapaw name, Big Thunder, as it more aptly describes his very large stature and personality. Big Thunder's unusual golden eyes sparkled with openness, laughter, and intelligence. He parted his straight, ink-black hair in the middle of his head, swept it around his broad face, and tied it in a ponytail that draped his massive shoulders and dangled halfway down his back. Unlike my Lakota, Shoshone, Crow, and Arapaho friends' northern reservation accents, Big Thunder spoke with a pronounced southwestern drawl.

In Tulsa, Big Thunder had created the foremost Indian theatrical training program in America. The program evolved naturally after Bob Hicks directed the play *Skins* for the Tulsa Indian Council on Alcohol and Drug Abuse (TICADA). The director of TICADA was Big Thunder's cousin Jay White Crow. After the successful production of *Skins*, Big Thunder and White Crow realized they were in a unique position to create something important for their people and, in that spirit, founded the American Indian Theater Company to provide training and opportunities in the theater arts for Indian actors, writers, directors, producers, artists, musicians and singers, dancers, set designers, costumers, and technicians. White Crow and Big Thunder also discovered that becoming involved in the theater arts and performing on stage was a great way for TICADA graduates to channel their energies into a regular, creative routine that would assist them with recovery from substance abuse—particularly when producing and performing in theater that addressed Indian concerns. First, Jay White Crow combined the Alcoholics Anonymous twelve-step program with traditional American Indian counseling and healing ceremonies such as sweat lodges that helped Indian abusers detox and get off alcohol and drugs. Next, Big Thunder brought many of the TICADA graduates—as well as other talented Indian and non-Indian people *without* alcohol or drug abuse history—into the theater program. Several of the members of AITCO were veterans of Kermit Hunter's *Trail of Tears*, the long-running outdoor drama portraying the heartbreaking trek of the Cherokee tribe from the southeastern United States to Oklahoma Indian Territory. Performed in a huge amphitheater nestled in the woods a few miles outside the Oklahoma Cherokee capital, Tahlequah, *Trail of Tears* was decades ahead of Chris Sergel's concept of producing a play with an American Indian cast. Moreover, the *Trail of Tears* production was a companion piece that paired with *Unto These Hills*, another full-Indian outdoor production held since 1937 in North Carolina, in the ancestral homelands of the Cherokee Nation. Together the dramas present a rich, dignified chronicle of the history of the Cherokee people and are also the longest-running Indian theatrical productions in America.

Big Thunder and the AITCO assembled a dedicated company of extraordinary young Indian actors and technicians in Tulsa and proceeded to produce popular theatrical works, such as *One Flew*

Over the Cuckoo's Nest, often casting American Indian actors in roles traditionally played by non-Indian actors. Gradually, however, the AITCO began producing original plays with American Indian themes, the most successful being Big Thunder's comedy revue, *Running on Indian Time*.

Big Thunder and I formed an immediate friendship and arranged for me to drive up to Tulsa as soon as I flew back to Texas from New York. Before he departed for Oklahoma, however, Big Thunder asked me to join the board of directors of the American Indian Theater Company. I immediately accepted his offer, and for the next two years, when not on stage in Wasserman's *Shakespeare and the Indians*, on tour with my one-man shows, *Seekers of the Fleece* and *Lakota*, or at the Eugene O'Neill Theater Center developing my musical, *Aldebaran and the Falling Star*, I was in Tulsa working with Big Thunder in preproduction on *Black Elk Speaks*.

During one of these early trips to Tulsa, I met the Cherokee actor Wes Studi while attending a sweat lodge his mother, Maggie, was conducting on their farm outside Tulsa. At the time Wes was training Morgan horses and I was immediately impressed with his excellent horsemanship, but I was even more impressed with the fact that Wes was a Vietnam War veteran who had written and published three educational, bilingual books for Cherokee children. Wes was also on the AITCO board of directors and, like me, would be cast in multiple roles in *Black Elk Speaks*. I had little idea at the time that four years later Wes would create the "Blackfeet warrior" role in the full-company debut of my mountain man musical, *Seekers of the Fleece*. After we moved *Seekers of the Fleece* from Cody, Wyoming, to Austin, Texas, Wes left the production and relocated to California to try to get into the movies. Almost as soon as Wes arrived in Hollywood, he was promptly cast as the "Bad Pawnee" in *Dances with Wolves*, the role that would make him a movie star. Wes was destined to become the most successful of the Indian actors to receive early training through AITCO. After the astonishing success of *Dances with Wolves*, Wes rode the crest of films with American Indian themes that followed in its wake. He had featured roles in *The Last of the Mohicans* and then starred in *Geronimo*. Since those successful films, Wes Studi has been at the top of the A-list of American Indian actors; indeed, Wes was one of the stars of *Avatar*.

In 1983, however, Wes was starring as Shakopee and helping Big Thunder and AITCO slowly fill the cast of *Black Elk Speaks* with American Indian actors. As the production gathered momentum, Chris informed us he had negotiated a production deal with Lindsay Law, the young man from New York who created the popular *American Playhouse* series on PBS. The plan was for Law's *American Playhouse* team to partner with Nebraska Educational Television to video-tape the AITCO production of *Black Elk Speaks* live and on location in the Black Hills for later national broadcast on PBS.

When I returned to New York in 1983 to officially audition for the role of William Bent, I met some of the Indian actors Chris had recruited for *Black Elk Speaks*, my favorite being the sardonic and venerable Apache actress, Marie Antoinette Rodgers. I auditioned for Chris and Lindsay Law in a loft on the Lower East Side of Manhattan, with Rodgers reading the role of William Bent's Cheyenne wife, Yellow Woman. I won the part, and the bond I established with Rodgers remained one of my most cherished until her death.

The role of Black Elk had been cast since the very beginning of Chris Sergel's involvement with the project. Soon after he bought the rights to the story, Chris traveled with Neihardt's daughter Hilda to South Dakota to meet with Black Elk's relatives in order to respectfully ask how they wished to see their famous grandfather depicted on stage and screen. Chris was particularly curious to discover the actor they envisioned portraying Black Elk.

Black Elk's grandchildren and great-grandchildren still live in his tiny cabin in Manderson, South Dakota, on the Pine Ridge Reservation. A large, close knit family, their Christian name is now DeSersa, but looking into Clifton's, Aaron's, Mitchell's, or Olivia's face it is easy to see their famous grandfather's features. And, on the subject of physical similarity, when Chris asked the DeSersas for a list of the actors they wanted to consider to play Black Elk, the grandchildren were unanimous in their choice: David Carradine!

In the early 1970s when the late David Carradine's hit series *Kung Fu* came on television each week, the entire DeSersa family would gather around the set and laugh about how much Carradine resembled their grandfather when he was a young man. Even Black Elk's elderly daughter, Lucy Looks Twice, agreed; Carradine was a ringer for her father. When they realized the striking likeness between Carradine and Black Elk, Chris and Hilda agreed: Carradine was their man. Coincidentally, Chris was an old friend of John Carradine (incidentally, one of John Ford's stock company of actors) and his brood of actor sons, David, Keith, and Robert.

David Carradine was very familiar with *Black Elk Speaks*. Even with the Black Elk family's blessing, however, he was genuinely concerned about a non-Indian taking the important part and was initially hesitant to accept it. David believed he should meet personally with the DeSersa family before any of them made a final decision. So Chris Sergel returned to Pine Ridge with Carradine for a private picnic on Wounded Knee Creek with the DeSersa family. Of course David and the DeSersa family became close, and the actor accepted the role.

Thus began an important ritual pilgrimage—one to which Chris Sergel remained devoted until his death in 1993: before mounting any production of *Black Elk Speaks*, Chris would first take new principle cast members, along with John Neihardt's daughter Hilda, to Pine Ridge to meet Black Elk's family in Manderson. From there, with Hilda and Black Elk's grandchildren leading the way, the entourage would head to the Black Hills and hike to the top of Harney Peak, the location of the holy man's power vision. At Harney Peak ceremonies were done with Black Elk's pipe, given to Chris by Lucy Looks Twice to empower him spiritually for the production of the play and motion picture. After ceremonies at Harney Peak—and other ceremonies conducted throughout the journey—we would trek down to Fort Robinson, Nebraska, to visit the location of Crazy Horse's murder in 1877. It was always chilling to hear Hilda read her father's epic verse, "The Death of Crazy Horse," in the very cell where the great chief was murdered.

Soon after winning the William Bent role in the Tulsa production I traveled to South Dakota with Chris, David Carradine, Big Thunder, Lindsay Law, and several members of Law's *American Playhouse* production team. We spent five days roaming western South Dakota and northwestern Nebraska conducting ceremonies, discussing the Indian wars, Black Elk, Neihardt, and the theater, and mounting Chris's script on the stage. When we returned to Rapid City we were delighted to learn that one of our most important wishes had come true: Will Sampson had agreed to portray Lakota warrior-chief Red Cloud in *Black Elk Speaks*.

Returning to Oklahoma was a homecoming for Will—or Sonny, as everyone in Tulsa called him. A full-blood Muscogee-Creek from Okmulgee, Oklahoma, Will's first film role was in 1975 as Chief Bromden in the film *One Flew Over the Cuckoo's Nest*. Prior to his breakthrough in movies, however, Will worked throughout the West as an oil field roughneck, construction worker, and rodeo rider. A self-taught painter, Will was selling canvases at an increasingly regular pace before a friend told him a casting director was looking for a very tall Indian for a movie role and suggested he audition for it. After his success in *One Flew Over the Cuckoo's Nest*, Will quickly rose to become the foremost American Indian actor working in film throughout the 1970s and 1980s. From the very beginning of his film career, Will was committed to portraying Indians realistically on screen and also helping fellow Indian actors in the performing arts. In 1983, while the American Indian Theater Company was in preproduction on *Black Elk Speaks*, Will was creating the American Indian Registry for the Performing Arts (AIRPA), specifically to create a central Hollywood location for Indian performers, producers, casting directors, and filmmakers to unite around common goals. Will's timing was perfect, as his registry got on its feet at the very moment Kevin Costner's Tig Productions was casting *Dances with Wolves*. Will's AIRPA has subsequently proven to be an invaluable tool for American Indian actors such as Wes Studi, Graham Greene, Russell Means, Floyd Red Crow Westerman, and Rodney Grant as well as scores of American Indian documentary filmmakers, technicians, costume designers, dialogue coaches, and others as Hollywood has increasingly sought Indian actors and advisors for feature and documentary films.

At six foot seven, Will made even Big Thunder look small. But as is often the case with very large men, Will Sampson was truly gentle and humble; when Big Thunder and I picked him up at the Tulsa airport for the first of his many fund-raising efforts on behalf of the American Indian Theater Company, Will genuinely blushed when people recognized him and asked for his autograph.

Will was also very ill by the time we started the fund-raising efforts in Tulsa for the *Black Elk Speaks* project. All I ever knew about his illness was that he had a rare skin disease with emphysema-like symptoms that made it extremely difficult for him to breathe. In the following months as we attended luncheons and banquets with David Carradine and other cast members raising funds for the production, Will and I became friends. During the short time I was privileged to know Will, the most I ever heard him talk was the day he described his hero, Jay Silverheels, to me. Will and I were seated next to each other at a Rotary Club luncheon, and I asked him what his inspiration was to create the American Indian Registry for the Performing Arts.

"Jay Silverheels—Tonto—was my inspiration," he quickly replied. Will informed me that even though few celebrate the fact, Jay Silverheels, a Mohawk, was the first Indian to actually portray an American Indian on television. But Silverheels was breaking ground for Indian actors long before the *Lone Ranger* television series started in 1949. His first film role was in 1940 with Errol Flynn in *Sea Hawk*. He served in World War II, but when it ended he returned to Hollywood and started working again. He even worked with Humphrey Bogart and Lauren Bacall in *Key Largo* in 1948. After his success in *The Lone Ranger*, Jay Silverheels started an organization in Los Angeles in 1966 called the Indian Actors Workshop and was always eager to help Indian performers get work in movies and television. Silverheel's prototype concept of the Indian Actors Workshop became Will Sampson's template when he created the American Indian Registry for the Performing Arts.

With Will signed on to the production, we had cast the entire ensemble of *Black Elk Speaks*. Chris was pleased we had accomplished his primary objective: aside from me, David Carradine, and two other non-Indian cast members, the entire thirty-person company was completely composed of Indians. Significantly, about the same percentage of the technical crew and administrative staff were also American Indians. Because of our landmark production company, it was decided that an Indian spokesman would step through the curtains before each performance and explain the show's structure. The spokesman would casually inform the audience that many generations of American Indian people had witnessed themselves depicted on stage and screen by Mexicans, Italians, Arabs, Anglo-Saxons, and scores of other ethnic nationalities. "Tonight," the spokesman continued, "American Indians will not only depict American Indian characters, but we will also depict *non-Indian* characters." (As a large percentage of our Tulsa audience was American Indians, this line usually brought howls of laughter and applause from the audience.)

Reversing stereotypical roles in *Black Elk Speaks* was a delightful, truly "Indian" touch, but, ironically underscoring the "becoming indigenous/playing Indian" theme of this book, it thrust non-Indian actors like me into ambiguous and truly comical territory concerning characterization. For example, I had worn a full beard for nearly fifteen years before arriving in Tulsa to play William Bent. Now, although the historical William Bent actually wore a beard, in order to remain true to the motif of the play, I had to *appear* to be an Indian portraying Bent, and this meant no beard. Complicating matters, when I arrived in Tulsa for rehearsals, I had suddenly been cast in a second part as the white newspaper reporter, John Finnerty. So, introducing several new twists to Phil Deloria's "playing Indian" insight, I was a non-Indian pretending to be an Indian while simultaneously pretending also to be a non-Indian. To accomplish this confusing task I had to submit to an hour of heavy "Texas mud" makeup each night to make my freckled, pink complexion disappear. Adding to the illusion, I had to wear a coarse, black, "Willie Nelson–style," pig-tailed, braided wig. Completing the comedic portrait, as the *Chicago Sun Times* reporter and Irishman John Finnerty I also remained in costume as an Indian in buckskin leggings, beaded war shirt, man-tan-makeup, and black wig. To become the reporter, however, I wore a tacky plaid sports jacket over my buckskins and a black derby atop my braided wig. My dear mother would not have recognized me. In fact, there were more than a few moments when I hardly recognized myself in the getup. But it worked. Indians loved the Finnerty character, so for that alone I was happy to be the clown.

Because of the diverse numbers of tribes represented in the *Black Elk Speaks* production, there were numerous sweat lodge ceremonies going on virtually every night after rehearsals. One night at a sweat I made friends with the lead singer of the Lakota Lone Eagle Singers and fellow cast member Harold Dean Salway. During this time I also met Ponca medicine woman Casey Camp Hornick. Casey was playing multiple minor stage roles in *Black Elk Speaks*, but she was already beginning to be known for her costume designs, a talent she would soon blossom into on feature films such as *The Trial of Standing Bear* and *Son of Morning Star*. Casey's real gift, however, revealed itself in sacred ceremony. Casey and her brother, former Oklahoma AIM leader and Trail of Broken Treaties veteran Carter Camp, were trained by the Lakota spiritual teacher Leonard Crow Dog to bring ancient wisdoms and ceremony to all people hungry for such things.

Destined to become famous as the designer-director of Broadway's innovative production of Disney's *The Lion King* and nominated for an Academy Award for directing the films *Frieda* and *Across the Universe*, Julie Taymor was an unknown but up-and-coming set designer in 1984. The spectacular set she designed for *Black Elk Speaks* was dramatic and sensitive to the spirit and artistic sensibilities of Indian people. The heart of the set was a very large drum that occupied center stage throughout the performance. From that centerpiece a ramp stage left steadily angled and ascended in a long and lovely sweeping curve until it reached the peak of the set, three stories high!

Sadly, Will Sampson had a problem with the set's height. Will's breathing condition made it extremely difficult for him to climb the three flights of backstage stairs to deliver his opening speech as Red Cloud. It took so much energy for Will to get to the top of the set that he barely had time to recuperate from the climb. Complicating matters, with his naturally soft voice it was difficult for Will to deliver his speech with any projection at all after ascending to the top of the set. Director Tom Brennan offered to re-block Will's position in order for him deliver the Red Cloud speech from a less stressful location on the set, but Will's commitment to *Black Elk Speaks* and portraying Lakota warrior and statesman Red Cloud with dignity motivated him nearly as much as his responsibility as a role model for young Indian performers; he felt it was important to stick with Tom's original stage direction and deliver the Red Cloud speech from the mountain peaks—the top of the three-story set. So it was decided that Will would have two assistants and an oxygen bottle to help him ascend the set each night. After a quick crowd scene in the opening sequence, I didn't appear on stage until halfway through the first act, so I volunteered to join my new Lakota friend Harold Dean Salway to help Will climb the mountain each night.

It was heartbreaking to see that giant, once-powerful man reduced to such a delicate state of health. But it was also truly inspiring to watch him gather his strength and move slowly, step by step, up the backstage ladder. Harold Dean and I would stop along the way for Will to place the mask over his face and breathe a bit of oxygen. Then we would move a little higher up the stairs. He hardly ever spoke and certainly never mentioned such a thing, but I got the distinct feeling Will considered this a small sacrifice compared to those of Indian leaders who had inspired him in life. Whatever his motivation, I will never forget his courage and devotion to his people and his art.

The American Indian Theater Company production of *Black Elk Speaks* was a huge success, attracting nearly ten thousand people—mostly American Indians—to the Tulsa Performing Arts Center for four performances. The successful production launched *Black Elk Speaks*, and the play continues to be occasionally performed to outstanding reviews and large audiences around the country. To this day, however, although we came very close on several occasions—once gaining an audience with director Robert Redford's representatives in New York—*Black Elk Speaks* has yet to be made into a major motion picture. I have no explanation for this except that the project lost its leader when Chris Sergel died on his seventy-fifth birthday, May 7, 1993. Respecting his final wishes, Chris's family returned Black Elk's pipe to the DeSersa family after his death.

Chris Sergel's vision of *Black Elk Speaks* may not have reached the silver screen during his lifetime, but he lived long enough to witness perhaps a more important vision realized when many of the Indian actors, costumers, and technicians who were in *Black Elk Speaks* blossomed in productions like *Dances with Wolves* after the show closed in Tulsa. Like Wes Studi, many of the Indian actors moved forward from the original dream of AITCO and *Black Elk Speaks* and made use of Will Sampson's American Indian Registry for the Performing Arts to become major artists depicting Indians more realistically on stage and screen. Chris Sergel's devotion to John G. Neihardt's *Black Elk Speaks* gave a generation of young Indian artists a dramatic and spiritual vehicle around which they could unite to learn the theatrical arts in order to create a revised, more sensitive, and more accurate depiction of their religion and culture. Sadly, Will Sampson lived only three more years after *Black Elk Speaks* closed in Tulsa. Will died at age fifty-three on June 3, 1987, in Houston, only weeks after surviving a heart-lung transplant.

The American Indian Theater Company's 1984 production of *Black Elk Speaks* occurred exactly ninety-nine years after Sitting Bull joined Buffalo Bill's *Wild West*. Following the chief's example, Indian performers such as Black Elk and Luther Standing Bear worked in various *Wild West* shows until motion pictures replaced that prototypical form of the Western. In both the *Wild West* and early motion pictures, Indians provided inimitable authenticity to the Western as the genre made the transition from living history to stage to arena to the silver screen to create the core mythology of the American nation. Being co-creators of the Western genre in the arena, Indians discovered that entertainment was a passageway to an ironic circumstance that would ensure the survival and the preservation of their way of life. During the intervening century between Sitting Bull's joining Buffalo Bill's *Wild West* in 1885 and the American Indian production of *Black Elk Speaks* in 1984, Indians portrayed either bloodthirsty savages or proud and noble victims in the mythological drama that formed the American heroic archetype. Indians thus gave birth to heroic characters like Buffalo Bill and John Wayne as they vanquished "the powerful and worthy foe" to continue the march of western civilization toward its "Manifest Destiny."

After Wounded Knee II in 1973 during the civil war on Pine Ridge Reservation, American Indians began to shift the focus of their quest for justice back into the realm of mythology. Thus, in a very real sense, the American Indian Theater Company's production of *Black Elk Speaks* represented Indian Country's very powerful post–Wounded Knee II assertion that they were not pacified, as it had been assumed they were after Wounded Knee in 1890. Nor were they mythologically impotent, as they had been depicted in motion pictures since the genesis of the art form. Instead, the Tulsa production of *Black Elk Speaks* boldly announced that Indians had made the transition into theatrical production. The production also audaciously declared that Indians themselves were finally in the position to express *their* version of the Western.

As evidenced by the immediate success of *Dances with Wolves* only six years after the American Indian Theater Company's production of *Black Elk Speaks*, it would appear that the play is yet another evolving part of the same "dynamic spiritual pattern" that John G. Neihardt described at the end of his long, mystical life. Now, as we rapidly move into the technological realms of the digitally interconnected virtual world of the future, *Black Elk Speaks* will continue to reunite us with the spiritual reality of the landscape of the Great Plains and connect us with the unexplored mythological legacy of the American West where the tall grass grows.

Notes

Introduction
Becoming Indigenous

1. Black Elk died in 1950.
2. Vine Deloria Jr., "Sacred Lands and Human Understanding," *Hoka Hey!*, Fall/ Winter 1992, 6.
3. Ibid.
4. Books about Buffalo Bill published between 1996 and 2006:
   a. L. G. Moses, *Wild West Shows and the Images of American Indians: 1883–1933* (Albuquerque: Univ. of New Mexico Press, 1996).
   b. Erik Stole, *Buffalo Bill: Myth and Reality* (Santa Fe: Ancient City Press, 1998).
   c. R. L. Wilson and Greg Martin, *Buffalo Bill: An American Legend* (New Jersey: Chartwell Books, 1998).
   d. Joy Kasson, *Buffalo Bill's Wild West: Celebrity, Memory, and Popular History* (New York: Hill and Wang, 2000).
   e. Thomas Berger, *The Return of Little Big Man* (New York: Little, Brown, and Co., 2001).
   f. Alan Gallop, *Buffalo Bill's British Wild West* (Gloucestershire, UK: Sutton Publishing, 2001).
   g. Bobby Bridger, *Buffalo Bill and Sitting Bull: Inventing the Wild West* (Austin: Univ. of Texas Press, 2002).
   h. Sandra Sagala, *Buffalo Bill, Actor: A Chronicle of Cody's Theatrical Career* (Bowie, MD: Heritage Books, 2002).
   i. Louis Warren, *Buffalo Bill's America* (New York: Alfred A. Knopf, 2005).
   j. Larry McMurtry, *The Colonel and Little Missie: Buffalo Bill, Annie Oakley and the Beginnings of Superstardom in America* (New York: Simon and Schuster, 2005).
5. Robert G. Athearn, *The Mythic West in Twentieth-Century America* (Lawrence: Univ. of Kansas Press, 1986), 271.
6. Neil Postman, *Amusing Ourselves to Death: Public Discourse in the Age of Show Business* (New York: Penguin Books, 1985), 10.

Part One

Epigraph. Frederick Turner, *Beyond Geography: The Western Spirit against the Wilderness* (New Brunswick, NJ: Rutgers Univ. Press, 1992), 273–274.

Chapter One
Flaming Rainbow, the Word Sender

1. *The Kansas City Star*, November 10, 1952, cited in Lucile F. Aly, *John G. Neihardt: A Critical Biography* (Amsterdam: Rodopi N.V., 1977), 171.
2. John Thomas Richards, *Luminous Sanity: Literary Criticism Written by John G. Neihardt* (Cape Girardeau, MO: Cape Concord Publishing House, 1973), 23.
3. Raymond J. DeMallie, "John G. Neihardt's Lakota Legacy," in *A Sender of Words: Essays in Memory of John G. Neihardt*, edited by Vine Deloria Jr. (Salt Lake City/Chicago: Howe Brothers, 1984), 110–111.
4. John G. Neihardt, *Black Elk Speaks: Being the Life Story of a Holy Man of the Oglala Sioux* (Lincoln: Univ. of Nebraska Press, 1979), 18–19.
5. Ibid., 43.
6. Ibid., 228.
7. Ibid., 270.
8. Roger Dunsmore, "Holy Man in History," in *A Sender of Words: Essays in Memory of John G. Neihardt*, edited by Vine Deloria Jr. (Salt Lake City/Chicago: Howe Brothers, 1984), 156–157.
9. Neihardt, *Black Elk Speaks*, xvii.
10. Ibid., xviii.
11. Richards, *Luminous Sanity*, 21.
12. Gretchen M. Bataille, "New World Prophet," in *A Sender of Words: Essays in Memory of John G. Neihardt*, edited by Vine Deloria Jr. (Salt Lake City/Chicago: Howe Brothers, 1984), 136.
13. Dee Brown, "The Power of John Neihardt," in *A Sender of Words: Essays in Memory of John G. Neihardt*, edited by Vine Deloria Jr. (Salt Lake City/Chicago: Howe Brothers, 1984), 10.
14. Ibid., 8.
15. Told to me personally by Julius Young.
16. Frederick Manfred, "Western American Darks," in *A Sender of Words: Essays in Memory of John G. Neihardt*, edited by Vine Deloria Jr. (Salt Lake City/Chicago: Howe Brothers, 1984), 40.
17. Dick Cavett, introduction to *All Is But a Beginning: Youth Remembered, 1881–1901*, by John G. Neihardt (New York: Harcourt Brace, 1972).
18. John G. Neihardt, *Patterns and Coincidences: A Sequel to All Is But a Beginning* (Columbia, MO: Univ. of Missouri Press, 1978), 1.

Chapter Two
Across the Wide Missouri

1. John G. Neihardt, *Black Elk Speaks: Being the Life Story of a Holy Man of the Oglala Sioux* (Lincoln: Univ. of Nebraska Press, 1979), 2.
2. Bernard DeVoto, *The Course of Empire* (Cambridge, MA: Houghton Mifflin/Sentry/Riverside Press, 1962), 390.
3. Ibid., 387.
4. Ibid., 391.
5. Ibid., 392–400.
6. Walter Prescott Webb, *The Great Plains* (Boston: Ginn and Co., 1931), 142–143.

7. Ibid., 153.
8. Vine Deloria Jr., *Behind the Trail of Broken Treaties* (New York: Delacorte Press, 1974), 85.
9. Ibid., 86.
10. Neil Postman, *Amusing Ourselves to Death: Public Discourse in the Age of Show Business* (New York: Penguin Books, 1985), 40–41; also see Richard Hofstadter, *Anti-Intellectualism in American Life* (New York: Alfred A. Knopf, 1964), 19.
11. Vine Deloria Jr. and Clifford M. Lytle, *American Indians/American Justice* (Austin: Univ. of Texas Press, 1983), 6–7.
12. Michael Pollan, *The Botany of Desire: A Plant's-eye View of the World* (New York: Random House, 2001), 6–18.
13. Hiram M. Chittenden, *A History of the Fur Trade of the Far Northwest*, 3 vols. (New York: Francis P. Harper, 1901); John G. Neihardt, *A Cycle of the West* (Lincoln: Univ. of Nebraska Press, 1991); and Bobby Bridger, *A Ballad of the West* (Austin, TX: Augustine Press, 1991).
14. Joseph Campbell, *The Hero with a Thousand Faces* (Princeton, NJ: Princeton Univ. Bollingen Series, 1968), 30.
15. Bruce Feiler, *America's Prophet: How the Story of Moses Shaped America* (New York: William Morrow, 2009), 1–24.
16. Neal Gabler, *Life, the Movie: How Entertainment Conquered Reality* (New York: Alfred A. Knopf, 1998), 29.
17. See Hiram M. Chittenden, *A History of the Fur Trade of the Far Northwest*, 3 vols. (New York: Francis P. Harper, 1901); John G. Neihardt, *A Cycle of the West* (Lincoln: Univ. of Nebraska Press, 1991); and Bobby Bridger, *A Ballad of the West* (Austin, TX: Augustine Press, 1991).

Chapter Three
The Road of the Emigrants

1. John G. Neihardt, *Black Elk Speaks: Being the Life Story of a Holy Man of the Oglala Sioux* (Lincoln: Univ. of Nebraska Press, 1979), 9.
2. Oren Lyons, *The American Indian in the Past, Exiled in the Land of the Free: Democracy, Indian Nations, and the U.S. Constitution* (Santa Fe, NM: Clearlight Publishing, 1992), 30.
3. J. Cecil Alter, *James Bridger* (Norman, OK: Univ. of Oklahoma Press, 1962), 209.
4. Hiram M. Chittenden, *The History of the Fur Trade of the Far Northwest* (New York: Francis P. Harper, 1901), preface.
5. Bernard DeVoto, *Across the Wide Missouri* (New York: Bonanza Books, 1947), 61–62.
6. John D. Unruh Jr., *The Plains Across: The Overland Emigrants and the Trans-Mississippi West, 1840–1860* (Urbana, Chicago: Univ. of Illinois Press, 1982), 4.
7. Ibid., 9.
8. Neal Gabler, *Life, the Movie: How Entertainment Conquered Reality* (New York: Alfred A. Knopf, 1998), 24–25.
9. DeVoto, *Across the Wide Missouri*, 61.
10. Lewis Paul Todd and Merle Curti, *Rise of the American Nation*, 2nd ed. (New York: Harcourt, Brace & World, 1966), 371.
11. Francis Parkman, *The Oregon Trail* (New York: Penguin Books, 1985), 42.

Chapter Four

The Iron Cyclops and the Lightning Slingers

1. John G. Neihardt, *Black Elk Speaks: Being the Life Story of a Holy Man of the Oglala Sioux* (Lincoln: Univ. of Nebraska Press, 1979), 8.
2. Walter Prescott Webb, *The Great Plains* (Boston: Ginn and Co., 1931), 185.
3. Lewis Paul Todd and Marle Curti, *Rise of the American Nation*, 2nd ed. (New York: Harcourt, Brace & World, 1966), 351.
4. Ibid.
5. Alan Trachtenberg, *Shades of Hiawatha: Staging Indians, Making Americans, 1880–1930* (New York: Hill and Wang, 2004), xii.
6. Dee Brown, *Hear That Lonesome Whistle Blow: Railroads in the West* (New York: Touchstone/Simon and Schuster, 1977), 22–23; also see David Howard Bain, *Empire Express: Building the Transcontinental Railroad* (New York: Penguin Books, 1999), 16.
7. Hampton Sides, *Blood and Thunder: An Epic of the American West* (New York: Doubleday, 2006), 49.
8. Brown, *Hear That Lonesome Whistle*, 24–32; also see Bain, *Empire Express*, 3–10.
9. Fred Reinfeld, *Pony Express* (Lincoln: Univ. of Nebraska Press, 1973), 13.
10. Ibid., 9–17.
11. Ibid., 9.
12. Ibid., 104.
13. Kenneth Silverman, *Lightning Man: The Accursed Life of Samuel F. B. Morse* (New York: Decapo Press, 2004).
14. Neil Postman, *Amusing Ourselves to Death: Public Discourse in the Age of Show Business* (New York: Penguin Books, 1985), 66.
15. Ibid., 65.
16. Ibid., 68.
17. Information on Edward Creighton comes from the Nebraska State Historical Society website biography, www.nebraskahistory.org/publish/publicat/timeline/creighton_edward_a.htm, March 1999; information on Hiram Sibley is from *Scientific American Supplement*, vol. XXI, no. 530.
18. Adele Nathan, *Building the First Transcontinental Railroad* (Chicago: Spenser Press, 1950), 59; also see Brown, *Hear That Lonesome Whistle*; and Bain, *Empire Express*.
19. Nathan, *Building the First Transcontinental Railroad*, 21–31.

Chapter Five

A Fierce Artfulness

1. John G. Neihardt, *Black Elk Speaks: Being the Life Story of a Holy Man of the Oglala Sioux* (Lincoln: Univ. of Nebraska Press, 1979), 194–197.
2. Walter Prescott Webb, *The Great Plains* (Boston: Ginn and Co., 1931), preface.
3. John D. Unruh Jr., *The Plains Across: The Overland Emigrants and the Trans-Mississippi West, 1840–1860* (Urbana/Chicago: Univ. of Illinois Press, 1982), 65–67.
4. J. Cecil Alter, *Jim Bridger* (Norman: Univ. of Oklahoma Press, 1925, 1973), 310–314; also see Dee Brown, *The Fetterman Massacre* (Lincoln: Univ. of Nebraska Press, 1962), 14–15; and Stanley Vestal, *Jim Bridger, Mountain Man* (Lincoln: Univ. of Nebraska Press, 1946), 220–240.

5. Bobby Bridger, *Buffalo Bill and Sitting Bull: Inventing the Wild West* (Austin: Univ. of Texas Press, 2002), 110–111.

6. Brown, *Fetterman Massacre*, 27–28; also see Bridger, *Buffalo Bill and Sitting Bull*, 113–119.

7. Ronald Goodman, *Lakota Star Knowledge: Studies in Lakota Stellar Theology*, 2nd ed. (Rosebud, SD: Sinte Gleska Univ. Press, 1992), 1.

8. Ibid.

9. Ibid., 2.

10. Ibid., 3.

11. Ibid., 25.

12. John G. Neihardt, *When the Tree Flowered: The Story of Eagle Voice, a Sioux Indian* (Lincoln: Univ. of Nebraska Press, 1951), 152–181; also see Goodman, *Lakota Star Knowledge*, 25–27.

13. Goodman, *Lakota Star Knowledge*, 1.

14. Ibid.

15. Neil Postman, *Amusing Ourselves to Death: Public Discourse in the Age of Show Business* (New York: Penguin Books, 1985), 25.

16. Goodman, *Lakota Star Knowledge*, 18.

17. Ibid., 17.

18. Ibid., 27.

19. Ibid., 26–27.

20. Ibid., 26–27.

Chapter Six
A Star Appears

1. John G. Neihardt, *Black Elk Speaks: Being the Life Story of a Holy Man of the Oglala Sioux* (Lincoln: Univ. of Nebraska Press, 1979), 228.

2. Modern revisionist historians have cast doubt that Cody ever worked on the bullwacker trains or rode for the Pony Express, but the circumstances of his life and the history of the bullwackers and the Pony Express certainly coincide, and I prefer to take him for his word and refer to his autobiography, William F. Cody, *The Life of the Honorable William F. Cody* (Lincoln: Univ. of Nebraska Press, 1978). Also see Don Russell, *The Life and Times of Buffalo Bill* (Norman: Univ. of Oklahoma Press, 1960); also, Bobby Bridger, *Buffalo Bill and Sitting Bull: Inventing the Wild West* (Austin: Univ. of Texas Press, 2002).

3. Tom McHugh, *The Time of the Buffalo* (New York: Alfred A. Knopf, 1972), 285.

4. Richard O'Conner, *Sheridan* (New York: Bobbs-Merrill Co., 1953), 213–214.

5. Dee Brown, *The Fetterman Massacre* (Lincoln: Univ. of Nebraska Press, 1962), 16.

6. Neal Gabler, *Life, the Movie: How Entertainment Conquered Reality* (New York: Alfred A. Knopf, 1998), 33–37.

7. Ibid., 38–39.

8. Ibid., 60.

9. Ibid., 64–65.

10. Ronald Goodman, *Lakota Star Knowledge: Studies in Lakota Stellar Theology* (Rosebud, SD: Sinta Gleska Univ. Press, 1982), 9–11.

Chapter Seven
The Showman, the Medicine Man, and the Messiah

1. John G. Neihardt, *Black Elk Speaks: Being the Life Story of a Holy Man of the Oglala Sioux* (Lincoln: Univ. of Nebraska Press, 1979), 214–215.
2. Stanley Vestal, *Jim Bridger, Mountain Man* (Lincoln: Univ. of Nebraska Press, 1946), 299.
3. Charles Eastman, *The Soul of the Indian* (Lincoln: Univ. of Nebraska Press, 1980), 157.
4. Vine Deloria Jr., *The World We Used to Live In: Remembering the Powers of the Medicine Men* (Golden, CO: Fulcrum Publishing, 2006), xxv.
5. Stanley Vestal, *Sitting Bull: Champion of the Sioux* (Norman: Univ. of Oklahoma Press, 1956), 151.
6. Ibid.
7. Vine Deloria Jr. and Clifford M. Lytle, *American Indians, American Justice* (Austin: Univ. of Texas Press, 1983), 42–43; it should be noted that some tribes object to the phrase "five civilized tribes" as it implies the remaining American Indian tribes were not civilized.
8. Dee Brown, *Best of Dee Brown's West: An Anthology*, edited by Stan Banash (Santa Fe, NM: Clearlight Publishing, 1998), 337.
9. Neihardt, *Black Elk Speaks*, 259.

Part Two

Epigraph. Daniel J. Boorstin, *The Image: A Guide to Pseudo-Events in America* (New York: Athenaeum, 1987), 37.

Chapter Eight
The Wizards and the Western

1. John G. Neihardt, *Black Elk Speaks: Being the Life Story of a Holy Man of the Oglala Sioux* (Lincoln: Univ. of Nebraska Press, 1979), 238.
2. Philip J. Deloria, *Indians in Unexpected Places* (Lawrence: Univ. of Kansas Press, 2004), 103.
3. Bobby Bridger, *Buffalo Bill and Sitting Bull: Inventing the Wild West* (Austin: Univ. of Texas Press, 2002), 403–405.
4. Jill Jonnes, *Empires of Light: Edison, Tesla, Westinghouse, and the Race to Electrify the World* (New York: Random House, 2003) 88–90 and 109–110; also see John J. O'Neill, *Prodigal Genius: The Life of Nikola Tesla* (New York: Ives Washburn, 1944, and Los Angeles: Angriff Press, 1973, internet volume).
5. Matthew Josephson, *Edison: A Biography* (New York: John Wiley and Sons, 1959), 159–164; also see Neil Baldwin, *Edison: Inventing the Century* (New York: Hyperion, 1995).
6. Jean Strouse, *Morgan: American Financier* (New York: Perennial, 1999), 182–184; also see Jonnes, *Empires of Light*; also see O'Neill, *Prodigal Genius*.
7. Josephson, *Edison: A Biography, 59–70*.
8. Ibid., 41-84.
9. Edmund Morris, *The Rise of Theodore Roosevelt*, (New York: The Modern Library

Paperbacks, 2001), 476.

10. Deloria, *Indians in Unexpected Places*, 62.

11. A. R. Fulton, *Motion Pictures: The Development of an Art from Silent Films to the Age of Television* (Norman: Univ. of Oklahoma Press, 1967), 8; also see Elizabeth Brayer, *George Eastman: A Biography* (Baltimore: John Hopkins Univ. Press, 1996); also see Carl W. Ackerman, *George Eastman: Founder of the Kodak and the Photography Business* (n.p.: Beard Books, 1930).

12. Frank E. Beaver, *On Film: A History of the Motion Picture* (New York: McGraw-Hill, 1983), 11; also see Gordon Hendricks, *Eadweard Muybridge: The Father of the Motion Picture* (New York: Grossman Publishers, 1975); also see Kevin MacDonnell, *Eadweard Muybridge: The Man Who Invented the Moving Picture* (Boston: Little, Brown, 1972).

13. Fulton, *Motion Pictures*, 7.

14. Beaver, *On Film*, 11–14; also see Gordon Hendricks, *The Edison Motion Picture Myth* (Berkeley: Univ. of California Press, 1961); also see A. Scott Berg, *Goldwyn* (New York: Alfred A. Knopf, 1989), 29; also see Josephson, *Edison: A Biography*.

15. Fulton, *Motion Pictures*, 45–60; also see Beaver, *On Film*, 44–50; and see Charles Musser, *Before the Nickelodeon: Edwin S. Porter and the Edison Manufacturing Company* (Berkeley: Univ. of California Press, 1991).

16. George N. Fenin and William K. Everson, *The Western: From Silents to the Seventies* (New York: Grossman Publishers, 1973), 53; also see David Robinson, *Chaplin: His Life and Art* (New York: McGraw-Hill, 1985), 135–145.

17. Fenin and Everson, *The Western*, 111–112.

18. Ibid., 109–121.

19. Ibid., 75–107.

20. Beaver, *On Film*, 100–103.

21. Deloria, *Indians in Unexpected Places*, 104.

22. Luther Standing Bear, *Land of the Spotted Eagle* (Lincoln: Univ. of Nebraska Press, 1978), 68–69.

23. Ibid., 293–294.

24. Bridger, *Buffalo Bill and Sitting Bull*, 432–435.

25. Deloria, *Indians in Unexpected Places*, 55.

Chapter Nine

The Dream Factory and a New Red Scare

1. John G. Neihardt, *Black Elk Speaks: Being the Life Story of a Holy Man of the Oglala Sioux* (Lincoln: Univ. of Nebraska Press, 1979), 240.

2. Philip J. Deloria, *Indians in Unexpected Places* (Lawrence: Univ. of Kansas Press, 2004), 50.

3. Alan Trachtenberg, *Shades of Hiawatha: Staging Indians, Making Americans, 1880–1930* (New York: Hill and Wang, 2004), 32–33.

4. Neal Gabler, *An Empire of their Own: How the Jews Invented Hollywood* (New York: Crown, 1988), 14–24.

5. Ibid., 28.

6. Deloria, *Indians in Unexpected Places*, 48–49.

7. Neal Gabler, *Life, the Movie: How Entertainment Conquered Reality* (New York: Alfred A. Knopf, 2004), 204–205.

8. Trachtenberg, *Shades of Hiawatha*, 214–215.

9. Gabler, *Life, the Movie*, 199.

10. Trachtenberg, *Shades of Hiawatha*, 214–215.

11. Ibid., 219.

12. Ibid., 225.

13. http://www.world wisdom.com/publicauthors/Charles Eastman.aspx; also see Raymond Wilson, *Ohiyesa: Charles Eastman, Santee Sioux* (Urbana: Univ. of Illinois Press, 1983); also see Kay Graber, ed., *Sister to the Sioux: The Memoirs of Elaine Goodale Eastman, 1885–91*, (Lincoln: Univ. of Nebraska Press, 1978).

14. Gabler, *Life, the Movie*, 67–68.

15. David Nasaw, *The Chief* (New York: Houghton Mifflin Co., 2000), 125–127.

16. Neal Gabler, *Winchell: Gossip, Power, and the Culture of Celebrity* (New York: Alfred A. Knopf, 1994), 102–103.

17. Gina Kolata, *Flu: The Story of the Great Influenza Pandemic of 1918, and the Search for the Virus that Caused It* (New York: Farrar, Straus and Giroux, 1999), 1–12.

18. James Green, *Death in the Haymarket: A Story of Chicago, the First Labor Movement, and the Bombing that Divided Gilded-Age America* (New York: Pantheon Books, 2006) 295–308; also see Marguerite Young, *Harp Song for A Radical: The Life and Times of Eugene Victor Debs* (New York: Alfred A. Knopf, 1999); also see Kenneth D. Ackerman, *Young J. Edgar Hoover, the Red Scare, and the Assault on Civil Liberties* (New York: Carroll & Graf, 2007); and see Leon A. Harris, *Upton Sinclair, American Rebel* (New York: Crowell, 1975).

19. Lois Palken Rudnick, *Mabel Dodge Luhan: New Woman, New Worlds* (Albuquerque: Univ. of New Mexico Press, 1984) 1–100; also see Lois Palken Rudnick, *Utopian Vistas: The Mabel Dodge Luhan House and the American Counterculture* (Albuquerque: Univ. of New Mexico Press, 1996); also see Christine Stansell, *American Moderns: Bohemian New York and the Creation of a New Century* (New York: Henry Holt and Co., 2000); also see Frank Waters, *Of Time and Change* (Denver, CO: MacMurray and Beck, 1998); Tony Lujan spelled his name with a "j," but Mabel Dodge Luhan spelled her name with an "h" because so many of her friends mispronounced her married name "Lu-jon."

20. Trachtenberg, *Shades of Hiawatha*, 286–287.

21. A. Scott Berg, *Goldwyn* (New York: Alfred A. Knopf, 1989), 107.

22. Alvin M. Josephy Jr., *A Walk Toward Oregon: A Memoir* (New York: Alfred A. Knopf, 2000), 95.

23. Ibid., 95–96.

24. Ibid., 96–98.

25. Gabler, *Empire of their Own*, 79–86.

26. Josephy Jr., *Walk Toward Oregon*, 96–97; also see Gabler, *Empire of their Own*, 311–322; and also see Greg Mitchell, *The Campaign of the Century: Upton Sinclair's Race for Governor of California* (New York: Random House, 1991), 369–372. Some film historians believe that William Randolph Hearst murdered the pioneer director of Westerns, Thomas Ince, in 1924. Insanely jealous of his mistress, the beautiful movie star Marion Davies, Hearst set up a vanity corporation, Cosmopolitan Studios, to produce and distribute her films, but suspicious of any man who came near his trophy, he kept Davies on a very short leash. Hearst suspected—perhaps correctly so—that Davies and silent film icon Charlie Chaplin were having an affair, and he believed they would not be able to disguise their feelings for each

other at a party. So the multimillionaire invited Chaplin, Davies, and a host of other Hollywood luminaries to a birthday celebration for Ince onboard his yacht, the *Oneida*. Complicating matters, however, Ince's and Chaplin's heads were reported to have a similar shape, and, intoxicated and confused, Hearst allegedly shot Ince by accident. Ince was discovered unconscious and reported to have over-eaten at his sumptuous birthday feast and had a heart attack. Ince was quickly and quietly removed from the *Oneida* to the home of a friend, where he later died and was immediately cremated. Kenneth Anger, *Hollywood Babylon* (San Francisco: Straight Arrow Books, 1975), 97–104.

27. Ibid., 98.

Chapter Ten
A WASP in the Wilderness

1. John G. Neihardt, *Black Elk Speaks: Being the Life Story of a Holy Man of the Oglala Sioux* (Lincoln: Univ. of Nebraska Press, 1979), 38.

2. Often suggested to me personally by Mr. Wasserman, playwright of *Man of La Mancha*, the stage adaptation of *One Flew Over the Cuckoo's Nest*, the screenplay for *The Vikings*, *Cleopatra*, and scores of other produced stage and film scripts.

3. Richard Hofstadter, *Social Darwinism in American Thought* (Boston: Beacon Press, 1944), 174–188; also see Robert G. Athearn, *The Mythic West in Twentieth-Century America* (Lawrence: Univ. of Kansas Press, 1986), 255–256.

4. Paul Van Develder, *Savages and Scoundrels: The Untold Story of America's Road to Empire through Indian Territory* (New Haven, CT: Yale Univ. Press, 2009), 227.

5. Garry Wills, *John Wayne's America: The Politics of Celebrity* (New York: Simon and Schuster, 1997), 310.

6. Alan Trachtenberg, *Shades of Hiawatha: Staging Indians, Making Americans, 1880–1930* (New York: Hill and Wang, 2004), xii.

7. Athearn, *Mythic West*, 54.

8. Ibid., 168.

9. Ibid., 169.

10. George N. Fenin and William K. Everson, *The Western: From Silents to the Seventies* (New York: Grossman Publishers, 1973), 130–143; also see James Cruze, "Making *The Covered Wagon*," *Film Yearbook 1924*, 19, 21, available online at www.cinemaweb.com/silentfilm/bookshelf/11_loc_4.htm.

11. Ronald L. Davis, *William S. Hart: Projecting the American West* (Norman: Univ. of Oklahoma Press, 2003), 177–178.

12. Fenin and Everson, *The Western*, 130–143; also see Cruze, "Making *The Covered Wagon*," 19, 24.

13. Randy Roberts and James S. Olson, *John Wayne: American* (Lincoln: Univ. of Nebraska Press, 1997), 79–80.

14. Neal Gabler, *Walt Disney: The Triumph of the American Imagination* (New York: Alfred A. Knopf, 2006), 116–128.

15. Roberts and Olson, *John Wayne: American*, 69–71; also see Scott Eyman, *Print the Legend: The Life and Times of John Ford* (New York: Simon and Schuster, 1999).

16. Fenin and Everson, *The Western*, 240.

17. Wills, *John Wayne's America*, 88–89.

18. Ibid., 37–38.

19. Roberts and Olson, *John Wayne: American*, 58.
20. Ibid., 61. Note: Even though the "football" aspect remains the same, the story of Ford's and Wayne's introduction changes incrementally when told by Ford's grandson Dan Ford, in his biography *Pappy*, again in biographer Scott Eyman's biography *Print the Legend*, and yet again in Garry Wills's *John Wayne's America*.
21. Ibid., 98.
22. Wills, *John Wayne's America*, 46.
23. Ibid., 67.
24. Roberts and Olson, *John Wayne: American*, 109; also see Andrew Bergman, *We're In the Money: Depression America and Its Films* (New York: NYU Press, 1971), 3–16.
25. Roberts and Olson, *John Wayne: American*, 103, 132.
26. Ibid., 70–71.
27. Philip J. Deloria, *Indians in Unexpected Places* (Lawrence: Univ. of Kansas Press, 2004), 107.

Chapter Eleven
The Indian "New Deal"

1. John G. Neihardt, *Black Elk Speaks: Being the Life Story of a Holy Man of the Oglala Sioux* (Lincoln: Univ. of Nebraska Press, 1979), xvii.
2. Whereas most tribes readily accepted citizenship, the Mohawks, suspicious of losing ground gained in treaties, declined the offer.
3. Lois Palken Rudnick, *Utopian Vistas: The Mabel Dodge Luhan House and the American Counterculture* (Albuquerque: Univ. of New Mexico Press, 1996); also see Christine Stansell, *American Moderns: Bohemian New York and the Creation of a New Century* (New York: Henry Holt and Co., 2000).
4. Frank Waters, *Of Time and Change* (Denver, CO: MacMurray and Beck, 1998), 86.
5. Philip J. Deloria, *Playing Indian* (New Haven, CT: Yale Univ. Press, 1998), 3–5; also see D. H. Lawrence, *Studies in Classic American Literature* (London: Martin Secker, 1924).
6. John Collier, *From Every Zenith* (Denver, CO: Sage Books, 1963), 126.
7. Vine Deloria Jr. and Clifford M. Lytle, *American Indians, American Justice* (Austin: Univ. of Texas Press, 1983), 100.
8. Vine Deloria Jr., *Behind the Trail of Broken Treaties: An Indian Declaration of Independence* (New York: Delacorte Press, 1974), 195–196.
9. Ibid., 196.
10. Ibid., 196–199.
11. Ibid., 199.
12. Ibid., 196–199; also see Deloria and Lytle, *American Indians*, 101.
13. Robert G. Athearn, *The Mythic West in Twentieth-Century America* (Lawrence: Univ. of Kansas Press, 1986), 29.
14. Ibid., 30–37.
15. Ibid., 78–83.

Chapter Twelve
A Clarion Call for Heroes

1. John G. Neihardt, *Black Elk Speaks: Being the Life Story of a Holy Man of the Oglala Sioux* (Lincoln: Univ. of Nebraska Press, 1979), 12.
2. Randy Roberts and James S. Olson, *John Wayne: American* (Lincoln: Univ. of Nebraska, 1997), 203–208.
3. Ibid., 209.
4. A. Scott Berg, *Goldwyn* (New York: Alfred A. Knopf, 1989), 367–368.
5. George N. Fenin and William K. Everson, *The Western: From Silents to the Seventies* (New York: Grossman Publishers, 1973), 11; also see 243–244.
6. Garry Wills, *John Wayne's America: The Politics of Celebrity* (New York: Simon and Schuster, 1997), 102–103, 108; John Ford was wounded by shrapnel while filming America's decisive victory over the Japanese during the Battle of Midway in the Pacific. Ford also shot the first color film footage of the destruction at Pearl Harbor. See Roberts and Olson, *John Wayne: American*, 266.
7. Roberts and Olson, *John Wayne: American*, 186; also see Dan Ford, *Pappy: The Life of John Ford* (New York: Prentice Hall, 1979); and see Ronald L. Davis, *John Ford, Hollywood's Old Master* (Norman: Univ. of Oklahoma Press, 1995).
8. Ibid., 188.
9. Ibid., 190.
10. Wills, *John Wayne's America*, 104.
11. Ibid., 106.
12. Roberts and Olson, *John Wayne: American*, 213. A disclaimer: I can personally relate to John Wayne's dilemma as his acting career began to blossom at the beginning of World War II, because I was enrolled in college when President Johnson began troop escalations in South Vietnam. I managed to maintain a 4-F draft status throughout the war until the lottery system of conscription provided me with a high enough number to spend a year with a 1-A, or on a "ready for service" list with no hopes of being drafted. Prior to the lottery, however, I signed my first major recording contract with Monument Records in 1967, the year the Vietnam War exploded, and the war definitely had a negative effect on my career because I could not support the success I was having with record sales by touring. To be fair, however, I avoided service, and because of this many conservatives would no doubt consider me a Vietnam draft dodger.
13. Ibid., 212.
14. Wills, *John Wayne's America*, 108–109.
15. Roberts and Olson, *John Wayne: American*, 213–214.
16. Wills, *John Wayne's America*, 110
17. Roberts and Olson, *John Wayne: American*, 304.
18. Ibid., 293.
19. Alvin M. Josephy Jr., *A Walk Toward Oregon: A Memoir* (New York: Alfred A. Knopf, 2000), 170.
20. Ibid., 185–201.
21. Ibid., 202–210.
22. Ibid., 211.
23. Daniel J. Boorstin, *The Image: A Guide to Pseudo Events in America* (New York: Athenaeum, 1987), 240.

24. Wills, *John Wayne's America*, 149.
25. Ibid., 156.

Chapter Thirteen
When Johnny Comes Marching Home

1. John G. Neihardt, *Black Elk Speaks: Being the Life Story of a Holy Man of the Oglala Sioux* (Lincoln: Univ. of Nebraska Press, 1979), 250.
2. Frank Waters, *Masked Gods* (New York: Ballantine Books, 1950), 432–433.
3. Ibid.; also see Lois Palkin Rudnick, *Mabel Dodge Luhan: New Woman, New World* (Albuquerque: Univ. of New Mexico Press, 1984), 314–315.
4. Palkin Rudnick, *Mabel Dodge Luhan*, 264–265.
5. Vine Deloria Jr. and Clifford M. Lytle, *The Nations Within: The Past and Future of American Indian Sovereignty* (New York: Pantheon Books, 1984), 180.
6. Ibid., 182.
7. Vine Deloria Jr. and David E. Wilkins, *Tribes, Treaties, and Constitutional Tribulations* (Austin: Univ. of Texas Press, 1999), 41.
8. Michael C. Burton, *The Making of a Liberated Mind, John Henry Faulk: A Biography* (Austin: Eakin Press, 1993), 67–68.
9. Larry Ceplair and Steven Englund, *The Inquisition in Hollywood* (New York: Doubleday, 1980), 150.
10. A. Scott Berg, *Goldwyn* (New York: Alfred A. Knopf, 1989), 432.
11. Ibid., 432–433.
12. Ibid., 433.
13. Neal Gabler, *Walt Disney: The Triumph of the American Imagination* (New York: Alfred A. Knopf, 2006), 451.
14. New Jersey congressman J. Parnell Thomas later went to jail for taking kickbacks and padding his government payroll; also see Alvin M. Josephy Jr., *A Walk Toward Oregon: A Memoir* (New York: Alfred A. Knopf, 2000), 233.
15. Berg, *Goldwyn*, 434.
16. Ibid., 435.
17. Garry Wills, *John Wayne's America: The Politics of Celebrity* (New York: Simon and Schuster, 1997), 196–197.
18. Ibid., 162.
19. Ibid., 197.
20. Dan Ford, *Pappy: The Life of John Ford* (New York: Prentice Hall, 1979), 164; also see Scott Eyman, *Print the Legend: The Life and Times of John Ford* (New York: Simon and Schuster, 1999), 246–255.
21. Wills, *John Wayne's America*, 162–163.
22. George N. Fenin and William K. Everson, *The Western: From Silents to the Seventies* (New York: Grossman Publishers, 1973), 249–251.
23. Josephy, *Walk Toward Oregon*, 220; Hearst and other anti–Roosevelt/New Deal newspaper attacks on the Marine Corps over Iwo Jima contributed greatly to the publicity campaign launched by the marines to capitalize on the popularity of the Joe Rosenthal photograph of the flag-raising on Iwo Jima as detailed in chapter 12.
24. Ibid., 221–222.
25. Vine Deloria Jr. and Clifford M. Lytle, *American Indians, American Justice* (Austin: Univ. of Texas Press, 1983), 103.

Chapter Fourteen
The Oracle of the Hearth

1. John G. Neihardt, *Black Elk Speaks: Being the Life Story of a Holy Man of the Oglala Sioux* (Lincoln: Univ. of Nebraska Press, 1979), 28.
2. Alvin M. Josephy Jr., *A Walk Toward Oregon: A Memoir* (New York: Alfred A. Knopf, 2000), 220–230.
3. Wallace E. Stegner, *The Uneasy Chair* (Lincoln: Univ. of Nebraska Press, 1974).
4. Robert G. Athearn, *The Mythic West in Twentieth-Century* America (Lawrence: Univ. of Kansas Press, 1986), 262.
5. Ibid. Note: The depiction of the American being forced to rely on his "Yankee ingenuity" when others can only depend on "book-learning" was in fact turned topsy-turvy during the Indian wars on the Great Plains. There, West Point graduates with brilliant Civil War records based on "book-learning" combat were repeatedly outwitted and defeated by Plains Indian military leaders such as Red Cloud, Sitting Bull, and Crazy Horse who employed ingenious guerrilla tactics.
6. Philip J. Deloria, *Indians in Unexpected Places* (Lawrence: Univ. of Kansas Press, 2004), 96–103.
7. Noted American Indian actor Jay Silverheels starred as Geronimo in *Broken Arrow*.
8. An April 2009 special edition of *Wild West* magazine rated *High Noon* number one in its list of the top 100 Westerns of all time.
9. *Wild West* magazine rated *Shane* as the eighth best Western of all time.
10. Neil Postman, *Amusing Ourselves to Death: Public Discourse in the Age of Show Business* (New York: Penguin Books, 1985), 78.
11. Neal Gabler, *Winchell: Gossip, Power, and the Culture of Celebrity* (New York: Alfred A. Knopf, 1994), 397; also see Lewis Paul Todd and Merle Curti, *Rise of the American Nation*, 2nd ed. (New York: Harcourt, Brace, and World, 1966), 810–811.
12. Josephy, *Walk Toward Oregon*, 232.
13. Ibid., 230–245.
14. Ibid., 245.
15. Ibid., 246.
16. Ibid.
17. Ibid., 247.
18. Ibid., 254.

Chapter Fifteen
The Searchers and the Captivity Narrative

1. John G. Neihardt, *Black Elk Speaks: Being the Life Story of a Holy Man of the Oglala Sioux* (Lincoln: Univ. of Nebraska Press, 1979), 215.
2. Fanny Kelly, *Narrative of My Captivity among the Sioux Indians*, edited by Clark and Mary Lee Spence (New York: Konecky and Konecky, 1990), xxxvi.
3. Many Americans claim a "Cherokee grandmother," implying a desire to somehow embrace the natural American state. As most captives taken by Indians were white women and children, a more accurate claim to Indian heritage would probably be an Indian grandfather. But non-Indian culture could more easily accept an Indian woman being taken by a non-Indian man than the other way around.

4. Frederick Turner, *Beyond Geography: The Western Spirit against the Wilderness* (New Brunswick, NJ: Rutgers Univ. Press, 1983), 233–234.

5. S. C. Gwynne, *Empire of the Summer Moon: Quanah Parker and the Rise and Fall of the Comanches, the Most Powerful Indian Tribe in American History* (New York: Scribner, 2010), 184–186. Perhaps the most famous—and ironic—American example of Stockholm syndrome is William Randolph Hearst's granddaughter, Patricia Hearst, who was taken captive by militant radicals and claimed she was "altered" into a bank robber and terrorist.

6. My son Gabriel attended Cynthia Ann Parker Elementary School in Houston, Texas, in the 1990s. Gabe's school is but one of many elementary schools named after Cynthia Ann Parker in the Lone Star state.

7. Scott Eyman, *Print the Legend: The Life and Times of John Ford*, (New York: Simon and Schuster, 1999), 449.

8. In 2008, the American Film Institute rated *The Searchers* as the "greatest Western of all time." In 2009, the AFI rated *The Searchers* number twelve on its list of the best 100 movies ever made. In 2009, a panel of ten Western historians rated *The Searchers* number seven in *Wild West* magazine's top 100 Westerns of all time. A sidenote to this is that if *High Noon* reflects the mood of the nation during the HUAC era, it is significant that *The Searchers* was released only a year after Rosa Parks refused to give up her seat on the bus in Montgomery, thus beginning the civil rights movement in the United States.

9. Randy Roberts and James S. Olson, *John Wayne: American* (Lincoln: Univ. of Nebraska Press, 1997), 424.

10. Garry Wills, *John Wayne's America: The Politics of Celebrity* (New York: Simon and Schuster, 1997), 268–269.

11. Ibid., 271.

12. According to Dennis Showalter, a former president of the Military History Society, in his synopsis of *The Searchers*, in *Wild West* magazine's April 2009 special collector's edition, "100 Greatest Westerns," Le May actually based his novel on the Elm Creek Raid in Young County, Texas, in 1846. Yet in his *Empire of the Summer Moon: Quanah Parker and the Rise and Fall of the Comanches, the Most Powerful Indian Tribe in American History*, S.C. Gwynne presents a substantial argument that *The Searchers* is indeed based on Cynthia Ann Parker's uncle, James Parker, and his decade-long, five-thousand mile search for his niece. Whether *The Searchers* is based on the Cynthia Ann Parker story, however, is ultimately irrelevant to my argument that the theme of the captivity narrative implies that deliverance in the wilderness is a major theme of the film. Sidenote: *The Searchers* was rated number seven on this list.

13. Wills, *John Wayne's America*, 252.

14. Ibid., 257.

15. Eyman, *Print the Legend*, 448.

16. Roberts and Olson, *John Wayne: American*, 420.

Part Three

Epigraph. Ian Frazier, *The Great Plains* (New York: Farrar, Straus and Giroux, 1989), 209–210.

Chapter Sixteen
Custer Died for Your Sins

1. John G. Neihardt, *Black Elk Speaks: Being the Life Story of a Holy Man of the Oglala Sioux* (Lincoln: Univ. of Nebraska Press, 1979), 28.
2. Alvin M. Josephy Jr., *A Walk Toward Oregon: A Memoir* (New York: Alfred A. Knopf, 2000), 254.
3. Ibid.
4. Ibid., 256–257.
5. Vine Deloria Jr. and Clifford M. Lytle, *The Nations Within: The Past and Future of American Indian Sovereignty* (New York: Pantheon Books, 1984), 194.
6. Ibid., 195.
7. Josephy, *Walk Toward Oregon*, 266–267.
8. Ibid., 267.
9. Ibid.
10. Deloria and Lytle, *Nations Within*, 206.
11. Neil Gabler, *An Empire of Their Own: How the Jews Invented Hollywood* (New York: Crown, 1988), 4–5.
12. Among Western film purists, the location of Marlon Brando's *One-Eyed Jacks* is as controversial as its subject matter because it broke with tradition and depicted a Western in the majestic Big Sur region of California rather than in the desert Southwest, northern Rockies, or on the Great Plains.
13. Actor Marlon Brando's career as an Indian rights activist began with the fishing rights movement in the Pacific Northwest.
14. Josephy, *Walk Toward Oregon*, 293.
15. Ibid.
16. Ibid.
17. Phil and Barbara Deloria, *Vine Deloria, Jr. Funeral program*, Foothills Chapel. Golden, Colorado, November 18, 2005; also see Vine Deloria Jr., *The World We Used to Live In: Remembering the Powers of the Medicine Men* (Golden, CO: Fulcrum Publishing, 2006), back cover biographical sketch.

Chapter Seventeen
A Librarian's Notebook

1. John G. Neihardt, *Black Elk Speaks: Being the Life Story of a Holy Man of the Oglala Sioux* (Lincoln: Univ. of Nebraska Press, 1979), 274.
2. Neil Postman, *Amusing Ourselves to Death: Public Discourse in the Age of Show Business* (New York: Penguin Books, 1985), 40–41.
3. Dee Brown, *When the Century Was Young: A Writer's Notebook* (Little Rock, AR: August House, 1993), 9.
4. Ibid.
5. Ibid., 51–52.
6. Dee Brown, *Best of Dee Brown's West: An Anthology*, edited by Stan Banash (Santa Fe, NM: Clearlight Publishing, 1998), xvi.
7. Brown, *When the Century Was Young*, 56.
8. Ibid., 56.
9. Ibid., 56.

10. Ibid., 100–101.
11. Ibid., 101–102.
12. Ibid., 103–104.
13. Ibid., 103–104.
14. Ibid., 135.
15. Ibid., 169.
16. Ibid., 172–173.
17. Ibid., 218–219.
18. Ibid., 219.
19. Ibid., 222.
20. Elaine Woo, "American West writer, Dee Brown, dies at 94," *The Los Angeles Times*, December 14, 2002.
21. John G. Neihardt, *Patterns and Coincidences: A Sequel to All Is But a Beginning* (Columbia, MO: Univ. of Missouri Press, 1978), 1.

Chapter Eighteen
The Trail of Broken Treaties

1. John G. Neihardt, *Black Elk Speaks: Being the Life Story of a Holy Man of the Oglala Sioux* (Lincoln: Univ. of Nebraska Press, 1979), 35.
2. Pete Fornatale, *Back to the Garden* (New York: Simon and Schuster, 2009), xvii.
3. Ibid., 127.
4. Vine Deloria Jr., *Behind the Trail of Broken Treaties: An Indian Declaration of Independence* (New York: Delacorte Press, 1974), 25–38; also see Jennings C. Wise, *The Red Man in the New World Drama: The great classic of the political and legal history of the American Indian,* revised and edited by Vine Deloria Jr. (New York, Macmillian, 1971).
5. Peter Matthiessen, *In the Spirit of Crazy Horse* (New York: Viking, 1983), 37–38.
6. Deloria, *Behind the Trail*, 24–44.
7. Ibid., 44–45.
8. Matthiessen, *Spirit of Crazy Horse*, 59–63.
9. Deloria, *Behind the Trail*, 48.
10. Matthiessen, *Spirit of Crazy Horse*, 53.
11. Ibid., 54.
12. Deloria, *Behind the Trail*, 203.
13. Matthiessen, *Spirit of Crazy Horse*, 258–259.

Chapter Nineteen
Dances with Wolves and *Avatar*

1. John G. Neihardt, *Black Elk Speaks: Being the Life Story of a Holy Man of the Oglala Sioux* (Lincoln: Univ. of Nebraska Press, 1979).
2. Vine Deloria Jr., *C. G. Jung and the Sioux Tradition: Dreams, Visions, Nature, and the Primitive*, edited by Philip J. Deloria and Jerome S. Bernstein (New Orleans: Spring Journal Books, 2009), 99.
3. Humberto R. Maturana and Francisco J. Varela, *The Tree of Knowledge: The Biological Roots of Human Understanding* (Boston: Shambhala Publications, 1998).

Index